BURGENLAND

When I first stood at Auschwitz-Birkenau the question that haunted me was not 'Where was God?' ... The question that haunts me today is 'Where is Man?'

Lord Sacks, former Chief Rabbi of the
United Kingdom and Commonwealth

You shall not stand idly by as the blood of your brother is shed.

Leviticus 19.16

Contents

Preface

At the toe end of Manhattan's Lower East Side, where evocative street names such as Delancey, Hester and Canal give way to East Broadway's Seward Park, there stands an impressive Art Deco building rising above the once overcrowded tenement blocks with their rickety exterior iron fire escapes. The building commands an unrivalled view from which to survey the collective sighs of the more than a million and a half Jews who lived here at the turn of the last century. It stands tall over the grand Eldridge Street synagogue and its community of Jewish families fleeing persecution and terror. Individuals seeking a new life, but also many who were trying to cling onto the world and language they had left behind. The first sign that this building is not the average New York high-rise is the bas-reliefs of Karl Marx, Friedrich Engels, Ferdinand Lassalle and Karl Liebknecht adorning the ornate frontage. Also clearly visible is the Hebrew lettering פֿאָרווערטס, spelling out *Forverts* in Yiddish.

This was the headquarters of *Forward* for about sixty years, between the early 1900s and the mid-1960s, the largest Yiddish daily newspaper in the world. It has now been converted into luxury apartments for a new generation of the upwardly mobile, mostly working in New York's nearby financial district. At the peak of its popularity, a quarter of a million copies were pored over every day. It was printed in the Hebrew alphabet, which would have been comprehensible to a large proportion of the world's Jews and certainly the population of the Lower East Side. Many would have only spoken or read Yiddish. Founder and editor of *Forward* until the late 1940s was Abraham Cahan, the prominent writer and socialist activist.

7

Cahan was determined to advance the cause and interest of the working man and did so through the paper's strong editorial and news coverage. Yet there was also another feature of *Forward* which gained enormous traction amongst a readership often struggling to come to terms with the overwhelming change in their lives and surrounding society. This was the agony aunt or advice column called the *Bintel Brief* (literally a bundle of letters).

On these pages, readers would be able to digest the answers given to those who had sought advice or presented dilemmas. The *Bintel Brief* ran until well into the 1960s and illuminates a world of bewilderment, often high comedy and of course a fair degree of tragedy, too. Fortunately for the non-Yiddish speaker, many have been translated.[1] Tucked away amongst a mother's complaint about a daughter who had to wear a crucifix to a job interview to stand any chance of securing the position, and the concerns expressed at a son or daughter dating someone who was not Jewish, was a letter of a different order altogether.

The writer started off by remarking that many years had passed 'since the sharp fangs of the mad beast destroyed a third of the Jewish people.' He asks whether it is appropriate to tell his young children of his own escape and the dangers he had had to face. The answer came back that his children were a great comfort and did not need to be burdened with the anxiety and sorrow. The response concluded that his children of course must be told everything, but that he should 'Let it go until later.'

It is as if those words formed an unspoken manifesto for my grandparents' generation and to a large extent that of my parents too. Wonderful, brave, strong people who deep down felt a duty to pass on their story – but not now, because it was all too painful. Like Moses' brother Aaron, this was a traumatised generation that fell silent in the face of overwhelming tragedy. Frankly though, even if the words could somehow be formed, it seemed somehow wrong to express them. After all, no one wanted to harm or even burden their own grandchildren. 'God forbid,' as my grandmother would have immediately added. She might even have muttered some scarcely audible imprecation under her breath to ward off the evil eye (*ha'ayin hara*). Like Cahan's newspaper, they were pressing forward and building a new life.

As time passed, so did many of those who were tasked with the long overdue obligation to tell the story at a later date. The letting go became more entrenched and harder to break. Why now? Why go into these stories? How could you explain the inexplicable? The inquisitive child – and I am afraid I did fit into that category – was fobbed off year after year with varied excuses. More time went by, more died and the memories of others faded. The voices of those left were diminished in strength and in powers of recollection. The blanket of silence remained firmly in place.

Being realistic, I probably never had any choice but to set about the task of uncovering their narrative. Certain disparate elements of the story have somehow lived with me for much of my life. Subconsciously, maybe some of its shadows have even shaped it. Sadly, too, as I have traced the dreadful racism suffered by my family across multiple generations, I have also heard the distinctive echoes of this history re-emerge in contemporary society with ever greater force. Extraordinarily enough, it is no longer exceptional to see hateful hashtags on social media accompanied by stomach-churning content, or slogans on placards at public rallies on our streets attended by self-proclaimed 'progressive voices' invoking what Hitler did to the Jews as a positive thing whilst at the same time accusing Jews, Zionists and Israel of being modern day Nazis.[2] Jewish Members of Parliament have been subjected to vile anti-Semitic abuse and ordinary people going about their business to physical attack on public transport or in the street simply because they are readily identified as Jews.[3] Today, every synagogue, Jewish school or community has to be protected around the clock from those who would otherwise attack or destroy. If we are to fulfil the solemn pledge of 'never again' it has become increasingly clear that we need first to understand what it is that we are forswearing and to come to terms with its anthropological foundations. Ultimately, this engages some of the most basic and destructive of all human traits – the fear, debasement and hatred of the stranger. The person that does not really look like or behave like us – the other.

What is found on these pages is the story of those who are not alive to tell it, which is at one and the same time a weakness and a strength. Inevitably, I have to start with an apology for any inadvertent errors or inadequate description of events incompletely recorded. I have had to search for the missing details and track down the available material as best as I could. In any event, armed with these thoughts and much more besides, I have for some years set about the task of assembling whatever I have been able to gather. At times the process has felt like a letter written with love to my dead grandparents or parents, or perhaps a long-lost communication received from them.

One of my first ports of call was the National Archives at Kew. Many of those who have poured their energies into this kind of endeavour will have marvelled at the ease of the internet access. Within minutes of undertaking some simple name searches, the files on my parents and grandparents were located. They would doubtless contain many of the details that I needed to start to unlock the story. The trouble was that although the files still existed and had been carefully stored, each was closed to view until 2053 by Lord Chancellor's instrument. More curious still was that the date of Lord Chancellor's Order was 27 November 2001, more than sixty years after the events presumably narrated in the documents themselves. It would seem someone had put their mind to the question of whether or not these records should be sealed at that time. It was said to be on the grounds that the files in question contained sensitive personal information that could substantially distress or endanger a living person or her descendants.

The closure of a file for over a hundred years is encountered from time to time but is not by any means a routine matter. It is fair to say that the National Archive clearly had my attention now. At least on some level, the bureaucrats appeared to agree with the advice from the *Bintel Brief*. The story, however, cannot wait until 2053. In any event, I could not.

Family Tree

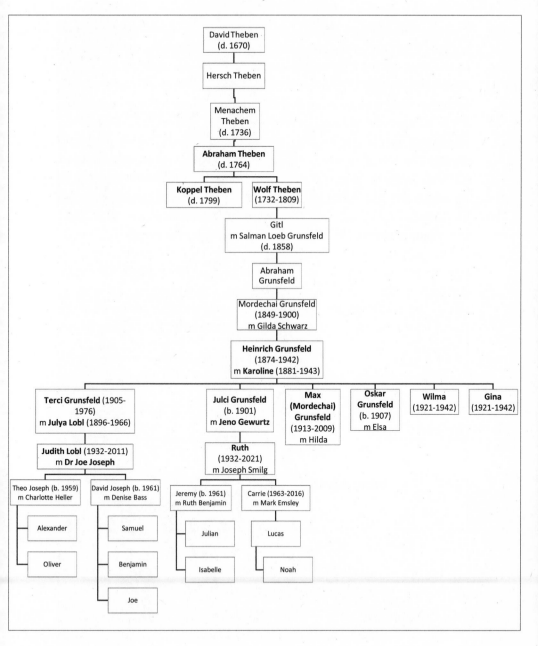

David Theben (d. 1670)
Hersch Theben
Menachem Theben (d. 1736)
Abraham Theben (d. 1764)
Koppel Theben (d. 1799)
Wolf Theben (1732-1809)
Gitl m Salman Loeb Grunsfeld (d. 1858)
Abraham Grunsfeld
Mordechai Grunsfeld (1849-1900) m Gilda Schwarz
Heinrich Grunsfeld (1874-1942) m **Karoline** (1881-1943)

Terci Grunsfeld (1905-1976) m **Julya Lobl** (1896-1966)
Julci Grunsfeld (b. 1901) m **Jeno Gewurtz**
Max (Mordechai) Grunsfeld (1913-2009) m Hilda
Oskar Grunsfeld (b. 1907) m Elsa
Wilma (1921-1942)
Gina (1921-1942)

Judith Lobl (1932-2011) m **Dr Joe Joseph**
Ruth (1932-2021) m Joseph Smilg

Theo Joseph (b. 1959) m Charlotte Heller
David Joseph (b. 1961) m Denise Bass
Jeremy (b. 1961) m Ruth Benjamin
Carrie (1963-2016) m Mark Emsley

Alexander
Samuel
Julian
Lucas

Oliver
Benjamin
Isabelle
Noah

Joe

Maps

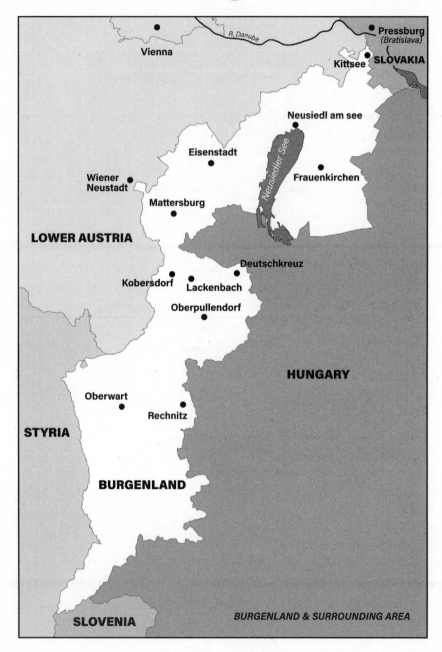

BURGENLAND & SURROUNDING AREA

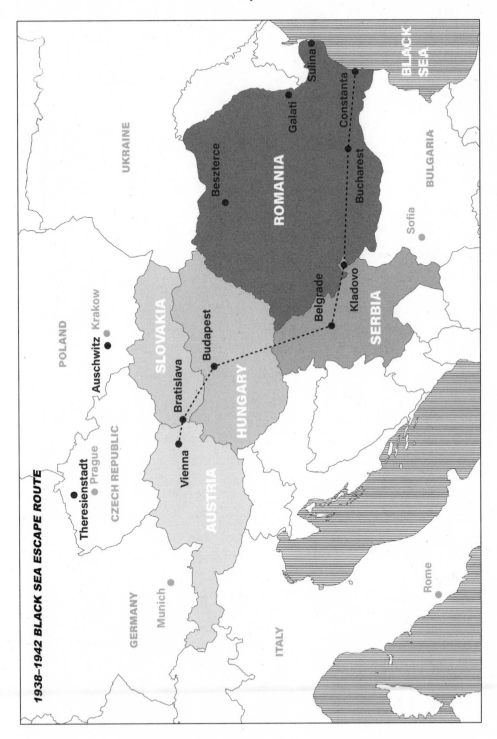

PART ONE
THE VILLAGE

1

The Photograph

There was a sepia-tinted photograph that had pride of position in my grandmother's bedroom and which had always captivated me as a child. The dressing-table on which it stood was itself a place of wonder, overflowing with old-fashioned sparkling brooches and sundry pearl necklaces. The image placed in a tarnished silver frame was positioned centrally and, on either side (much to my amusement) were two polystyrene shapes in the form of a head. At the time I didn't know that these were wig stands. In fact, as a child I didn't know that my grandmother, as an orthodox Jew, wore a wig. She had splendid, tightly brushed short brown hair. As a seven-year-old I just thought this was all her own. She lived with her sister, Julci, who always was simply called Auntie. They were as inseparable as twins, doing everything together. Terci and Julci. Grandma and Auntie. (The 'c' in both is an affectionate diminutive rhyming with 'lychee'.)

The long-preserved family portrait triggered many thoughts in my curious mind, but I was fascinated to see my mother, Judith, or Judy as everyone called her, at more or less my own age. She could be seen on the far left of the front row leaning into her mother and wearing a sailor dress with a neat little bow matched by a similar arrangement in her hair. Even better, I thought I could glean or perhaps imagine from my mother's expression that she was a little bit of a naughty child. Yes, of course she was formally dressed, as indeed was everybody else, but she was half looking away from the camera as though she did not altogether want to be there. It seemed that, held by her mother's gentle hand, she was both leaning in and somehow holding her distance all at the same time. At the far right of the front row my Auntie Ruth could be seen standing next to her mother, Julci. Behind my mother stood my grandfather, Julya suited and wearing a smart hat, his ears awkwardly sticking out at the rim. Further along the back row to the right (second from the end) stood my favourite uncle, Max. There was, however, no doubt as to the major attraction as far as I was concerned, it was my great-grandfather, Heinrich, in the front row sitting arms folded next to my great-grandmother, Karoline. Heinrich with his kindly smile, neatly trimmed moustache and fabulous felt hat, something of a cross between a Fez and a more traditional Polish Kashket, which added a wonderful touch of the exotic to the gathering.

Being taken away from the everyday is of course extremely attractive to any young kid, and a trip to see Terci and Julci in Southport at their somewhat grandly named Sandhurst Hotel, a kosher boarding house which they ran together for many years, was just such an occasion. Southport is found on the windswept Lancashire coastline, just north of Liverpool and south of Blackpool. In my own hazy memory, there was always some rain involved in whatever activity had been planned for the day. The red-bricked Sandhurst Hotel, consisting of two large houses, occupied a prominent corner plot on Leicester Street, just a short hop from the seafront, and an important place in my young imagination. I recall its neat gardens that wrapped around the entire building and the many bay-windowed rooms that no doubt attracted something of a premium. Like Tevya's legendary house in *Fiddler on the Roof*, it had a main staircase 'going up', which guests used, and a second staircase 'going down', for anyone other than paying residents. During the longueurs of the school summer holidays, whilst our father would carry on his work as a doctor in London, the rest of us would decamp to Southport. We would arrive by train, the very last of the passenger steam trains, and walk the short distance to the hotel. Holidays there were never dull. Not only were we all ensconced at the seaside with its endless beaches but there was also the diversion of the Land of the Little People. This was a strange Lilliputian model village where everything was reduced in size for children to wonder at. The Land of the Little People had it all: a railway bridge across a mini lake with roaring model steam trains, a manicured cricket ground; and even a miniature biscuit factory.

The main attraction though for the many loyal guests, and indeed for my brother Theo and I, was the Viennese cooking that featured so prominently on Terci and Julci's menu. Long-bearded Rabbis would come from far and wide for it. Anyone who has had the misfortune of eating what might be referred to as old school kosher food will testify to the fact that all taste is in essence expunged; the poor meat is beaten into surrender before being served up and the cakes can be heavy, laden with artificial colour and preservative. Not so with Terci and Julci; they cooked with love but also with what can only be described as *elan*. Whether serving up a schnitzel or goulash, they worked at great speed and in the full knowledge that what they produced was simply very good. Somewhat bizarrely, they even managed to infuse certain traditional dishes like Lancashire hotpot and shepherd's pie with enough paprika and spice to lift them out of the ordinary. They cooked to an audience and frequent loud applause. After Terci had finished in the kitchen, she would pass from table to table, exchanging small talk in her inimical *mittel-Europa* accented English. It was something of a mix between Austrian-German and Hungarian but with a distinct sing-song in the cadence. A simple sentence asking a guest if he or she wanted chicken or lamb chops for dinner involved passing up and down the entire musical scale and a fair few howlers of mispronunciation, which would endlessly amuse by brother and me.

Ours was, however, a small, tight-knit family and I was of course conscious that the strange foreign accents and the back story as refugees marked us apart from many others untrammelled by such burdens. My mind would often wander back to that photograph, which Terci had kept so close to her. Above all, it was the sheer size of the assembled group that struck me. Who were all these people that I never saw and indeed were not really spoken of? Despite my curiosity, I never asked her where it was taken, let alone when or in what circumstances. I doubt very much whether at that age I would have been able to frame the questions in any meaningful way, or make much sense of any response, but perhaps even then I could sense that this was forbidden territory. I cannot recall being told not to ask Grandma about those gathered in the photograph. Nevertheless, for as long as I can remember, an invisible barrier always served to prevent discussion of days long left behind.

Half a lifetime later, I resolved to try to shatter this conspiracy of silence and work my way through the many questions I had about the history of my mother's family. As a teenager, I had become transfixed by the story of one of my uncles, Martin, who had – as family legend would have it – fled Austria in the 1930s to fight the fascists in Spain. In my adolescent mind, it seemed that his armed resistance was the only family lore truly worthy of attention. Only when I grew a little older did I turn to consider the story of my mother and her parents. There were half-preserved garbled tales of a struggle to escape from Nazi Europe and of a desperate fight to survive. Yet my questions always seemed to be rebuffed or impossible to answer. This was not a subject for discussion in a family at one and the same time studiedly turning its back on the past, whilst not being able to escape it either.

After many failed attempts, my last hope rested with my Uncle Max, by this time in his mid-nineties and living in a care home in the quiet back streets of a Tel Aviv suburb. One day, I dropped him a line to tell him of my plan to sit down with him and take down whatever I could of his life story. I needed to make sense of the shadows. When I finally got an opportunity to fly out to see him, it was in the middle of August, definitely not the best time to be in Tel Aviv with its oppressive humidity and stifling heat beating down from an endless blue sky. Most visitors at this time wisely do not stray from the beach and its bustling bars. As tempting as this was, I instead grabbed a taxi which drew up outside a fairly non-descript mid-sixties building. I asked for Max at the reception, was given a warm welcome and told he was waiting for me in the communal cafeteria lounge with its Formica tables and upright plastic chairs.

As I turned the corner, I could see Max shuffling towards me leaning heavily on his aluminium walking frame cushioned at the feet with two worn tennis balls. His clear blue eyes lit up with joy. I suspect that he did not receive so many visitors and that this was a particular pleasure. We had hardly sat down together when Max wasted no time in telling me that there was no need to worry about my project because he had written everything down and that he had a copy ready for me to take home. He then showed me with more than a measure of pride a typed manuscript which looked to be about forty pages and was simply headed *My Life*.

My first reaction to this was that Max writing an autobiography would amount to something of a linguistic triumph. He spoke several languages fluently, but all told he had the least command of English, which he spoke with a strong German accent and awkward syntax. Max had an indomitable spirit and impressive energy and was proud of the fact that he was one of the most active in the care home's yoga and pilates classes. Nevertheless, his typing skills were not of the highest order. So as was explained to me, Max had turned to Joseph, his Filipino care-worker, to type up his life story, dictated by Max in his broken German-English. Joseph himself was a wonderful man, kind and compassionate; he had looked after Max for several years at the home and was genuinely fond of him. I never suspected, however, that he possessed any hidden literary talents; he was not a master of any of Max's native tongues and all in all I did not have high hopes for this manuscript.

We sat together in the cafeteria and caught up on the family gossip. As Max had a visitor from abroad, this attracted a degree of attention from other resident *kibbitzers*. A *kibbitzer* is Yiddish for an interferer, someone who chips in with views and advice from the side, particularly when not asked for. Like so many Yiddish expressions, the derivation is not without some controversy. It is said by some to originate from Central European cafés where elderly men would meet and play chess, only to have the next move shouted out and suggested vociferously by *kibbitzers*. A really good *kibbitzer* is someone who proffers advice without knowing anything of the real issues or situation at hand. This of course takes a degree *chutzpah*, or cheek. The *kibbitze*r rarely lacks this quality.

After a little while, I felt that it would be wise to ask a few questions – by way of an insurance policy in case not all was revealed in his typed manuscript. I asked him about Lackenbach in Austria, the village where my mother was born. Max responded with great excitement that he had returned there some years ago and that he had taken a photograph of the house my mother was born in and had sent it to her. My mother had spent a whole lifetime running away from anything connected with her childhood and had never mentioned Max's visit there to me. Max then drew me a little closer and told me that it was all written down. He patted the photocopy of his life story, sitting on his lap, and finished by saying in a very serious voice, 'But you know that we are directly descended from the Thebens of Pressburg.'

This did not have quite the immediate impact on me that Max was no doubt expecting or hoping for. I had to confess that the name did not mean anything to me. I was not even sure exactly where Pressburg was, either. Max then told me that the Thebens were a supremely wealthy merchant family in Pressburg, today Bratislava, the capital city of Slovakia on the Danube. The Thebens, he continued, were leaders of the Jewish community who both consorted with the Hapsburg Emperors of the day and were rabbinical scholars of great renown in their own right.

I was digesting this information when one of the *kibbitzers* sitting nearby piped up with a large measure of sarcasm that *he* was a direct descendant of Moses Mendelssohn, the great eighteenth-century Jewish philosopher of the Enlightenment. There was a good deal of laughter from others at this. Max was understandably somewhat affronted by this unwelcome interference. He turned to me and told me to ignore the man, who Max said had been a brilliant lawyer in his day but was now *tsemisht*, pointing his forefinger to his temple and turning it as he spoke. *Tsemisht* is another great Yiddish onomatopoeic expression which means all mixed up or confused and is often used of an elderly person who has lost his or her full grip on reality. It is, however, flexible in meaning and can also be used of a person talking gibberish at the end of a heavy night on the town. It is fair to say that Yiddish does not exactly conform to contemporary notions of acceptable language or political correctness. Indeed, those who spoke Yiddish would probably identify this as one of its core strengths. It is nothing if not earthy.

The damage, however, had been done. Hubris can of course be dangerous at the best of times, but in a Jewish old age home it is practically lethal. In an instant, a fair few other fantastical suggestions were being called out by way of famous mythological or biblical ancestry. Max smiled weakly. He recognized he had lost this particular battle and asked me to take him back to his room where we could talk quietly. We did so and had the most precious of conversations, talking for some hours. I took detailed notes but above all it was wonderful just to hear his voice, even though age had left it quite thin and reed-like. He intermingled stories of his long life with complaints of his many ailments and symptoms. Then suddenly, he stopped, looked at his watch and said it was time for evening prayers. Max remained an observant orthodox Jew all his life. He only agreed to moving into a residential home if it had a synagogue on the premises. So we paused our conversation and I walked slowly beside him to the in-house prayer hall. We recited the prayers together with his fellow residents, a number of whom had been teasing him just a short while before and then, seeing he was tired, I left him.

It is to my great shame that I took home his photocopied manuscript and did not really study it closely. As I had suspected, the English was all too often hard to follow. Worse still, I saw from my brief scan that the pages were not sequentially numbered, some had been copied twice whilst others it seemed had not been copied at all. As a result, there were frustrating gaps in the story that could not be easily understood, whilst other sections were repeated verbatim as if by way of some kind of coded emphasis. Regrettably, when I got back to London, life and work took over and I put my notes and his manuscript away.

Only a few months later, I was arguing a case many miles away from home when I got a call from my mother telling me that Max had died peacefully in his sleep. He did not quite make it to a hundred. I was upset but also felt so foolish. I had not finished what I had set out to do when I went to see him. I had not followed up on the many questions I had. Of course, I did not know then that this would be our last conversation, but that is not much of an excuse. Soon after, I fished out his manuscript from the back of my desk drawer. I read it through properly for the first time and saw that amongst its scattered pages was an outline of a family tree stretching back in a continuous line from the Thebens of Pressburg through to the many successive generations who lived in Lackenbach in Austria and ending with my own boys and those of my brother, born nearly three hundred years later. The time had now come. I had to follow the story that Max had outlined, fill in the gaps and make sense of what he had written down for me. Throughout, I have been helped by the extraordinary kindness of strangers but above all, on the many occasions I have stumbled or thought I had reached yet another dead end, I have somehow felt Max's frail hand gently placed on my shoulder guiding me ever onwards, so allowing me to recount this story to the very end.

2

Herr M

My first thought was to start my journey by heading off straight to Lackenbach. I was armed with a photograph taken in front of the house my mother was born in and another of the house itself, which Max had given me. I imagined walking up and down the streets of this little picturesque village until I could match these pictures with today's reality. I even harboured the somewhat unrealistic notion of standing outside the front door and being invited in by the present owners to talk. Nevertheless, before any worthwhile exploration could be undertaken it would be necessary to get hold of as many of the historical papers and archives as possible to guide the search in the right direction. This meant I had to start not in Lackenbach, but a few kilometres away in the provincial capital of Eisenstadt.

Although the main purpose of the visit was to inspect the records for traces of my mother's family, no trip to Eisenstadt would be possible without hearing some music in the great *Haydnsaal*, in the fabulous baroque palace, Schloss Esterházy, with its extravagant frescoed ceilings, highly decorated walls and more gold leaf than might be thought strictly necessary for present-day tastes. Prince Nikolai Esterházy was Joseph Haydn's patron for nearly thirty years, allowing him to hire and conduct his own orchestra of about a dozen musicians, as well as ensuring that the *Haydnsaal* met the composer's own exacting requirements. Whilst acting as *Kappellmeister* for Prince Nikolai, and after that for Prince Nikolai II, Haydn composed a body of now largely unknown operatic works, which presumably fulfilled the twin purpose of pleasing his patrons and keeping his mistress, the soprano Luigia Polzelli, at the estate. However, he also wrote there some of his most influential music, a series of symphonies, oratorios including The Creation, and spectacular Masses written each successive year for the name day of Prince Nikolai's wife, Maria Joseph of Lichtenstein. As well as these great public works, Haydn composed his piano sonatas and a little over sixty string quartets at Eisentadt. Incredibly enough, these seem to have been written for Haydn's own satisfaction and were never performed for an employer who had no taste for either. Given the importance of Haydn in the whole history of classical music and the importance of Eisenstadt to Haydn, it is no exaggeration to say that Eisenstadt was midwife to the age of the classical tradition.

There are many who speak eloquently of the acoustic in the Musikverein of Vienna, which is indeed splendid. There is nevertheless something tremendously moving about sitting in the very hall built for Haydn and hearing the music composed for that stage. We made sure on our arrival that we got tickets for a lunchtime concert there and I asked politely whether they would be playing Haydn. The answer came, 'Here, it is always Haydn.' Quite so. It was high summer when I was there with Denise, my wife. Before the concert, we visited the Eisenstadt archives. The state records were held until very recently in a grand neo-classical building on the Europlatz, a stone's throw from our hotel. As any visitor walks up the steps towards the entrance, there is a clearly visible pale-yellow memorial with the sombre inscription: 'Each victim should serve as a warning and an obligation to us all, so that intolerance and racial madness never arises again. Never forget.'

We arrived as the doors opened early in the morning, introduced ourselves and asked to see the files kept there relating to my mother's family who had lived for generations in this region. We were asked for their names with all relevant spelling variations and so wrote down Lobl and Grunsfeld, spelt both with and without an umlaut, respectively my grandfather's and grandmother's family names. To our complete surprise, half a trolley-load of brown folders were brought to our reading table. Somewhat jarringly, we also spied another trolley laden with black box files, each marked with a white Star of David at the top of the spine. The folders on our trolley, were, however, organised differently: each had the metal bar and hook at the top to suggest they must once have hung neatly in an office cabinet, in strict alphabetical order. Each contained the records of a specific family or business. I took up the first. It was marked on the front cover as forming part of the Burgenland, Lackenbach archive. A neat hand identified the file as dealing with the records of my grandfather's household, said to consist of Julya, his wife, Terci, his daughter, Judy, and his own mother, Johanna. This particular file contained the records relating to his house in Lackenbach. It was marked with the reference number 'EZ 136'. A quick internet search decrypted this as an 'Einlagezhal number', the land registration numbering system in Austria. As we turned the pages, we could see the address of Julya's house in Lackenbach, recorded as Berggasse, 18 and the endless detail relating to the dispossession of this property. Other files dealt with different family members and the businesses they had owned.

Leaving aside the raw emotion of holding these files in my hand, which had plainly been meticulously stored and produced with such ease, it became clear that there was too much to comprehend and digest in one sitting. We asked permission to take copies away to examine them carefully back home with the help of friends able to read the highly stylised pre-war gothic German script. The archivist in charge could not have been more helpful or encouraging. She insisted I contact her with any further questions that I might have.

It was a productive morning and the Haydn concert immediately afterwards capped it off. The sun shone and luck was clearly on our side. In a buoyant mood, I even popped into one of the many shops selling traditional Austrian wares and purchased some collarless linen tunic shirts. My wife gently teased that the look of a local artist clearly suited me.

Opposite the Schloss there is a well-appointed restaurant in the former stables, complete with a shaded terrace and a fabulous view of the then sun-drenched Esterházy palace. Denise and I took a table and settled down for a somewhat self-congratulatory late lunch. We tucked into some delicious lake fish, ordered a bottle of *gruner veltliner* and got chatting to the two gentlemen on the next table. Our conversation was in a mixture of English and German and no doubt aided by the fact that each of us had drunk a few glasses of wine. Our three boys often despair of our tendency to strike up conversations with total strangers.

The two men were smartly dressed retired businessmen in their seventies. The younger of the two, Herr M, told us he was born in 1944, and had worked as a European director for a multinational corporation and had so lived abroad for a number of years. As a result, he clearly spoke the better English and from time to time would translate a few sentences for the benefit of his friend. Herr M asked me what we were doing in Eisenstadt, which is not exactly on the main Austrian tourist trail. I told him that I was here for two reasons, for the music and to go to my mother's birthplace in a village not far away. For a little while he talked knowledgeably about the music of the Burgenland – Haydn, Liszt, Bruckner, and the great violinist Joachim all having lived in this part of the country. He asked me where my mother had been born and I told him Lackenbach. When he heard me say this his eyes lit up and he turned to his friend and said in German that he knew it, that I was in truth a Burgenlander, 'Ninety per cent (*Neunzig prozent Burgenlander*)!' he exclaimed. He then told us he had been born in a village only about six kilometres away from Lackenbach, at which point there was more exclamation and a symbolic raising of a glass.

Herr M then drew himself closer to me and said, 'You know, before the war, Lackenbach was full of Juden.' He hissed the last word. I felt physically sick, like someone had kicked me in the stomach. I had never heard this word expressed before, in German, with all its dreadful historical venom. I was still trying to catch my breath and he continued, 'You know what I mean, Juden... Jews. They stood in the street and stuck together.' He then made a gesture linking the forefingers of his hands together indicating what he meant. 'They did no work, the only business they did was funny business.' At this he cupped his right hand behind his back to indicate someone receiving a back-hander or illicit payment. 'You know, Hitler was very clever, he knew how to deal with them.' At this he paused for just a split second before finishing, 'He fucked them.' This last he spoke in barely a whisper and accompanied the words by sticking his thumb between his second and third fingers. And then he sat back.

I looked at him for what seemed like an eternity but was most likely just a few seconds. I took a deep breath and responded.

'You know what you have said is obscene and evil. I am a Jew; my wife is also a Jew and we are proud to be Jewish. The Hitler you have praised murdered half my family in Lackenbach. Took them away and was responsible for their murder in cold blood. Just so that you know, not that it is particularly relevant, they had worked hard, ordinary, honest lives and lived in peace in the town for hundreds of years. What you have said is disgusting.'

It was now Herr M's turn to be astonished. Maybe it was the wine. Perhaps it was all the ludicrous Burgenlander small talk. I think at the moment he leant over to me, we had still been chuckling about my being described as a thoroughbred local. I suspect he was deceived by Denise's blonde hair, blue eyes and more than passable conversational German. He did not expect this. He clearly thought he was in like-minded company and free to speak. His friend who had understood enough of the conversation (but had not in any way tried to stop Herr M), looked mortified.

Herr M tried one last riposte. 'I never said all Jews were like this. Some of my good friends are Jews and not all of them were lazy.' He may have tried to say more, but I waved him away with a hand gesture and turned my back on him. We paid and left, whilst he was still quibbling over some minor item on the bill.

I was still shaking with rage and hurt. There were so many other things I could have said and would have wanted to say but of course did not. Reminding him of the memorial at the entrance of the state archive would not have been a bad place to start. Still, I could then see in sharper focus, perhaps for the first time, the darkness that often lay not far beneath the surface of this tale of rural life in Austria. Herr M was born in 1944, after all the Jews had been taken away. There were no Jews at all in Lackenbach in his lifetime, let alone standing in the street. This hatred was handed down to him in his mother's milk. What is more, Herr M was not some tattooed skinhead fascist. In just the same way that my Jewishness took him by surprise, so I was caught out by his racism. He was a middle class, suited, classical music loving retired businessman with a tennis-playing daughter living in England. I just didn't expect it, just as my own family did not see the storm coming their way in the 1930s.

What was perhaps a little clearer to me though, was that this part of Europe never really accepted the notion of a strongly identifying religious and ethnic minority living side-by-side but distinct from the culture of the majority. Perhaps just as shocking is that when you look up the Lackenbach website for some account of the town's past, there is a dedicated section on its Jewish connections stretching back hundreds of years right up until March 1938, which concludes, 'Little is known of the expulsion of the Jews ... after the so-called Anschluss... Nobody returned after 1945.' Prejudice and deep denial remain close companions in this neck of the woods.

3

Esterházy's Jews

The half-hour drive from Eisenstadt to Lackenbach passes through the wine country of the Burgenland and its many princely chateaux, never far from present-day Hungary. The proximity with the border serves as an important reminder of the frequency with which these lands changed hands from Austria to Hungary and back again: my grandmother, and indeed most of the family, spoke both languages fluently. With the dream-like shores of the *Neusiedler See* only a few kilometres to the East, today you can see row upon row of vines planted with its famous Blaufrankisch grape. They are occasionally broken up by rows of sunflowers collectively bowing their heads at the late afternoon sun. At the approach to Lackenbach, the Leitha hills in the distance provide a natural backdrop which a landscape artist of the nineteenth century would have thought worthy of attention. At the village entrance with its neat little square, manicured lawns and carefully curated collection of local shops, there is a sign for its principal tourist attraction, the Esterházy hunting lodge, the *Jaeger Schloss*.

After meandering a short distance down the marked gravel path, a visitor will come upon a handsome low brick structure and a wonderful garden planted with red and white roses. This was perhaps a patriotic gesture, being the colours of Austria, or maybe even a nod to the discourse between the babbling brook and the forlorn lover of Schubert's *Die Schöne Müllerin* who had sought peace of mind in just such a scene. In tune with its function, it is a more modest affair than the family's neighbouring palaces. The cool waters of the gently flowing and shaded Selitzbach complete the idyllic setting.

The Schloss was built by Count Nicolai towards the start of seventeenth century, when the Esterházy dynasty was only in its infancy. Through a felicitous money match, Count Nicolai become the lord of the village. Yet it was his victory at the battle of Lackenbach in 1620 against the rebellious Protestant Prince Gabor Bethlen that saw the start of the stratospheric rise of the family fame and fortune. The Hapsburgs increasingly looked to the Esterházys as a bulwark against both its Protestant and Ottoman enemies.

The politics of the seventeenth century hold the key to the story of both the rise of the Esterházy family to the very top of European aristocracy and to the history of my family in this part of the world. The Ottoman Turks had for over a hundred years occupied large swathes of Hungary including Buda, half of modern-day Budapest. There were large-scale invasions by the Ottomans and counter-attacks by Hapsburg troops aided by multiple European Catholic allies who gathered their forces under the banner of the Holy League. The Ottomans had allies of their own. They were assisted by a largely Lutheran Protestant uprising led by Imre Thokoly in Transylvania who had established a Kingdom in Upper Hungary, thereby putting even greater pressure on the Hapsburg armies.

Victories against the Turks were loudly celebrated throughout Europe. Defeat was also tasted regularly. Candia, the final city in Venetian hands in Crete, fell to the Ottomans in 1669 after a twenty-year siege that figured large in the Western European imagination, with a great foretelling of the end of days.

In the summer of 1683, Vienna itself was besieged for about sixty days and looked distinctly vulnerable.[1] The Ottoman troops had apparently tunnelled through the major outer fortifications. Vienna faced 'a barrage of cannon, musket shot, bombs and grenades which changed the face of the fairest and most flourishing City in the world, disfigured and ruined most part of the best Palaces and chiefly those of the Emperor'.[2] The siege was ultimately relieved by the arrival of Polish forces under King John III Sobieski alongside soldiers of the Imperial Hapsburg army, strengthened by the legendary heroics of Count Starhemberg, whose family reappears some two hundred and fifty years later in this story.

After this triumph, the Hapsburg forces along with their allies turned their attentions to recapturing Buda from the Ottoman Turks. A lengthy campaign followed, the Ottomans were forced to retreat and the city was once more under Hapsburg rule, as was reinforced in the Peace of Karlowicz in 1699. Following the liberation of Buda, the Hungarian legislature met at Pressburg in 1687 and as a token of gratitude for the removal of the Ottoman yoke, the Diet recognised the Hapsburg's hereditary right to the Hungarian throne, thus allowing the dual kingdom to take hold.

The consequence for the Jews of Buda was appalling. It is estimated that half of the few thousand Jews living there at the time were murdered or sold into slavery by the conquering Imperial army. Whether real or imagined, the Jews were believed to have profited from trade with the Turks, and then understood to have sided with and fought alongside the Muslim invaders. This perception may have been strengthened by the mythology surrounding Shabbatai Zvi, a Cabbalist and self-proclaimed Jewish Messiah. At the age of twenty-two, Shabatai Zvi declared himself to be true saviour of the Jews and embarked on a lengthy pilgrimage to Cairo and then Jerusalem. Many thousands joined him as fanatical and devoted followers. In anticipation of what was widely thought to be the year of the apocalypse in 1666, he embarked on a journey through Central Europe, only to stun his acolytes by converting to Islam and living out his days in Constantinople. This abandonment of his old faith was at first met with disbelief and sent shockwaves across Jewish communities in Europe[3] but also provided Catholics with yet another stick with which to beat the infidel – as it showed in their eyes that the Jews were not even steadfast in their apostasy and that there was only one true Messiah, Christ himself.

The destruction of the Jewish community of Buda was not a one-off tragedy, it was reflective of the mood of the widespread and politically led religious hatred of the time – all too often with half an eye to the potential for economic gain which followed such persecution, especially when debts and contracts were routinely cancelled. In 1668, there were large-scale riots in Vienna clamouring for the Jews to be sent packing out of the city. Whether reluctantly or not, in February 1670, Emperor Leopold I signed a decree for the expulsion of all Jews from Vienna and Lower Austria to be completed by Corpus Christi the following year, 1671. When the Jews of Vienna were allowed to return in 1673, they were subjected to punitive taxation.

It is in this wider context that the remarkable story of the Esterházy family's protection of the Jews living on their estate lands must be seen and understood. Count Paul Esterházy, the son and heir of Nicolai, was instrumental in the defeat of the Turks. As Imperial Field Marshal and Commander in Chief of the army of Southern Hungary, he was one of the heroes of the relief of the siege of Vienna and in the recapture of Buda from the Ottomans. Like his father, he was fiercely loyal to Emperor Leopold I and became an essential cog in the Imperial regime uniting Austria and Hungary under Catholic domination. Titles were showered on Paul – first Count Palatine of the Holy Roman Empire and then Imperial Prince. It was not just aristocratic honorifics that were bestowed on the family but vast swathes of land. From the more modest origins of his father Nicolai, in the space of a generation Prince Paul became the largest of all the Hapsburg landowners and his combined holdings were the size of a small modern European nation-state. That position was then further consolidated by the royal grant of the status of *Fideikomiss* over the entire estate, a form of trust which allowed the Esterházy lands to pass intact and crucially largely tax-free from generation to generation, until its abolition by the Nazis in March 1938. The establishment of the *Fideikomiss*, however, did have another consequence relevant to this story; namely that the land, their principal source of capital wealth, could not in substance be sold. Ultimately, this made them an asset-rich, cash-poor family, with cashflow depending heavily on what could be raised by way of feudal taxes, rent from tenant farmers or the money markets.

The equipping of armies, building of palaces at Lackenbach, Eisenstadt and Ferstod and then furnishing them with quantities of expensive Italian and Dutch art consumed large sums of money. Prince Paul turned to one of the most reliable financiers of the day to meet his requirements. This was Samson Wertheimer, an orthodox Jew and one of the most prominent court Jews or *Hoffaktors* as they came to be known. These were wealthy merchants who performed the dual function of lending money to the royal houses and aristocracy of Europe as well acting as an intermediary between the Jewish communities and their rulers, presenting pleas and petitions.

Samson Wertheimer originally came from Worms in present-day Germany. He was the nephew of Samuel Oppenheimer, one of the principal financiers to the Hapsburg Emperors in the second half of the seventeenth century.[4] Their finance house was based in Vienna. At the end of the seventeenth century, however, the Wertheimers and Oppenheimers could count themselves amongst the most powerful banking families of Western Europe. Samson Wertheimer was said to be a cautious financier who eschewed some of the riskier ventures of his uncle but nevertheless lived in grand style and maintained houses in Vienna, Eisenstadt and elsewhere. In the sole known surviving portrait, dating from the early 1700s, he is shown with a long flowing beard, resplendent black robes adorned with a heavy chained medallion and court-like bands.[5] His long-fingered right hand is seen holding a quill pen, no doubt tending to some pressing matter of business. Whilst he holds his gaze straight ahead, the composition seems to suggest that the letter he is signing rests on top of a tray of vital correspondence, perhaps to or from the Emperor himself.

A first-hand account survives of a visit of a young cousin to Samson Wertheimer in Vienna in the 1700s.[6] He was overwhelmed by the splendour of his lifestyle. He reported that the house was guarded by a detachment of ten soldiers of the Imperial Guard. He referred to Wertheimer as having a white beard and being dressed in 'the Polish style'. He was described as a learned man who had also built many synagogues and supported Jewish communities as far off as Jerusalem. The cousin also noted that no Jew was allowed to stay a night in Vienna without the permission of either the Emperor or Wertheimer.

Wertheimer's services went beyond the business of simply lending money. In 1701 Wertheimer was said personally to have negotiated the dowry of 1,000,000 florins on the marriage of Leopold's brother-in-law, Duke Charles Philip, to the daughter of the King of Poland.[7] At the turn of the eighteenth century, on the death of his uncle, he was appointed Imperial Court Factor and became one of those principally responsible for effecting supplies of equipment and uniforms to the Imperial Army. It was Samson Wertheimer to whom the Emperor looked to pay off the Empress's debts and even redeem certain of the crown jewels which had been pawned.[8] In short, he was a trusted financial adviser handling the most confidential and delicate personal matters for the Hapsburg and Esterházy families.

Samson Wertheimer's position had a further material consequence. As a result of his financing of Prince Paul's affairs, an agreement was reached between the two which resulted in Prince Paul in 1690 issuing a Letter of Protection, or the *Schutzbrief*, as it was known. The *Schutzbrief* gave permission for Werthemer to build a synagogue in his house in Eisenstadt, the *Wertheimer hausshul*, which remarkably and almost alone of all the former synagogues of Austria, still stands today. The synagogue is unusual not just because it has survived but also for its dimensions and design. Situated on the first floor of an ordinary-looking seventeenth-century house, there is nothing on the outside that prepares the visitor for what is within. The synagogue is more like a private chapel than the traditional Jewish communal meeting place. It is nearly twice as high as it is wide with an ornate yellow painted walls, decorated ceiling and stunning chandelier. There is the traditional ark to house the torah scrolls, a *bimah* or podium in the centre from where the main prayers would be recited and then just one wooden bench, presumably for the family members and a row of chairs behind, perhaps for guests. All this was designed to meet both the letter and spirit of the permission granted, namely for a household place of worship.

More importantly still, Prince Paul set out the terms under which Jews in general – not just the Wertheimer family – could live in peace and under protection in Eisentadt. The territorial scope of the protection was expanded over the next few years, first to include Mattersdorf in 1694 and in due course covered a series of Burgenland villages where the Esterházy family owned land and held political sway. Lackenbach, too, became a protected community with a grant at the beginning of the eighteenth century to build a synagogue and a cemetery. These villages became known as the *Seben Gemeinden*, the Seven Communities, and consisted of Eisenstadt, Mattersdorf, Lackenbach Frauenkirchen, Deutchskreutz, Kobersdorf, and Kittsee. Lackenbach and Mattersdorf were home to the largest Jewish populations.

Formal decrees of feudal protection like the *Schutzbrief* were by no means unknown in Europe or even in this neighbourhood at the time. Indeed, without such a document there was no legal right for a Jew to live in Hungary as they were not afforded the rights of citizens.[9] In 1627, Paul's father Count Nicolai had granted limited protection to the Jews of Lackenbach, which laid out a series of financial terms on which Jews could live on his estate there. In 1687, Count Batthyany in nearby Rechnitz similarly granted permission to 36 Jews to live on his lands. Examples can be traced further afield, in particular in the communities of Worms, Mainz and in Brandenburg.[10] It is of course possible that Wertheimer, who came from Worms, looked to past precedent, as presumably did Paul himself.

Nevertheless, the direction of travel in this document differed from other such instruments. In the *Schutzbrief,* the Jews on these lands were not only afforded protection but also wide-ranging freedoms to practise their religion openly and 'celebrate all your Jewish ceremonies'. The Jewish communities here felt no compulsion to assimilate and carried on strictly orthodox lives. They became known as the *Schutzjuden* – the protected Jews. As long as they paid feudal taxes to the Esterházys, they enjoyed a *Heimatsrecht,* a legal right of abode on a designated part of the Esterházy's lands and the right to earn a living on any part of the wider estate.[11] What is more, the right to establish a household was generally interpreted as being hereditary, which in turn led to a stable and permanent population of specific families that can still be traced back today.[12]

Jews in these Burgenland communities could settle, marry, and live a life without fear of eviction.[13] These Jewish communities were permitted – even required – to supervise and police themselves. In Lackenbach, the Society of Israelite Firemen ran their own volunteer fire service and the Rabbi himself was proud to serve in this capacity.[14] This regulated separation of Jew and Catholic in such a small village gave rise to odd situations frequently occupying the border of tragedy and comedy. In 1774, a complaint was made by two local Christian residents to the Esterházy estate manager about the lack of skill of the Jewish firemen after a fire had caused damage to several houses. It seems that following the failed attempts to control the fire, a mass brawl broke out and the Esterházy estate regent had to mediate and impose fines on all and sundry.

Disputes within the community were to be resolved by a Jewish tribunal under Jewish law with the fines imposed being split two-thirds for the Esterházy rulers and one-third for the Jewish community. Without doubt this was a radical package, extending the boundaries and norms in relation to the treatment of Jews.

When it came to day-to-day work, Jews were allowed to engage widely in commerce and crafts. Under these arrangements, they could make and sell kosher brandy, wine and beer. Also listed were more traditional occupations such as tailor, shoemaker, furrier, lace-maker, barber, doctor and goldsmith.[15] In addition to the specified liberty to build synagogues,[16] there was permission to employ a rabbi and build Jewish schools, further provision for the maintenance of a Jewish cemetery, a ritual bath (a *mikveh*),[17] and for Jews to have their own ritual slaughterer of meat, a *shochet*.[18] The Jews of the day were allowed not only to slaughter cattle but to pickle, preserve and sell the non-kosher parts of the animal to non-Jews, which in turn gave rise to frequent accusations that Jewish butchers were undercutting their Christian counterparts when selling non-kosher meat.[19]

There was in addition some fairly enlightened social provision to prevent excess indebtedness and to encourage cleanliness in the Jewish quarter.[20] The community was also permitted to elect its own political leader. known as the *Judenrichter*, who had a ceremonial mace carried before him to mark his position.

These were the first Jewish communities in Hapsburg lands to obtain such broadly stated social and political autonomy and retained it until March 1938. Long before emancipation was given statutory force in Austria-Hungary in the mid-nineteenth century, the *Schutzbrief* lit a pathway for Christians and Jews to live side by side under the law according to their own respective customs. In time, it led to the development of many local regulations and practices. The Jews of Eisenstadt were allowed on the Sabbath and other festivals to draw a metal chain across the street, closing off their section of the town and so being left to their own devices and worship. The chain can still be seen today at the entrance of the Judengasse. The community in Eisenstadt also developed a strict prohibition on all forms of gambling, which was only relaxed during the eight-day winter festival of Chanukah, when it was traditional to play games for money including the spinning of the *dreidel*. The rabbis, however, in a very concession to popular demand, would permit gambling for just one additional day after the festival had ended. At the end of the ninth day, with a firm knock of a wooden staff on the floor of the synagogue, it would be announced that the usual rules once more applied.

In Kittsee, a tradition developed that the synagogue services were conducted in complete silence so as to ensure spiritual concentration. The only time a name was called out was after someone had died. In other words, each Jewish community was permitted to regulate for their own spiritual rest, quietude and entertainment. This was a charter of freedom which had practically no parallel in the rest of Europe at this time. It allowed the Jews to express themselves over generations – in their religion, but also in commerce, the arts and in due course in politics, too.

In return for the right of residence, the Jewish community was required to pay certain specified annual taxes, called the *Schutzgeld*, or protection money, which was set annually and varied from village to village. In

Lackenbach, it was a lump sum paid collectively by the whole community which had to be raised from the inhabitants, the majority of whom were plainly indigent and in the words of one of the Esterházy administrators, 'owed more in florins than they had hairs on their head'.[21] Scraping together these not insignificant sums each year was clearly a significant struggle, but this was also fertile ground for the development of a trope of feigned poverty; that Jews did always have money that could be shaken out of them but merely pretended to be poor out of cunning and a desire to hold on to their ill-gotten wealth. This image still takes a powerful grip on the imagination of many in parts of Eastern Europe today and specifically Poland, where it is seen as quite normal to carry around a 'lucky Jew' in your wallet. This is a small figurine of an orthodox Jew that for best effect should be held upside down on the Jewish sabbath so as to encourage the coins to fall out of his pockets.

Whilst onerous, the lump sum was not the only form of taxation to which Jews were subjected on these lands. There were specific levies such as for the building of houses, as well as an expectation that at New Year and other special occasions such as notable feast days gifts of fruit, game, sugar, and coffee would be delivered (which were generally distributed amongst the Esterházys' household retainers).[22]

Furthermore, thirty pounds of pepper was to be produced annually. Pepper was much in demand as an exotic and expensive spice from the East. In this region procuring such quantities of pepper would have likely involved contacts with Venetian or Ottoman traders. It must be assumed that Samson Wertheimer's connections would have allowed the Jewish community to pay a tax in this form and provides another example of what seems to have been a symbiotic relationship. A list of non-Jewish taxpayers from 1715 in Lackenbach shows that there were only twenty persons recorded on it. It seems that a material proportion of the Esterházy's tax take would have come from the arrangements set out in the *Schutzbrief*.

The issuance of the *Schutzbrief* marked the near high point of the power of Samson Wertheimer and his cousins the Oppenheimers. Sixty years later, the considerable fortunes of the Oppenheimer and Wertheimer families had come to an inglorious end. This often witnessed arc of fortune served to reinforce the notion that as a Jewish businessman or financier, the heights you rose to only signified how far you had to fall. First, the Oppenheimers were falsely accused of intrigue by Cardinal Kollonitz, a notorious old school anti-Semite.

One of Samson Wertheimer's nephews was imprisoned, but the trumped-up charges did not yield any result. This did not suit those who still owed them money. The Emperor then defaulted on his debts, refused to pay anything further and set up a commission of inquiry, which predictably concluded that it was the Oppenheimers who owed the state, rather than the other way round, leading in the end to the family being forced into bankruptcy.[23]

The Wertheimers ultimately fared no better. Samson's son, Wolf Wertheimer, was ambitious and perhaps too eager to prove himself to his father. He expanded the business and opened offices in many cities across present-day Germany. It was this that ultimately led to his ruin and the bankruptcy of the family business. On 25 August 1722, Wolf Wertheimer concluded a huge loan to the Elector Max Emmanuel of Munich with detailed and careful provision of security in terms of tax revenues. The loans were refinanced and increased in size over the years and inevitably ultimately fell into default. Despite the intervention of the Emperor who put pressure on the Court of Munich, repayment was simply not forthcoming and most likely not possible. Wolf Wertheimer had overstretched and had to then declare bankruptcy himself in 1733 when his own creditors pressed for repayment of the monies he had borrowed to lend to the Elector.

For thirty years, Wolf Wertheimer sought compensation and justice. It looked like he would finally make headway on the death of Elector Charles Albert in 1745 and the succession of Maximilian Joseph III. A new commission of inquiry was established and in 1754 promissory notes to a value of 3,700,000 florins were issued, payable only in 1764. Wolf Wertheimer died in 1763 before any payment was made. The will of Samson Wertheimer's grandson, Samuel Wolf Wertheimer, records that he died in poverty 'through unfortunate times and bad luck'.[24]

It would then seem that the short period between 1690 and 1710 was the only time when the confluence of wealth, influence and religious observance could have led to the establishment of these seven protected self-governing Jewish communities. Their survival under the protection of the Esterházy family for so long has to be seen as truly remarkable, especially as the tension between Jews and Christians in these villages was never far beneath the surface. The records of the Esterházy Estate show that frequent petitions and complaints were made by the Christian villagers to the local estates managers. At the extreme end, attempts were made to persuade the Esterházy family to rescind the *Schutzbrief* altogether and eject the Jews principally on grounds of the well-worn tropes of Jews spreading disease and undertaking dishonest business practices.[25] These were invariably rejected. In 1741, the stakes were raised by an unsuccessful petition to the Hungarian Diet to expel 'these godless vermin' from the Burgenland, and a long stand-off between Prince Paul Anton and the Jewish communities was only resolved in 1749 when the Prince agreed to renew the *Schutzbrief* on payment of a further not inconsiderable sum of 100 ducats.[26]

In 1772, the battleground shifted to mass protest against the forced conversion of a young Jewish girl from Lackenbach simply referred to as Malchel. It seems that this time the organised resistance was successful and the kidnapped girl was retuned to her parents. On other occasions, the complaints made were more prosaic, such as infringements of the terms of the *Schutzbrief*. These included the objection made to the Jewish brandy seller who set up his stall too early in the morning, said to amount to unfair competition. Each petition to the Esterházys was investigated and dealt with.

So it was that in this somewhat remote rural corner, for the greater part of two hundred and fifty years generations of Jews lived amongst, but at the same time largely separate from, the Christian population. They were allowed to worship openly and according to orthodox custom and rites. By the early eighteenth century, just short of half the population of Lackenbach was Jewish. In the mid-nineteenth century, they made up the majority. With some ebb and flow, this remained the position in March 1938.

There are occasional references in the communal records to members of both sides of my mother's family, Grunsfeld and Lobl, living in Lackenbach in the eighteenth century. The very earliest gravestones would only record the Hebrew first name and patronymic of the deceased. The Jews at this time had not yet been forced to take German names. This was introduced by a decree dated 23 July 1787 under Joseph II which forbade Yiddish or Hebrew names. In due course a list of sufficiently identifiable names was circulated that Jewish families would have to choose from and if they didn't, a name would be assigned. So it was that my maternal grandmother's family took the name Grunsfeld – literally green field. When, a hundred and fifty years later, the Nazis felt so secure in spotting a Jewish sounding name, it was because these names had been forced upon the Jews and were clearly recognizable as such.

The name Lobl, my maternal grandfather's, appears to be somewhat more idiosyncratic, however. It is not at all clear how this name met with the approval of the authorities. It is a Yiddish diminutive meaning 'little Lion' derived from the German word for Lion (*loewe*) and so most likely a reference to the Lion of Judah, which today is the civic symbol of Jerusalem found emblazoned everywhere in the streets on the lampposts and drain covers. What it was definitely not was a Germanic name.

In a handwritten life story of my great-grandfather Moritz Lobl, born in 1853, it is recorded that many members of the wider family had settled in Lackenbach for as long as people could remember. Moritz served as the elected President of the Community. He was a store owner on Berggasse, the main street, and appears to have dedicated much of his life to trying to alleviate the living conditions of the poor in Lackenbach, albeit not always with success. One of his principal responsibilities was to buy in timber to distribute to those who could not afford to heat their homes and so he had the idea of purchasing more expensive beechwood than the local pine wood, which was in plentiful supply. But the beechwood was heavier and gave off more heat. Walking through the village one day, Mortiz was dismayed to hear a poor woman complaining that this newly purchased timber was too heavy to carry to the fire, and that he should be forced to lie down and bear the weight of it on his ample stomach. This was above all a conservative community and he soon learned his lesson and went back to the old ways, much as everyone else did. According to Moritz, Berggasse – where many of the family lived – was known locally has 'Lobl Hill'.

In Islam, the muezzin will call the faithful to prayer at night and each morning. Likewise, church bells will mark the start of each service. There is no precise equivalent in Judaism, which requires ten adult men in attendance before formal prayers can begin. Instead, for generation after generation, at first light on the Berggasse in Lackenbach, the beadle of the community could be seen walking up and down the gentle hill and heard knocking on the door with his silver-handled staff calling out, '*Lobl zeit tzum shul.*' (Lobl, time to get to synagogue). Prayer, religious learning and a modest living from local commerce was a sufficient diet for these family members living in Lackenbach and across the centuries they could not detect anything that endangered the very particular protection they enjoyed.

4

The Blood Libel of Orkuta

On 19 June 1764, a five-year-old boy called Istavan Balla disappeared from the fields of Orkuta, a remote village nestled in the Carpathians. Orkuta lies in the rugged and empty north-eastern reaches of today's Slovakia, about 300 kilometres from the capital city, Bratislava, but at the time was part of the Kingdom of Hungary ruled by the Hapsburgs. Tragically, two days later the boy's naked dead body was discovered in the most horrific circumstances, with a rope around his neck and multiple stab wounds. Eyewitnesses described the boy as having nineteen knife wounds on his legs and seventeen stab wounds in his back. Others gave evidence that on the day of his disappearance, the boy 'had been seen talking to a Jew'. The Jews of the nearby town of Szedikert were immediately held responsible, thirty people were detained and charged with the murder of the child.

For several hundred years, the disappearance of a child and discovery of a dead body had been linked in parts of Europe with the accusation that Jews engaged in ritual killing of children at the time of the Passover festival, so that they could use the blood of an innocent to make the unleavened matzo bread necessary to celebrate the exodus from Egypt. Other incidents recorded that the blood was used by Jews '*ad suum remedium*', to make up some kind of apothecary's brew.[1] The end result of such accusation was depressingly predictable. Torture, conviction, hanging, riot, and slaughter. On occasion – as in Norwich in 1144 – mass suicide of the Jewish community appeared to be the only way out. Unlikely perhaps as it might seem, this grotesque mythology was to a material extent England's contribution to the ever-growing panoply of anti-Semitic motifs. In twelfth-century England, a series of these dreadful accusations were levelled against various small Jewish communities in

Norwich, Gloucester, Bury St Edmonds, Bristol and Winchester, and for a while at least helped to make these towns sites of Christian pilgrimage. The Blood Libel, as it came to be known, was even given a full airing in Chaucer's Prioress's Tale. After the expulsion of Jews from England in 1290, the fashion for these show trials soon passed to France with far more murderous consequence. From France, the trail continued eastwards through the Rhineland, then driving south into Hesse and Bavaria ultimately turbocharged by Lutheran pamphleteering and then across Europe.[2] Even with the advance of the Enlightenment in the eighteenth century, the Blood Libel retained an obstinate grip on the imagination of rural communities, but not generally amongst the higher reaches of the Church.

The Blood Libel possessed a grotesqueness which acted as a powerful reinforcement of Jews as the very image of otherness and inhumanity. Since no human could act in this way, it demonstrated beyond argument in the eyes of many that Jews were not really like God's other creatures or deserving of any mercy. Indeed, because of the ritualistic nature of the alleged practice, the image seared in the mind was of devilry or the anti-Christ. For the many afficionados of Bach and followers of the gospel of St Matthew, there was moreover an ancient religious justification for such treatment. In Bach's Matthew's Passion, composed forty years before these events, Pontius Pilate declared himself to be innocent of having anything to do with the killing of Christ, whilst the Jews who stood before him demanded that God's son be crucified and cried out in unison that his blood 'would be upon us and our children'.[3]

The image of the blood-thirsty Jew lusting to kill the innocent out of perverse compulsion has been a perpetual feature of the anti-Semitism of the Christian era and still flourishes today. The acknowledgment on the part of the Jews, according to Matthew's Gospel, that they accepted full responsibility for the consequences of the murder of Christ added a further dimension and has acted as both effective prompt and a salve to the conscience to many participating in acts of extreme cruelty towards Jews.

The Orkuta case had its own particularities. To begin with, as would have been well understood by the accusers, the Passover festival closely tracks the timing of Easter. June is not the time of Passover, which traditionally takes place in late March or early to mid-April, and so the 'matzo baking' thesis had to be recast completely to fit the particular facts. It was therefore asserted that the blood of the child must have been needed for the Jewish festival of Shavuot, which follows Passover, in May or June, but which does not have anything to do with unleavened bread, or indeed blood.

Shavuot is traditionally the festival celebrating the Jews' exit from the Egyptian wilderness, entry into the Promised Land and the giving of the law at Mount Sinai. This generally involves nothing more dangerous or sinister than eating copious amounts of sweetened baked cheesecake, symbolising the land of milk and honey. Nevertheless, for hundreds of years, the Jewish communities of Central Europe had all too frequently been subjected to violent attack by Christians around the time of this festival. This dated all the way back to June 1096, at the time of the First Crusade, when the priest Gottschalk led a band of Crusaders first through the Rhineland and then through Hungary on their journey to Jerusalem, leaving in their wake death, destruction and forced conversion. It is therefore plausible that the timing of the Orkuta affair, also in June, has to be seen in this light.[4]

The next and perhaps critical blow was that certain 'Jewish minded Christians' came forward to testify that the stab wounds on the boys appeared to form patterns that resembled – according to their understanding – Hebrew letters. Voluble witnesses were common in such cases. Stab wounds forming Hebrew lettering, however improbable, less so. A trial in the town where the body was found would follow. The accused would understand only too well that the process could not be expected to conform with even the most basic notions of natural justice.

The timing of this trial was also significant. It followed the Papal Nuncio's investigation and detailed deprecation in 1758 of the whole Blood Libel mythology. After a spate of notorious accusations in Poland in the early eighteenth century, Pope Benedict received an impassioned plea for Papal intercession from Jacob Selig, a Polish Jew.[5] The Pope commissioned one of his closest colleagues – the Franciscan Cardinal Lorenzo Ganganelli, Councillor of the Holy Office of the Inquisition – to conduct a full inquiry into the truth or falsity of the Blood Libel accusation. In March 1758, Cardinal Ganganelli reviewed the recent spate of cases, reiterated in the strongest language that there was no basis or truth or doctrinal underpinning in the false accusations and also warned against the receipt of evidence at trial obtained from Jews who agreed to convert to Christianity under torture.[6]

In the face of obvious danger, the Jews of Szedikert sought outside help from a leading Jewish businessman, asking him to intercede with Maria Theresa. They turned to Abraham Theben, the person who sat near the top of the family tree that Max had set out in his life story and had alluded to with such pride as his direct forebear. In Max's description, Abraham Theben was the plenipotentiary of the tight knit Jewish community of Hungary, a man of exceptional wealth and influence. I was intrigued to discover the true extent of his power in such matters, which would also provide an insight into the standing of the Jews under the Hapsburgs at this time.

It is worth considering how Abraham Theben came to be in a position to plead for the accused. The family name Theben referred to the nearby spectacular hill-top castle town of Devin only a few kilometres from Bratislava towards Vienna, on the confluence of the Danube and Morava rivers. The founder of the Theben family was David Theben, who died a violent death in 1670, leaving a young infant son Menachem who became the head of the small Jewish community in Devin. He was given the task of negotiating and then signing in 1730 formal terms to govern the relations between the Jews and their Christian neighbours. Abraham Theben was the eldest of Menachem's four grandsons and it seems outgrew life in Devin. In the early to mid-eighteenth century, Abraham settled in Bratislava, which at that time was the German-speaking capital city of the Kingdom of Hungary and known as Pressburg.[7] Its wide avenues and splendid baroque palaces would have impressed any visitor. Abraham Theben came to Pressburg to make his mark and succeeded in some style.

He appears to have made his fortune over a number of years by securing and operating quasi- monopolistic rights to the output of the prestigious royal textile factories of Linz.[8] At their height in the eighteenth century, it is estimated that over 18,000 spinners were employed in Linz in the Imperial textile business.[9] Understandably, as a result of his wealth and position Abraham Theben became the leader of the Hungarian Jewish community and performed the role of intermediary with the Imperial Court of Maria Theresa, a notorious anti-Semite. Towards the end of her life and reign in 1777, she said of the Jews 'I know of no greater plague than this race, which on account of its deceit, usury and avarice is driving my subjects into beggary.'[10] No doubt these prejudices would have made his job near to impossible at times, especially as he was himself an orthodox practising Jew with a full beard and would doubtless have dressed in the traditional manner.

Whatever her personal views, Maria Theresa had little choice but to engage with Abraham Theben. It was his cloth that kept the cold off the backs of the Imperial Army, and it was to him that she would turn to enforce the collection of the hated Toleration Tax, also known as 'the Queen's gold'. This was a form of poll tax initially set in 1749 at two florins per head for Jews but then raised again and again in 1760 and 1778, such that it was eventually four times the initial minimum guaranteed total. This was the ever-increasing price paid by Jews to be tolerated in the Hapsburg lands. A key feature of this tax was that she made the Jewish leaders responsible for collecting the prescribed amount per capita and handing it over to the State in a formal ceremony in the main square of each provincial capital city. Thus, any shortfall in the gathering of taxes measured against census records was to be borne by the Jewish elders and not the State. This imposed serious financial risk on Abraham Theben, but at the same time provided him with considerable status and clout.

Abraham Theben's position of tax collector, provider of army uniforms and leader of the community would therefore have enabled him to request an audience with the Empress and raise his concerns about what was happening in Orkuta. The Empress generally resided in the Hofburg in Vienna, but in 1764 she had convened the Hungarian Diet or Parliament which sat at Pressburg. As a result, the meeting between these two took place in Pressburg rather than Vienna. Apart from meeting on home turf, Abraham Theben had another precious card in his hand. He would have known that the Empress had convened Parliament because she herself was desperately short of money, following the considerable expense of having her son Joseph installed as Holy Roman Emperor in Frankfurt in April 1764.[11] As was often the case with the Hapsburg rulers, Parliament had not met her request in full.

It is reasonable to suggest therefore that Abraham Theben would have met the Empress with a measure of cautious optimism. The whole accusation was without any rational basis or evidence and the arrest of an entire community would be a stain on a forward-looking society. He would have had reason to think that Maria Theresa would be inclined to try to see her way through this distant provincial difficulty, if only for financial reasons. Furthermore, he also had the Pope and Cardinal Ganganelli on his side. I suspect that many an advocate would have been only too eager to accept this brief on behalf of the accused.

It is always a mistake, however, to underestimate the power of prejudice. The accusers themselves were not without weapons in their armoury. A local painter had been asked to depict the dead boy and did so graphically, showing the multiple stab wounds of the deceased. The artist interpreted what he saw as spelling out in Hebrew letters; 'God is one and one must be killed.' Maybe this was thought to be a demonic distortion of the Jewish *shema* prayer asserting the oneness of God. In any event, the finished painting was sent to Maria Theresa, who saw it as strong proof that a ritual killing had indeed taken place at the hand of the Jews. She was so moved that she kept the painting in her personal collection. As the weeks and months went by, members of the Jewish community of Szedikert were subjected to horrific torture. Some confessed their guilt, others agreed to convert. The most gruesome story was perhaps that of Moses Josefovitch, who was tortured for ten successive days and died on the rack, but without making any admission of guilt or seeking conversion.

Abraham Theben pleaded the case for the accused with scarcely any success. Twenty-one of the thirty accused had been forcibly converted to Christianity and had been released. Forced conversion was considered to be an appropriate 'sentence' and was often demanded of all the members of the accused's family. The remaining defendants it seems either died under torture or languished in prison refusing to renounce their faith. Only a small part of the records of the Orkuta Blood Libel Trial have survived. The Hungarian State archives hold a handful of documents relevant to these events and inquiries of the Austrian State Archives confirmed that a large number of records from certain date ranges have been lost. Nevertheless, the diligence of the archivists in Vienna unearthed for me one handwritten document in a beautiful Latin legalese script, dating from November 1764.[12] It records in part the confirmation of prison sentences for certain clearly Jewish-named prisoners from Szedikert and the release of others. There is a clue as to how this document, has survived. The second page bears an archive reference to a date in the 1880s. It seems that this document was taken out of the records over a hundred years later and then filed elsewhere and has only recently been digitised by reference to its correct date.

Abraham Theben died only a few years after this attempted intercession, apparently still bitter at the injustice. It is also possible that he felt his standing in the community had been undermined. He was almost certainly being too harsh on himself; the awful affair was followed by some lasting reforms. Maria Theresa instituted successive bans on the forcible conversion of Jews to Christianity and this trial was said to be the last time that judicial torture was used, though it was not legally prohibited by the Hungarian Diet until 1790.[13]

Still, the underlying sickness never disappeared, but only remained in remission. A hundred and twenty years later, on 1 April 1882, shortly before Passover, a fourteen-year-old Calvinist village girl disappeared from Tisza Eszlar, about 150km south of Orkuta in the same remote corner of Hungary. Rumours began to circulate once more that Eszter Solymosi, the missing girl, had been murdered by no fewer than thirteen Jews of the town in their synagogue as part of a ritual killing connected with the Passover festival. An inquiry began and, through the most doubtful of means, it was said that Moric Scharf, the fourteen-year-old son of the synagogue caretaker Jozsef, had confessed to seeing his own father forcibly holding down the girl as she was beheaded by the town slaughterer whilst her blood was collected in a cup normally used for religious blessing. This confession was obtained after Moric had been sequestered away from his family and persuaded to convert to Christianity and give false testimony. The central plank of Moric's evidence was that he witnessed all this through the keyhole of the synagogue door, which was shown to be palpably false.[14] This fantastical tale became the subject of yet another remake of the same ageless plot line. To be fair, there was uproar. Liberal voices despaired at this kind of embarrassing nonsense being pursued whilst the Western world looked on aghast and demanded concrete facts rather than baseless allegation.

On 7 May 1882, Geza Onody rose to speak in Hungary's Parliament. He was the representative from Tisza Eszlar itself, and part of Hungary's newly formed Anti-Semitic Party. He addressed the floor in support of an unsuccessful motion to expel all Jews from Parliament. It was a much interrupted and somewhat rambling speech, but the essential line taken was that Jews were vagrant criminals quite outside of society and had no place in Parliament or indeed in Hungary. Liberal Party MPs in the government tried to shout him down, but he continued. Onody's principal point was to try to draw parallels between the terrible murder in Orkuta in 1764 and the disappearance of the girl without trace in Tisza Eszlar. His trump card was the painting of the murdered boy in Orkuta, which he reminded everyone could still be seen in the national collection. He gave a graphic account of the multiple stab wounds observable in the painting, the so-called Hebrew lettering, and finished by saying that it should be remembered that the accused in each of these cases were not really Hungarian at all but were Poles, Polish Jews. There was considerable commotion at this in Parliament and a call for facts not fantasy.

A month after this shameful speech, a body was found in the local river. It was identified by several as being that of Eszter Solymosi, even though her own mother denied this and continued to maintain the charges against the Jews of the village. Despite the accusation of ritual beheading, the head of the corpse remained firmly attached and there was no sign of any attack, or murder. Tragically, she had simply drowned.

Echoes of the blood libel and Tisza Eszlar affair never quite disappeared and still reverberate in Hungary. In 1941 a Nazi propaganda film was planned to tell the story of Tisza Eszlar as established fact, but the project never really got off the ground. Yet today, Eszter's grave is a place of pilgrimage for the ultra-right-wing nationalists of the Jobbik Party in Hungary, with its questionable pro-Russian stance and which in the 2018 election was the second-largest party in Parliament garnering 19 per cent of the vote. In 2012,[15] Jobbik MP Zsolt Barath delivered a five-minute speech in the Hungarian Parliament about the Tisza Eszlar affair, saying that foul play had never been ruled out, just not proven. Others in his party have complained bitterly about the continual discussion of the deportation of Hungary's Jews in the last months of Hungary's participation in the Second World War, exhorting people simply to get over it.

What of the painting itself? In writing this book, I sought doggedly to try to track it down. I knew that it had been kept by Maria Theresa and so I thought it was really just a question of discovering the whereabouts of her collection. I contacted both the Austrian and Hungarian National Archives, without success. I then had the idea of speaking to the archivist at the Albertina in Vienna, which houses a large part of what had been the Hapsburg art collection. The last time any record is made of the painting is in the early 1930s, after which the trail simply goes cold. It seems it had been kept in Budapest. The answer in the end was perhaps only to be expected. By this time, the painting was no longer on public display but stored in a large warehouse in Budapest as part of the Hungarian National Archive, along with many other paintings and artefacts no longer considered suitable for display. This was referred to as Depository 41. In December 1944, the Soviet Army encircled Budapest and with an ever-tightening squeeze, amidst some of the bloodiest fighting of the war, took the city in February 1945. Artillery rained on the German troops who had dug themselves in near the National Archives in Becsi Kapu Square, obeying a Stalingrad type order of no retreat. Along with thousands of German soldiers and much of Budapest itself, all the paintings in Depository 41 were engulfed in flames and destroyed.

5

Beards and Bayonets

After the death of Abraham Theben in 1764, two of his sons –
ambitious men in their early thirties – took over the family textile
business. Koppel was said to have been extremely imposing in
appearance, a tall man with penetrating eyes and a lengthy beard
falling down onto his chest.[1] Wolf was the younger and more serious
of the two. Each of the brothers was a workaholic. They lived close
to one another in the Jewish Quarter of Pressburg enclosed by its
heavy gates and under the watchful gaze of the Counts of Palffy
residing in their fortified castle at the top of the hill. From the street
outside, a candle could be seen in the window burning away in the
small hours. Often a queue would form of people seeking advice or
some kind of assistance. By all accounts, the two of them expanded
their interests far beyond cloth and oversaw a dramatic rise in wealth
and influence. They started a new business brewing beer, became close
financial advisers to many of the Hungarian barons and extended their
operations as far as The Netherlands. With such widespread interests,
they learnt and spoke Court German rather than dialect Yiddish.
One of the local tax records gave Koppel Theben's wealth alone as
being in excess of 50,000 gulden. This was approximately twice the
total amount of the Toleration Tax owing in a year from the entire
Hungarian Jewish community.[2]

Koppel and Wolf were no longer merely presenting petitions to
the Court as their father had; they could count themselves amongst
the monied elite of the Hapsburg Empire. They belonged to that
last generation of the *Hoffaktors*, businessmen who had the right
of audience at the Imperial Court. Quite unlike the image of the

Hoffaktor made familiar by Hannah Arendt – a class apart, divorced from the needs of their own community – they, like many others in their position, remained true to their religious faith and identity.[3] They were seen in the corridors and halls of the Hofburg in Vienna dressed in the black frock coat of the orthodox Jew.

When I sat with Max on that last occasion in Tel Aviv, he clearly enjoyed recounting this part of the family story. Much of it had the feeling of fable passed down from generation to generation. There was a feel-good factor to these tales, allowing the audience to indulge in the fantasy that whatever their own poverty or position in life, there was one person, or in this case two, who had had the ear and respect of the Emperor. For a long time, I had to rely pretty much exclusively on Max's uncorroborated account of their lives. But with a measure of persistence, it soon became apparent that recounting the lives of notable figures in Jewish European history had been a popular genre of literature between about 1880 and the mid-1930s and much of this learning was then summarized and captured in the Jewish Encyclopaedia, first published in 1906. By dint of their larger-than-life personalities, the Thebens featured prominently.

Accounts of the family often referred to a full-length biography of Koppel Theben by Joshua Levinson, written in Hebrew and published in Warsaw in the 1890s. Eventually I succeeded in purchasing a copy and even though the binding was no longer secure and many of the pages fell loose into my nervous hands. I have been able to get this biography translated and was finally able to cross-check every detail of what Max had told me and had written down. Reading this material only served to reinforce what I felt Max took particular pleasure in; namely the theatrical air that emerges from the many individual incidents.

There is the fairy-tale-like encounter in the dark winter days of 1783 between Koppel Theben and Emperor Joseph II, recorded in most accounts of Koppel Theben's life but almost certainly apocryphal. Joseph II was renowned for touring across his domains to see the conditions under which his people lived. One of these trips involved a visit to nearby Pressburg, where, accompanied by his entourage of courtiers, the Emperor rode on horseback through the town on market day. According to the legend, the Emperor – to his surprise – saw Koppel Theben tending a stall below the sign of the Cross, selling alcohol and cakes. Joseph is said to have stopped when he recognized

Koppel Theben and said, 'What's this? Do you also trade schnapps now? So pour me one!' Koppel Theben explained that he was doing a favour for a poor Christian woman who was looking after a sick child and had no other way of keeping her stall open for business. The Emperor is said to have replied, 'We too want to be nice to those for whom my Jew has been so nice.' Joseph proceeded to make a generous purchase from the stall and all his courtiers followed suit, showering Koppel with gold coins such that the old woman was speechless when she returned.[4]

This story sits easily alongside the already not inconsiderable *Hoffaktor* mythology. The friend and confidant of the Emperor selling schnapps beneath the sign of a Cross and the shower of gold coins – it all has the air of pure fantasy. Yet the very fact that these stories were handed down, mixing fact with a large dose of fiction, shows how great the need was for the idea of a Jewish leader who could talk to emperors and princes to address some of the harshness of the Jewish lot, and move so easily between the Jewish and Christian communities. Certainly, this was a balm and delight to Max.

Another incident well illustrates Koppel's eye for drama. In 1794, after the death of Emperor Joseph II, a draft decree had been prepared which mandated the closure of all Jewish shops in Pressburg. This led to a hurried journey by coach and horse to Vienna to present a petition of complaint to Emperor Leopold. When they succeeded in securing a promise of the reversal of the decree, Koppel rushed back to Pressburg on a Friday and arrived at the very beginning of the Jewish Sabbath when all work must cease. He is said to have burst into the synagogue just as the newly elected Rabbi was about to give his inaugural address to the community. Regardless, he announced his news and demanded that the time of the commencement of Shabbat be extended for thirty minutes in order to enable storekeepers to open their shops, if only for a few minutes, as a gesture of celebration of their hard-won freedom.[5] As Koppel stood there, and the Rabbi looked on, there can be little doubt of the deep impression on everyone present as to where the power in the town's community really lay.

The opportunity for some material amelioration of the condition of the Jews of Hungary arose during the short reign of Joseph II (who became Emperor in 1780 on the death of Maria Theresa). Legislation introduced by Joseph dealt with life and liberty of the Jews living in the Hapsburg Empire.

Between 1782 and 1789, Joseph II issued eight separate decrees regarding the condition of the Jews in his lands with separate provision and treatment in each. They covered communities across the Empire, from Vienna to Hungary and Bukovina in the East, to the Polish province of Galicia in the North and Italy in the South. [6] They were designed to replace the ad hoc system of protection of wealthy landed families which had hitherto prevailed, such as the *Schutzbrief* issued by the Esterházy princes nearly a hundred years before. As such, there was aristocratic opposition to this new legislation, the fear being that this development was likely ultimately to interfere with the existing private system of raising of taxes from the Jewish population. [7] At the end of the day, the princely families and Vienna were competing to collect the same tax dollar from a poor population of local Jews and irrespective of Joseph's reforms, there was to be no reduction in the annual Toleration tax of 80,000 florins. [8]

The underlying objective for the Jewish community was complex. In May 1781, prior to the promulgation of the first of these decrees, Joseph II signed a statement of his policy towards the Jews which set the tone for much of the subsequent legislation. Amongst other things, it sought the mandatory replacement of the Jews' 'national language' by the legal language of each province for use in any official document or legal instrument or contract. Hebrew would only be retained for their private worship. The stated aim of his policy was to encourage or force Jews into society, widening their economic participation and therefore making them more useful to the State. [9]

An important feature of these decrees is that each was (to a differing extent) negotiated by representatives of government in dialogue with the leaders of the Jewish communities in the respective territories. In Hungary, a Commission of Inquiry headed by Count Johan Csaky was established to make recommendations and hear complaints about the provisions that had already been implemented in other parts of the Hapsburg lands. The larger the community, the more extensive the discussion. The Patent for the Jews of Hungary was debated for nearly eight months from the autumn of 1782 to the spring of 1783 before it was finally promulgated in Hungarian, German and extraordinarily enough, in Hebrew[10] – the only Hapsburg law ever to have been issued in that language. Part of the delay was caused by the difficulty in collating information on the school system of the Jewish communities in Hungary. It was well understood that the Patent would to a material extent cover and interfere with the existing provision of education, and there was considerable debate as to whether Jewish schools should be allowed to continue to exist at all. One suggestion, eventually abandoned, was that Jewish children should be made to sit on benches at the back of the classroom of schools established by the Church in order to ensure that everyone learnt the same curriculum. [11]

The Hungarian decree was finally published on 31 March 1783. The key themes were education, language and the permitted forms of economic activity. Provision was made for Jewish schools, including the standardisation of curriculum and supervision by public officials. Jews were also to be allowed for the first time to attend public schools.[12] Likewise, greater freedom was conferred with regard to the ability of Jews to work in more or less all forms of trade in town whilst excluding them from traditional occupations in the countryside, 'in order to protect the poor tax paying population from the destructive deceitfulness of the Jews'.[13] As regards language, the Patent was clear, official documents were to be written in Hungarian, Latin or German but not Hebrew. Further measures were to be taken to advance the policy of assimilation; 'so that the children of Israel attending the new schools forget the Yiddish language whether they like it or not.'[14] It was, however, the final article that caused the most immediate controversy and offence:

> All distinguishing marks that have the aim of differentiating the sons of Israel from other people are null and void. His Majesty permits them to carry a weapon but on the other hand orders them to shave off their beards and other manifest signs of their belief.[15]

To make matters worse, this all took place just before the festival of Passover and was to be enforced by the police forcibly shaving those who refused to comply.[16] It seems that those in power were very much wedded to the notion of using humiliation as a means of control and subjugation of the stranger in their midst.

There was understandably considerable disquiet that a Toleration Decree – which was ostensibly designed to enhance the rights of Jews living in Hungary – contained provision of such a nature. It should also be contrasted with the Esterházy's *Schutzbrief*, which although written nearly a hundred years earlier, did nothing of the sort. The goal of greater civil liberty in the mind of Joseph, however, seemed to be inextricably linked with the enforced loss of identity. The irony surrounding this particular requirement would not have been lost on the community. Less than a generation earlier, in 1764 under Empress Maria Theresa, a regulation had been issued making it *mandatory* for married Jewish men to sport a beard, so distinguishing Jews from non-Jews as they went about their business. The first violation would carry a fine of twenty-four Reichsthaler for the wealthy and bodily punishment for the poor. If caught a second time, expulsion or imprisonment would follow. [17] The political treatment of Jews in Central Europe across the ages suffered consistently from this kind of split personality disorder – you were either too Jewish and insufficiently assimilated or not Jewish enough.

It is also not exactly clear what was intended by the reference in the Toleration Decree to the other manifest signs of belief, but it is a fair interpretation that this was aimed at the orthodox Jewish practice of the wearing of *payot* (ringlets of hair that curl down around the ears) and *tzitzit* (a fringed cornered vest like undergarment). The community of Pressburg looked once more to its leaders to press their case with the Imperial court.

Accordingly, on 22 April 1783 Koppel and Wolf Theben travelled to the Imperial Court to protest and explain the position that it would not be acceptable to require orthodox Jewish men to shave off their beards or their ringlets and so abandon their own religious practice and identity. [18] They attended the Imperial Court dressed in full court costume, including powdered wigs, but so as to not to suffer from any excess of pride, underneath their finery they also wore their *tachirichim*, a white linen garment, the traditional shroud used for the burial of all, rich and poor alike. They took with them a petition signed by many in the Hungarian Jewish community.

An account of this meeting was given in an article written in 1932 based on primary sources, which like so much else, sadly did not survive the Second World War. [19] It is said that Koppel and Wolf Theben challenged the Emperor as to the true and valid scope of Imperial decree and gently reminded Joseph II of the somewhat contradictory history of this provision. By way of an opening shot, they asked whether the Emperor believed that a man's beard or facial hair ought properly be the subject of legislation, either by way of mandatory or proscriptive provision.[20] As far as opening shots go, it was a pretty good one. Joseph had no ready answer and asked Koppel and Wolf how they would have the law altered. Some discussion ensued and six days later the law in Hungary was amended so as to remove the restriction. This was more liberal than the Toleration Decree for Vienna in the Province of Lower Austria, which retained the prohibition on the wearing of beards.[21] This was a small but important victory on the path towards the acceptance of religious minorities living according to their own rites and custom.

At the same time, a further issue of Jewish legislation came to the fore: whether or not Jews would be permitted or required to serve in the Hapsburg army and if so, on what terms. In 1781, Wilhelm Dohm, a leading Prussian bureaucrat and advocate of the Enlightenment, published an influential pamphlet in which he argued in general terms for equal treatment but made the observation that, 'Jews should not ask for equal rights in a society which they declined for religious reasons to defend in times of need.'[22] The argument ran that so long as Jewish religious practice proscribed service in the army, they could not expect to be free from prejudice or treated with equality. The religious argument focused mostly on the requirements of the Jewish Sabbath and also the inability of Jews to eat the same foods as Christian soldiers.

This was another area of law that grabbed the attention of Joseph II. He was persuaded that the essence of the argument advanced by Dohm had force. Joseph faced extensive threats from Prussia and the Turks and – especially with his ambition to gain the Danubian Provinces for the Empire – urgently needed to overhaul the Austrian military machine. In August 1788 he therefore adopted a resolution requiring Jews to perform military service. The terms, however, were remarkable:

Without any further considerations, the Jew as a man and as fellow citizen will perform the same service that everyone else is obligated to do. His religion will not thereby suffer. He will be free to eat what he will and will be required to work only on that which is necessary during the Sabbath, much the same as the Christians are obligated to perform on Sundays.

Not only this but Jewish soldiers were issued with special uniforms, no doubt produced under the direction of Koppel and Wolf Theben, which were free of the type of cloth prohibited by the Bible (any mix of wool and linen).

It might be thought that this new decree and its extensive concessions could not be reasonably objected to. Nevertheless, the leaders of the Hungarian community stood once more in opposition. It is not possible now fully to understand all the underlying motives of the communal leaders and not enough contemporary records remain to reach any satisfactory conclusions. No doubt there were many that saw the threat of assimilation in having their young men go off to serve the Emperor. There would have been others only concerned that such military duty was not compatible with the service of God.

Koppel and Wolf saw the issue differently. To them the real question was that of full citizens' rights. Jews had always been singled out for oppressive separate treatment by way of special legislative control and in particular taxation through the Toleration Taxes; the state could not have it both ways. Either these laws and taxes had to be abolished so that Jews were treated equally in all spheres of life, or Jews should be entitled to a special exemption from military service. This was not an easy hand to play and would become all the more difficult after the death of Joseph II in February 1790 and the accession of Leopold to the throne.

Koppel's first step in the summer of 1790 was to convene an assembly of the Jewish leaders throughout Hungary.[23] This ended with a Petition being sent to the new Emperor requesting that the Jews of Hungary be given full and equal rights of citizenship in order to permit them to become full participants in and defenders of the Hapsburg Empire. This Petition did not meet with success, although it can be safely assumed that in the fevered atmosphere of the French Revolution, which did result in the universal conferral of civic rights, that attention would have been paid to this kind of talk.

After the failure of his Petition, Koppel decided that the next port of call would be the Hungarian Parliament, which he addressed in 1792. The theme remained more or less constant; likewise, the Hungarian nobility's opposition to the idea. Count Batthyany, whose family controlled the lands around Pressburg itself and whose impressive castle sits atop of the hill overlooking the old City, was most vocal. As far as he was concerned, the Jews were not worthy of serving the flag and anyone not worthy of serving the flag was not entitled to any rights of citizenship.[24]

By this time, Francis II had succeeded the short-lived Leopold II and been crowned as Emperor of Hungary in a lavish ceremony in Buda in June 1792. The Hapsburgs were doing battle once more with the Turks, and after France had declared war on Austria in April 1792, the need for soldiers was greater than ever.

Koppel Theben requested one further audience with the new Emperor Francis to plead his case. He prepared for this meeting by fasting for a week. He also instructed communities throughout Hungary to fast and pray for the success of the mission. The only account which I have read of the meeting itself – which is not corroborated by contemporaneous records – details how Koppel Theben addressed the Emperor with a most solemn speech listing how every ruler in history who had sought to treat the Jews with unfair, oppressive laws had ultimately come to a sorry end. He referred to the Pharaohs, Nebuchadnezar and Titus, and then is said dramatically to have been interrupted. Emperor Francis was astonished and asked Koppel if he dared to come to threaten him and raise his voice. Koppel is said to have responded as follows, 'No, I am not shouting but the pain of the people of Israel is crying out of me. Even myself as a sixty seven year old man with nine children I will serve the Emperor's army, but we ask Your Majesty for the same rights as all other Hungarians.' With this, he fainted.[25] His health thereafter deteriorated and never properly recovered. He was taken to Karlsbad, known for its curative waters. but this did little for him. He was then taken to Prague where he died in 1799 and is buried.

Predictably, his plea fell on deaf ears. However, whilst the seeds of the underlying argument had been planted, it took many years to find acceptance. A petition was presented by the Hungarian Jewish community to parliament in 1810 seeking the abolition of the Toleration Taxes and the grant of full rights as citizens to its Jews. This, too, was rejected. It was not until 1846 that the Toleration Tax was abolished, and full citizen rights would not be granted for nearly seventy years after Koppel's death.

What then finally of Wolf Theben in this story? From what is known, Wolf appears to have been a profoundly religious man dedicating his life to those in the community in greatest need. Together with his role in the family business and his communal work he was also a *mohel* and was said to have circumcised more than 1300 boys in his lifetime. He also undertook a pilgrimage to Jerusalem, which would have been arduous voyage. No account of what he saw there survives, but no doubt he would have visited what remained of the Hurva Synagogue built by pious Jews from Europe but burnt down by the Ottoman authorities.

Amongst his many children he had a daughter called Gitl. In due course Wolf managed to secure a suitable match for Gitl; a young and energetic Rabbi, Salman Loeb Grunsfeld, who was Max's great-great-grandfather. In 1804, ten years after the inauguration of the previous Chief Rabbi, which Koppel had dramatically burst in on and interrupted, it was necessary to look once more to fill the position of Chief Rabbi of Pressburg. Wolf campaigned to secure his own son-in-law the job. Salman Loeb had already served as Rabbi in nearby Kittsee, another of the seven towns under Esterházy protection. Salman Loeb was by marriage related to the most influential Jewish family in Pressburg and might have been thought to have been a shoo-in. Nevertheless, the community instead chose an unknown firebrand, Moses Schreiber who over the years became known as the Chatam Sofer. Through his strict interpretation and continual rejection of any attempts to reform or reshape everyday observance and practice, the Chatam Sofer would change forever the course of Orthodox Judaism and is firmly linked with his most famous strap line – that all change should be resisted (*ein chadash*, 'nothing new'). He was to become one of the most famed Rabbis across all of Europe, revered in the Haredi movement today.

It is hard to resist the temptation to see this as something of a fork in the road. It led in due course to an ever-widening chasm between those in Judaism who followed the Jewish law to its ultimate degree without reform or change, and those who could not accept such strictures in the modern world. Arguably, the election of the Chatam Sofer was the midwife to the Hungarian Neolog Movement, which came to dominate the Hungarian Jewish community and later Reform Judaism. Ironically, it became a factor in the wider move towards assimilation most often detected in the larger urban communities for many of whom this ultra-strict orthodoxy just did not resonate. It is not clear why it was that the community rejected Wolf Theben's own son-in-law. At this distance, it requires a measure of speculation. Still, there is a strange family connection that might just provide some explanation.

One of Abraham's daughters had married yet another dazzling Rabbi of the age, Mordechai Eybeshutz. The trouble here was that

Mordechai was the son of Yonatan Eybeshutz. He was one of the great scholars of Prague but had been accused of secretly being a follower of Shabbetai Tsvi, the preacher who had swept Central Europe a century earlier with a promise of redemption for the entire house of Israel, only finally to convert to Islam and then denounce Judaism. Any form of family connection with this false messiah, however slender, would have been seen as militating very strongly against an applicant for a prominent rabbinical position. In any event, the upshot was that Moses Schreiber was preferred to Salman Loeb, who went off to serve as a Rabbi in a nearby provincial town and eventually settled in Lackenbach, where he is buried in the Jewish cemetery.

As a footnote to this and by way of reinforcement of the strength of these connections, Max noted that Mordechai Eybeshutz died young and did not himself have any children. So when Salman Loeb and Gitl moved away from Pressburg and started their own family, they named their eldest Abraham in honour of Abraham Theben. In turn, Abraham named one of his sons Mordechai, supposedly in honour of Mordechai Eybeshutz, and the name Mordechai then passed down through alternate generations. As is common in Jewish families such names are passed down from grandfather to grandson, it being considered unlucky to carry the same name as your own father. Max's Hebrew name was Mordechai, named after his grandfather. He was therefore, albeit it has to be said somewhat indirectly, named after Mordechai Eybeshutz.

Of the wealth of the Theben family, little is known after this short and glorious interlude. As has already been noted in the case of far more resplendent banking families in Central Europe, there was much volatility and almost no generational continuity. Unlike the property rights of Esterházy's protected Jews, each business dynasty was heavily reliant upon the grant of personal concessions and licences from royalty who themselves were reliant on this form of income in order to secure money independently of parliaments and the leading aristocratic families.[26] These were insecure riches and after Koppel's death it is said that his house was broken into by those trying in vain to find evidence of ill-gotten gains.[27] Like Ozymandias, transient power and financial ruin seem to have been the epitaph of nearly all the *Hoffaktors*. What can be said with some assurance from Max's family tree is that the rabbis and small-town shopkeepers appear to have prevailed over those engaged in high finance or international business.

Wolf Theben died in 1809 at the ripe old age of 77. This was a time of profound crisis in Pressburg. The city faced attack from Napoleon's troops, plague and disease was rife and the great comet of 1811 only served to add a sense of deep foreboding and end of days. The Chatam Sofer was newly installed and redoubled the quotient of daily prayer in an attempt to give reassurance. He wrote an account of these days and of the deeply moving eulogy he delivered at Wolf's funeral.[28]

I went to Bratislava to try to find any trace of Koppel or Wolf Theben. Practically all that remains of the once vibrant Jewish community there now lies buried underground. Literally so. By the bank of the Danube, slightly raised on a hillside there had once stood an old cemetery in which Karl Marx's family lay side by side with Wolf Theben's, but this was desecrated and destroyed in the course of the Second World War – the only surviving gravestones being that of the Chatam Sofer and his immediate family. These were dug up and preserved in a small corner plot. Nearly twenty years ago, an impressive mausoleum-like memorial was built underground to house these few gravestones. Ultra-orthodox Jews still come from far and wide in large numbers to say prayers and ask for guidance. Scattered in front of the Chatam Sofer's grave are hundreds upon hundreds of small, crumpled pieces of paper filled with plaintiff petitions.

I spoke to the caretaker there as he tried to hurry me on and lock up after what looked like a slow day. Ever the optimist, I asked him where I could find any information about the gravestones of the former leaders of the community and mentioned the Theben family. He went off to a storeroom and produced a well-worn, dishevelled looking publication and handed it to me without fuss.[29] In its torn pages is the following information. At the height of the deportations to the death camps in 1943, a member of the Jewish community of Bratislava, Robert Neumann, decided to pass from grave to grave of the Old Cemetery and transcribe the headstones in order to keep this as a permanent record of those who had contributed so much to the rich past of the town. This simple but remarkable act of defiance then remained in the records of the Jewish community, practically forgotten, until it was chanced upon by those working on the Chatam Sofer Memorial. Turning the pages of this book in the dark, musty underground graveyard, I stumbled on the beautiful wording of the headstone of Wolf Theben, albeit this has been translated from its original Hebrew to German, to Slovak, and finally to English.

Under this stone rests a devout soul, a godly scholar
Reb Wolf Theben

When his time came, joy was turned to the bitterest regret and delight became pain. We grieve for a person who became strong like a lion and rushed toward the Torah and the ten commandments. He led his children with a fair hand and was a faithful leader of his brave community. He was faithful in his dealings with meat so that he could perform circumcisions in Israel. They met in front of his gate and around his table. He generously and kindly supported many of the poor. He has turned away from us, they've taken his beauty and his wonderful crown. Then, as in absolute clarity he finished his journey. On Tuesday, the 26th of Adar he was torn from this fragile life, but his soul lives on among those who live forever. May he be joined with everlasting life in the Lord's garden.

Emancipation to World War

O Mensch! Gib Acht![1]

The Compromise of 1867 which created Austria-Hungary allowed Hungary a free hand in regulating its internal affairs. The Hungarian Parliament acted swiftly and passed a series of liberal reforms including legislation to confer full and equal rights on the Jewish population. This seemed to bring to an end hundreds of years of civil struggle and ushered in a lifting of restrictions on what work could be undertaken, which towns could be inhabited, what dress could be adopted and which schools attended. It also led to the repeal of the very last remnants of centuries of discriminatory taxation which had been exacted without scruple. In Hungary, Act XVII of 1867 simply declared that 'The Israelite inhabitants of the country are ... entitled to the practice of all civil and political rights as the Christian inhabitants.' Any law to the contrary was abrogated. Similar legislation was passed in Austria and many other countries in Western Europe. This movement became known as Emancipation.

This would, at least superficially, appear to have been the victory that so many had been fighting so hard for, including Koppel and Wolf Theben seventy-five years earlier. It is not easy, though, to evaluate the effect of the Emancipation on life in the small provincial villages of the Burgenland such as Lackenbach and the rest of the Seven Communities, tucked away in the westernmost part of Hungary. In this corner of Europe, significant freedom of cultural and religious expression had been established nearly two hundred years earlier under the local charter of the Esterházy Princes. The advent of the railways and the consequent pull towards the big city in all probability were more influential in everyday life for many than the new liberty. The rural population in these parts was falling as an ambitious generation migrated to find work or pursue their professional, cultural or political dreams. It is not surprising that what is written about the Jewish experience in this period focuses on the flowering of expression in a wide variety of artistic and professional fields in the capital cities of Vienna and Budapest.

It also cannot be forgotten that the optimism of this brilliant new era was short-lived. The legislation took effect at a time when the influence of enlightened liberal values had already peaked. Twenty years previously, Karl Marx wrote *On The Jewish Question*. Marx argued that Jewishness had to be eradicated from society in order for society itself to be free. According to Marx, emancipation involved the liberation of society from what he charmingly called 'Jewing'.[2] By this he meant embedded Jewish characteristics of financial swindling and 'huckstering'. Marx obtained a position in London as correspondent for the *New York Tribune* and gave free rein to his anti-Semitic views, linking Jews to all manner of delinquency and financial dishonesty. There was also a disturbing and unprintable biological element to his views.[3] A good deal of the mud thrown from the left and right of politics stuck.

Emancipation was followed almost immediately in 1873 by a serious financial crisis across Western Europe, discussion of which often focused on the supposed or imagined responsibility of Jewish bankers and merchants. These sentiments were no doubt fuelled by the publicity given to prominent events such as the Rothschilds' successful organisation of the purchase by Britain of a nearly 50 per cent shareholding in the Suez Canal Company. The significant social and economic after-effects of the crash lingered for more than a decade. In Hungary, the market turmoil was accompanied by an agricultural crisis, giving rise to extreme poverty in rural communities. It also saw the Esterházy's own wealth and power much reduced. Six hundred and thirty major works of art were transferred by the Esterházy family to the state at a deeply discounted price to establish the Hungarian National Art Gallery under the terms of a complex agreement concluded by Prince Nikolai, which nevertheless improved his liquidity.[4]

This was a far better outcome than that faced by the Batthyany family, who faced financial ruin and had to sell much of their land and estate at Rechnitz. In Austria, the crash brought down the merchant house of the newly ennobled Baron Gustav Epstein, one of the richest Jews of Vienna, residing in splendour in his brand-new Palais Epstein on the Ringstrasse not far from the Palais Ephrussi, which Edmund de Waal has written about so movingly.

In England, Anthony Trollope, the great Victorian observer of this new age, published in 1875 perhaps his most brilliant and scathing novel, *The Way We Live Now*. In this tale, Trollope recounted the dishonest exploits of the odious Augustus Melmotte, the presumed Jewish railway speculator, with his awkward foreign accent, dreadful greed and gauche social manners. Trollope never expressly identifies Melmotte as a Jew (although in his private sketch notes he describes his wife as 'the fat Jewess'). Nevertheless, this ambiguity is perhaps precisely the point. No one quite knew where he came from or who his family was – a sure sign of trouble for the Victorian reader. There are hints of his German ancestry linking him to well-known Jewish financiers of the same origin. His ruthlessness was further emphasised by his predatory Jewish sidekick, mischievously called Cohenlupe, and the fact that he did not scruple to swindle Breghert, another Jewish banker, out of his fortune. This publication was received with admiration by an adoring public.

This was not wholly dissimilar to the overwhelmingly favourable reception of the stage adaptation of *The Lehman Trilogy* in New York and London in 2018 following the financial crash a decade earlier. This was a dazzling, skilful and often relentless production, which at the climax showed the Jewish immigrant traders cum financiers standing on empty banker's boxes, reciting the Jewish *kaddish* prayer of mourning, whilst hundreds of ordinary workers with quiet dignity faced personal ruin. All this despite the fact that many years had passed since Lehman Brothers was in Jewish ownership. Each work was said to hold up a mirror to the bankruptcy of contemporary values. Neither was thought by critics to propagate classic anti-Semitic themes, even though each to differing degrees repeated timeless damaging references to Jews' 'foreignness', their supposed lack of probity, trustworthiness, obsession with money and coldness to the suffering of others outside the faith or family. One scene from *The Lehman Trilogy* particularly sticks in the mind, that of the founders of the finance house supposedly looking to profit from the human misery, death and destruction caused by the American Civil War of the 1860s.

There would have been many from the Vienna of the *fin de siècle* who would have instantly recognised and applauded this almost pathological depiction of the grasping foreign-accented moneylender, the 'bloodsucker', and would above all have celebrated that it was written by a playwright born into a Jewish family.[5] It takes one to know one, many would have muttered under their breath.

What can be said is that the legislation proved an ineffective way to change either social attitudes or the political dialogue. Perhaps it always has been and always will. There were only fifteen years between Emancipation and the renewal of the Blood Libel accusation in Tisza Eszlar in 1882, and the accompanying outbreak of mob rule. By this time, Augustus Rohling had published *Der Talmudjude*, which sought to reinforce the Blood Libel mythology by suggesting that the requirement for ritual murder of Christians was in fact contained in the Talmud itself, an integral part of the canon of Jewish law. In nearby Pressburg, with its large Jewish population, following the disappearance of the girl there were murderous riots on 28 September 1882 resulting in several deaths and mass destruction of Jewish property. In August 1883, after it had become clear that the Jews of Tisza Eszlar had been falsely accused of murder and so freed, violence broke out once more across Hungary – in Pressburg and Budapest, as well as Sopron, only a few kilometres from Lackenbach in the Burgenland. There was precious little integration or communal spirit in evidence. Everyone knew where the Jewish houses and shops could be found (a depressing fact which would become relevant sixty years later.)

In the 1880s, Pressburg was also home to the first society in Hungary dedicated to an anti-Semitic agenda, with its own newspaper to peddle its views, the *Westungarischer Grenzbote*. In the end, less than a generation had passed from Emancipation and the banking crisis of 1873 before the rise of Dr Karl Lueger as Mayor of Vienna, with his particular brand of anti-Semitic politics, which marked a deadly serious turning point, too little understood both then and now.[6] As the nineteenth century came to a close, it was not possible to stand on a populist platform without adopting an overtly racist anti-Semitic stance.[7]

Karl Lueger unquestionably shaped the political debate of the time and without him many of the subsequent horrors of the twentieth century might well have taken a different course. Born in 1844, Lueger, or 'Handsome Karl' as he was all too frequently called, was a charismatic lawyer from Vienna who started his political life as a member of the Liberal Party. However, his political ambition fast outgrew the traditional landscape and in the early 1890s he established the Christian Social Party. He was above all a populist politician, and as he rose through the ranks, he noted that focusing on what was called the 'Jewish Question' only served to increase his appeal. He first learnt this lesson when asked to attend a meeting of the sister organisation in Hungary, the Christian Social Union.

When the first speaker rose, a Hungarian politician called Komlossy, he embarked on an anti-Semitic tirade which produced a standing ovation lasting several minutes. Lueger asked the chair how he should follow that and was told that more of the same would go do down well.[8] This was a lesson he applied consistently thereafter. He was elected repeatedly as mayor in the 1890s, only for Emperor Franz Josef to refuse to confirm his election – Franz Josef loathed Lueger and his anti-Semitic politics but as time passed he had more pressing problems closer to home after the suicide at Mayerling of Crown Prince Rudolf, his only son and heir apparent, and then later the assassination of his beloved wife Empress Sisi. Ultimately, after five successive election victories and with the support of Pope Leo XIII, who was said to have kept a photograph of Lueger on his writing desk, he was confirmed as the Mayor of Vienna in 1897 and remained in that position until his death in 1910.[9]

Lueger was the master of identity politics and declared himself the enemy of the Jews, opposed to their prominence in public life. One of his central themes was to forge an unbreakable link in popular imagination between Jews and socialism.[10] Thirty years later, this was modified, albeit only slightly, under the Nazis with their incessant reference to Jewish Bolshevism. Lueger revelled in the polarisation of politics. He wrote the playbook that practically every populist politician has followed since. Perhaps the most significant idea developed by Lueger was that being strongly disliked by a clearly identified section of society was itself a powerful means of strengthening and even expanding your own support base. He put his finger on a democratic paradox: the more you are hated by one group, the more you can be loved by those who identify with your particular brand of politics.

According to his narrative, the Social Democrats were the enemy of Austrian civilisation. He is said to have brutalised Vienna with his anti-Semitic rabble rousing and transitioned this primal hatred and fear of the other, the stranger, into mainstream politics. Prior to the expansion of the suffrage in Austria in 1882, only 3 per cent of the population had the right to vote. As suffrage increased, so did the noisy exploitation of popular anti-Semitism.[11] Lueger spoke directly to the petit bourgeois of Vienna in a way that no other politician had ever done. Many long after him would imitate his manner of discourse. He switched back and forth at will from outright attack to a knowing sneer. For example, when a city-wide medical check-up of schoolchildren was proposed, Lueger opposed it – 'the danger exists that Jewish doctors would inspect the girls too closely.' Nothing more needed to be said.[12]

Prominent newspapers such as the *Deutsche Zeitung*, previously known for its liberal politics, adopted a brazenly anti-Semitic editorial line. The mainstream press that despised him and his politics was referred to by him only as 'the Jewish press'.[13] With these menacing turns and tricks, he weaponised the constant attacks on his brand of politics as being the work of the dark combined forces of the Jews and socialists ranged against him. Even today we are still by degrees under Lueger's spell, as the supposed Jewish control of the media remains one of the most stubborn of all anti-Semitic canards. Lueger managed to bring together a diverse range of anti–Semitic forces in the 1897 election, combining forces with the far-right nationalists led by Georg von Schonerer who advocated union of Austria with Germany and the expulsion of Jews and immigrants. This alliance managed to unseat Viktor Adler, the Jewish leader of the Social Democrats, from government and only served to increase his popularity.

Lueger is well known for his retort, 'It is up to me to decide who is a Jew.'[14] This was aimed in two directions at one and the same time and was sufficiently pithy to be taken up with relish by Hermann Goering in the Third Reich.[15] First, it was a response to those who accused him of hypocrisy for accepting hospitality from certain members of Jewish high society whom he counted amongst his friends. Perhaps more relevantly, though, it was a deadly serious remark directed to the many in Vienna who imagined they could avoid Jewish taint through baptism, placing distance between themselves and their racial origin in whatever ways they could. Many asserted that they were not really Jewish because they did not practise the religion or had even converted to Christianity. Amongst wealthier classes there was a commonly held view that assimilation, acting, dressing just like one's neighbour and joining the same clubs and societies was the only effective means of addressing anti-Semitism. Equally, it was frequently heard that someone or other now living in the grand cities was born to Jewish parents but was not Jewish themselves and may indeed have proclaimed themselves ashamed of so called 'Jewish characteristics' from the 'old country'. With a nod to *The Merchant of Venice*, this might be thought of as the 'Jessica complex'.[16]

None of this mattered to Lueger and his many fanatical followers. In many ways, the person seeking to suggest to the world that he or she was not really a Jew was most despised of all. Adolf Hitler, living in straitened circumstances toward the end of Lueger's time as Mayor of Vienna, was impressed. He took note, and eulogised both Lueger's craft and his politics in *Mein Kampf*. His observations of the Mayor could be applied to many populists on today's political stage. Hitler wrote: 'Lueger had a rare knowledge of men and in particular took good care not to consider people better than they are.' Propaganda, Hitler continued, 'had to adjust its intellectual level .... to the most limited intelligence among those it is addressed to.'[17] There are too many today versed in the dark arts of social media messaging who recognise and practise Hitler's advice.

Until 2012, there was a section of Vienna's famous Ringstrasse named after Karl Lueger. This perhaps reflects the central place he held in the Viennese psyche. It would often be heard said that Lueger was a bit of an anti-Semite but a terrific mayor. Happily, Lueger's name has now been removed from the Ringstrasse and a more honest discussion can take place of the havoc he wrought.

Perhaps the most striking manifestation of this new populist strain of anti-Semitism related to the treatment of Gustav Mahler, the greatest conductor and composer of the day. Mahler's parents were orthodox Jews from Bohemia, but Gustav Mahler had converted to Catholicism in order to advance his career prospects. This was referred to some years earlier by Heinrich Heine, the romantic poet, as 'the ticket to European civilisation', but this was fundamentally to misunderstand the changing nature of the anti-Semitism of the *fin de siècle*. To Lueger and many who supported him, this was more a matter of race and what was said to be an excess of power and control, rather than religious affiliation by choice. [18] As soon as Karl Lueger took office, he moved against Mahler. He refused to allow Mahler to conduct the annual Philharmonic benefit concert or a concert in honour of Empress Elizabeth, assassinated in 1889. He did not consider Mahler to be sufficiently German to safeguard its music. Emperor Franz Josef was implacably opposed to Lueger and asserted his authority by appointing Mahler as principal conductor of the Vienna Court Opera (predecessor to today's State Opera).

Over the next twenty years, Mahler had to put up with all too frequent visceral anti-Semitic attacks and a vociferous opposition to a Jewish-born outsider holding a position of such prominence. There can be little doubt that there were also artistic reasons aplenty that underscored deep division in Vienna. There always were as the Viennese took their music seriously. Mahler was considered by many to be too modern and innovative. There was an extremely lively debate at the Opera as to whether Wagner's long works should be played in their entirety or truncated. Mahler was firmly on the side of the purists and abjured any edits. Equally, his endless rehearsals and drive for perfection often proved unpopular with the musicians.[19] Nevertheless, in the eyes of far too many and a depressingly growing section of the press, his original sin was that he was a Jew who had forgotten his true place with all this talk of Emancipation. It has been observed that some of this torment can be heard in Mahler's minor chords and the faintly masked sense of foreboding of his great early symphonies.[20]

In the summer of 1907, Mahler's daughter died of scarlet fever; in August of that year Mahler finally had had enough and resigned from the Vienna Opera; by December 1907 he had left Austria for New York. He was replaced as Principal Director by Felix Weingartner. A cartoon in the *Alldeutsches Tagblatt* showed the new conductor cleansing the Opera House with a pair of shearing scissors cutting off the head of a large, hook-nosed Jewish looking member of the orchestra, whilst in the background dozens of others awaited their fate. The depiction of the shearing scissors had a double meaning: Jews in the orchestra would now be cut out and a new approach could finally be taken to shortening Wagner's four-hour epics.

Ignaz Seipel, who would in due course become Federal Chancellor of Austria, was leader of the Christian Social Party in the 1920s. He stood in Austria's post-war election on an anti-Semitic platform that could have been scripted by National Socialist party members in the 1930s. The manifesto declared, 'The corruption and power mania of Jewish circles, evident in the new state, forces the Christian Social Party to call on the Austrian people for the most severe defensive struggle against the Jewish peril.' Indeed, such was the mania of populist anti-Jewish feeling that it was widely understood that any organisation with the word 'Christian' in it shared those views. When the president of the American branch of the YMCA visited Hungary, he was met by Miklos Horthy, a rising star of Hungary's politics and who later as Regent of Hungary played a decisive role in the fate of the remaining Jews in the Second World War. Horthy welcomed his visitor, saying that he was proud to receive a delegation from such an important anti-Semitic organisation in the United States.

There would have been many living in Jewish communities in the provinces who would have considered these anti-Semitic outbursts in Vienna, Budapest or Pressburg to be worrisome but largely an irrelevance to their life. At the risk of over-simplification, away from the urban centres, Jewish life at the turn of the twentieth century appeared to fall into one of a number of camps. There were many, perhaps the majority, who simply sought to carry on as well as could be managed, without any regard to the politics of the day. Others, and this was most prominent in the younger student population, opposed the Christian Social Party principally through membership of the Social Democratic Party or the early exploration of Zionism following the ideas of the Viennese journalist, Theodor Herzl. Others still continued the deeper advancement of orthodox Judaism as a bulwark against new ideas. In contrast, for many seeking a life in the great cities, an abandonment of the old ways was seen as the only means of progress. My family in Lackenbach appear to have explored each of these pathways except for the last. They rejected any form of assimilation and remained steadfast in their faith and identity.

It would be wrong to think of life in the provinces as mired in poverty or daily grind. That came during the First World War and its aftermath. Prior to that, these small Burgenland villages could count on the stable and profitable business of farming and the local wine industry. At the close of the nineteenth century, there was also an important practical development which was to be of some significance to my mother's family and many others. The Esterházys decided in order to stabilise their finances that in exchange for a land transfer fee, they would sell freehold interests to those living on their lands in places such as Lackenbach.[21] This was something that the family took advantage of, and over the next thirty years, different members purchased various houses on Berggasse, the main street. It resulted in an unusual feature of life in this region; namely a high proportion of Jews owning the properties they lived in. This was a matter bitterly complained about by Walter Rafelsberger, an Austrian Nazi who from April 1938 was placed in charge of the State Property Commission with responsibility for expropriation of Jewish property.[22]

Life there was by no means devoid of cultural links either. Franz Liszt came to Lackenbach for piano lessons and to give small concerts, whilst his father Adam earned a living as a local trader. Joachim, the violinist virtuoso, grew up in the neighbouring town of Kittsee and in his childhood he absorbed many of the Hungarian melodies which were to become so influential in the music of his great friend and colleague Johannes Brahms. Karl Goldmark, composer of the opera 'The Queen of Sheba' and a body of string quartets, grew up a short distance away in the Jewish community of Deutschkreutz, as did the much-loved Hungarian poet and playwright, Lojos Doczi, who was made a baron by popular demand. There seemed to be much to indicate that life could continue here, well-insulated from the turbulence of the wider world.

Every account I have read of Jewish life in Lackenbach appeared to centre on the synagogue itself, on Templegasse. The synagogue was rebuilt after a fire in 1810. The community continued to increase in both numbers and prosperity and the 1860s saw a major renovation and decoration of the interior. The community turned to Adonijah Kraus, born in Lackenbach, but who had since moved to Vienna to make his name. The records show that Kraus, apart from financial recompense, required his employers to keep him in plentiful supply of libations, the precise nature of which can be inferred but were never expressly stated. He insisted that only with such supplies could he guarantee the flow of his artistic inspiration. No doubt the Rabbis thought this an unusual arrangement, but the results were spectacular. Nothing could prepare a visitor who saw the plain whitewashed exterior walls for what was to be found inside, after climbing a narrow staircase to the synagogue entrance.

Frescoes covered the north and west walls with a moving depiction of Jerusalem under a bright blue sky framed with two luscious palm trees in the foreground. Separately, there was a representation of Isaac on Mount Moriah and other key scenes from the Bible. On the ceiling further frescoes were added, illustrating passages from the Bible with accompanying Hebrew script. In keeping with the fashion of the times, everywhere you looked there was another depiction of Zion, the Jewish homeland. Otto Abeles was a well-known music critic and journalist from Vienna. He wrote for a number of Vienna's leading newspapers including the *Wiener Morgenziet*. He came to Lackenbach in 1927 to write a piece about the synagogue and its famed interior.[23]

Even though it was not his first visit and he could see signs of damage to the paint from excessive moisture, he was still spellbound. He observed the Turkish-looking columns, expansive arches, the highly decorated chandeliers and elaborate Holy Ark with its two large silver candlesticks. Inside the Ark were twenty-four scrolls. Max still wrote of his wonder at the building seventy years after he had departed, never to see it again. There can be little doubt all of this would have cost a significant sum and gives some idea of the standing of the community at the time.

The Jewish community records of Lackenbach have been preserved in part and are held today at the Central Archive in Jerusalem. It would appear from these ledgers – written in a mixture of German, Hungarian and Hebrew – that many made a monetary contribution to assist in the renovation. The precise amounts are not recorded. It seems that a flat levy was imposed and once collected, a tick besides the member's name indicate that they had paid up. My family's forbears played their part in this levy and the religious life of the town. Some taught, others served as communal leaders. Among the most prominent of these was Rabbi Tovia Schwarz, a judge or *dayan* in the religious court and also head of the yeshiva in Lackenbach for nearly forty years, until his death in 1885.[24] Tovia Schwarz's daughter, Gilda, married the twenty-five-year-old Mordechai Grunsfeld on 12 November 1865 in Lackenbach. Just under ten years later, Heinrich was born, my great-grandfather, who can be seen sitting in the very centre at the front of the family photograph described earlier.

There were only about half a dozen thoroughfares in Lackenbach, and principal amongst them was *Berggasse* (Hill Street). The church stood at the top end and on each side of the broad tree-lined street were the local shops and stores providing for those who lived in Lackenbach and its surrounding vineyards and farms. An annual list of business proprietors in the first decade of the last century shows name after name of Jewish family businesses. Ignaz Kohn owned a bakers and soda water bar, there was Hacker the butcher, Fuchs the shoemaker, Weiss the tailor, Kornfein the confectioner, and Tauber the meat slaughterer. There was also a kosher Inn at Berggasse, 9, where Julius Deutsch, the prominent socialist leader, was born and grew up.

The Grunsfeld family appear to have led a moderately prosperous life. My maternal great-grandfather Heinrich Grunsfeld at Berggasse 14 owned first a printers' shop and then a haberdashery business. My paternal great-grandfather Moritz Lobl ran the grocers and spicers. Some years later, my grandfather Julius took over the haberdashery business, which he ran from his own house located a little further up the hill on *Berggasse*. The pattern of local life was clear. Landowning, wine making and farming was quite separate from inn or shop keeping or the local cafe and restaurants, which were predominantly in Jewish ownership. In economic terms, the Jews characteristically played the role of mediators between the countryside and those who lived in the town and village.[25]

Max described the haberdashery business as having enjoyed a measure of success. They bought cloth from the wholesale warehouses in Vienna and sold it to a wide range of Jewish and Christian customers in Lackenbach. It was common to see poorer peddlers who travelled from village to village to sell cloth and wares. Heinrich by all accounts was a generous and trusting man. He felt he owed anyone plying such a precarious trade a chance to get on his feet and so would give them cloth and only ask to be paid when they had made a sale.[26]

There was some but not much integration between the Jewish and Christian communities of Lackenbach. On a practical level, religion separated them. To describe my family as having been orthodox would not really do the subject justice. Of course, they would only eat meats prepared in accordance with the laws of *kashrut*, but this was just the tip of the iceberg. Max described that they had an arrangement with a local farmer to purchase the milk from his cows, which no doubt suited all parties. Nevertheless, for this to meet strict religious requirements, Max's family would turn up at his farm and milk the cows themselves. Exactly what the farmer made of this can only be imagined.

War came in 1914 and brought catastrophic destruction for the Austro-Hungarian Empire. The Hungarian half of the population of the dual monarchy, which at the time included Lackenbach, bore the greatest part of all casualties. Across France and Britain, each little village has its own war memorial. It is no different in Lackenbach. On the grass lawn in front of the yellow painted walls of the church, there stands a record of those who lost their lives for Emperor and Empire. Slightly faded in the white stone, each of the fallen is recorded, amounting in total to about fifty soldiers. This was a nearly a third of all those of fighting age in the village, a large number being killed in the first year of the conflict. There are Christian and Jewish sounding names, reflecting the make-up of the population.

Heinrich was born in 1874 and was too old for front-line combat in the First World War but was nevertheless in 1915 drafted into the Hungarian Army. He served first as a medical orderly and then was transferred towards the end of the conflict to work in an administrative capacity in a Military Hospital in Vienna. This meant living in Vienna for the latter part of the war and its immediate aftermath.

The principal impact of the war in the city was hunger. There was a lack of food as a result of the lengthy Allied blockade of German ports, and supplies were entirely insufficient for daily needs. The Social Democratic Party of Austria (no doubt with an eye to events in Russia) organised a series of protests and then a general strike in January 1918 (*die Jannerstriek*). They demanded increased food supplies, better working conditions and above all an end to the war itself. The strikes were widely supported but broken up, and Austria stumbled towards the devastation of national defeat. If this was not enough, Austria then had to meet the deadly impact of the 1918-1919 flu pandemic. The social distancing and closure of public spaces which we have had to adopt in order to deal with coronavirus came quite late to Vienna. The first cases of the flu were detected in February 1918, but strict measures were only in force for about four months from September 1918.

Towards the end of 1918, Heinrich was installed in a flat in Vienna and invited the family to visit him over a weekend. Max, who was only just five years old at the time, remembered this trip vividly. On the Sunday, Heinrich organised a trip to the cinema for the family, the first time for Max. (Lackenbach would only get its own cinema about ten years later.) He remembered sitting there watching a scene which involved an elaborate dinner table overflowing with food. With all the shortages that everyone at that time had to live with Max's eyes widened and he prodded his father and called out in a loud voice which could be heard by all near to them; 'Papa are they celebrating Passover?' For the five-year-old Max that could be the only conceivable explanation of such plenty at a time of widespread privation.

Both during and after the First World War, the sourcing and shortage of food was a constant obsession. There was also of course reduced demand for haberdashery, and the basic standard of living for all deteriorated dramatically. In order for Austria to pay for its vast civil service and food coupons for the discharged soldiers, the Government resorted to the printing press. Vast amounts of currency were printed, leading to the hyperinflation of the early 1920s. My grandmother was a teenager and could recall her own father's despair looking at a suitcase filled with entirely worthless banknotes. Money was rapidly replaced by a barter system. My grandmother was tasked with taking food by train to Vienna to her own father and whilst there to exchange flour from the farms of Lackenbach for tobacco and salt, which would then be brought back to the village and used in further exchanges.

For this purpose, flour was essentially the base currency and of course having somewhere for the storage of flour was important. My grandfather, Julya, understood this and persuaded his father Moritz to take out a bank loan to purchase a barn for the purpose. This turned out to be a disastrous decision. Some years after the war, Julya and his younger brother Victor went on an outing one Sunday to the nearby Pinkafeld aerodrome to see first-hand these splendid new machines take off into the skies. One of the pilots who had just landed at the airfield told them that from the vantage of the cockpit he had seen a fire raging from the North, in the direction of Lackenbach. They left promptly and on their return saw the family barn had burnt down and with it their entire stock of flour and shop merchandise. Whether it was the result of an accident or arson was never known. The financial consequences, however, were severe for the family. I do not know for certain, but I suspect that Julya must have felt some considerable degree of personal responsibility for persuading his own father to take on debt at this precarious time. Whilst his brothers left Lackenbach to study and start new lives in Budapest and Vienna, he remained behind to take over and run the family haberdashery store for the next twenty or so years. In 1931, he then married my grandmother, my mother was born shortly after and they began their own little family adventure, living in a small house in Lackenbach.

In a photograph which my cousin Tom managed to dig up from his attic in the United States, my grandfather, grandmother and mother can be seen together looking pretty much like any other young family starting out together. Julya in a smart suit, shirt and tie, which I assume he wore for work in the shop; my grandmother Terci wearing a housewife's pinafore and my mother standing in between, holding her own's mother's hand, protected by them both.

7

12th February Battalion

Wir wollten nur das Paradies auf Erden[1]

At the start of *Beware of Pity*, Stefan Zweig's only full-length novel, he introduces the reader to Anton Hoffmiller in a Viennese café on the eve of the Second World War. To the outside observer, he is yet another of the many tens of thousands who had fought in the 1914-1918 War but had now fallen on hard times. Nevertheless, as in Coleridge's *Ancient Mariner*, we quickly learn his tale of past error and misjudgement, in this case taking us back to the very last days of the Hapsburg Empire. Fundamentally, this is an allegorical tale. Hoffmiller's disgrace is symbolic of the fall of a whole nation, even though that is scarcely ever mentioned. It hangs in the air. Zweig skilfully weaves the disasters of the past generation through the present. In the end, with all the hurt he has caused, the soldier feels that he has no choice but to do penance by throwing himself headlong into battle. To his further shame, Hoffmiller survives. Worse still, he is awarded the Order of Maria Theresa, which he sees as being wholly undeserved. At its core, *Beware of Pity* exposed a number of the fault lines of Austria's complex national psyche, with excessive pride, the continuous dependence on sugar coating and an unhealthy obsession with past glory each playing its part.

Many have attempted to identify the moment where Austria's slide into the abyss reached the point of no return. There was the hyperinflation of the early 1920s followed by the crash of 1929, the rise of Hitler to power in Germany in January 1933, and the exhausted surrender of Austria's Chancellor, Kurt Schuschnigg in February 1938 to Hitler's demands, to name but a few. Yet still this is to ignore the importance of the crushing of the doomed Social Democrats in February 1934, referred to as the Austrian Civil War.

There is a powerful painting by Oskar Kokoschka – *Anschluss, Alice in Wonderland* – which makes the case.[2] Kokoschka was a so-called 'degenerate' artist who had to flee the Nazis and painted the work from exile in England.[3] Vienna, his city, lies ruined in flames. In the foreground, the observer sees a baby being carried in a mother's arms, in a full gas mask. Others cower, and three civilians stand with only soldiers' tin helmets for protection. They represent three muses who see, speak and hear no evil. The front-page headlines on the sandwich board of a newspaper vendor can be seen proclaiming; 'Our Times'. The date given looks like 1938, but the last digit has a '4' painted on top of it. It looks like an imaginary dial has been turned backwards so as to replace the '8' with an over painted '4. In Kokoschka's eyes what was reaped in this firestorm was sown in 1934.

The small, landlocked Austria which emerged in 1919 was, from an economic point of view, always on its knees. Most soldiers returned from the front without jobs, and firearms were in abundant circulation; out of this maelstrom, a number of rival informal armed militias emerged. On the ultra-right wing of politics, there was the *Frontkampfer* (the Front Fighters) led by the appropriately named Hermann Hiltl. There was also the monarchist *Heimwehr* under the leadership of Count von Starhemberg, distantly related to the hero of the siege of Vienna two hundred and fifty years previously. These groups excelled in anti-Semitic demonstration and terror, a particular favourite tactic being lightning raids on the cafes of Vienna known to have a Jewish clientele to beat up whomsoever they could catch.[4]

As regards the left, in 1923 the *Republikaner Schutzbund* (the *Schutzbund* or Protection Union) was formed. Its principal function was to act as an armed defensive bulwark against the increasingly militant nationalist and proto-fascist *Frontkampfer* and *Heimwehr*. Kurt Schuschnigg observed many years later that central government for a decade after the war was too weak to do anything about this and was largely reduced to simply looking on. These private armies had access to an abundance of ex-service weapons and would hold frequent rallies, particularly at weekends. Often these would end with marches and stylised shows of strength. These were rival gangs jostling for territorial control.

The *Schutzbund* was established on military lines with companies, battalions and regiments in each of Austria's nine provinces, 80,000 members at full strength.[5] There were of course demonstrations of force by the *Schutzbund* in Vienna – where the largest formations and central administration were concentrated – and there would have been no real opposition on such occasions. The municipal politics of Vienna were more or less completely in the hands of the Social Democrats. By 1932, they had garnered just shy of 60 per cent of the vote in Vienna's twenty-one municipal districts.[6] So much so, it was known as *Rotes Wien* (Red Vienna). This moniker was somewhat misleading; the Social Democrats above all were a democratic socialist party and quite separate from the much smaller Austrian Communist Party, aligned to the Soviet Union. What is more, a large number of those who voted for the Social Democrats were not predominantly working class or even necessarily socialist, but were at least in part voting against the far-right nationalists. This was perhaps most marked in the three districts of Vienna with the highest proportion of Jewish voters, which turned most decisively towards the Social Democrats during the 1920s and 1930s, and which were not particularly working-class. [7]

Irrespective of the demographics, the socialist control of the city gave rise to all manner of important innovation, particularly in the field of housing. Teams of architects designed and built large-scale social housing projects known as *Gemeindebauten* built in both working class and bourgeois neighbourhoods, enabling tens of thousands of people to escape shameful living conditions.[8] Perhaps the most famous was Karl Marx Hof, built in the fairly genteel Nineteenth District. One of the most notable features of these large-scale projects was the low density of the accommodation, allowing each housing association to provide amenities such as kindergartens, doctors' surgeries and laundrettes. There was also material improvement in the regulation of the working week to an eight-hour day and the proviso for one day's mandatory holiday per week. Vienna was the poster child for what could be achieved through collective government effort to improve the lives of the ordinary working man and woman.

As regards the Burgenland, a truce had been agreed by the coalition parties governing the province such that no marches or demonstrations would take place there and that it would de facto operate as a de-militarised zone. But as far as the *Frontkampfer* were concerned, the border country province of the Burgenland was very much the front line.

They advocated that the Burgenland should once more be returned to Hungary, reversing the settlement reached between Austria and Hungary at the end of the war. In their eyes, this region was not predominantly German-speaking and had large populations of Jews and Roma.

As for the *Schuztbund*, this had been banned by the right-wing government of Miklos Horthy in Hungary; accordingly, a number of the truly committed had slipped over the border into Austria. The Burgenland was a tinder box and a recruiting ground for both factions. The military commander and founder of the *Schutzbund* was the blond-haired, blue-eyed Julius Deutsch, himself Jewish and born in Lackenbach. He was a highly decorated officer in the First World War and then War Minister in the Social Democratic Party government formed in May 1919. The force of his personality persuaded many others in the region to join. Amongst his recruits was my great uncle Martin, the younger brother of my grandfather Julya.

Practically nothing survives of the life of Martin in Lackenbach. The meticulous handwritten records kept by the mohel who performed the circumcision ceremony on the Jewish boys born in Lackenbach at the time indicate that he was born in early September 1903, Julya being some seven years his elder. Martin would have left school and most likely Lackenbach at about the age of sixteen, sometime in 1919 or 1920; the local Jewish school adjacent to the synagogue did not cater for students beyond that age. The most obvious option for Martin would have been to work in a nearby Burgenland town on the Austrian side of the border. This is exactly what Max did, working as a textile manufacturer's apprentice in nearby Mattersdorf. Martin followed the path of socialist activism and became a journalist. He wrote for the *Arbeiter Zeitung*, the principal daily newspaper for the Social Democrats of Austria, although the records prior to 1945 are incomplete and from 1938 largely destroyed. In any event, Martin became more and more influenced by and involved in the socialist politics of the day – and specifically the militant *Schutzbund*.

In January 1927, the Burgenland truce between the *Schutzbund* and the *Frontkampfer* fell apart spectacularly. The *Frontkampfer* announced that they would be holding a demonstration on Sunday 30 January in the small village of Schattendorf, right next door to Mattersdorf and halfway between Vienna in the north and Lackenbach to the south. The *Schutzbund* called out their battalions to come in force to Schattendorf for a show-down. Although impossible to establish with certainty, it is highly likely that Martin would been in

Schattendorf with the thousands of other *Schutzbunders* that day to see off their bitter rivals.

The *Schutzbund* set up their temporary headquarters in Schattendorf at the Moser Inn and the *Frontkampfer* in the Tscharmann Inn, only about five hundred metres apart. There were skirmishes and fist fights at the train station, no doubt with each group receiving reinforcements by train from north and south. The Schutzbunders drove the Frontkampfers back and were marching back into town loudly singing, 'Down with the Front Fighters, down with the Christian dogs, and monarchist murder boys.' As the Schutzbunders marched down the main street of Schattendorf and past the Tscharmann Inn, they were heard taunting their rivals; 'Come out if you dare and let's have it out.'[9]

Then in full view of numerous eyewitnesses, shots were fired out of the windows of the *Frontkampfer* headquarters. Two were killed, including a six-year-old called Josef Grossing, an innocent bystander. Five others were injured. Three *Frontkampfers* were arrested and put on trial. They admitted firing the shots but pleaded self-defence, which on the evidence, certainly in relation to the innocent boy of six, presented something of a forensic challenge. At the trial, the defendants were represented by Walter Riehl who was a parliamentary national deputy, a leading member of the Austria National Socialist Party and a rabid anti – Semite. In 1931, Riehl would call for the compulsory castration of any Jew who had sex with an Aryan girl.[10] In July 1927, he managed to secure the acquittal of the three defendants on all charges.

This led immediately to the socialists declaring a general strike. Spontaneous demonstrations began in Vienna, leading ultimately to the burning of the Palace of Justice in violent protest. The army intervened and dozens were shot and killed. Julius Deutsch saw the danger in this moment and appeared before a baying crowd standing atop a fire engine imploring them to disperse peacefully. To no avail, by this time many in the *Schutzbund* had lost faith in the rule of law and had begun to take matters in their own hands.

As Austria plunged into deeper economic depression, the political landscape deteriorated in tandem. In September 1929, the Christian Social Party proceeded to form a right-wing coalition block, bringing Starhemberg's *Heimwehr* with them. With deadlock between the two main rival political parties – the Christian Social Party and the Social Democrats – the diminutive Chancellor Englebert Dollfus in March 1933 moved to suspend Parliament. This was the only real platform of power left for the Social Democrats. Austria now faced rule by decree, in what the socialists termed Austrofascism. The right responded by banning the *Schtuzbund* itself and imprisoning many of its members. The endgame was fast approaching.

On 12 February 1934, a police raid was conducted in Linz to try to find some of the hidden cache of firearms amassed by the *Schutzbund*. Numerous arrests were made. In Vienna, similar raids took place with the *Heimwehr* taking the lead. The *Schutzbund* considered they had little choice but to rise and make a last stand to defend their position on their home turf in Vienna with such weapons as they had.[11] Rather than surrender their service rifles, they barricaded themselves into the vast, newly built housing projects in Karl Marx Hof, Viktor Adler Hof and in the Florisdorf suburbs. Chancellor Dollfuss ordered the Austrian army to shell the housing blocks indiscriminately. The *Heimwehr* duly obliged and also surrounded the buildings with snipers. Julius Deutsch would explain years later the manifold reasons for the revolt's lack of success; chief amongst these was said to be the failure of the workers' districts of Briggittenau to the north to rise up to protect one flank and similarly in Wiener Neustadt to the protect the south. More realistically, the ill-equipped and amateur *Schutzbund* was simply outnumbered and outgunned by a regular army. Thousands were either killed or wounded in a wholesale slaughter including many innocent families. The battered *Schutzbund* surrendered four days later and in the ensuing months thousands were arrested and put on trial. Significant numbers were executed.

After this, there were only really two realistic pathways: the continuation of Austrofascism or unification with Nazi Germany. G. E. R. Gedye was the *Daily Telegraph*'s correspondent in Central Europe living in Vienna and in *Fallen Bastions*, his account of the history of Austria in the early twentieth century, he pinpointed 12 February 1934 as the critical pivot. Events moved rapidly after this failed uprising. As a direct response, the Government formally banned the Social Democratic Party and arrested its leadership. On 25 July 1934, Dollfuss was assassinated in a failed coup when fifty Nazis disguised in the uniforms of Austrian police entered the Chancellery and shot the Chancellor. For twenty-four hours it was unclear whether the attempted coup d'etat would succeed. But some semblance of order was restored and Kurt Schuschnigg who shared much of Dollfuss' views on the right of politics succeeded as Chancellor.[12] It needs to be recalled that the Social Democrats had won the 1930 general election, the last to be held in Austria before the war, with over 40 per cent of the vote and well above 55 per cent of the vote in Vienna. Nevertheless, after February 1934, they were completely crushed. All that remained was the half of the population associated with political parties on the right, or terrified silence.

For the Jews of Austria, February 1934 was yet another disastrous moment. Already blamed for the financial crash in 1929 followed by the collapse of the Jewish-owned Creditanstalt in 1931, the events of 1934 only served to reinforce, in the minds of far too many, the ready notion of an unholy trinity of Jews, bolshevists and bankers. It was well known that a large proportion of the senior cadre of the Social Democratic Party in Austria was Jewish and this made it easy to portray them as a dangerous fifth column and the cause of the nation's ills.

In the aftermath, a small band of fighters fled Vienna. Amongst these was Julius Deutsch, the commander of the *Schutzbund,* and Otto Bauer, the leader of the Social Democrats. The remarkable story of Deutsch's escape was recounted in the British newspapers. Seriously wounded in the eye and scarcely able to see, he somehow found his way to Brno, crawling on hands and knees across the border between Austria and Czechoslovakia.[13] Although Deutsch claimed to have done this unassisted, logic dictates that he could not have succeeded alone. He must have been assisted by a small cadre of trusted 12 February fighters. For those who escaped, there was no real possibility of returning to Austria; facing trial there would have been suicide. The banned *Arbeiter Zeitung* set up a samizdat press in Brno for distribution to the faithful. Some of those in exile stayed in Czechoslovakia, many others fled to Moscow.

Trying to find out more about Uncle Martin's story as a teenager eager to discover tales of derring do was probably my first attempt actively to find out more about what had happened to my Austrian family. As an adolescent, I was gorging on a diet of books written by those who had been witness to the Spanish Civil War – George Orwell, Ernest Hemingway, Arthur Koestler. I was young, impressionable and consumed by the lost Republican cause. I remember talking to everyone and anyone about it, when one day my mother casually responded – as if merely recommending another book I might want to look at – that her father's brother had fought the fascists in Spain with the International Brigades. I am sure my jaw dropped. I wanted to know more, everything, well, actually *anything*, but my mother said that the only thing she knew was that he had left Austria in the 1930s to fight in Spain. She thought that he may have survived the war, possibly emigrating to Australia where there was distant family. For many years, my every attempt to follow this up yielded precious little. I recall many years ago, when I was still living with my parents, writing a letter to Uncle Max on the off chance that he could help. He replied that he could not add to my knowledge as Martin had left Austria without trace and added somewhat cryptically that the real heroes were those who somehow survived without a gun in their hand. A fair measure of persistence, the extraordinary help of friends in Spain and a good slice of luck, however, have allowed me to piece together Martin's armed struggle against fascism.

As matters turned out, Martin did not have long to wait after the disaster of February 1934 before being called to arms.

In July 1936, the world's attention turned to Spain, when an uprising of the extreme right nationalist rebels sought to overthrow the democratically elected Republican government. It was not long before the complexity and bitterness of the Spanish Civil War was added to by the development of a deadly proxy war between forces funded and often armed by the fascists of Germany and Italy and the communists of the Soviet Union. The Soviet Union, through Comintern, organised over 40,000 volunteers from Europe and beyond to come to fight for the Republicans. They were, largely, committed socialists and communists, but there was a large contingent of about 8,000-10,000 anarchists, too.

The volunteers who came to fight joined International Brigades that were generally formed along national lines. Put in a wider context though, the international volunteer force constituted less than 10 per cent of the total Republican army and it is worth recalling that the International Brigades themselves were made up of a blend of volunteers from overseas and Spanish troops.[14] Julius Deutsch was one of the first to volunteer with the International Brigades. Given his exceptional military experience in the First World War, his organisation of the *Schtuzbund* and his high profile in the socialist movement, he was accorded the rank of General.

None of this information got me any closer to finding out specifically what had happened to Martin. Just when it seemed that every inquiry had run into the sands, I stumbled upon an academic study, *Jews*

Who Served in the Spanish Civil War, which listed country by country those Jews identified as having served in the International Brigades. The overall conclusion was that of the 40,000 or so who came from around the world to fight and serve as auxiliaries for the Republicans, extraordinarily enough approximately one quarter were Jewish. The largest contingents of Jews who went to Spain to fight came from Poland and then the United States, each with their large populations of Jews and well-established Bundist tradition. Jewish volunteers from Britain, Palestine and Austria also figured prominently. Naturally, Julius Deutsch's name was to be found amongst those who came from Austria to fight. Four pages on in the list, was the name of Martin Lobl. Contrary to my mother's sketchy account, he was said to have been killed in action. No further details were given.[15] Yet again, this brought me back to the drawing board or, more accurately, the archives.

The most complete biographical record of those who went from Austria to fight in Spain, both Jew and non-Jew alike, has been drawn up by the remarkable Hans Landauer.[16] In Landauer's biographical list, about thirty-five names below that of Hans Landauer himself, Martin Lobl was again identified. This time, there were more details. His date of birth was given as September 1903, which matched the record from the Lackenbach mohel book. He was recorded as having been a journalist by profession and as having come from Sweden to Spain in December 1936, where he had fought with the XIV and XI International Brigades and attended officers' school in Albacete (also known as the Tower of Babel, for obvious reasons). More than thirty years after I had asked my first questions about Martin, these new details finally enabled me to cross-check his records with those held in the National Archive of Spain.[17] It all matched: Martin had made his way to Spain to fight with the Brigades.

The details of Martin's service in Spain were something of a breakthrough and allowed me to put together further elements of the story. The first detail that needed explanation was why Martin had arrived in Spain from Sweden. This initially seemed unlikely but turned out to have a logical explanation. Many of those involved in the fighting in February 1934 had fled Austria for Moscow and joined the communist party. They were then put to work in factories and when the call came from Comintern for volunteers to fight in Spain, a large contingent of those who responded to the appeal were the Austrian *Schutzbunders* living in exile in the Soviet Union. An illegal transportation organisation was set up, and arrangements were made for these *Schutzbunders* to travel to Leningrad, then to Finland, to Sweden and then to Spain. So, one of two explanations seems likely: either Martin had been living in Moscow in 1936, or he had travelled there, perhaps from exile in Czechoslovakia, just so that he could get to Spain. We cannot know for certain, but one way or other it seems he travelled from Sweden to join up in a group organised by the Soviet Union.

The volunteers first gathered at the San Ferran Castle in Figueres where the majority of the International Brigaders assembled before being assigned to a battalion and unit. Unlocking the first piece of the puzzle allowed the remaining missing fragments to fall into place. A short account of the training of the Austrian fighters was recorded by Karl Bauer, a diminutive fighter from Vienna a few years younger than Martin. He spoke of meeting up with a number of Austrian comrades at Figueres in December 1936 and specifically named Martin Lobl amongst the group there, who then together formed part of a machine gun unit.[18]

The record of Martin having attended officers' school is also relevant. Those who attended officers' school generally had previous military experience and so were considered suitable to lead others into battle. This would certainly fit with Martin's prior role in the *Schutzbund*. It is unclear how long Martin remained at Albacete, but then another surprising detail emerged. The archivists in Vienna who had with great diligence collected all the materials relating to Austrian resistance to fascism wrote to me, with wholly unnecessary apologies for having taken so long to find what I was looking for. Incredibly enough, they had attached a newspaper article from *Le Soldat de La Republique,* a Comintern newspaper, written by Martin Lobl in December 1936. A photograph of Martin still eluded me but at long last I did have some of his words. It was a short, frothy but gently ironic piece. He wrote of a football match that had been hastily arranged at Albacete between the soldiers of the International Brigades and the Spanish Republican troops. He described the good atmosphere and determination on the part of the Brigaders to show that men from many countries could come together not just in support of the Olympic ideal but equally in the fight against fascism. He regretted that the 'international bourgeois press' had not come to see the game as no doubt they, too, would have been impressed with the indomitable spirit of what he mischievously called these 'Red Barbarians'. As to the score, the German/Austrian team beat the Spanish soldiers 6-2. Apparently, a re-match had been requested and agreed to.[19]

Now that I knew that Martin had served with the XIV and then XI International Brigades, it was possible to follow his trail. The XI International Brigade was the first to be formed of international volunteers and saw more fighting than practically any other. It was created in October 1936 at the outset of the Civil War. The Brigade was divided into various battalions, of which the two most prominent were the Edgar Andre Battalion, under the legendary Hans Kahle (Hemingway's inspiration in *For Whom The Bell Tolls*), consisting largely of German and Scandinavian fighters, and the 12 February Battalion (its German name was the *Zwolfte Febuar*), the majority of whom were Austrian. The dominance of German and Austrian fighters in the XI International Brigade was such that the regimental song was in German. They were formed in Albacete, the chatter in the streets was heard predominantly in German and the Austrian medics there outnumbered the Spanish. The link between Martin's past and the 12 February Battalion seemed to be an obvious fit. It made perfect sense.

The XI International Brigade were soon called up to their first deployment. The Nationalists attacked Madrid on 8 November 1936, crossing the Mazanares River from the West and attempting to batter their way into Madrid through its largest public park, the Casa de Campo, in a frontal assault. There was desperate fighting; first in the Casa de Campo and then in University City, with clashes moving from faculty building to faculty building. It has been recorded that the Republican troops used thick library books to fill jute sandbags for protection against the Nationalist snipers, the bullets apparently rarely penetrated beyond 350 pages.[20] The battle to save Madrid lasted about two months until it became clear that neither side could achieve a decisive victory. The Republicans' regular forces were reinforced by Russian air cover and the arrival of nearly two thousand from the XI International Brigade. They suffered heavy casualties but became known across the world as the face of the International Brigaders. It was said of the Germans and Austrians that time and again they were asked to prove – and succeeded in showing – their stomach for battle. These were fighters who had seen fascism up close in their own lands. Their fight was personal, not just ideological.

The reference to Martin also having fought with the XIV Brigade was less easy to understand. The XIV Brigade was mostly made up of French volunteers, known as the Marseillaise Brigade and there is no obvious reason why Martin, a veteran of the 12 February 1934 fighting in Austria, would have served with a French unit.[21] In addition, the timing does not quite fit either, as the XI Brigade was formed *before* the XIV Brigade. It is of course possible that the XI Brigade had already moved up to Madrid by the time Martin arrived in Albacete in December 1936 and so perhaps the best explanation is that Martin initially had to join whichever Brigade was being formed at the time and then transferred into the 12 February Battalion as soon as the opportunity arose.

After the Republicans stopped the Nationalists from taking the capital in early 1937, the next major engagements were the attempts made by the Nationalists to encircle Madrid rather than storm it. Principle amongst these were the Battles of the Corunna Road and Jarama in which both the XI and XIV Brigades fought. By this time, the 12 February Battalion of the XI International Brigade consisted of four companies, each named after one who had fought in the streets of Vienna in 1934. Martin had transferred to fight in this Austrian unit as a machine gunner. The fact that he continued to serve as an officer in a front-line unit also said a good deal about his politics. From December 1936, the Soviet paymasters exerted an ever-greater degree of control over those fighting against the fascists. Political commissars were appointed to watch over the fighting troops with orders to purge anyone who displayed any form of doctrinal disloyalty. It was said that these purges were conducted with same energy as that shown in the Soviet Union.[22] Martin obviously survived this test, too.

Then, in the miserably cold concluding months of 1937, the Republicans looked to turn defence into attack. The two lines of Republican and Nationalist forces had more or less stabilised. To the east of Madrid, the Republic front line formed a dagger-shaped salient pointing towards the Republican Mediterranean coastal strongholds. At the tip of the dagger was the small town of Teruel, which other than its geographical position held no strategic importance, and at the outset was defended only by about 8,000 of Franco's soldiers.[23] Since the Nationalist forces in the salient were ranged deep into Republican territory, they were essentially surrounded on three sides. This fact, and the importance of obtaining a clear victory, and the need to divert Nationalist forces from an impending attack on Guadalajara, all led to the Republican forces planning to take Teruel, encircle the

Nationalists and push back the enemy front line. The Republicans under the command of Hernandez Saravia committed something in excess of 100,000 troops to this battle. In the language of the casino, the Republicans went 'all in'.

On 10 December 1937, the XI International Brigade was put on alert for the attack on Teruel, although to begin with they were held in reserve. The Loyalist Republican forces launched their offensive on 15 December, a week before the Guadalajara attack was due to begin. The snow had already been falling when the attack began. Initially, the Republican Army met with success. On 17 December the Nationalists abandoned their positions on the surrounding hillsides and retreated into the town. By 21 December 1937, Martin's company of the 12 February Battalion had entered the centre of Teruel. Their advance was broadcast across the world; Ernest Hemingway, a frequent visitor of the XI Brigade, was there with them. I have been fortunate enough to obtain an extremely fragile original copy of the dispatches from Spain which Hemingway wrote for the American weekly, *The New Republic* in 1937 and 1938, often having to crawl on his hands and knees to reach the necessary vantage point and tell the story. He described what he saw as 'cold as a steel engraving, or wild as a Wyoming blizzard'.[24] Robert Capa, the famous war photographer was also there. Likewise, Paul Robeson who treated the troops to the Internationale and renditions of his famous *Show Boat* number Ol' Man River, with altered lyrics.[25] The news was splashed across the AP newswire and *New York Times* with a fanfare announcing this significant defeat of Franco's forces. *The Times* in London on 23 December 1937 carried the story that the Republicans had announced that Teruel had fallen into their hands. Clement Attlee, then leader of the Labour Party in Britain, who had himself earlier that month gone to visit the Brigaders in Spain, sent a telegram of congratulations.

In reality, the free press had celebrated too soon. The centre of town had been flattened but had not been fully captured. There was intense fighting from house to house but small pockets of Nationalist forces stubbornly held out, particularly in a cluster of buildings in the southern part of the town around the Bank of Spain and the Convent of Santa Clara. Robert Capa took a series of photographs in Teruel in December 1937, showing the Republican soldiers fighting through destroyed buildings whilst on the lookout for sniper fire. Both sides were severely impeded by extraordinary weather conditions.

Temperatures stubbornly hovered between minus 10 to minus 20°C. Nearly four foot of snow fell, forming drifts which impeded visibility and obstructed both sides' ability to bring in armaments. It was not until early January 1938 that the very last of the Nationalists surrendered in Teruel. And the besieging Republican forces were soon to become the besieged.[26]

On 24 December 1937, the Republican Army considered that the battle for Teruel itself was to all intents and purposes over, but also that they had to reinforce and hold the high ground on the exposed ridges which overlooked the town, so as to be ready to repel any counter-attack. The fighting transferred to two strategic hilltops which Hemingway described as 'odd thimble shaped formations like extinct geyser cones which protected the city'.[27] These were La Muela to the southwest and El Mueleton de Teruel to the northwest, which had previously been fortified by the Nationalist forces. It took the 12 February Battalion together with the largely American Lincoln Battalion a full week from Christmas Eve to New Year's Eve to dig their way through the deep snow to reach the summit of La Muela, driven on by their slogan that the quality of the fighter always wins over the quality of the enemy's armour. Their orders were to hold the summit at all costs.

The expected Nationalist counter-attack began on 29 December 1937. General Varela's Nationalists advanced with tens of thousands of troops re-deployed from the aborted planned attack on Guadalajara and assisted by German and Italian aircraft continuously strafing those dug in on the barren hillsides. Although ill-equipped and with insufficient clothing, the XI International Brigade repulsed attacks on 5 and 6 January 1938 with resultant heavy loss of life on both sides.

The next wave of attacks came on 17 January 1938. By this time, each side had thrown everything into the attack and defence respectively. In the meantime, the 12 February Battalion had been withdrawn from La Muela and redeployed together with a company of Catalan anarchists to the desperate defence of El Mueleton on the other side of Teruel. Over three murderous days, the 12 February Battalion repulsed eleven separate attempts to gain the heights. The Austrians in the 12 February Battalion fought for each inch of that hillside. The Polish General Karol Swierczewski, known as General Walter, said they fought the most stubborn and powerful battle they ever had to fight.[28] One of those there recorded that 'There were no real positions there. We just lay straight on the mountain – or sometimes among the rocks. There was hardly any soil, no more than some twenty or thirty centimetres. We had no chance of digging positions in the cold. We were right up on the rock.'[29]

No artillery or tanks, on either side, could make it through snow-packed hill-side tracks. Radiators froze and cylinders cracked in the cold. Six hundred vehicles were said to be snowbound between Teruel and Valencia on the coast. This was a true infantry battle with frostbite as much the enemy as the rifle bullet. The ensuing fighting in abominable conditions was just about the bloodiest of the Spanish Civil War. Hemingway, who looked on helpless from below, said that it was 'a position sold as dearly as any position was sold in any war.'[30]

Finally, on 19 January 1938, the Nationalists broke through and by the evening of the next day, El Mueleton fell into their hands. Still the XI International Brigade was not finished. Between 25 and 27 January 1938, they tried themselves to counter-attack before the Nationalists had fully dug in. The Republican troops by this time were completely exhausted. There were even sporadic reports of mutiny. By 7 February 1938, it was clear that the battle was lost, the Nationalists were in complete command and the Republican forces had suffered a fatal hammer blow.[31]

It proved to be the decisive turning point of the war, leaving the Republicans in full retreat. Landauer recorded that on the eve of the Battle for Teruel, the XI Brigade had 920 foreign volunteers in its ranks, including 226 Austrians. He also listed the dozens upon dozens of Austrian nationals of the 12 February Battalion who died defending their position at El Mueleton in January 1938. Named amongst the dead is Martin Lobl, fallen on the snow-covered hills of Aragon with no grave to mark him. He had become in Hemingway's words, 'part of the earth of Spain',[32] one of an estimated 60,000 Republicans who lost their lives in the battle.[33]

The defeat of the socialists in Spain left the field to the agents of the far right in Europe; Martin was just one of the many who had fought with all they had to hold back this tide. With this much altered military landscape and balance of power, it would soon become apparent quite how vulnerable those who remained behind in Austria were.

PART TWO
FALLEN

8

Doorstep Condition

Each family has its own morning routine, taken for granted by those accustomed to it. My father began each day in front of a cup of coffee, half a grapefruit, a piece of cold brown toast, together with some unappetising cottage cheese, all pushed carefully to one side as he scoured the paper with a silent intensity not devoted to any other activity. This was long before *The Times* was published in tabloid format, giving rise to an elaborate ritual of folding and unfolding the pages in such a manner as to avoid any possibility of them being dunked into coffee or smeared with buttered toast or worse still, his dietetic spread.

Just as my father was held transfixed by the daily news, I was – as a child of nine – ever curious as to exactly what was holding his complete attention. What was he looking for? It was certainly not the sports pages or the stock prices that absorbed him so totally. Was it domestic news or the ebb and flow of world politics? It might even be that he was double-checking that there was simply nothing relevant in the newspaper. He would often say, 'No news is good news.' I would sometimes try to scan his face for clues. There was no possibility of actually getting hold of the newspaper or any part of it whilst my father catalogued its contents before he left for the surgery.

So it was that I started to get up at the crack of dawn to creep down the length of the corridor of our apartment, being careful not to wake my father, and have a read of the paper before everyone rose for breakfast. If I succeeded, I would sit by the front door cross-legged and examine the pages for signs, for the mystical clues that gripped him each and every day. When I heard my parents getting up, I would fold the newspaper diligently, silently replace it just outside the door and go to the kitchen to start laying the table for breakfast.

The creeping and tiptoeing was critical. There were a fair few rules in our household, but one was sacrosanct and repeatedly invoked by my mother; 'Do not wake up your father.' To be fair there was good reason for this first commandment. He was a GP, and as required would tend to the sick at their homes round the clock. The notion of a doctor undertaking such home calls whilst the rest of us sleep soundly has now all but disappeared but was then not uncommon. As a result, my father would regularly have to drag himself out of bed in the small hours to visit patients and when he finally got back home, he was not to be disturbed for anything, except another patient. The first question at breakfast always related to how many times his slumbers had been interrupted the previous night.

I remember sitting at my cross-legged doorway vigil one morning, reviewing the contents of the day's newspaper, when I looked around and saw my father standing over me wearing a profoundly quizzical look. Thinking back on it now, he must have wondered what on earth was happening and why I was not asleep. I mistook his expression for one of irritation: someone else had devoured his precious paper and perhaps even read the very print off it. I immediately folded it with exaggerated care and handed it to him, saying, 'Here it is, in doorstep condition.' No more was said, but that was the end of my early morning newspaper routine.

Instead, as part of a silent pact between my father and I, for my tenth birthday I was given a wonderful miniature radio which became my pride and joy. Quite possibly this was the only time my father had himself organised a specific present, a task otherwise left to my mother. I used that instead to follow the news, particularly on the World Service with its wonderful introductory tune. I think I felt comforted to know that whatever had happened overnight around the world I would be the very first in the family to learn of it. Above all, however, I used it to listen to all the early morning 'progress' of England's overseas winter cricket tours. There was something inevitable about being told by Christopher Martin Jenkins, the Test Match Special commentator, that there was more bad news for English listeners.

I am not sure I ever paused to think how strange it was to grow up in this news junkie environment. It was certainly not joked about, or even discussed. I think now that many of my mother and father's generation were determined never again to be caught out by the march of world events. Perhaps in the 1930s they had been reading the wrong journals or had placed too much weight on the ill-founded reassurances of communal leaders. Whatever the cause, the great majority missed the critical signals until it was largely too late. In fact, as a teenager in Germany, my father *had* been digesting the news in the aftermath of Hitler's rise to power and urged his own father to make arrangements to leave whilst they still could. Many others in the community rebuked my father for saying this, pointing out that no one else was packing their bags, and scolding him for presuming to know more than others.

As circumstances deteriorated over the course of 1938, my grandfather even wrote to one of his brothers who had left Europe for Peru. He tested the waters to see whether his brother thought it advisable for the whole family to come out and join him there. His brother strongly cautioned against the idea, saying that things were really tough for him and that they were better off where they were. Their town Rabbi also lent his weight to the side of those inclined to stay, saying that anyone was free to go to America, so long as they were happy to work as a cinema attendant. After all, what else was there to do in the land of the free? Who knows, maybe my father even felt a misplaced sense of guilt that he had not pressed sufficiently the need for everyone to pack up and leave or unfairly blamed himself that he had not fully understood the politics of the day, until everyone was overtaken by it. All this fed into another of my father's traits; once he had made his mind up on some subject or other, his view was fixed, immutable. So, all those years afterwards, each day he read the newspaper in complete silence. Cover to cover.

9

White Flags

Fremd bin ich eingezogen
Fremd zieh ich wieder aus[1]

On Friday evening 11 March 1938, Max along with all the men in the family went to synagogue in Lackenbach, as they did every week. The women did not accompany them; by tradition they would have been preparing the evening meal in their respective homes. In the Jewish religion, the Friday evening service is unlike many of the other regular services. It is a relatively speedy affair as far such things go, about an hour in duration, but full of song welcoming the Sabbath. Over that short service, Max's whole life was to change. Likewise, the lives of his family and entire community.

Max emerged from the synagogue into the clear crisp moonlight. At this time he was living with his parents, Heinrich and Karoline, about five minutes away at Berggasse, 8. He started the short walk home from the synagogue on Templegasse to their house around the corner on the parallel street. He walked through the narrow alleyway dividing the two streets and turned the corner to join Berggasse. Since his brothers-in-law also lived on the same street, just a half a dozen or so houses up the hill, no doubt everyone would have been walking together, enjoying the moment of rest at the end of the working week. As Max turned the corner, the mood turned to horror. As far as his eyes could see, half the houses on Berggasse were draped in Nazi Swastikas – the *Hakenkreuz*, as he called it. These were not just makeshift flags but made of heavy cloth that had to be suspended from flag poles. All this required more than a moment's planning and preparation. Max understood in a flash that for many in the village this was a moment that they were eagerly awaiting. People that his family had lived side by side with for so many years had, it seemed, turned in the time of a brief synagogue service.

Berggasse was to all intents and purposes divided into two halves: the lower section towards the main square being largely inhabited by Jewish families and the upper part, nearest the Church, with only Christian families, most of whom were now flying the swastika. It is not possible to comprehend Max's stupefaction – and he was certainly not alone in experiencing a catastrophic sense of shock. Where had this come from? Each non-Jewish household publicly declaring their hateful allegiance in this manner.

The closest study of the press that morning would not have assisted Max to anticipate these events. The final issue of *Die Judenpresse* – the local weekly newspaper written for the Jewish communities of the Burgenland – was published on Friday 11 March 1938. It was stock full of advertisement and articles looking forwards to the festival of Purim, which was to begin a few days later on the evening of 16 March. Purim is a festival celebrating deliverance of the Jewish people of Susa in the Persian Empire from genocidal threat about two and a half thousand years ago. With dreadful historical irony, the persecution of the Jews of Susa had begun with the taunt of an ambitious local politician, Haman, that the Jews were strangers in their midst that had been scattered over the corners of the earth but who obeyed their own rules and not those of the Emperor and so deserved to be eliminated.[2] Equally, there was little of note in Robert Stricker's highly regarded Zionist-leaning weekly from Vienna, *Die Neue Welt*, also published that day. There was lengthy coverage of the debate on Palestine in the English House of Commons and copious advertising imploring readers to stock up on unleavened bread (*matzo*) from Schmidl in good time for the festival of Passover, which followed a month or so after Purim. There was, however, a short front page article referring to the plebiscite that Chancellor Schuschnigg had just announced would take place that Sunday, 13 March 1938.

In order to understand that announcement and the events of the evening of Friday 11 March 1938, it is necessary to track back one month. On 12 February 1938, Hitler had summoned the Austrian Chancellor Kurt Schuschnigg to his mountain retreat in Berchtesgaden, near the border of Germany and Austria. This was only a matter of days after he had assumed supreme command of the German armed forces. Schuschnnigg turned up dressed in a full winter ski outfit providing an unconvincing cover for his trip at short notice to Germany.[3] Hitler tore into Schuschnigg, threatened Austria with the kind of devastation wrought in Spain unless Schuschnigg acceded to his demands. He insisted on the appointment of Seyss-Inquart – an Austrian Nazi – as Minister of Security; the official merger of the Austrian Nazi Party with the Fatherland Front and the release of all Austrians convicted for the assassination of Chancellor Dollfuss, or participation in the July 1934 revolt, or imprisoned for membership of the Nazi Party. Schuschnnigg was told that the terms would not be altered one iota.[4] An exhausted Schuschnnigg signed the Protocol agreeing to these terms at 11pm, one hour before the deadline expired. As Schuschnigg was escorted back to his car to leave for Vienna, Herr von Papen, then German Ambassador to Austria, commented to him, 'Well now you have seen what the Führer can be like at times. But the next time I am sure it will be different. You know the Führer can be absolutely charming.' As he was driven down the mountain, however, Schuschnnigg was under no illusion that there would be a next time.[5]

Included amongst those released under the Protocol was Tobias Portschy, who would fulfil the role of tormentor-in-chief in the Burgenland; first of the Jews and then the Roma community. He was a lawyer and party activist in his early thirties with a full round face and a receding hairline. A Burgenlander from Unterschutzen born into a large and poor Protestant family, he joined the Nazi party in 1931 but had found himself in and out of prison since 1933. From about 1935 he had assumed the unofficial position of Gauleiter for the Burgenland region. A rabid anti-Semite, he had written widely of the need to expel Jews from Austria and was also unremitting in his verbal attacks on the Roma of the region. One of his tasks from 1936 was to co-ordinate the drawing up of lists of prominent Jews and activists in the region, together with photographic identification.[6]

On Wednesday 9 March 1938, in a final futile act of defiance and after a belated dialogue with what remained of the Social Democrat leadership, Schuschnigg declared that a plebiscite would be held in Austria just days later, on Sunday 13 March, to establish whether the Austrian people wished to join with Germany or remain an independent nation. Predictably, Schuschnigg's action was enthusiastically welcomed by Dr Desider Friedman, the President of

Austria's Zionist Organisation, who said that every Jew would be expected to do his or her patriotic duty to vote against Anschluss.

The unintended consequence of Schuschnigg's announcement was to accelerate Hitler's plans for the invasion of Austria. On Thursday 10 March 1938, a meeting of senior representatives of the Austrian Nazi Party took place in Vienna and those present, including Portschy, were told that Berlin had sanctioned the taking of all necessary measures in anticipation of the seizure of power including, if necessary, the use of force. German troops were to be in Vienna two days later. Portschy and his fellow Nazis in the Burgenland needed little encouragement. The next day he organised and spoke at a rumbustious rally of 14,000 people in Eisenstadt protesting against Schuschnigg's plebiscite.[7] This was significantly more than the entire population of Eisenstadt and gives an idea of the both the organisational reach of the local Nazi Party and its widespread support. The police – under the ultimate orders of Seyss-Inquart – stood by. The violence spread into Deutschkreuz and Mattersburg, nearby communities in the Burgenland. In Hornstein, which neighboured Eisenstadt, a larger banner was raised above the main street decorated either side with swastikas reading, 'Jews not wanted'. It seems the residents of Lackenbach were also ready with their flagpoles and flags.

By the evening of Friday 11 March, while Max was ensconced in the synagogue and shut off from the outside world, the worst had happened and nearly half of Lackenbach eagerly welcomed it. The Austrian Government surrendered to Germany's threats and cancelled the planned plebiscite. At 7.30pm, Schuschnigg made a radio broadcast announcing that the German government had issued a further ultimatum requiring President Miklas to nominate as Chancellor a person designated by Germany, and that in order to avoid bloodshed, the Austrians would comply. Seyss-Inquart was in the room standing over him as he spoke to ensure compliance.[8] Schuschnigg concluded his broadcast with these words: 'So I take leave of the Austrian people with a German word of farewell uttered from the depth of my heart: God protect Austria.' A moment's silence followed this and then the second movement of Haydn's Emperor Quartet was played. It was an old recording, a softer rendition of Deutschland Uber Alles.

An aircraft was waiting at Aspen aerodrome to fly Schuschnigg out of the country, but he refused to leave. He would soon be arrested by the Gestapo and whilst he survived the war, he suffered greatly at their hands. By nightfall Seyss-Inquart had replaced Schuschnigg, and he had had Portschy installed as the Governor of the Burgenland. Meanwhile, the centre of Vienna was draped in the Swastika.

Later that evening in Vienna at the Café Louvre on the corner of Wipplingergasse and Renngasse, a number of journalists and reporters gathered. This was a café favoured by the foreign press and had been the haunt of Theodor Herzl, the founder of modern Zionism, who had practically set up office there. At their own regular table, their *stammtisch*, sat the American journalist William Shirer, then working for CBS. He was talking animatedly with a number of his circle when Emil Maass, his former assistant of many years, joined them. Maass, in response to the news of Schuschnigg's resignation, said 'it was about time.' Then to William Shirer's horror, he turned over the lapel of his jacket to reveal a hidden pin. Discarding the Austrian flag, he had previously worn, Maass pinned the Nazi emblem in its place, now willing to display it openly. Major Goldschmidt, a trusted colleague of Shirer and source of inside news, himself Catholic but with a Jewish father, expressed his disgust. He stood up to say he was going home to fetch his revolver.[9] This was not a pronouncement of armed resistance but of surrender. He left to shoot himself. William Shirer later recorded in his diary that his fellow CBS broadcaster Ed Murrow, that night in a quiet bar in Vienna off the central Kartnerstrasse, had seen a man take out a knife in front of everyone and slit his own wrists.

G. E. R. Gedye was the *Daily Telegraph*'s correspondent covering Austria and Central Europe. Perhaps of all the British journalists writing about the region his was the deepest insight and understanding. He spent the evening wandering around Vienna. He followed a baying mob of nearly 100,000 marching through the centre of the city singing the Horst Wessel song. The crowds then descended on the Jewish quarter in Leopoldstadt chanting anti-Semitic slogans. Many could not bear to see this and ended their own lives. By July 1938, the Archbishop of York and Bishop of Chichester had written to *The Times* with credible reports that since Hitler had taken power in March more than 7,000 Jews had committed suicide in Vienna alone.[10] Deliverance from expulsion and annihilation must have seemed very remote that Purim.

The next day, Portschy would have fully expected that the German army would have arrived in force in Austria as planned – yet there was still no sign of them and so the putsch would have to be enforced from within Austria and not externally by the Wehrmacht. Somewhat belying the reputation for ruthless efficiency, the German tanks had ground to a halt near the border a few dozen kilometres from Linz. A major mechanical fault had developed in the motorized heavy artillery and the tanks were caught up behind them.[11]

None of this bothered Portschy, who was itching to get going. He announced first thing on 12 March by auto-diktat published in Lackenbach that the Jews of the Burgenland region were required to leave not later than 18 April 1938. This was a striking pronouncement. It was the first unambiguous expression of a comprehensive policy of expulsion of Jews anywhere in the Reich, and it did not originate in Germany but in rural Austria. It took place a full year and half before the start of the Second World War and several years before the mass deportation of Jews from urban centres. Moreover, it was simply announced without any legislative or legal basis, not by a German but by an Austrian. It was in essence the expression of a local party leader who sought advancement and wanted to be noticed.

On the evening of 12 March, Portschy sent a cable to Hitler. He expressed his gratitude for the rescue of Austria from extreme distress and the wish that in return the Burgenland would show its gratitude and allegiance to him. Portschy drove forward Nazi policy in this small, easternmost region of Austria with considerable determination. His work was to catch the eye of Eichmann, who was dispatched to Vienna in the next few days. He was not the only leading Nazi to have been impressed with Portschy's work.

Dr Wilhelm Frick, the author of the Nuremberg laws, accepted an invitation from Portschy to come to the Burgenland on 6 April 1938 to inspect the success of the local Nazi party. Frick first of all had the brass to visit the socialist stronghold of Neufeld Steinbrunn to explain to the unemployed factory workers there that under the Nazis they would all have work. The nature of this work was not spelt out. Then he went to Eisenstadt. This time, nearly 60,000 were reported to have gathered in Eisenstadt's parade ground to cheer, although some were heard to have been disappointed when they saw they were cheering Wilhelm Frick. They had been promised a leading Nazi figure and had assumed it would be Hitler himself. In anticipation, the town's buildings were festooned with Swastikas, celebratory fireworks were arranged for the evening and Portschy presented Frick with a signed photograph album filled with images of cheering Burgenlanders as a commemoration of the visit.[12]

So it was that the Austrian Nazis first seized power in the Burgenland, a day before The 8th Army of the Wehrmacht poured into Vienna and two days before Hitler, himself of course Austrian-born, came to address a packed, close to hysterical crowd in the Heldenplatz. It has been estimated that more than one and a half million lined the streets for Hitler's cavalcade, nearly half the total population of the whole country.

The local Austrian Nazi party, under orders from Portschy in Eisenstadt, took full control of Lackenbach over the weekend of 12-13 March 1938. Max recalled that the Jewish shops, which would otherwise normally be open for business, were ordered to remain closed on the Sunday. Max was ordered to present himself that day at the local police station. He went with his father, Heinrich and his brother-in-law, Julya. It was explained to them that the Jews had to pay all taxes immediately and leave the Burgenland by 18 April 1938 and not later because the creation of a *Judenrein* (Jew-Free) Burgenland was intended as a special birthday present from the Austrian people to Hitler, whose birthday was celebrated as a national holiday on 20 April. Before the meeting, Max's parents' house had been searched by the Gestapo, who had expropriated or simply stolen any money or jewellery they could find. At the police station, my great-grandfather Heinrich spoke out when he heard what was being demanded. He asked the Gestapo chief how the Jews could afford to pay taxes and pack up and leave when the police raided their homes and confiscated all they had. This was met with the response that Jews always had a way of finding more money.

Max sought to persuade his own parents that they, along with his younger twin sisters, had to leave Lackenbach immediately and stay with friends or contacts in Vienna until the situation became clearer. Max, my grandfather Julya, my grandmother Terci, and my mother would stay behind in order to try to take care of the family business and shops and try to raise some money by selling as much of the stock as they could. Only a few days later Heinrich, Karoline and the twin sisters, Wilma and Gina, were loaded onto trucks by the local police and taken to Vienna. Some of those transported with them tried to escape over the border into Hungary but were turned back by Hungarian border guards. Others found themselves marooned on barges afloat on the cold Danube, unable either to leave or return.

Before they were torn apart, however, there was one thing that had to be organised, a family photograph. There is no date recorded on the copy that I have and so I cannot be certain precisely when or where it was taken. But there are clues in the photograph itself. It could not have been taken earlier than 1938 because the youngest in the photograph, Eva, was only born in 1937 and appears to be wearing her first shoes. It could not really have been taken after April 1938 because this group would no longer all be together. Accordingly, it makes sense that this photograph was taken in Lackenbach in the weeks following the Anschluss at a time when the family group already knew that they would have to leave their hometown, and that any reunion was unlikely to be soon, if ever.

This was the image that each would take with them, not knowing where. This was the photograph that ended up on my grandmother's dressing table and which I would sneak in to look at as a child. It does not yield its secrets readily. On further reflection, the setting is extremely formal and the men in the back row do look sombre. Nevertheless, Heinrich and Karoline, my great-grandparents at the front and centre, appear confident and reassuring as if to say, 'We will all survive and be together again.'

The next days in Lackenbach must have been hard to face, surrounded by loathing and charged with fear. A local villager, who was nine years old at the time, commented that practically the whole of the Christian population of Lackenbach supported the Nazi Party: 'They glorified Hitler.' [13] Max recorded his particular disgust that the anti-Semitic mob appeared to be swollen by many he had known growing up as religious Catholics and even former socialist Schutzbunders. Although Max did recall that when someone tried to attend Church in a Nazi uniform, he was practically thrown out by a member of the Esterházy family, who had stood up for tolerance and decency for many centuries. It was also apparent that there were a number of others in Lackenbach, mostly amongst the wealthier residents, who clearly took no pleasure from the situation and distributed food to those in need.

The pressure to leave immediately was fuelled by rumours that Jewish men within a certain age range were going to be rounded up and arrested before the date of compulsory deportation. This was not idle speculation. On 31 March 1938, the Jews of nearby Frauenkirchen and Deutschkreuz were arrested and taken to a concentration camp at Berg. Max's brother Oskar was also now in great danger. He had had a heated altercation with a local policeman he knew well over many years but who clearly revelled in this latest political turn. The policemen approached Oskar and tried without success to confiscate Oskar's tefillin and tallit on his way to prayers at the synagogue. The policeman made it clear his time in Lackenbach was over and that he was a marked man. Oskar had no choice but to go into hiding immediately.

The speed of implementation was relentless. The synagogue was closed down. On 15 March 1938, a new Burgenland Provincial Administration ordered the confiscation of all Jewish bank deposits, the closure of Jewish businesses, and the prohibition of the sale of foodstuffs or the restitution of debts owed to Jews. The administration also directed that control of Jewish shops be transferred to a local *kommissar*. As a result, Julya and Max would have struggled to raise money through the disposal of any part of the family business. Long-standing customers would explain that they had nothing against the family personally, but they would not now settle their overdue accounts. Julya, it seems, was unable to sell any of his furniture or stock, or pay taxes. A ban was imposed by the local authorities on trading with Jews and the great part of the village were too scared to do other than abide by it. On 23 March 1938, the Jews of the Burgenland were stripped of their citizenship and the right to vote. The same applied to the Roma. This of course included the forthcoming plebiscite announced on 13 March 1938 and due to take place across Austria on 10 April 1938.

The festival of Passover took place from 15 to 22 April 1938. Max records that he, Julya, my mother and grandmother had a lonely Passover meal together in Lackenbach at my grandfather's house at Berggasse 18. Max did, however, add one telling detail. The Jews of Lackenbach had been ordered to leave not later than 18 April. Anyone staying after that date did so at great peril. Nevertheless, he recalled that one evening when they had sat down to eat, a policeman, maybe even the same person who had tormented Oskar earlier, peered through the net curtain of the ground floor window of their house to see what was happening inside and who remained within. They had overstayed the mandated departure date of 18 April, so this must have been an extremely tense moment. I suspect there was a temptation to try to hide. In any event, Julya decided to invite him in and perhaps to the surprise of all parties, he accepted. He sat down, shared a glass of wine in silence and then got up and left. The next day he returned to inquire after a rather nice piece of furniture that he could not but help notice in the corner of their living room. Being unable to either take it with him or sell it, Julya told him he could keep it.[14]

The remaining members of my family – including my mother, grandmother and grandfather – left Lackenbach immediately after Passover. They were amongst the last 35 Jewish families to leave and no doubt having stayed a few days beyond Hitler's birthday ruined his present entirely. When each town or village in the Burgenland achieved its stated objective of expulsion, it raised a white flag to show that it had been purified. On 25 April 1938, Lackenbach raised its own white flag.[15] By the time all this happened, the bonds of decency had been broken with remarkable ease.

Among the more extraordinary accounts of these terrible days is a short film by Elisabeth Fraller entitled *Remembering and Forgetting,* made in 2007. Fraller was born in Lackenbach after the Second World War but spent most of her adult life in Vienna and beyond. She says that she knew nothing of the Jewish past of the village as nobody spoke of it. The only story she had heard which made any reference to the Jews of Lackenbach was the dark warning from a classmate in primary school who told her of a Jewish cemetery located at the end of a deserted overgrown lane further up the hill beyond the Church. The boy told her that there was a skull which hung from the gate of the burial ground and that if any child were to enter, they would die and end up hanging from the gate themselves. Fraller decided many years later to return to Lackenbach and film the older residents sharing their recollection of the expulsion of the Jews in 1938. There are four interviewees, all in their eighties. A good deal of the power of the film is that each person is allowed to tell his or her story almost entirely without interruption. The narrators appear to show a measure of remorse and shame for what happened. An ageing group, quietly facing their past.

The film is a poignant exploration not so much of collective memory but rather collective erasure. Each interviewee recalled that the Jews had been kind and, in many cases, good employers in the village. In the lifetime of those interviewed, a majority of the total population of

Lackenbach had been Jewish. Each described how Jews and non-Jews lived side by side with a high level of interaction in business. Many of the local villagers had worked together with Jews or in their shops or households. Both Berggasse and Neugasse, two of the main streets were, they said, almost entirely populated by Jewish shops. One elderly man recalled that he went to the Jewish bakery for special breads and cakes at different times of year including the special Passover matzos.

One lady recalled how the Jewish family she was employed by, the owners of a bakery, were especially thoughtful and kind, and how, one day in 1938, she helped them prepare to leave. The next morning, she came to work as usual and saw that her employers had baked a special loaf of bread for her to take. They had all gone and the house was empty. The family left a note saying they were sorry they had nothing else to give her. After the Jews were expelled, she said, there was a free-for-all. People took away all the stock, machinery and furniture they could lay their hands on.

Each person interviewed predominantly narrated the events in the third person or passive mood. Things happened without any individual agency or even witness. The Jews left. No individual actually did anything or saw anything. One young boy looking on recalled many years later that the Jews didn't even seem to care that they were being thrown out. They seemed to accept their fate. [16]

There were, however, a few small cracks in the collective version of events told by those interviewed. There was the story of Propaganda Karl, as he was known, who could be seen marching up and down the streets shouting 'Sieg Heil' whilst everyone apparently stood by and watched. There was the villager who was nicknamed 'Hundred Per Cent' (*'Hundert Prozent'*). With a wry smile, the elderly farmer being interviewed recalled how, in the run-up to the 10 April 1938 plebiscite, she walked around the village with a placard reading 'Hundred per cent'. This was a reference to the fact that any district which voted 100 per cent 'Yes' in favour of the Anschluss was promised a photograph personally signed by Hitler. The efforts of *'Hundert Prozent'* were in vain, as old lady Steiglitz in the village apparently voted 'No'. In the end, only 61 voters in the whole of the Burgenland were brave enough to vote against the Anschluss and it should be noted that 291 out of the 327 districts in all Austria did receive their signed photograph of the Führer. By this time, the unification of Germany and Austria under Hitler was endorsed publicly not only by Cardinal Innitzer, the head of the Catholic Church, but remarkably also by Karl Renner, the leader of what remained of the Social Democratic Party and many of the former Schutzbunders. Whilst there was no doubt strong public support for the new plebiscite, the election was not a free one. In many county districts such as Lackenbach, voting took place in public and without even the pretence of a secret ballot. In Vienna, whilst there were voting booths, Nazi officers stood close by to oversee how people voted and generally instil fear. [17]

Also telling was the attempt by the filmmakers to find a trace of the site or remains of the old synagogue of Lackenbach. The search led to a wooden gate besides a row of relatively newly built houses and a suspicious villager looking on at the film crew. Nothing remains of the synagogue but an obscure and modestly sized plaque laid by the Jews of Vienna. One of the interviewees took the film crew to her house and proudly pointed out that in her garden she had kept what she referred to as a 'holy stone' which she and her husband took from the rubble of the synagogue when it was blown up in 1938. She said that many others took away stone or bricks for their own private use commenting that this was for certain what had happened, otherwise how did one think that Lackenbach looked so beautiful today. She continued in a somewhat matter-of-fact manner pointing to her garden stonework: 'It's a decent memorial.' She lamented that the Jews had to leave the village observing that 'We were integrated with all of them. There was not such a hatred like there is today.' She was being interviewed in 2007 when no Jews could be found living in the entire region.

In the film credits, Elisabeth Fraller gave thanks not only to those she interviewed but to the surviving Jews from Lackenbach to whom she had spoken about their own experiences, and from whom she had sought advice and guidance in making the film. Included amongst these, to my surprise, was Max. He had never spoken to me about this project or his involvement in it.

10

Closing Time

Anyone who has conducted research in libraries or archives will know that each has its own code. Trespass at your peril. Strangely enough, silence rarely features amongst the inviolable precepts. There is the constant sound of laptop typing, muted mobile phone conversations and the persistent whispering of those who are employed full time to keep on top of an ever-increasing mountain of material. In some of the places I went to in the course of my research, there were so few people at the reading tables that the administrative activity was an entirely pleasant distraction. In collections focusing on Holocaust material, the titles of the books on the surrounding shelves would often mean it was a relief to hear ordinary conversation about the everyday, with not even a hint of mass slaughter. Nevertheless, there is one unbreakable rule of all libraries and archives across the globe. It is that closing time must be obeyed.

One of my first ports of call was the National Archive of the History of the Jewish People in Jerusalem. This collection holds papers and materials assembled from a number of the prominent Jewish communities of pre-war Europe. I thought that going there would assist me in my quest to track down the last days of the Jewish communities in Lackenbach and the Burgenland and what happened to them thereafter. I took the no 42 bus which dropped me at the impressive entrance to the Givat Ram Campus where the National Archives are housed. I followed the signs as best as I could into the main entrance, somewhat optimistically thinking that documents of such historical significance would be kept in this state-of-the-art shiny new building complete with cafeteria. I was to be disappointed. Each inquiry was met with a puzzled expression until eventually I was led back outside into the scorching midday heat and to a row of old Nissen huts. I was then conducted to a subterranean corridor of reading rooms equipped with old-fashioned spooled microfilm document readers.

After filling in the requisite forms, the librarians brought up several boxes of microfilm for me to read through. I asked about photocopying and got an odd look. I was told that no one did that anymore: researchers simply took out their mobiles, photographed whatever was on the screen and looked at it later. This technique proved useful and I gathered a large amount of historical material from Lackenbach stretching back nearly three hundred years and which was mostly recorded in Hebrew – not German or Yiddish but Hebrew, which was taught, written and spoken as the lingua franca of this community, looking across the centuries East to Jerusalem. There were details of my family and their contribution both spiritual and financial – but I was still unable to find answers to my questions about the events of March 1938 and their immediate aftermath. Those helping me there could see that I had not quite found what I needed and so after a bit of further explanation I was given the next destination on my idiosyncratic trail; the archive of the National Holocaust Memorial Museum in Washington.

There is another important rule of historical archives. The researcher has to identify in advance the particular collection they require so that the librarians can prepare the materials for the reader's arrival. This is of course not always easy as you don't really know what you need until you have it, but I did this as best as I could and once more I was shown some invaluable records, letters and photographs through the diligence of the archivists there. Yet still the precise details of what had happened in March 1938 eluded me and on my last day before I had to head off for work in Washington, the head librarian asked me if there was anything else I needed.

I explained once more my frustration and perhaps having got a little more used to the world of archives I used more precise language because she then said to me that it was obvious what I needed was not the archives of the Burgenland but those of the *Israelitische Kultusgemeinde Wien* (IKG) in Vienna, as this was the next port of call for the Jews deported from Lackenbach. A microfilm copy of this archive was held in Washington as well as in Vienna and would most likely contain the personal details and records of my relatives. She then said that the only trouble was that the material needed to be ordered in advance and that it would not be ready until 2pm that afternoon at the earliest. It was the record – on microfilm in alphabetical order – of all the Jews of Vienna who had ever registered with the IKG. Over a hundred thousand files all told. I muttered some question about closing time and was reminded that it was 4.30pm sharp.

As good as her word, the boxes of microfilm arrived at my desk at 2pm. I was shown to one of the microfilm readers and was asked if I knew what I was doing. I thought that my experience in Jerusalem made me something of an expert and confidently answered in the affirmative. The boxes were carefully labelled in alphabetical order with name ranges. I think I can say I have never worked as fast in my life. I sped through hundreds upon hundreds of pages of microfilm in order to find the records of my relatives, the Grunsfeld and Lobl families. The trouble was that when it came to the Grunsfelds, the records had to be found amongst the many almost identically named families. Some with and some without an 's', some with an accent here or there. When it came to the Lobl family, there were simply dozens of records bearing the exact same surname.

Each record told its own desperate story and there was I speeding through each one to get to where I needed to be. It was a powerful illustration of the most basic and obvious point; the vast scale of the suffering. The human brain is not adept at processing mass despair or destruction. As a general rule, we are better at focusing on an individual, a family or a village. Yet here I was, spooling through record after record of families born in or outside of Vienna; a seemingly endless catalogue, yet itself only a tiny part of the pitiless pile. I saw the brief handwritten story of Emil Lobl, then Emmanuel Lobl, Erich Lobl, Jacob Lobl, Johann Lobl and then right in front of my eyes was the hand of Julius Lobl, my grandfather born in Lackenbach on 28 November 1896. Fine, steady handwriting.

I can be confident from the content of these records that my grandfather never contemplated that these precious pages would ever be read or considered by future generations. The information given is spare and without embellishment. Each person's file is recorded on a pre-printed form but completed by hand by the named individual. A husband or father would complete the form for each member of his immediate family. So my grandfather filled out his form on behalf of himself, my grandmother Terci and my mother. It is written in a thick black ink. It recorded that he arrived in Vienna from Lackenbach on 25 April 1938 and they were all living together at Grosse Schiffgasse, 6 in the Second District of Vienna. Then I found Max's records. Max had filled out his own form in his more spidery hand, recording that he was single and had been running his own business for the past four years in Lackenbach, that he had arrived in Vienna 23 April 1938 and that he was living at Tandelmarktgasse, 12, likewise in the Second District.

The forms contained a myriad of detail, dates and fragments of a story I had yet to unlock. The only trouble was that it was now 4.10pm. I had been given the first warning call of the approach of the end of library hours. I thought that the obvious answer to this was to take my phone out and start taking photographs of the pages of microfilm on the reader. I was then stopped by the kind researcher at the neighbouring table. He asked me what on earth I thought I was doing, when all I had to do was use the computer to save multiple pages onto a thumb drive. This took a few more precious minutes but in the end I copied hundreds of pages of these detailed forms. As I saved the very last pages of the family files, I was told over the tannoy system (a bit like my law exams) to stop everything. It was now 4.30pm. After thanking everyone for their immense help, I walked out into a humid Washington spring afternoon, with something of an adrenalin rush and armed with further clues held securely on a memory stick. I would now be able to trace the next chapter of the story.

11

Vienna's Spring Pogrom

אֵיכָה יָשְׁבָה בָדָד, הָעִיר רַבָּתִי עָם[1]

The extended family and a few thousand others from various towns of the Burgenland arrived in Vienna in late April 1938 with what little they could carry and no means of support. Their destination was a far cry from the Vienna known to tourists today, with its grand boulevards and opulent cafes. They were bound for the tightly packed pullulating Jewish quarter, home to a significant proportion of Vienna's 200,000 Jews. After Warsaw and Budapest, this was the largest pre-War Jewish community in Europe. Particular to Vienna, however, was the very rapid growth over the prior seventy or so years.[2] In common with many large cities today with significant immigration, less than one in six of the Jewish population of Vienna at this time had a mother or father born in the city. This was a gathering of exiles from all parts of the former Hapsburg domains seeking work and shelter. The size of the community and its considerable growth was at one and the same time a strength and a fatal weakness.

It seems that the *Israelitische Kultusgemeinde*, the Jewish Community Centre, must have assisted the family in finding accommodation provided by local volunteers. The fact that they were split up into several different apartments a few roads apart suggests that favours had to be called in and that not for the last time they had to rely heavily on the kindness of strangers. Each address given on the forms secured from the Washington archives was found in the Second District of Vienna, also known formally as Leopoldstadt and more informally as *die Matzo Insel* (The Matzo Island). This stretch of land in the centre of Vienna forms part of an island squeezed in between the Danube Canal and the Danube River. Perhaps the most well-known landmark in this part of Vienna is the Prater Gardens with its Prater Wheel of *Third Man* fame. A series of bridges cross the Danube Canal connect the Jewish quarter with Vienna's inner city.

The geographical position of this slice of Vienna as a Jewish district was no accident. It allowed former Hapsburg rulers of old to be satisfied that the Jews of Vienna were sealed off and kept apart from the majority population by a natural barrier. This had made the re-admittance of Jews into Vienna nearly three hundred years ago more palatable. In 1938, the pre-existing geographical separation of Jew and Christian in Vienna made the Nazis' work much swifter.

Julya managed to secure accommodation for himself, Terci and my mother in an apartment right next door to the grandly decorated Hungarian Synagogue, known as the *Schiffschul*, the focal point for Vienna's orthodox community. Heinrich and Karoline together with the twins Wilma and Gina were just around the corner at Lilienbrunngasse, 9 and Max was nearby. Each of these apartments would have been crammed full, Lower East Side fashion, with multiple families; orthodox Jews abiding by the demanding intricacies of the rules of kashrut mixing with those for whom these strictures meant little; the elderly and sick alongside the newly married; wailing children and those who drifted in and out for a few nights only before moving on. Some of these houses had well over a hundred people recorded as living there, albeit in multiple apartments. Rumour and news travelled fast in these streets, and this, too, played its part in what followed.

The entire family as well as most of those who arrived with them would have been beholden to charitable organisations to get by. I remember a conversation many years ago with my grandmother, who told me of her own sense of shame at having to go to soup kitchens to eat and seeing ladies queuing up in true Viennese style in their finest furs. It is estimated that in Vienna 40,000 each day depended on these soup kitchens.[3]

These streets today retain nothing of their former hustle and bustle. Accommodation is largely found in apartments built towards the end of the nineteenth or beginning of the last century. Many of the buildings have an entrance courtyard and a janitor. The older apartment blocks have handsome wrought-iron balconies on the upper floors. There are still a few orthodox Jews walking around, some wearing frock coats and wide-brimmed fur hats. There are even a few small informal prayer rooms or synagogues in operation, which have been rebuilt or re-formed in recent years. Missing, however, is any sense of a thriving or functioning Jewish quarter. A statue of Admiral Tegetthoff rises high above the Prater Gardens in the 2nd District. That rarest of breeds, a naval hero of a landlocked country, Tegetthoff has a telescope at his eye and casts his gaze into the middle distance. In the 1930s, a popular Viennese anti-Semitic jibe was that he was looking in vain to find anyone who was not a Jew. Today, the Admiral need not have such concerns.

It is painful to describe the Vienna that awaited the family on its arrival. Fear and loathing were everywhere. Personal physical danger was the day-to-day reality and had to be managed in whatever way possible just to get food on the table. It clearly would have been safer to stay indoors out of harm's way, but the overwhelming priority was to get out in the streets, obtain something for the family to eat – and plan an escape. This was undoubtedly hazardous. Long queues formed outside embassies or consulates, full of desperate people being beaten by sticks as they waited to see if they could advance their hoped-for exit.

The Nazi takeover of Vienna following the Anschluss in March unleashed an orgy of populist violence as well as the swift implementation of the racist legislation that had been in place in Germany since the implementation of the Nuremburg Laws of 1935. In most accounts of this era there is a laser focus on the events surrounding *Kristallnacht*. In reality, Vienna had already gorged itself on hatred and violence several months earlier. These were the days of Vienna's Spring Pogrom. It has never really been labelled as such. Pogroms in the popular imagination belonged in Russia or the far reaches of the Hapsburg Empire, not to the city of Mozart, Strauss and Mahler. But Vienna's particular version involved a fetishistic display of cruelty and brutality. What took place could almost be described as a festival of anti-Semitism of a type not seen in Vienna for hundreds of years, if ever. The main actors in this violence were as much ordinary Viennese and the local police as Nazi officers and Nazi paramilitary groups. All restraint on human behaviour appeared to have been abandoned. What had started in Karl Lueger's Vienna about thirty years before with offensive, dehumanising words and images, had mutated into deadly physical blows.

One story records that various Rabbis were rounded up by the mob and forced to clean the lavatories of the oldest synagogue in the centre of Vienna with their phylacteries.[4] Others had to clean the police headquarters' latrines using brushes soaked with acid solution that cut into their bare hands whilst a cheering crowd looked on calling out, 'Work for the Jews at last. We thank our Führer for finding them work.' The Chief Rabbi of Vienna, Dr Taglicht, was seen in the streets on his hands and knees scrubbing the pavements. He had a sign around his neck declaring 'I am a Jew.' Communal leaders begged the Chief Rabbi to allow others to take his place but he demurred, saying he wanted to perform this small act of cleaning up the mess of the world.

The extent to which the Viennese were willing participants in these events could not have been predicted. This even included a number of the former socialist Schtuzbunders who were now seen marching on the streets in Nazi uniform. Hitler arrived in Vienna on 14 March 1938 and established himself at the Imperial Hotel. There were many hundreds outside, several rows deep, screaming his name. Only a few hours after his arrival, the Archbishop of Vienna Cardinal Innitzer emerged from a large black limousine outside the hotel and as he entered gave the Nazi salute to the loud cheers of the crowd. This was quite a turn for the Cardinal who previously, as Rector of the University of Vienna, had closed the University for a whole year following violent anti-Semitic attacks. The tram which trundled around the Ringstrasse now sported a catchy advertising banner in support of Hitler's unification plebiscite saying, 'All of Austria on 10 April of course is saying Yes.'

Gedye, who had reported the frenzied demonstration accompanying the night of the Anschluss, was soon to be deported by the Nazis, but was able to file this account of the violence:

It is not so much the brutalities of the Austrian Nazis... it is the heartless, grinning soberly dressed crowds on the Graben and Karntnerstrasse, the Strube's Little Man class of Austrian, the fluffy Viennese blondes fighting one another to get closer in to the elevating spectacle of an ashen-faced Jewish surgeon on hands and knees before half a dozen young hooligans with swastika armlets and dog whips that sticks in my mind. His delicate fingers which must have made the swift and confident incisions that had saved the life of many Viennese, held a scrubbing brush. A storm trooper was pouring some acid solution over the brush and his fingers.

Another sluiced the pavement from a bucket, taking care to drench the surgeon's striped trousers as he did so. And the Viennese – not the uniformed Nazis or a raging mob, but the Viennese 'little man' and his wife – just grinned approval at the glorious fun.[5]

My father-in-law, Henry, was ten years old in April 1938. He lived with his mother in Hollandstrasse, a stone's throw from where my own family was living. It was a little apartment block in a smart street near to the Salztor Bridge, connecting the Jewish quarter with central Vienna. He told me of his terrifying daily run from the local school to his house, chased all the way by other kids wearing Nazi Youth uniforms or other such identifying paraphernalia. Despite the constant tormenting, school continued, although classes were now segregated with Jews not being allowed to study with Christian children. School served as an enforced period of daily truce during which acts of violence could not easily be perpetrated, but the final bell served as the notice of a resumption of hostility. Even reaching home did not guarantee safety. The janitor of Henry's building – whom he had known from childhood – was to be seen pointing out to the baying mob which flats were occupied by Jews. Not that this would ordinarily be necessary because Jewish families generally obliged by displaying a *mezuzah* on the door frame. According to a report in the *Jewish Chronicle*, one of the preferred methods of terror at this time was for gangs to force Jewish shop owners to open up their store in the small hours of the morning, then loot it and smash in the windows.[6] This epidemic of lawlessness and looting gave rise to sufficient cause for concern that on 6 May 1938, Gauleiter Buerckel, the Commissioner for Austria, issued a proclamation that Jewish shops would now be under the protection of a special detachment of the SS on patrol in Vienna. One can assume this would have been a cold comfort.

A seventeen-year-old boy called Harry Gruenberg was out on the streets of Vienna and found himself at the wrong time and place and witness to a shocking collapse of all decency. He saw an excited crowd gathered in a circle laughing, jeering and shouting. Curious to see what was happening, he approached. He saw in the centre of the circle an orthodox Jewish man on the pavement, being kicked to a pulp. The elderly man tried to get up and begged for help. A young blonde woman dressed in a blue suit moved into the centre of the circle as if to come to his aid. Instead, she stood over the man and urinated on his face to the applause and whistles of those gathered.[7]

Jewish shops were marked as such in capital letters in white paint so as to enable the Viennese to carry out their boycott. One young woman was seen being forced to kneel outside her shop with a sign around her neck reading, 'Please do not purchase from me. I am a Jewish sow.' In another nearby shop window, there could be seen a middle-aged lady forced to sit for five hours with a sign round her neck warning others, 'I am an Aryan, but a swine, I bought in this Jewish shop.'

Within days of the Anschluss, on 14 March nine Jewish judges were summarily dismissed from the higher courts. A few days later, Jewish lawyers were banned from appearing in criminal courts. Doctors, university professors and teachers fared no better. A high proportion of the Viennese Philharmonic were dismissed or had disappeared. Bruno Walter, the maestro conductor, had fled Berlin in 1933. In 1936 he had become the artistic director of the Vienna State Opera. By luck, March 1935 found him conducting abroad, having had time to conduct Mahler's Ninth Symphony one last time before he departed. Walter, however, was clearly a target for the Nazis. In his absence, they arrested his daughter as some kind of leverage, but after an international outcry she was released. Mahler would not be heard again in Vienna for another seven years.

Whilst violence and terror were the order of the day on the street, the operation against key political, business and communal figures was overseen by the Gestapo from its headquarters at the Metropole Hotel, just on the other side of the Danube Canal from the Jewish quarter. The Gestapo was heavily reliant upon the list of prominent names drawn up over the years by the Austrian Nazi Party.[8] Opposite the Metropole was the well-known café *Johann Strauss*, which had in better times been popular with a Jewish clientele. Ironically, after March 1938, it was one of the very few Viennese cafés not to forbid entry to Jews. Few, however, would have been foolish enough to sit there.

Political opponents, such as former Prime Minister Schuschnigg, were held at the Metropole for several months. Less fortunate were those socialist journalists and writers who had not fled Vienna after the events of 1934. Hans Pav was the former sports editor of the *Arbeiter Zeitung*. He was arrested and tortured by the Gestapo and eventually agreed to lead them to where Kathie Lechter, one of its political directors was hiding underground. She was then arrested and tortured. Attention quickly turned to the principal leaders of the Jewish community of Vienna. Dr Desider Freedman, a prominent Zionist, was the President of the Community and Robert Stricker, a lawyer and Zionist activist, was the Vice President and also in 1919 a Member of the Austrian Parliament for the Jewish National Party. Each was arrested, sent to Dachau and subsequently murdered. Louis de Rothschild, the head of the Rothschild family in Vienna, was taken to the Metropole from his Palais in Prinz Eugen Strasse and imprisoned in March 1938. He was released in May 1939 after the receipt of a ransom believed to be the largest ever paid (US$21,000,000). He was one of the relatively few prisoners to be freed from that building, reportedly after the personal intercession of the Duke of Windsor with Hitler himself.

Thousands of others were either murdered on site or sent to languish at Dachau concentration camp. The horrific conditions of Dachau were not a particularly closely guarded secret. Much was written in German and foreign newspapers or socialist journals in 1933-1938 about the conditions at Dachau, Buchenwald and other camps.[9] The Nazis were not nearly so bashful about this coverage as has been generally assumed to be the case. The assumption that practically all remained hidden until its discovery in the last days of the war in 1945 is simply not tenable.[10] Equally false is the notion that once a prisoner entered Dachau, he or she never returned. Many were imprisoned there and released when it suited those in command. A section of Dachau was reserved for 'twicers', people who had been re-arrested.

The threat of Dachau was publicly dangled in order to discourage all forms of political opposition and to encourage Jews to re-double their efforts to leave the Reich. One popular establishment in Vienna was even renamed Café Dachau.[11] German newspapers would report prominent people who had been sent to Dachau, no doubt in order to encourage others to offer no resistance. This was a time when the preferred Nazi policy was to solve the so-called Jewish question by rapid forced expulsion, and Adolf Eichmann would be the key architect of its implementation. *The Times* in London reported on 2 June 1938 that another special train had left Vienna the previous day for Dachau with about 700 passengers on board, mostly Jews. The same article recorded that in the prior two weeks alone about 4,000 Jews had been arrested for questioning.

The arrest of Jews in Vienna was not only an instrument of terror, it had a fiscal goal. As a result of a decree issued on 30 March 1938 by Seyss-Inquart, if a Jewish business owner had either fled or was in prison, then a manager could be appointed by the State to take care of their affairs. On 26 April 1938, a further decree was passed to make provision for the forced Aryanisation of Jewish enterprises. In another sadistic twist, as was reported once more in *The Times*, if a Jewish business was confiscated, the owner had to pay a levy equivalent to a ¼ of its value to obtain permission to leave the Reich. [12]

This fevered atmosphere of fear and hatred gave an opportunity to a thirty-three-year-old junior but ambitious officer who wanted to make a name for himself and get noticed by the Nazi hierarchy. He had taken note of the operation carried out by Portschy in the Burgenland, speed and terror being the chief ingredients ensuring success. Adolf Eichmann arrived in Vienna in August 1938 and established the Central Office for Jewish Emigration in the former Rothschild Palais. This clearly appealed to Eichmann's own sense of self. When seeking to terrify or impress no doubt terrified people summoned to his office, he would refer to himself as the Tsar of the Jews; and what better place to carry out his work than the home of the imprisoned head of the Rothschild family?[13] Those seeking to leave Vienna had to obtain an entry permit or visa from the place of destination as well as an exit permit from the Nazi authorities and this in turn meant running the gauntlet of Eichmann's Central Office for Jewish Emigration.

This was the daily reality that faced nearly two hundred thousand Jews in Vienna, my family included. They were not only seeking to obtain permission for themselves to go anywhere that would take them but also to obtain similar permits for their nearest and dearest. Their task was made a lot harder by the fact that from 24 May 1938, the Jews' Austrian citizenship was revoked and few, if any, countries allowed them to enter. On 1 April 1938, Goering and Goebbels spoke at a rally at the Nordwest Bahnhoff in the middle of the Jewish Quarter to start the campaign for the plebiscite on 10 April. To great cheers, it was announced that within four years all Jews would either have left or been eliminated from Vienna and that it would once more be a German city. The location for the rally was of course deliberately chosen. Jews stayed in their homes and turned off their lights in protest. At the site of another light being turned off chants of '*Jude*' rose in the crowd. It was clear to all Jews that they had to leave. Where to and how?

Each day a new rumour would do the rounds – of the possibility of emigration to some or other corner of the globe, whether it be Brazil, Argentina, Cuba or the Dominican Republic. More often than not, these stories were unfounded, but each had to be explored even though it involved personal danger queuing up outside embassies and hours of waiting.

Max was a committed Zionist, and he was holding out to get to Palestine. Max's journey into the Zionist movement was a fairly well-trodden path amongst Austria's Jewish community. After leaving the local *Gymnasium*, in 1930 he went to the famous yeshiva in Pressburg to study for a little over two years. He did not particularly enjoy it and told his father so, in what must have been a difficult conversation. Heinrich suggested that Max instead go to work as an apprentice in the textile business in Mattersdorf, about forty kilometres from Lackenbach, and so enhance his skills in a useful trade. Max did, and soon also became heavily involved in the local Zionist youth movement in Mattersdorf. It is perhaps little surprise that the most popular Zionist youth organisation was *Betar,* which in Austria had a particular leaning towards organised military-style discipline, weekend camps, marching and drills of a very similar kind that had been otherwise seen in the Schutzbund. In the early 1930s, Dollfuss the Chancellor of Austria, resplendent in his military uniform and feathered hat that added several inches to his height of four foot eleven, could be seen at a passing out parade for the latest volunteers.

The founder, leader and prime influence of *Betar* was Vladimir Jabotinsky, the firebrand Revisionist Zionist who had publicly set himself up as a rival to the mainstream leaders of the Jewish Agency and specifically to Chaim Weizmann and Ben Gurion. Jabotinsky was, to say the very least, a divisive figure. The clash was in part one of egos but there were also fundamental political differences, too. Ben Gurion was tied to the labour movement and saw Zionism primarily as an expression of agrarian socialism combined with Jewish nationalism. He advocated territorial compromise with the Palestinian Arabs, so that each side would have its own state. Jabotinsky did not share these views and made his opposition plain, splitting the Zionist movement into two when such division was rightly seen as extremely damaging. Likewise, he did not agree with Ben Gurion as to how a Jewish State would be established. Jabotinsky was unabashed in stating the view that, if necessary, a Jewish state would have to be established by force. Ben Gurion gradually came a lot closer to these views. Nevertheless, he would never agree with the methods deployed by those like Menachem Begin, Jabotinsky's political successor, founder of the Likud party, future prime minister of Israel and a commander in the *Irgun Zvai Leumi* (abbreviated as an acronym in Hebrew to *Etzl*) or worse still, those in the Stern Gang who openly advocated terror. Jabotinsky died in the United States in 1940 long before the creation of Israel in 1948. The grudge between these two factions continued even after Jabotinsky's death, as Ben Gurion held out for nearly twenty-five years before agreeing to having his body taken for state burial in Israel at Mount Herzl. His fierce resistance to the cult of Jabotinsky was perhaps best summed up in his tart response to those seeking the dead man's repatriation: 'The land of Israel needs living Jews not dead bones.' Indeed much of the bitterness between voices on the opposite ends of the centre and left and on the right in Israeli politics today can be traced back to this feud.

Max's first plan was quite simple. He obtained work as a volunteer in the Jewish Agency for Palestine in Vienna to help indigent Jews leave Vienna. The Jewish Agency was the organisation that, albeit under the strict control of the British Mandatory Authority in Palestine, issued immigration visas for those seeking to start a new life in Palestine.

On the face of it, Max's long-standing connection with *Betar*, the Zionist youth organisation structure, held him in good stead for this work. He also spoke German, Hungarian and passable Hebrew and presumably appeared to be a good candidate for working at the Jewish Agency, particularly if it did not cost them anything in wages. It seems that at least as far as Max understood the position, things were going to plan. On Max's *Israelitische Kultusgemeinde* emigration questionnaire form, he recorded that he wanted to go to Palestine and that he had already submitted a visa application to the Jewish Agency. Through his work, Max had also befriended an official working at the Passport Section of the British Consulate in Vienna who was prepared to support his application for a permit and vouched, falsely no doubt, that Max was going to undertake secretarial work for the British Government in Palestine.

The relationship between those working at the British Consulate and Whitehall was complicated; likewise, the relationship between the British Consulate and the Reich. After the Anschluss, the British Viennese Legation was closed, leaving a Consulate General with a manifestly inadequate number of personnel for the present crisis. This was headed up by Donald St Clair Gainer who had recently been transferred from Munich. In correspondence with Whitehall, Gainer tried to give some indication of the pressures that his staff were working under and recognized that complaints from London that his staff were not rigidly following protocol and procedures had some real foundation. Gainer accepted that all his staff had 'some pet Jew' they tried to help, one way or other.[14] There is a small clue from the news reports of the time as to who it was that might have been helping Max at the Consulate. On 18 August 1938 it was reported in the German newspapers that Captain T. J. Kendrick, a Passport Control Officer at the British Consulate, had been arrested by the Gestapo and taken to the Metropole Hotel for questioning over irregularities in the issuance of visas and permits. On 21 August 1938 he was released and expelled from the Reich.[15] He was lucky to have escaped with his life.

What Max could not have realized at the time was that his application to the Jewish Agency for a permit to go Palestine was basically doomed to failure from the outset. There were two reasons for this. The first being the general antipathy between those working for the World Zionist Organisation and the Jewish Agency supporters of Chaim Weizmann and David Ben Gurion on the one hand and the Revisionist Zionists supporters of Jabotinsky on the other hand. This would have included of course people like Max who were signed up members of *Betar*, the youth organisation of the Revisionist Zionist movement. With so few permits available for distribution, very few, if any, Jabotinsky supporters were lucky enough to receive one. They were in essence reserved for supporters of Ben Gurion's political party, the *Histadrut*. The second reason was the ever-tighter controls imposed through numerous shifts and changes to British policy in Palestine. I have searched in vain the Central Zionist Archives in Israel for the details of what happened to Max's application to the Jewish Agency. What is clear, though, is that no permission was given to Max to enter Palestine from Austria and no doubt Max soon came to understand that he would not after all be receiving any such permit.

12

Shuttered Gates

As Max assessed his position, the picture facing the Jews of Europe under Nazi rule remained bleak and the options slim to non-existent. The political crisis was accompanied by a hardening of the international – and critically the British – attitude towards refugees.

To its great credit, British immigration policy following Hitler's accession to power in Germany had for some years been just about the most generous in all of Europe. Since 1933, Britain had been instrumental in providing asylum to many tens of thousands of German refugees, principally Jews, fleeing Hitler's persecution. In response to Hitler's ascent to power in January 1933, Britain announced modified immigration procedures into Palestine specifically designed to facilitate persons fleeing Germany. In particular, this was directed towards either manual labourers or those arriving with a specifed amount of capital.[1] Between 1933 and 1936, it is estimated that over 32,000 German Jews emigrated to Palestine. [2] In a memorandum written in 1935, an official in the Foreign Office described the policies adopted in Palestine as 'our contribution to the refugee problem'.[3] In addition, British policy was liberal in its attitude to admission of German Jews onto its own shores. A further 10,000 refugees from Nazi persecution were given shelter in Britain itself in the period from 1933 to 1937. It needs to be stressed that this was at a time of widespread unemployment and so it would have been easier in some ways for the politicians to turn their backs on those in desperate need of help.

However, in March 1938, following the Anschluss, a major shift of policy took place and the doors were systematically shut to the Jews of Germany and Austria. Lord Beaverbrook's *Daily Express* rhetorically inquired of the nation in March 1938 where people stood with its editorial strap line of 'Shall All Come In?' The newspaper noted the sad stories emerging from Vienna but questioned, 'Where will it end?'[4] Lord Beaverbook did not have to wait long for an answer.

From 2 May 1938, a new restriction was imposed: Austrians could no longer arrive in the country without a valid visa; from 21 May 1938, the same applied to those arriving from Germany. The response to the Anschluss had been debated in Parliament and likewise discussed in Cabinet.[5] On 16 March 1938, the Home Secretary Sir Samuel Hoare advised Cabinet that in the wake of the Anschluss a new wave of Jewish refugees could be expected in Britain. Whilst some sympathy was expressed in Parliament and in Cabinet for the plight of the Austrian Jews the feeling was that immigration had to be tightly controlled to avoid the creation of a 'Jewish problem' through a rise in anti-Semitism in Britain.

After the Cabinet discussion, this dual task was taken forward by the Home Secretary, in consultation with Jewish communal leaders. On 1 April 1938 Sir Samuel gave advance notice of his intention to adopt new rules requiring refugees to hold a valid visa before arrival at a British port. The argument was advanced that it was necessary to discriminate very carefully as to the sort of refugee to be admitted in the country in order to avoid a flood of the 'wrong type' which would itself 'give rise to a serious danger of anti-Semitic feeling being aroused in this country'.[6] Profoundly sad as it is to note, the leaders of the Jewish community consulted by the Home Secretary are recorded in the notes of a critical meeting as having endorsed this approach, at least in part. Notably amongst those echoing these sentiments was none other than Otto Schiff, himself a German refugee from Frankfurt who had founded the Jewish Refugee Committee in 1933 and who observed to the Home Secretary that the imposition of a visa

> ...was especially necessary in the case of the Austrians who were largely of the shopkeeper and small trader class and would therefore prove much more difficult to emigrate than the average German who had come to the United Kingdom.[7]

Otto Schiff might have had my own grandparents in mind. In any event, the Home Secretary did not accede to the argument to make this nice distinction between Jews coming from Austria and not Germany and in due course imposed a universal visa requirement covering the whole Reich. Maybe he had in mind Otto Schiff's hypocritical warning that 'It was very difficult to get rid of a refugee once he had spent a few months in the country.'[8]

Britain was not alone in wrestling with the problems raised by the growing refugee crisis. In late March 1938, President Roosevelt of the United States invited representatives of governments around the world to a special international conference which aimed to establish a committee facilitating the emigration of refugees from Austria and Germany. This was the Evian Conference of 6-15 July 1938. There was already a significant measure of support expressed in the mainstream press in both the United States and Britain, calling for action to assist the Jews in their plight. It was argued that something had to be done to address the admission of Jews into Palestine.

Hitler himself, clearly with a large measure of calculated mischief, welcomed the Evian Conference when it was announced, no doubt seeking to place other nations on the spot and sow discord:

I can only hope and expect that the rest of the world, which displays such deep sympathy towards these criminals will show enough generosity and translate its sympathy into real aid. We on our part are willing to leave all these criminals in the hands of these countries; as far as I am concerned even on luxury ships.[9]

Whilst the invitation expressed the hope that governments could work together with private organisations to address the emergency, critically it also stressed that 'no country would be expected or asked to receive a greater number of immigrants than permitted by existing legislation.' The terms of the invitation itself appeared to have predicated the outcome.

Delegates from over thirty countries attended the conference held at the Royal Hotel overlooking Lake Geneva. The nations responsible in the main for the oppression of the Jews and the crisis itself (notably Germany and Poland) were not invited but stood on the sidelines, some attending with observer status.[10] Russia was invited but declined to attend. The national delegates sat at a large horseshoe-shaped conference table covered with green baize and behind each representative sat two rows of advisors. In the manner of a secret auction, delegates were asked during the course of the conference, initially in confidence, to submit the numbers of refugees that their country would accept.

To encourage this effort, those in the room heard from numerous aid organisations and representatives of the Jewish communities of Vienna and Berlin. The contrast between the surroundings of this luxurious lakeside hotel with its palatial gardens reached by its own private funicular railway and the devastated lives under discussion must, presumably, have made at least some feel uncomfortable. No one hearing the first-hand accounts from Austria could have been under any illusion about the dire position faced. The delegates were told of four hundred Austrians summarily expelled from the Burgenland who were then marooned on a barge on the Danube, within sight of three frontiers but unwelcome at all of them; unable either to go back to where they had come from or to proceed to safety in a new land. The *New York Times* reported that these were 'people without a country, human flotsam adrift on an international stream, they symbolize with dramatic literalness the urgency of the present refugee problem.'[11]

One of the delegates representing the Jews of Vienna was Berthold Storfer. His presence at Evian might have been thought to be something of a curiosity. He was not a politician and did not at this time hold any official communal position. He was instead a fixer and to boot was not Jewish. Although born to Jewish parents, he was baptised as a Christian, a move that he considered would open the way for him into the wider business world. A wealthy businessman in his mid-fifties, he had been decorated in the First World War for his services in logistics and supplies to help the Hapsburg army on the Romanian-Russian front. After the war, he established himself as a banker in Budapest and came to serve as financial adviser to the governments of both Austria and Czechoslovakia. These were of course landlocked countries and his extensive connections in maritime transport served him well.

It was therefore logical in the early days for the Jewish community to turn to Storfer to find ships to enable serious numbers to leave Vienna.[12] He came to the notice of Eichmann himself, who increasingly over the next years leant on Storfer to make the arrangements which would enable Eichmann to achieve his policy of ridding Vienna of all its Jews. Storfer in turn worked more and more closely with Eichmann's office and eventually the great part of all transportation one way or another came to pass through him.[13] This has led to vigorous debate as to whether he should be seen as a rescuer of thousands of lives or a quisling collaborator. It is next to impossible to address this in a rational manner divorced from the extreme context of the time, but history appears to have been too unkind.[14] Eichmann's Office controlled all emigration from Austria and practically anyone who escaped did so only with its permission. What Storfer did was to work directly with Eichmann, but the evidence appears to show he did so to save lives, and without caring if anyone had the right papers or not.

At Evian, Storfer's role was a little different. He emphasised that if an agreement was reached as to which countries were willing to admit the refugees, there would be no difficulty in organising the necessary transportation. To the consternation of those present, Storfer read out a demand that he had been given by Eichmann that a minimum of 40,000 Jews must leave Austria before the autumn.[15] It was hoped this would focus everyone's mind, but instead it had the exact opposite effect and made some delegates feel distinctly uncomfortable that they were being asked to yield to Nazi blackmail. In the meantime, back in Vienna, the Jewish community observed a fast day on 9 July 1938 praying for the success of the mission at Evian.[16]

There were probably only three countries that could effect material change at this time: Britain, France and the United States. As regards the United States, its policy was to preserve its existing fixed quota system. The United States stood by the merger of the previously separate quotas for German and Austrian refugees but otherwise made no headline announcements. The British delegation noted the desired objectives of the Conference but stated that its work could not either replace or interfere with the work of individual countries or that of the League of Nations High Commission for Refugees. Britain also made it clear that the solution to the problem could not lie in Palestine and that whilst some inquiry had been made of East Africa as a possible destination, this, too, could not provide meaningful asylum. This was all highly unsatisfactory.[17] The whole point of the conference was to find consensus for urgent solutions and not to list barriers. More shocking was that the British Ambassador to Germany, Sir Nevile Henderson, met with Ribbentrop in Berlin at the commencement of the conference and before the delegates had even spoken, he indicated that 'no country was prepared to receive the emigrating German Jews.' [18] Ribbentrop and no doubt Hitler took careful note.

After the key speeches had been given, the Conference heard from each of the remaining country delegates. One after the other stood up and took the cue from the leading nations. Peru said that the United States had set a wise and cautious example. Australia's representative stated that they did not have any homegrown racial problems and had no intention of importing one. Brazil only wanted baptized Christians. On it went. The final tally was almost uniformly depressing and negative. One exception was Mexico, which under the Socialist President Cardenas had been the only country at the League of Nations to lodge a formal protest against the Anschluss. Mexico indicated that it would be open to establishing a Jewish settlement of 1500 families in Tabasco. Nevertheless, back home, there was such a strong adverse reaction that this plan was in due course abandoned. A short while after the conference, the Dominican Republic announced that it was willing to accept up to 100,000 Jewish refugees, most of them settling in agricultural communities such as Sosua. This remarkable and extraordinary act stood out against the overall rejection by one country after another of making any direct and immediate change to its policy. The only material positive statements were made by those attending from the Caribbean or Central and South American states.

Various pleas were advanced including that of allowing an immediately increased immigration of refugees into Palestine and exploring the possibility of identifying an uninhabited area under present colonial administration which could also be used for admittance and settlement of refugees. The notion of emigration from Germany to Palestine was also picked up by Alfred Rosenberg of the *Volkischer Beobachter*, one of the principal mouthpieces of the Nazi propaganda machine. Rosenberg made it clear that any such idea should be opposed, as Jewish emigration to Palestine would lead to riots there. It seems that at this stage the Nazi policy had been in alignment with the position of the Palestinian Arabs' nationalist demands and in opposition to the Zionists.

As if to reinforce the sensitivity of these discussions, the build-up to and duration of the Evian Conference saw a significant escalation of violence in Palestine, with dozens of Arabs and Jews killed in attack and reprisal in Tel Aviv and Haifa.[19] On 12 July 1938 it was reported that the Committee for the Defence of Palestine had sent a telegram to Evian from Damascus pleading that the doors of Palestine remain firmly shut to Jewish refugees. On 15 July 1938, the Evian Conference adjourned without any plan in place except to hold a meeting of the Intergovernmental Committee for Refugees in London in August 1938. Considering what was at stake, and the urgency of the situation, this amounted to setting the bar at a very low level. Storfer returned to Vienna without having achieved what he had set out to do.

At some time in August 1938 a new rumour began to circulate, that a Viennese lawyer by the name of Willy Perl was calling for members of *Betar* to come forward to go to Palestine on a transport he was organising over land and sea, and that the operation would not be for the faint-hearted. Max immediately volunteered. Willy Perl was himself a staunch supporter of Jabotinsky and was organising an illegal transport operation to bring Zionist youth volunteers to Palestine even if it meant breaking through the British naval patrol of the coastline there. Willy Perl's archives are also held in the archives of the Holocaust Museum in Washington. The story told in these papers is an unlikely one and it is to him that Max owed his life. One of the first that Willy Perl would turn to for help in chartering a vessel to take this group to Palestine was Berthold Storfer.

13

Af Al Pi

On a warm evening in mid-August 1938, an excited crowd gathered outside Vienna's impressive colonnaded main train station, the Sudbahnfhoff, in the southeast of the city. Most of them in their late teens or early twenties, they formed a tightknit group dressed in a scout-like uniform of shorts, dark grey shirts and cravat. In all, there were more than eight hundred young Jews that evening preparing to leave Nazi Europe, on their way to Palestine to fulfill their dream of starting a new life.

For many, this would have been the first time they had been separated from their family. Under clear advance instruction, each was told to bring three weeks' provisions but was restricted to what could be carried on their back. No suitcase or other luggage was allowed. As a result, those standing outside the station could be seen chatting animatedly, weighed down by over-stuffed rucksacks, no doubt in part filled with the product of their mothers' cooking. Standing amongst them was Max.

Each person had also been given a blue cotton square with a yellow border to sew onto his or her uniform. The badge depicted a proud standing lion framed by the Star of David, the script at the bottom limited to just three words written in Hebrew: '*Af Al Pi*.' The words broadly translate as 'In spite of everything' and were taken from one of the slogans of Jabotinsky's New Zionist Organisation, calling for mass migration to Palestine in spite of all the difficulty.[1] '*Af Al Pi*' was the rallying call of those engaged in helping Jews get to Palestine even if this had to be in breach of quotas and limits imposed by the British.

Once the whole group had arrived, they filed through the vast marbled halls of the station concourse and onto an awaiting train for Fiume on the Italian coast, all in plain view of the German soldiers patrolling the station. Nobody stopped them. They were waved through and escorted onto the platform.

This was the first large-scale undertaking organised by Willy Perl. Ever confident of his own success, he was not there in person that evening to supervise the proceedings, but was instead in London, already planning the next voyage. Willy Perl practised as a lawyer on the fashionable Stubenring in the centre of Vienna. He was also the leader in Vienna of the New Revisionist Organisation's youth group *Betar*. Little is known of Perl's skills as a lawyer, but he does appear to have had certain qualities in super abundance – a scant regard for rules, a large dose of bare-faced cheek and an instinct for survival against the odds. Loosely translated back into Yiddish, this might be encompassed by the word *chutzpah*.

The story of this particular odyssey began very shortly after the Anschluss and the arrival of the Nazis on the streets of Vienna. On 16 March 1938, Adolf Eichmann arrived in Vienna and established a special *SonderKommando* unit in Department II/112 of the *Sicherheitsdients*, the Nazi intelligence service known as the SD run by Heinrich Himmler. The SD formed one of the key branches of the Reich Security Main Office, (the RSHA) which employed Eichmann. Amongst his first tasks was to gather the intelligence necessary to enforce the departure of Vienna's two hundred thousand Jews. His unit was provided with lists of Jews to be arrested and interrogated, assisted by the full resources of the Gestapo, the Nazi Secret Police.[2] Unsurprisingly, this included the entire Jewish communal leadership in the offices of the *Israelitische Kultusgemeinde*. He acted swiftly and with a cold ruthlessness that became his trademark throughout the Holocaust. Eichmann not only arrested the communal leaders but also took with him the organisation's files for analysis to pave the way for further arrests.

In May 1938, Perl received a demand that he attend a meeting with Eichmann at the dreaded Metropole Hotel, Gestapo Headquarters. Few summoned to the Metropole left unscathed; many never left at all. He was summoned together with several of the senior leaders of the Jewish community in Vienna. Perl guessed that the reason for his summons was his involvement in establishing a Jewish boycott of

German goods prior to the Anschluss. In fact, Eichmann was in the main looking for information about others who had to date eluded the Gestapo.

Eichmann took Perl into a room, alone. He held his gun to Perl's stomach and started counting to five. He said he would give Perl a second navel unless he gave up the whereabouts of two specific people he was looking for. Those Eichmann had named had indeed been instrumental in the boycott, but fortunately each had to Perl's knowledge already managed to escape the country and so Perl was able to truthfully say that they were no longer in Vienna and he did not know where they were. Eichmann told Perl that they would continue the interrogation after they had searched the offices of the New Zionist Organisation on the Biberstrasse, near the Stadtpark in Vienna. Perl was escorted there in an armoured car under guard. He was now clearly in desperate trouble. When they reached the offices, he was marched up the narrow staircase and saw Tury Deutsch, the secretary of their organisation. Perl thought the game was up, as the Gestapo would no doubt find a whole pile of records linking them with the boycott. Not for the first (or last) time, Perl got lucky. As soon as Tury Deutsch discovered that Perl had been summoned to Eichmann at the Metropole, he realised that he would not have enough time to dispose of or burn the most incriminating papers before the Gestapo came to Biberstrasse. Instead, he had the idea of placing them all openly in voluminous piles of dull unfiled material on the floor beside his desk. Remarkably, this trick of hiding in plain sight worked. As Perl looked on, the Gestapo systematically removed the irrelevant administrative contents of the filing cabinets but failed to examine what lay before their eyes.[3]

Perl was nothing if not a chancer. His next gambit was to tell Eichmann that the Gestapo needed him alive and not dead because he himself was heavily engaged in an elaborate operation to help Jews leave Vienna. In saying this, Perl was of course greatly exaggerating the stage his little group were at and their capacity to put anything in place, but he calculated that anything that might achieve this end would be of interest to the Nazis. Eichmann gave Perl one day to put forward his proposal. Perl typed up a very formal looking Memorandum in triplicate which is held today in Washington and presented it to Eichmann with a flourish. The Memorandum was an overly ambitious and impractical plan, involving the charter of a series of ships to bring nearly a thousand Jews a week out of Vienna to Palestine. Eichmann's reaction to this was completely dismissive. He told Perl that; 'These transports are out of the question. We don't need a centre for criminals in Palestine. The Jews will be atomized.'[4]

Perl, however, was not to be discouraged and next took his plan to a wholly improbable level of bluff. He told Eichmann that he had already had promising discussions with senior officials in Berlin and that they would be displeased if Eichmann did anything to interfere with or impede these transports. Eichmann was ever keen to advance his career. It seemed he did not want to incur the wrath of those in Berlin he was trying to impress, and so once more he allowed Perl a short period of time to deliver. Perl and his inseparable comrade Moshe Gallili planned the next steps. Perl and Gallili had been working together on and off since 1936 without proper back-up on small-scale transports from Europe to Palestine. Their first venture involved just sixteen young men leaving Vienna by train in 1937 for Athens. From there a fishing boat took them to the shores off Palestine. At this point, Gallili waded onto the beach and ran from house to house knocking on strangers' doors whispering that they had just escaped Nazi Germany and seeking shelter. This was all pretty ramshackle Boy's Own stuff and could not have prepared Perl or indeed Gallili for what they now attempted to pull off.

The two of them set off to Berlin to try to persuade the Ministry of Finance of their plans to organise mass transports for Jews to leave Austria. Central to the plan was to obtain permission to change Reichmarks into foreign currency to pay for the ship charters required for these transports. They did not present this exclusively as a plan to send Jews to Palestine but rather as being consistent with Nazi policy of forced emigration. They explained that to the extent that Jews went to Palestine, this could not be objected to by the Germans as it would only serve to embarrass the British, who were opposed to such immigration. Remarkably enough, after a series of meetings they received the agreement they needed. In order to achieve this, they obviously suppressed what had passed between Perl and Eichmann and they also used forged correspondence with Greek shipowners as supposed proof of their advanced preparation. This was gambling with high stakes. Triumphant, they returned from Berlin to Vienna and presented the Ministry of Finance's consent to Eichmann, who then agreed to allow Perl a chance to deliver on his plan.[5]

From this speculative and implausible game of bluff, exaggeration and falsehood, Perl not only managed to secure his own release from the Gestapo but also permission to exchange foreign currency to secure ships to take Jews out of Vienna to Palestine. Nevertheless, Perl had little doubt of two things, that if he was not in fact able to successfully secure such shipments, his fate in Dachau was assured and that he had next to no time to deliver on what he had promised.

There was only one aspect of his plan that Perl felt he could deliver without difficulty; namely, thousands of people seeking the chance to leave Austria for Palestine. The logical place to start was of course the youth volunteers and community leaders in the *Betar* movement. The call went out, and Max – alongside hundreds active in the movement – answered it. They first gathered for a weekend camp to receive instruction for the voyage and then they made their last-minute preparations and farewells.

Max and the rest of the *Betarim* assembled late at night for the start of their journey. The train took the group to the border of Austria and present-day Slovenia at Arnoldstein. There it stopped and everyone waited. Nazi soldiers ensured everyone stayed aboard, despite the suffocating heat and lack of any proper water or sanitation. Max and his companions were told that the reason they had been kept at the border was because the British Government had persuaded the Yugoslav Government not to allow the train to cross. They had not been told the truth.

A fraud had been perpetrated on Perl's amateur group. They had chartered a ship, SS *Socrates*, to take the whole group from Fiume to the shores of Palestine and had made a down payment of US$10,000 to secure the vessel. They had made careful inspection of what were thought to be ship's plans to ensure that it could indeed safely carry over a thousand people from Fiume to Palestine. They had been scammed by unscrupulous businessmen and had paid the money over to people who had no ownership interest whatever in the SS *Socrates*. No ship was on its way to Fiume to collect these hapless refugees. This was a complete disaster for Perl and all those, including Max, patiently waiting under guard on the sealed train.

Perl, in London when the train was caught at the border, was then told of the crisis. On Jabotinsky's direct orders, he flew to Italy and then travelled to Arnoldstein to try to resolve the situation.[6] The organisers of this group can be seen in photographs sitting around a table in Arnoldstein at a nearby café. Given the circumstances, they all look tolerably relaxed, but no one could doubt that unless Perl came up with some instant solution this unforeseen setback could cost hundreds of lives. Each day Eichmann telephoned Perl and screamed down the phone, threatening to come down to Arnoldstein and take charge himself. Without a ship in place, he threatened to order the train to be sent directly back to Dachau. Perl's group had to find a solution quickly.

After the train had been kept waiting at the border for about a week, Perl reached out to Berthold Storfer. Reading between the lines, Storfer presumably saw this as an opportunity to exercise greater control and obtain more influence over the entire operation. Storfer himself had contacts with various willing Greek shipowners and he managed to make contact with a Mr Davaris who was amenable to considering this charter and its very particular cargo. Davaris arranged for another ship to be dispatched for Fiume, and – even more remarkably – agreed that the US$10,000 already given to the fraudsters would be accepted as the down payment for the new charter, and that Davaris himself would recover the money from people whom he described as unworthy smalltime crooks. On this basis, Perl could breathe again. He told Eichmann that a ship, the SS *Draga*, had been found and was making its way directly to Fiume. The vessel arrived two weeks later and took on board the group of two hundred and eighty Poles who had been patiently waiting in hiding in Fiume.

But the SS *Draga* came too late for Max. One day before its arrival, Eichmann simply lost all patience. Perl managed to persuade Eichmann not to send the train straight to Dachau by invoking the biblical story of Masada and the threat of some last desperate stand at the border. It is not clear why or how this affected Eichmann, but in the end what happened was that after a three-week wait at the border, Max and the rest of his group were turned round and dispatched by train back to Vienna.

Max returned home to Vienna towards the end of September, when everyone thought he had at last escaped. This journey must have cost the family precious sums they could ill afford to part with and inevitably everyone must have vested their own fragile hopes in Max's successful escape. No doubt there was a fair bit of shame too. One of Max's fellow companions, Berta Seigel, recorded the scene of her return to Vienna:

The worst thing was to go up that staircase to face my mother again who (in her mind) had already seen me in Israel. As it was

6am when I knocked on the door, my family thought it was the Gestapo. They would have preferred to have been fetched from home themselves to seeing me return. My mother started crying and could not stop for a long time. She said that she at least thought I had been saved and now she understood that this, the only way, did not work either.[7]

The SS *Draga*, however, *did* make it to Palestine. It was not carrying the thousand or so that Perl had planned but only 281 passengers.[8] One person had managed to escape from Max's heavily guarded and locked train at Arnoldstein through a window. He got to Fiume and joined the waiting Poles. The journey was one of the first to deploy the technique of transferring those on board onto smaller vessels as the larger ship approached the twelve-mile coastal limit of British Mandate territorial waters. The Polish refugees were also amongst the first of the illegal immigrants to land on the beaches north of Tel Aviv, which had been scoped out by the Revisionists in Palestine. The captain of the landing craft signalled their arrival off the coast in Morse code to those waiting on the shore. The code used was the opening words of the anthem of the nascent Jewish state, *Hatikva* (the Hope).

Although the stated objective of the Arnoldstein transport had clearly failed, the sea voyage as ultimately carried out served as a test case for the techniques used in many subsequent operations. Perhaps given the earlier amateur operations described above, Perl and Gallili needed a semi-dry run. In any event, Perl was sufficiently emboldened to plan further transports and he promised Max and the other *Betarim* first berth on the next boat out. The SS *Draga* itself undertook more than one such clandestine voyage to Palestine and was even involved in the transport that ultimately took Max out of Austria.

In my last conversation with Max that late afternoon in the quiet of his old people's home, I remember a point when he, already tired of my questions, told me that I would find everything I needed in his papers. For a long time, I thought that he had been referring to his typed life story, a copy of which he had just given me and which did indeed mention this failed journey. But long after his death I found myself wondering whether I was mistaken in my interpretation of what Max had said. Eventually I read and then re-read the notes I had taken during our conversation and was struck by the fact he had seemed to imply that there was another, quite separate record that he was referring to. But where would he have left such a record? Somewhere he trusted, no doubt, perhaps with his only son Tsvi, who was living the dream working in alternative medicine in California or at a relevant archive or museum?

There was a distinct danger of my hunch becoming a time-consuming wild goose chase. When I got hold of Tsvi in Northern California, he had no knowledge of these supposed records. I then turned to exploring institutional sources. Israel has a museum for practically every subject and often more than one, with only a slender distinction between them. I had assumed at one stage that these were places of refuge for a rainy day but there are precious few of those in that part of the world. Any weekend when I had a few moments spare, I would ring up archivists in Israel and explain what I was looking for. First it was Yad Vashem, then the National Archives and after that the Museum of the Diaspora. Generally, I received a sympathetic audience, but on more than one occasion the voice at the other end of the phone would convey a bewildered sense that this might be an elaborate waste of everyone's time. Still, even when I was unsuccessful, more often than not I was put in touch with another and then another, and so the search continued.

Months seemed to pass and then I was told that any records connected with *Betar* might found in the Jabotinsky Institute in Tel Aviv and that I should speak to the archivist there, Amira Stern. I rang and told her I was calling about my uncle, Max Grunsfeld. She told me she would make some inquiries and ring me back. It was a Sunday morning, an ordinary working day in Israel. A short while later, my phone rang. Amira told me that the records I was looking for belonged to Mordechai Grunsfeld, Max's Hebrew name. She said that she had in her hand his diary and some other personal effects he had donated to the Museum, which she would be happy to show me when I was next over there. She was so matter of fact, but my heart had skipped a beat. I felt I could hear Max saying; 'I told you, and you simply did not listen. What took you so long to work it out?'

As soon as I could, I made a trip to Tel Aviv. I went to the Jabotinsky Institute situated on the somewhat run-down King George Street, which these days mainly offers passers-by endless variations of massage. On the second floor of a corner house can be found a deserted museum, where the silence is broken by the occasional visit from a bunch of bored looking army conscripts fixated with their mobiles. Amira came to greet me and showed me Max's *Af Al Pi* cotton square that he would have worn on his *Betar* uniform on that train. It was on display in the Museum amongst other photographs from that time. Amira then asked me to come with her to the archive room. Wearing cotton gloves, she took out a small fragile notebook with spidery handwriting in pencil on its front page. This was Max's diary from 1938, written in German in the faintest script. Turning each page, I thought it would disintegrate at my gentlest touch. Whatever doubts I had previously held about writing this story evaporated the moment I held this diary in my hand. I could not let go now.

PART THREE
ESCAPE

14

The Next Boat Out

Max did not have to wait long for Willy Perl to start organising the next boat out of Vienna. Perl was intent on keeping his promise to all those he had failed in the late summer of 1938. It must have been clear to Max that this remained his only realistic option of getting to Palestine, even though as far as the British were concerned it involved illegal entry. When Max returned from the border at Arnoldstein in September 1938, the last handful of legitimate visas were being issued by the British Consulate for entry into Palestine for that quota year. They were only available to teenagers. Once more, there was no joy for Max.

Nevertheless, on 28 October 1938 Max submitted a signed form to the Emigration Department of the *Israelitische Kultusgemeinde* recording that he was intending to emigrate to Palestine at the end of October 1938. Max also confirmed, falsely as it so happened, that he was in possession of all valid travel documents and visas. He confirmed that he was in possession of a valid passport issued in Mattersburg with an expiration date in June 1939.

Things then moved quickly. Max must have got word from Perl that they should be ready once more to leave in a matter of days. Two days later, on 30 October 1938, Max went back to the Emigration Department and signed a further document stating that he was travelling as a single passenger to Palestine. He is described as being 'from the earlier transport'. Presumably this would have made his position clear, without expressly saying in as many words, that he was one of those who had tried but failed to leave Vienna on the Arnoldstein transport, albeit without a valid entry visa to Palestine. Max had to pay 20 Reichsmark, said to be the required application fee. What was not recorded, however, was the true position as regards the details of Max's proposed transport. Officially, the *Israelitische Kultusgemeinde* was opposed to the illegal transports to Palestine organised by people like Willy Perl, as they had good reason to fear that the British would simply deduct these numbers from the established visa quota. But the processing of the application fee and the fact that the application form was countersigned by someone at the *Israelitische Kultusgemeinde*, would tend to indicate that at least on this occasion they turned a blind eye to those leaving in this manner.[1]

For Max to be in a position to leave Austria, however, first he had to obtain all the relevant permits and stamps from Eichmann's Central Office for Jewish Emigration. This required a visit to the Palais Rothschild at Prinz Eugen Strasse, 22, which Eichmann in August 1938 had requisitioned and looted of its art and silver.[2] At this point Eichmann's duties had moved away from intelligence work in the SD and instead was given executive responsibility. In his case this involved the enforced expulsion of Jews from Vienna. Eichmann had taken careful note of the possibilities opened up by having one coordinated office to process emigration applications. He used this to operate his particular form of psychological and physical control so as to ensure that before the last stamp was applied, the applicant was relieved of every last penny. The Central Office operated on the twin principles of fear and extortion.[3] Outside the Central Office the SS paraded up and down with whips and dogs. They frequently beat up those queuing up just for sadistic pleasure and to sow panic.

The methods of the Central Office were considered by Berlin to be an outstanding success. At a meeting on 12 November 1938 attended by Heydrich and Goering, it was noted that in the few short months in which the Central Office had operated, just shy of 50,000 Austrian Jews had been expelled from the country in contrast to 19,000 German Jews from the whole of Germany in the same period.[4] Heydrich was only able to marvel at this work and Goering noted that this would enable Vienna – 'one of the Jewish capitals so to speak' – to be dealt with by the end of the year. Eichmann's methodology was noted and rewarded. He was promoted and asked in March 1939 to go to Prague to oversee the same job there that he had performed in Vienna.

Max's journey from his accommodation in Leopoldstadt to the Central Office would have been filled with dread. He walked the three kilometres there in part to save money and in part to avoid any confrontation on the tram. He also made a detour around the Stadtpark and the Belvedere, the two main parks on the route as these were now forbidden to Jews. He would have walked past many of Vienna cafes that now carried signs that Jews were not welcome (*Juden unerwünscht*). I recall my father-in-law, Henry, telling me how shocked he was when he saw such a sign in his favourite café, at the Sacher Hotel, today a very pleasant destination for tourists seeking to sample their famous chocolate cake.

There can be little doubt that Eichmann derived particular pleasure from establishing himself in the Palais Rothschild, whilst the head of the Rothschild family languished in a cell at the Gestapo headquarters in the Metropole Hotel. None of this symbolism would have been lost on those in power and those oppressed.

The main offices were on the first floor. Those many hundreds each day entering the building to complete their applications for exit permits had to walk through the front hallway and then up a grand, red-carpeted staircase. Jews though were strictly forbidden to walk on the carpet. Instead, they had to tread carefully on the stone flooring at the edge of the tread, not holding the handrail either, as Jews were considered unclean. At the top of the stairs Max was ushered from one desk to another garnering the necessary permits and paying over what was required as he went.

Dr Franz Meyer, a prominent member of the Jewish community of Berlin, had been sent to visit Eichmann to see for himself the methods deployed and report back what people could soon expect in the capital city. In evidence at Eichmann's trial, he described the system as akin to an automated production line:[5]

> You put in at the one end a Jew who still has capital and has, let us say a factory or a shop or an account in the bank, and he still passes through the entire building from counter to counter, from office to office – he comes out the other end, he has no money, no rights, only a passport in which it is written: ' You must leave this country within two weeks; if you fail to do so, you will go to concentration camp.'

Max was himself 'processed' as described and then funnelled into a room on the left-hand side of staircase and there he stood in front of

Eichmann himself, seated at his desk in his black SS uniform. Eichmann would boast to Hagen in a letter, the same person with whom he had visited Palestine in 1937, that he should not worry because he kept

> ...these gentlemen here on the run, on this you can believe me... I have them completely in my hands, they dare not take a step without first consulting me. That is as it should be, because then much better control is possible.[6]

This was the final ordeal, the last station. Max had witnessed Eichmann's explicit threats to send those on the train at Arnoldstein straight to the camps and had every reason to tremble. Eichmann looked Max up and down asked him where he was emigrating to. Max answered to Palestine. Eichmann responded, 'I am pleased be to be getting rid of you, as the Jews have been stealing from the Reich for years and now at last you are able to steal from one another.' With this he applied the final stamp. Max, with every document in order, left the building. As he examined his exit visa, he understood perfectly well that he had just two weeks to leave the country or face Dachau.

Of course, Perl knew perfectly well that he was in a race against time to make the last arrangements for this replacement transport to Palestine, or everyone would face the consequences, including himself. He had an idea for a radical change of route and plan. Instead of a passage via the Italian port of Fiume, as he had attempted on the failed Arnoldstein transport, this time he would take the passengers on Danube steamboats downstream to a Romanian Black Sea port and then transfer to seagoing vessels for the voyage to Palestine. Perl's initial thinking was that since the Danube downstream of Vienna was an international waterway under the supervision and control of the European Commission of the Danube, the riverboats could not be intercepted in their voyage after they left Austria and that this would greatly simplify not only the successive border crossings but also the position as regards visas.[7]

The help of Dr Paul Diamant was enlisted to organise the Danube leg of the journey. The sea leg was to be organised by the Greek shipowners who had come to the rescue on the prior voyage from Fiume. In the meantime, Eichmann was breathing down their necks. Eichmann summoned Perl's team to his office and demanded to know when they would finally leave, indicating that he was losing patience and that they only had days to bring this to an end. Eichmann thundered that the Arnoldsteiners, the organisers and their families 'had for too long poisoned the good German air of the city'.[8]

The main difficulty encountered was that whilst passengers could apparently travel on the Danube through Czechoslovakia, Hungary and Yugoslavia without a valid end visa, such a document was definitely required for those intending to transit through Romania. It was at this time that the plan was hatched to purchase 'end visas' from a friendly Consulate on the express understanding that the passengers were secretly going to Palestine and not elsewhere. In other words, the Consulate would receive cash and the passengers a route through Romania. The Liberian Consulate came to Perl and Diamant's assistance and for 10,000 Reichsmark, issued a thousand such end visas.[9] So it was that by the end of October 1938, the arrangements had been concluded for seven hundred and fifty passengers in Vienna to board two Danube steamboats called the *Melk* and *Minerva* and leave Austria. Max was amongst them, and indeed for many of the passengers this was the second embarkation.

Max, like every passenger, had in his possession a forged ticket for what was described as a special transport to Liberia departing on the *Ostbahn*, the Eastern Railway. Max's ticket was numbered 00106 and records the date and time of departure as 4 November 1938 at 21.00 hours. Max kept this ticket along with his *Af Al Pi* cotton square. Both were on display at the Jabotinsky Museum. Max recorded in his diary that they left by train on the Ostbahn on Friday evening 4 November 1938 and the next day they boarded the *Melk* at Fischamend, a small market town a dozen or so kilometres out of Vienna at the confluence of the Fischamend Canal and the Danube, today near to Vienna's airport. It was here that they started their journey of hope. They took on board such provisions as they could arrange and naturally a torah scroll as well.

Soon the *Melk* gently steamed around the corner of the river bend by Devin's ruined castle, a view familiar to Max's beloved Wolf and Koppel Theben from generations past, and across the border into Czechoslovakia. A few hours later they glided past Pressburg and Max saw white sheets hanging out from buildings on the riverbank on which was written in German: 'Now that the Jews have gone we all have enough bread to eat.' This was the city where Max had studied, and which had such a proud tradition as the cradle of Jewish learning in Europe. Even without Nazi occupation, it seemed that Pressburg had been infected with the same contagion.

The *Melk* continued its journey down the Danube, past Budapest, Belgrade, then to Galati in Romania and finally to the Black Sea port of Salina, where Max boarded the MS *Eli*. At this point another group of passengers arrived. One hundred and twenty-five spectres came on board. They had been released from Dachau on the condition that they too left the Reich immediately. Many were sick and barely in a position to endure the voyage but given the choice between such a journey and a return to Dachau, there was not much hesitation. Originally, it had been intended that they would travel on the SS *Draga*, which after its passage from Fiume in September had returned for a second voyage to Palestine. Given their need for medical attention, however, it was decided to allow the SS *Draga* to leave first and for the MS *Eli* to leave a few days later once some medicines had been purchased in Romania. This required a transfer of passengers between the vessels. It is not clear on what basis the selection was carried out. Max stayed on the MS *Eli* and as a youth group leader, would most likely have been a good choice for someone to make the necessary arrangements for those who had arrived in such a poor state.

A postcard of the *Eli*'s voyage shows a dozen young men holding onto or leaning over the rail on the deck of the vessel. The vessel's name written in Greek can be seen on the life buoys above their heads. It can be assumed that this photograph records some of the senior leadership of the transport. A few are in military uniform, one of them being Shmuel Targanaski, a commander in the *Irgun Zvei Leumi*, the underground paramilitary organisation closely linked to Jabotinsky's Revisionists who had travelled back from Tel Aviv to accompany this group back across the sea. In the top right of the postcard is the *Betar* insignia or seal. The postcard presents a confident picture of Jews being rescued by their own.

Below deck, the situation was distinctly less accommodating. This was a cargo vessel converted to carry desperate immigrants by a local workforce in Romania. Wooden platforms were built along the sides of the cargo holds. Each platform level was reached by a series of ladders. Triple bunks were built on each level, only the height of one metre separating one bunk and the next above. The next row of bunks would be built 75 cm from the next. There was little room to move about except for a central area. Each level was given a scheduled time to go on deck to wash, catch some fresh air and exercise, although all this was subject to change or cancellation if another vessel should happen to be nearby. As events in Europe deteriorated over the next year and matters grew more desperate, the arrangements on these vessels became ever more crowded and unsanitary.[10]

Max noted in his diary they waited for three or four tense days at the port. It was not just the delay that worried them. Whilst at the port they learnt that that just days after leaving on their journey, violence and destruction had once more erupted in Vienna and right across the Reich. The newspapers and radio broadcasts all carried news of the terror and destruction which had exploded during the night of 9 November 1938, Kristallnacht, the night of broken glass. There was no doubt in anyone's mind that they had to leave, but what of those they left behind? On 14 November the MS *Eli* departed Salina bound for Palestine and not of course Liberia, as their papers stated officially.

15

The Life of Sarah

There was a tight crush consisting mostly of young men in the smallest of communal spaces in one of the makeshift converted holds beneath the deck of the *Eli*. The air was dank and such was the darkness that it was not easy to make out people's faces. Just an occasional shaft of light here and there and a flickering bulb left on permanently to avoid accidents at night. Many, either out of religious conviction or curiosity, had pressed close to a makeshift bench where the Torah scroll containing the five Books of Moses had been laid out. Others were not able to stand and simply lay in their bunks taking in what they could. As is customary, seven men in sequence had been called up to witness the reading of the biblical scriptures and to say a short blessing at the beginning and then end of each recitation. It was inevitable that the whole religious service would take place below deck as passengers were not allowed on deck for prolonged periods and in any event the spray of seawater would have destroyed the precious scroll.

After the reading of the designated weekly passage of the Bible (*parsha*) had finished and before the conclusion of the Shabbat service, it would be usual to expect a sermon. This was no synagogue and there was no serving Rabbi amongst them. Nevertheless, there was an expectant air. After a long pause, reluctantly a young scholar came forward who seemed to be known by a fair number of those gathered. Whilst Max many years later recalled the service and its sermon, there is no record of the name of the man who gave it.

The amateur preacher spoke at first in a halting voice:

'The Torah is filled with accounts of the words of those called upon to act when feeling distinctly unqualified to fulfil any such duty. I am like this before you. There are many more learned than me amongst you and also many others more devout and observant. So, I ask your indulgence and forgiveness. It would not though be right for us to finish reading from the Torah and to end our prayers without saying a few words about this week's parsha and anyway, what else are you going to do today? It is not like you are in a hurry to go anywhere.

You are no doubt thinking that it would be a lot easier today if we were reading from Sefer Shemot (the Book of Exodus). My task would be helped if right now we were hearing of the great deeds of Moses, Moshe Rabenu, who with God's might led the people of Israel out of Egypt and freed them from the oppression of the Pharaoh. It would be so much simpler, if divine providence allowed me to draw a direct parallel today between those who sought to destroy us in the past and today's Nazis. The Amalek of our times. A curse be on all their names.

No, that would be too convenient. Instead, we have just been reading this Shabbat from parsha Chayee Sarah, the life of Sarah, the wife of Avraham, which paradoxically opens not with her life, but her death and ends with the search for a wife for Isaac. We are told in the first verse that Sarah died in Kyriat Arbah, today Hevron, at the age of 127 and that Avraham came both to mourn and deliver a eulogy. It might then be thought that the account would continue with some words to help us understand what we have all learnt from the life of Sarah or the rites that followed her death. Surely this would be the occasion for some reflection of the fact that she was uprooted from her birthplace in Mesopotamia to start all over in a new country, with a new name, as she would no longer be known as Sarai but as Sarah. These are things everyone here can understand as we face our new lives. Perhaps we could have all reflected once more of her following Avraham into Egypt where she had to pretend to be his sister not wife, a false tale that very nearly ended with her being raped. Then there was her extraordinary struggle in life to bear children and the complexities of her relationship with Haggar, her maidservant who then became pregnant with Ishmael. Maybe also we could have once more thought of her joy at the birth of Isaac and her distress no doubt at the extraordinary account which we read last week of Avraham going to Mount Moriah with the intention of sacrificing their child. We

149

might also find that there would be some discussion of the comparative worth of internal and external beauty. But this is not the direction of travel at all. None of it. Instead, what follows is a somewhat legalistic account of Avraham negotiating with Ephron, the Hittite, for a burial plot for his beloved departed wife. It is to be frank pretty business-like and does not contain words that soar to the skies or plunge deep into the heart. This is transactional. The Torah even descends into what might be thought are unbecoming details – the discussion about the exact price and the counting out of the silver shekels. So, what is this all about? Why the endless prosaic detail about an event of this magnitude?

I would like to share some thoughts with you. Perhaps this is made all the more relevant because of who we are and our present situation. Avraham opens his dialogue with the Hittites saying that he is a stranger amongst them and he would wish to find a burial plot in order to bury his wife. He was a stranger in the same way that you will be when you arrive in Ha'aretz. The customs, practices, food, and yes of course the weather will be in degrees strange to you. Sorry, a very bad pun. You too will find yourself as Avraham did. Hopefully not burying loved ones, but nevertheless a stranger in a strange land. In response, Ephron offered him the burial plot without charge. Although he did mention the value of the land and observed that four hundred shekels should not be allowed to come between friends. Avraham, however, was insistent on paying his way. He measured out four hundred shekels of silver in front of all the witnesses gathered and then sealed the purchase of the cave of Machpelah in Hevron which can be visited today. Only then did he bury his wife.

There are two aspects of this story that I wanted to focus on.

The first is that Avraham having come from Ur in Babylon would have been broadly familiar with the customs and practices of the old country. According to the Hammurabi Code, which had been in place as long ago as 1750 BC, there were strict rules governing the alienation of land which had to be sold in a particular ceremony or manner involving the weighing out of the price and had to witnessed too. No doubt Avraham wanted to take every step he could to make sure this was done in accordance with the formal legal requirements in order to make the contract enforceable. What is more, if Ephron the Hittite was, as would seem to be the case, a Chieftain, then under the Hammurabi Code it was at least arguable that the sale might in any event be invalid as a Chieftain could not alienate land. Avraham it seems was taking care because of the extreme importance of securing a burial place for his Sarah. It also has to be recalled; Avraham was initially offered land without any charge, but he refused it. This is significant too. There are many occasions in life when we lean heavily on each other. We are all the stronger for it. Certainly, Avraham famous for his open tent, was a great expounder of this philosophy. Nevertheless, we also know that there are times which go far beyond hospitality but engage business dealings when we have to pay our way and do things by the book. The formality of this transaction is a useful lesson to us. Avraham understood perfectly well that this was a business occasion and that the offer of the gift of land was not appropriate and might well not secure for him anyway the desired objective – an eternal burial shrine.

The Torah, however, does not stop there. Be open as well. Avraham not only paid Ephron the full value of the four hundred shekels, incidentally ten times the price paid for Joseph as a slave, he did so by counting out the money aloud, openly and in front of all present. Avraham acted in a fully transparent way so that no one could say otherwise. He leads us by example. Be honest, faithful and open in your dealings. Indeed, it is said that the practice of counting out money in front of witnesses continued right into the late Middle Ages with the bankers of Florence on the Ponte Vecchio.

Now you are all looking at me quizzically. Many of you are crazed with thirst and hunger. You have nothing by way of belongings apart from what you are wearing and to be honest none of you look like you are wearing your Shabbat best. You are muttering how can we even think in terms of our business dealings? The answer to this is obvious. This is precisely the moment when you have to think of it. You are weak. You think that others have taken pity on you and someone owes you a favour in any event. Maybe your judgment is impaired. This might have been Avraham too. He had just lost his dear wife of many years. He was a stranger amongst the Hittites. He was desperate to complete the burial rites and say the prayers of mourning. He could easily be forgiven for thinking that this was a somewhat exceptional situation. His compass, however remained intact and he understood what was required and acted accordingly. Carry his example with you always.

The second aspect I wanted to mention is the significance of Ephron the Hittite in this story. Some confusion is sown by the reference to

Hittites in the Bible, people who had migrated from Central Anatolia, presumably as a result of the loss of their lands to Egyptian invaders at around this time. Most of you here today will know the story of King David and Uriah the Hittite. David behaves disgracefully towards his loyal Hittite captain and in the end pays a heavy price affecting the lives of multiple generations of his offspring. Nevertheless, in this story I suggest we are perhaps being told something different. Avraham and those with whom he arrives, have come to live in a land which is not empty. As we learnt last week, Avraham had already spent time living with Avimelech, the Philistine in Beer Sheva. Leaving aside the historical anachronism of the reference to the Philistines, who would not arrive from Crete for several hundred years after the death of Avraham, the fundamental point remains. Different tribes have always had to live together and had to do so as best as they could in peace and harmony. Of course, we know that these fine wishes have had to withstand significant pressures over the years, and you will recall that battle after battle is described in detail in the Book of Samuel in particular. Nevertheless, we too are arriving in a land which is not empty. We know that today there is endless bitter conflict between Jews and Arabs, which tragically not long ago resulted in many Jews being killed in Hevron itself. Yet still, like Avraham we are bound to take every step to strive to live together in harmony. To respect each other, not take advantage of one another and to see the human quality in each person you live with or next to or carry out business dealings with. After all we are all of us, Jew, Christian and Arab made in Hashem's image. May we all learn from our wise fathers who taught us there are only three pillars for a good life – justice, truth and peace. I wish you all a Shabbat Shalom.'

16

Kristallnacht/Kristalltag
November 1938

Dort wo man Bücher verbrennt,
Verbrennt man am Ende auch Menschen[1]

Max had every reason to fear for the safety of those he left behind in Vienna. In the short space of four or five months during which he was fully occupied in finding a way to get to Palestine, the situation had clearly deteriorated for the Jews living there. My mother, Judy, was living with her parents Terci and Juyla next door to one of the oldest synagogues in the Second District. Her cousin Ruth was living a few streets away in the same area. None of them could have known quite how vulnerable this would make them.

The version of Kristallnacht which has been now become fixed in the mind from numerous images of burning synagogues, television documentaries, museum exhibitions and as taught at schools, does require some adjustment; certainly as regards Vienna. The overwhelming destruction seen on the streets has to be seen in the broader context of an escalating series of violent incidents in the months leading up to Kristallnacht in November 1938, and those incidents themselves have to be examined alongside the never-ending flow of extreme laws and measures introduced against the Jewish population of Austria. Furthermore, in Vienna, the night of broken glass was in fact predominantly a series of coordinated attacks in broad daylight during the course of the late morning of 10 November rather than the night of 9 November 1938.[2] It was not so much Kristallnacht as Kristalltag.

The new laws and measures brought into effect in Austria in the build-up to November 1938 should be seen as a deliberate policy of increasing the pressure on the Jewish population designed to bring about a mass forced departure. In April 1938, all Jewish children were expelled from non-Jewish schools. On 26 April 1938, the first of a series of measures was introduced to force what was described as the Aryanisation of Jewish enterprise at prescribed prices and exchange rates, which represented only a fraction of the value. On 20 May 1938, the Nuremburg race laws were extended to Austria. My father-in-law Henry remembered the summer of that year as being exceptionally hot, when a series of new orders came into effect which prohibited Jews from entering parks or going to any public space, including the city's swimming pools.

Then from 23 July 1938, every Jew had to carry with them an identity card which was marked on the front page with a 'J' for 'Jew'. All male Jews had to adopt the name 'Israel' and the females, 'Sarah'. This required everyone to undertake a process of registration, which in turn also meant endless hours of queuing up outside local police stations. In turn, this allowed passers-by to hurl insult or worse. One potential way out of this was thought to be baptism. On the day after this new law was introduced, Reverend Hugh Grimes in the Anglican Church in Vienna baptised 129 people. This was more than his entire congregation of a little over a hundred. In total it is thought that he baptised 1800 Jews, so saving the lives of many.

Soon the focus switched to individual professions. On 16 September 1938 a new decree was issued which forbade Aryan nurses or doctors from seeing Jewish patients in hospitals. The Jewish community was ordered to build a new hospital to look after their own, but of course had no money to do so, as it had been confiscated by the many other measures dealing with property. On 27 September 1938, attention was turned to the removal of all Jewish lawyers from the list of those allowed to appear in court or give legal advice.[3] All of this added to the sense of isolation, and the inability to continue to live any semblance of a normal life in the absence of redress in the courts. On 5 October, the passports issued to all Jews resident in the Reich were declared invalid and had to be reissued. Once more this required the process of registration and provided further opportunity for casual violence.

A glimpse of the endless queuing up for registration or permits can be seen in a photograph taken at this time outside the Polish Consulate in Vienna. It shows a line of hundreds stretching as far as the eye could see down a wide boulevard. Most would have arrived at 5am at first light.[4] In the picture several plain clothes SD officers can be seen walking up and down carrying sticks and no doubt spitting out some choice words or perhaps worse. There is also in view a café open for business in the midst of all this on the side of street where everyone is waiting patiently for the queue to move forward. It might have been thought that they would be doing brisk business, but instead the owners displayed in the window two neat swastikas and the sign 'Jews Forbidden'.

Attempts were made to widen the popular appeal of the principal themes of anti-Semitism. On 2 August 1938, Seyss-Inquart and Gauleiter Odilo Globocnik, both Austrian-born Nazis at the very top of the command structure, opened a grand exhibition at the Nordbahnhoff in the Jewish Second District, entitled '*der Ewige Jude,*' the 'The Wandering Jew'. In truth, the only itinerant aspect of this display was the exhibition itself, which had made its way from Munich where half a million passed through the doors, then to Vienna and finally onto Berlin. Odilo Globocnik had been teased as he grew up for his obviously Slavic name and subsequently strived to be more Aryan than the next. He became a senior member of the SS, a loyal lieutenant to Eichmann, and was said to be responsible for the deaths of up to a million Jews in the Holocaust. The giant poster which covered the entire façade of the building depicted an orthodox Jew begging for money with one hand and carrying a torah scroll in the other, the velvet cover of which depicted the hammer and sickle.

Inside, there was plenty to entertain the masses. There were exaggerated cartoon displays of the supposed features of a Jewish face with particular focus on a grotesque portrayal of noses and lips. Space was dedicated to reminding the curious of prominent Jewish communists such as Leon Trotsky and supposedly Jewish Hollywood actors, such as Charlie Chaplin, who was not in fact Jewish but had of course satirised Hitler and so presumably in the eyes of the organisers was as good as. The local press coverage underscored the importance of the exhibition, noting that the choice of venue where Jews would come pouring into the city from Galicia and the provinces could not be more important.

In this fetid atmosphere it was only a few short steps to the recommencement of physical attacks and threats witnessed in the spring of 1938. The generation of fear was a central plank in Eichmann's wider policy and so when such attacks took place, more often than not a blind eye was turned.

As summer turned to autumn there would be more frequent raids at night on people's homes looking for property to confiscate. The ruse most often adopted was to suggest that property found had not been properly accounted for under the Aryanisation laws. Henry, who was eleven at the time, recalled the sound of jack boots on the corridor in the early hours of the morning outside their small apartment at Hollandstrasse, 8 in the Second District. A sound he said he could never forget. It was the Gestapo. They demanded that the door be opened or they would break it down. Once inside the apartment, they ransacked it looking for money but found none. Henry recalled that his own mother opened a cupboard which had some fancy Rosenthal china in it and offered this instead. This was flatly rejected and likewise the odd unimpressive remaining silver ornament. They said they really had quite enough of all that already. Instead, they walked off with his mother's bed linen. Henry spoke of the ever-present psychological torment. Most nights that summer, gangs roamed the streets of the Jewish quarter looking for someone to beat up and singing aloud their favourite Nazi song; 'Today Germany belongs to us... Tomorrow the whole world.'[5]

Yom Kippur, the Jewish Day of Atonement, began that year at nightfall on 4 October. As would be expected, a very large proportion of Vienna's Jews would be found in synagogue beginning their fast and prayers. This was the moment chosen to strike at those praying in the 17th, 18th and 19th Districts. Police entered several synagogues in a co-ordinated action and ordered those present to leave immediately and go straight down to the Danube, where they were told there were ships ready to take them to Palestine where they belonged. The congregants had got some way towards the river when they were told that the order had been revoked and they could return. Mass arrests also returned as a tool of intimidation. In the second half of October about 2,000 Jews were arrested in the Second District for no apparent reason and taken to the local police station. They were only released when they had given an update as to when and how they intended to leave the country. This operation had to be suspended because very quickly the police realized they were just not able to process that number of people.

Then came the attacks on the synagogues themselves. On 15 and 16 October, the synagogue in Odeongasse in the Second District just a few streets away from where my mother was living was broken into and ransacked. The same happened in the prayer room at Flossgasse. On the evening of 15 October, the violence came to the synagogue right next door, when the windows of the main entrance to the Shiffshul were smashed. On the 16th, in the middle of the afternoon, the synagogue in Templegasse was set ablaze. The perpetrators were naturally never found or apprehended. All of this violence in October was merely the dress rehearsal. Once more it could be said that Vienna led where Berlin followed.[6]

On 30 October 1938, Eichmann issued an order that any Jew in Vienna who was either stateless or a Polish national had to leave within 24 hours. This was later extended to four weeks because of the obvious impracticality of the original deadline. These decrees were mirrored across the Reich. Tens of thousands of Polish nationals living in Germany were taken by truck to the border and told to walk across into Poland. There were three crossing points designated for this forced expulsion. Amongst this desperate crowd was my then teenage father, who was born and had lived all his life in Fulda, Germany, not far from Frankfurt. Nevertheless, because his own father was a Polish national, my father was designated as a Pole, not German and so required under these new laws immediately to leave Germany.

My father remembered the chaos at the border with families trying not to get separated, with some being pushed across into Poland whilst others remained behind. He told me how one of his sisters was caught up in a surge of people striving to get across the border and how someone in their group reached out and dragged her back, so most likely saving her life. My father also remembered the bitter cold and having to camp out in fields without shelter at the beginning of winter. Those at the border had been rejected both by Germany and Poland so were stuck in a no man's land, and such was the confusion they did not even know themselves whether they were better off in Germany or Poland. *The Times* reported the plight of those being deported but noted that at Katowice, one of the three border crossings, the situation had been resolved by 31 October with all those remaining at the border being sent home.[7] Others were not so lucky and had to wait at the border in the cold until January 1939.

The worst conditions at the Polish border crossings were found at Zbaszyn. Amongst the crowd there were Szendel and Riva Grynszpan who had been forcibly deported from their home in Hanover to the border. They wrote of these horrific scenes in a postcard to their son Herschl living in Paris, which he received on 3 November 1938. On 7 November 1938 Herschel purchased a revolver and shot Ernst vom Rath, an official at the German Embassy in Paris, five times. There are two rival theories with regard to the motive for the assassination. The first and predominant theory is that it was the act of a desperate man in protest against the treatment of the Jews, including his parents at the border and that although he had intended to kill the ambassador, instead he shot and fatally wounded the first person he encountered; namely vom Rath. The second is that the shooting was a *crime de passion*, with vom Rath and Herschl being clandestine lovers. The seventeen-year-old Herschl with some skill elaborated on the latter story, thus thwarting the plans of Hitler and Goebbels for a show trial.

As vom Rath hovered between life and death, shortly before midnight on 9 November, the head of the Gestapo, Heinrich Muller, issued an order for an organised raid on the synagogues of Germany for the purpose of seizing communal archives that could then be used to facilitate the arrest of 20-30,000 wealthy Jews. At 1.20am Heydrich added a few details to the order stating that the security forces should prevent looting and should protect property. These orders would have served little purpose in Austria as Eichmann had in July 1938 already seized all Jewish communal records. Equally, those with any possessions had already been arrested or threatened with arrest.

Nevertheless, this served as the required pretext to unleash the next and perhaps most famous round of Nazi pogrom activity on the night of 9 November 1938 and then during the following day on 10 November, now known universally as Kristallnacht. As soon as the news of vom Rath's assassination broke, there were many who feared the worst. The German press prepared their groundwork with strongly worded attacks on Churchill, Duff Cooper and Arthur Greenwood, linking them to a Jewish plot to murder vom Rath. William Strang in the Foreign Office on 9 November wrote to Sir George Ogilvie Forbes in the British Embassy in Berlin, who in the absence of Sir Nevile Henderson was acting ambassador. Strang suggested that a senior diplomat should intervene and speak to the Nazi leadership calling for restraint. Ogilvie Forbes considered that any such intervention would only make matters worse for those British nationals living in Germany and not improve the position of the Jews anyway.[8] Nothing was said and the events unfolded over the next twenty-four hours. Ogilvie Forbes seems afterwards to have felt a measure of guilt for his silence.

All but one of Vienna's forty-nine synagogues and sixty prayer halls were burnt down or attacked by the early afternoon of 10 November 1938.[9] It appears that the majority of the destruction of property took place between about 11.00am and 12 noon on Thursday 10 November by means of a series of coordinated attacks.[10] The dominant method used was the throwing of hand-grenades through shattered windows and then the setting of furniture on fire. The largest and perhaps most famous of all the synagogues in the Second District of Vienna was the Leopoldstadter Tempel with its triple façade, ornate dome and Moorish style decoration and columns. It was destroyed by a large bomb at 11.30am. The force of the explosion was such that pieces of masonry and granite weighing up to half a ton were thrown down the street. The memorial plaque at the site today states that nothing remains except the foundation stone of the building.

Next it was the turn of the Schiffshul synagogue on Grosse Shiffgasse. This was right next door to where Judy was living. The Schiffshul was designed and built in the mid-nineteenth century. Perhaps having been designed and built at a time before Emancipation, it was somewhat unusual, in that the façade on the street did not give any indication that this was a house of prayer. Instead, from the street all that could be seen was a nondescript front entrance leading to a courtyard. The entrance would have been locked that morning. The synagogue was built facing into the courtyard, away from the view of the street. The destruction of this particular synagogue certainly required a little more forward planning and knowledge. It could not plausibly be explained as a spontaneous act of violence by a mob running through a street.

My mother was with her cousin Ruth that day. At about 12 noon, rioters broke through the main entrance into the courtyard and then the synagogue. The torah scrolls were then taken out and burnt in the street in full view of all. Grenades were tossed in and a huge blast could be heard coming from inside the synagogue itself and what was left was then set ablaze. Judy and Ruth were told to stay in their room and away from the window. They only obeyed half of these instructions. They looked out of their window at the back of their apartment building facing away from the street front and saw the flames enveloping the neighbouring synagogue. Yet still they had to remain in their room as it was clearly too dangerous to leave.

The food bank, for the tens of thousands who like my mother's family who had little or no means of keeping themselves, was housed in the nearby synagogue on Krumbaumgasse and was next on the list. It, too, was set on fire. Systematically, one by one, each synagogue and prayer hall was razed.

The destruction was not restricted to synagogues. Jewish shops, which had for some time been marked with visible signs as to their ownership, were looted by the hundreds. As in the Spring Pogrom there were reports of rape and violent physical attacks meted out by Nazi street gangs. It was estimated that ninety Jews were killed that afternoon. More than six hundred reportedly took their own life. About 8,000 others were rounded up and arrested. Those who witnessed the violence in either Vienna or Berlin were under no illusion that this was pre-meditated and organised and not some spontaneous demonstration. Mr Kirkpatrick, one of the chargé d'affaires in the British Embassy in Berlin described the scene with striking crassness: 'It is rather like watching a side show at an exhibition, where you pay so much to break as much crockery as you like.'[11] Throughout there appears to have been far too little attention paid to the clear and obvious danger to life.

Ruth Maier, a schoolgirl wrote of that day in her diary. She woke up thinking it would be her special day, as it was her eighteenth birthday. Instead, as news spread of the attacks, they were all sent home from the Jewish school she attended. In the streets she saw a lorry packed with Jews standing up and being driven off, like livestock to the slaughterhouse.[12] My father-in-law remembered being sent home from school with his friends that afternoon. Outside the school gate a gang of Nazi youth were waiting with sticks and knives, chanting '*Sau Juden*', an anti-Semitic chant used since the early Middle Ages and one which had given rise to its very own genre of obscene art. It loosely translates as dirty Jew or Jew pig and is often associated with drawings of Jews in the farmyard suckling from a pig. Henry was not about to debate the ancient origins of the '*Sau Juden*' imagery and ran for it. They chased him and his friends. He got separated from them and as they bore down on him, he had reason to be fearful for his life. He ran into the first apartment building he could find with an open door, rang a doorbell and asked to be protected from the Nazi youth. Once again, a complete stranger saved his skin.[13]

1. The family photograph at Terci's bedside- back row left to right; Juyla, Oskar, Gina, Wilma, Max, Jeno. Front row left to right; Judy, Terci, Olga, Eva on her lap, Karoline, Heinrich, Julci, Ruth.

2. Sandhurst Hotel, Southport.

3. Burgenland farmlands at sunset.

4. The Esterhazy Schloss in Lackenbach by the cool waters of the Selitzbach.

5. Samson Wertheimer.

6. The interior of Lackenbach Synagogue in 1890s.

7. Oskar Kokoschka's painting *Alice in Wonderland*, depicting the horror of 1938 and its origins in 1934.

Above: 8. A family photograph outside Berggasse, 18 in Lackenbach, in the mid-1930s.

Left: 9. Terci, Julya and Judy outside Berggasse ,18 in Lackenbach in mid 1930s.

10. Republican soldiers inside the ruins of the Governor's Palace at Teruel, the last bastion of Fascist resistance, 3rd January 1938.

11. Soldiers in the trenches above Teruel, January 1938.

Above left: 12. A Nazi rally in Eisenstadt on the afternoon of 11 March 1938, the day before German troops crossed into Austria.

Left: 13. Hitler's triumphant reception in Vienna, 14 March 1938.

Below: 14. Former Schutzbunders in Nazi uniform marching in Vienna in April 1938 under a banner supporting Hitler.

15. Jews scrubbing streets of Vienna, March 1938.

16. Willy Perl (right) and Paul Heller (left) on Max's train held at the border at
Arnoldstein, August 1938.

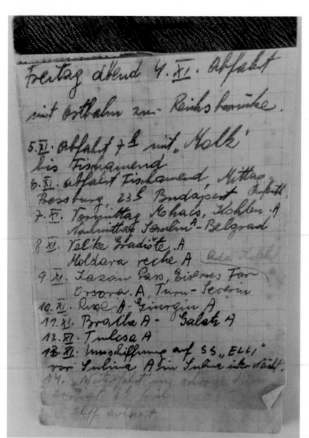

Left: 17. The front page of Max's handwritten diary.

Below left: 18. Max's Af Al Pi badge, which he wore when he left Austria with Betar.

Below right: 19. Max's forged train ticket.

20. The crew of the *Eli* with Targansky and the Irgun rescuers.

21. A wedding on the deck of the *Eli* at sea.

"We're here" smile comes from two refugee children; 250 of them arrived at Liverpool-street from Vienna yesterday. They will stay with London families.

This document of identity is issued with the approval of His Majesty's Government in the United Kingdom to young persons to be admitted to the United Kingdom for educational purposes under the care of the Inter-Aid Committee for children.

THIS DOCUMENT REQUIRES NO VISA.

PERSONAL PARTICULARS.

4214

1818

Name LÖBL JUDITH

Sex F.   Date of Birth 17.12.1932.

Place Vienna

Full Names and Address of Parents

LÖBL Julius and Therese,

6/4, Gr. Schiffgasse. Vienna II

Above: 22. Judy's Kindertransport documentation recording her arrival in England in December 1938.

Left: 23. Ruth's arrival in England in December 1938, as reported by the *Daily Express*.

Below left: 24. Rabbi Solomon Schonfeld, the rescuer of many thousands of Jewish children.

Below right: 25. Inventory of possessions taken of Berggasse 18, including Judy's dolls (highlighted).

14/12/45

Anlage 5

Warenaufnahme Julius Löbl am 1.Juli 1938.

26. Julya (far right) in his suit, tie and overcoat at Constanza, 1939, ready to depart Europe.

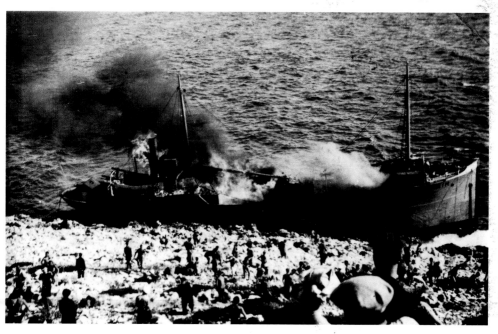

27. The *Rim* on fire off the island of Simi, near Rhodes.

P. 252.

THE PALESTINE POLICE FORCE.

APPLICATION FOR AN ORDER OF DEPORTATION.

No. 24

1. Full name (and aliases) *JULIUS LÖBL*

2. Father's name *Moritz Löbl*

3. Mother's name and maiden name *Johanna Nussbaum*

4. Present address in Palestine *Sarafand*

5. Occupation (state if unemployed) *Merchant*

6. Place of birth (village or province) *Lackenbach, Burgenland, Germany*

7. Full address in country of origin *6. Grosse Schiff st. Vienna Germany*

8. Date of birth *28. XI. 1896*   9. Religion *Jew*   10. Married or single *married*

11. Present nationality, and how acquired *German*

12. Full names, addresses and occupations of references in country of which he/she is a national

Rudolf Gerbach, merchant 6. Gross Schiffstrasse Vienna

13. Name of Omdah (Mukhtar) or Sheikh (name of tribe in case of Sudanese or nomad Arabs)

14. Places of residence twelve months prior to entry into Palestine *as above in prison ?*

15. Present circumstances (destitute or otherwise; state whether in possession of money or other valuable property) *no*

16. Date of last departure from country of origin *4. II. 39*   17. Date of entry into Palestine *19. 8. 39.*

(P.T.O.)   GPP. 4705—16000—18.12.37

28. The front page of Julya's deportation application, including the two prison mug shots numbered 146.

29. Max and Julya in Palestine, May 1941.

30. A portrait of Wilma, date uncertain but presumably before she left for Kladovo.

Hebrew text on flags: חזק ואמץ (left flag), תרי״ד עם ישראל חי (right flag)

Brückner J.

SOPRON
TORNA UTCZA 14

Above: 31. Gina (left) and Wilma (right) (circled) amongst the Kladovo group at Sabac.

Left: 32. Heinrich and Karolina's engagement photograph in 1890s.

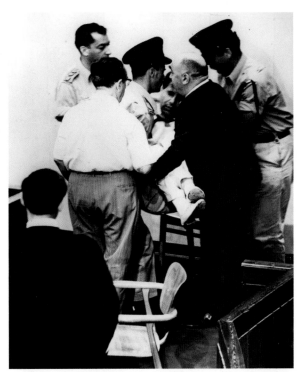

33. A witness faints in the public gallery at Eichmann's trial, Jerusalem, April 1961.

34. Eichmann giving evidence at his trial in Jerusalem, sitting behind bulletproof glass.

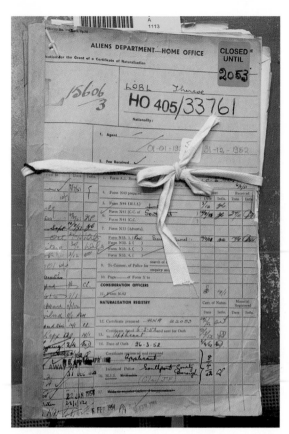

Left: 35. Terci's Home Office File, sealed until 2053.

Below: 36. Judy (front centre) and Ruth (second left) smiling with a group of their school friends in Southport.

The only synagogue not to have been razed in this violence was the Seitenstettengasse Synagogue just across the Danube Canal in Central Vienna's First District. It was ransacked, with the ark and furniture all destroyed but was not set ablaze. There are various explanations for this, the most plausible being that it was too near a neighbouring Church in a narrow street for arson to have been an option. Nevertheless, it is remarkable that the structure of this wonderful building did largely escape damage that day and throughout the war. It has a somewhat unusual architectural design for a synagogue. It was built in the round and remains a beautiful and peaceful place to visit or pray at today with its slightly over the top blue and gold domed ceiling. Having said this, it is perfectly in keeping with the city itself. Vienna has always had a penchant for a bit of show.

One aspect of Kristallnacht which has been the focus of less attention in the published literature was that the organised violence also extended to the Sudetenland, which had only one month previously been absorbed into the Reich. Under the careful co-ordination of Konrad Heinlein, the local Nazi Governor, once more there were grotesque scenes of synagogues being burnt and Jews being forced to crawl on hands and knees across the border into Czechoslovakia whilst being spat on by the local gendarmerie.[14] Heinlein then issued an order that all synagogues still standing and which were no longer in use as result of this expulsion should be handed over to Sudeten German Sports Clubs.[15] This was predictable and yet it was just one more breach of the principles established under the Munich Agreement, which amongst other things had ensured the right of Jews living in the Sudetenland to continue to do so if they desired.

As the violence petered out on the late afternoon of 10 November 1938, the following communiqué was issued in Vienna after Goebbels called to an end to the violence:

In the course of the day the Reich Commissar Gauleiter Burckel arranged for raids in the homes of many Jews. In these raids large amounts of arms, Communist literature and illegally possessed foreign currency were found. The success of these raids shows that mildness and tolerance towards the Jews are entirely out of place. If in future Jews are to avoid harshness, which is now justified, there remains for them but one course – to get out of Vienna as quickly as possible.

At the same time, a fine was issued of 1 billion Reichmarks payable collectively by the entire Jewish community to the State for their responsibility for Kristallnacht. This was the equivalent of £80,000,000 in 1938 and just under £5 billion today. This sum clearly could never be paid but would pave the way for further expropriation of assets. In addition, complex arrangements were made with regard to insurance claims. Goering was both incensed and embarrassed at the prospect of foreigners, including Jewish-owned companies, making insurance claims for the damage suffered or for theft. It seems that Goering was keen to give the impression to the outside world that he found the destruction of Jewish property to be needless and insupportable. Goering even went so far as to send Major General Bodenschatz, one of his most trusted liaison officers, to London in late November 1938 on a top-secret mission to explain to Whitehall that as a result of Kristallnacht he had tendered his resignation to Hitler.[16] This was treated with a great deal of scepticism. Nevertheless, in case it be thought that Goering had become somewhat soft hearted, the point he wished to make through Bodenschatz to those who listened in London was that Kristallnacht had been a disaster as far as he was concerned because so much of the merchandise destroyed in Jewish shops turned out to be owned by non-Jews, having been supplied on terms of sale or return, and they would now have to be compensated. Worse still, the destruction of so many shop fronts meant that three million Reichmarks of Belgian glass had to be ordered, which was a waste of precious resources.

All this required delicate handling as far as Goering was concerned. He did understand that it was hard to contemplate valid contractual claims being denied without damaging what remained of Germany's commercial reputation. In response, on 12 November 1938 Goering summoned the heads of leading German insurance companies to Berlin to explain that claims made by non-Jews for loss of property would be met, but that whilst Jews in the Reich could make claims no money was to be paid over to them and instead would be paid directly to the State as part of the huge fine imposed. This was then put into law by the wonderfully euphemistic Ordinance for the Restoration of the Appearance of the Streets.[17] The insurers had rather hoped that they would be able to keep part or all of the money themselves.[18]

Joseph Goebbels wasted little time in the immediate aftermath in implementing yet further measures and restrictions against Jews in terms of the living they could earn which would come into effect as from 1 January 1939.[19] He then noted in his diary for 11 November 1938: 'We'll wait for the reactions abroad. For now, there is still silence, but the uproar will come.'

He did not have to wait long. The orgy of destruction, plunder and physical violence was fully reported in the English newspapers; likewise, the arrests, deportations and the explicit threat of the Reich Commissar. *The Times* reported on 13 November 1938 that two trains with 1,400 Viennese Jews had left Vienna on 12 November 1938 for Dachau. Donald St Clair Gainer, the British Consul General in Vienna, reported back to London of the scale and severity of the persecution. The total number of Jews held at Dachau, Buchenwald and Sachenhausen was now estimated by David Yarnell of the American Quakers to be in the region of 35,000.[20] He reported that those in Dachau would potentially be allowed to leave if they could demonstrate they were able to leave for another country.[21] On 16 November 1938, Bertha Bracey, the Chair of the Germany Emergency Committee, reported of her meeting with Lord Halifax the Foreign Secretary in which she found him to be fully appraised of the poor conditions faced by those imprisoned in the concentration camps in Germany.[22]

There was no more room for any ambiguity as to the present position and the consequences of countries such as Britain failing to act. There was a united front in the condemnatory press coverage of the acts of Hitler and his coterie.[23] This really did seem like a turning point, in contrast to the coverage of the Czech Crisis two months earlier in 1938. The *Daily Mail* had for a number of years since the rise of Hitler struck a somewhat neutral or even supportive tone for the direction that Germany was taking, but it could not stomach this and joined in the chorus of revulsion.[24]

There was a similar reaction in the American press. The *New York Times* carried the story on its front page for three successive days and President Roosevelt declared his shock. There was blanket coverage in the European press, even from countries such as Portugal under right-wing dictatorship, condemning the stain on European civilization resulting from Hitler's orchestrated murderous acts.[25]

By contrast, the Viennese edition of the *Volksche Beobachter*, a Nazi newspaper which had previously been banned in Austria by Schuschnigg, joyfully reported that Germany had settled its score with the Jews for the Paris murder. It carried pictures of a caricature of a

Jew under the headline, 'The Jew is Germany's enemy.' Ominously, it also reported on how the rest of the world treated Jews with its own concentration camps, closed borders and deportation.[26] This had been a repeated Nazi refrain, which was aired extensively at the time of the Evian Conference in June 1938, that no other country would admit the Jews of Germany or take steps to resolve what it referred to as the Jewish Question.

Nevertheless, such was the strength of the world's reaction that questions were raised at the highest level in the Reich and it was felt that something had to be done to address public concern. First, almost laughably, the SD intelligence services sent out a questionnaire trying to gauge public reaction to the riots, but the response was – patchy. Many were too frightened to express an opinion. Not so Johannes Popitz, the Prussian Finance Minister, who demanded that Goering punish those responsible. Goering responded by asking Poptiz if he wanted to punish Hitler himself.[27] When the responses did trickle in, there was unease felt at the high level of sympathy that this action had generated with the oppressed Jews, particularly in observant Christian communities. This was not what was expected at all. In due course some perfunctory attempts were made to hold criminal trials to demonstrate that there was still some semblance of a legal system in Germany, but by and large these were formalities without conviction or punishment.

The consequences of Kristallnacht also played out at the diplomatic level and at the Foreign Office. Sir Nevile Henderson, the German ambassador, was absent from Berlin in the critical period between November 1938 to February 1939. Henderson was, to say the very least, a controversial character in the history of the Diplomatic Service. Both Henderson and his then Undersecretary, Ivone Kirkpatrick, were strongly associated with Chamberlain's policy of appeasement. When Henderson arrived in Berlin in 1937, he was something of a hit and a favourite amongst the leadership of the Reich. Just as important as the Chamberlain connection was Henderson's strongly held anti-Semitism and anti-Slavism (Chips Channon pithily described him as being pro-German, anti-French, and anti-Jew), which permitted him on more than one occasion to appear as Hitler's apologist. He considered that Britain was being played by the Jews to manoeuvre the country into an ill-advised war with Germany. He also thought that it was the Jews and Communists who were responsible for whipping up an unmerited anti-German feeling in the country. Worse still, he held private discussions with the German ambassador in London during which he opined that the treatment of the Jews might be 'regularized in an orderly and systematic manner'.[28]

Lord Halifax, the Foreign Secretary, even said of himself that he had always been 'rather anti-Semitic'.[29] Astonishingly, Henderson wrote to Halifax on the day after Kristallnacht to suggest that the time was ripe for Britain to make a comprehensive offer to return former German colonies.[30] This supine form of diplomacy was also on display a few months earlier in connection with the Sudeten Germans. So it was that on 10 May 1938 Ivone Kirkpatrick told Prince Bismark Germany should tell them what they wanted as regards the Sudetenland and that the British Government would then lean on the Czechoslovak Government to yield.[31]

As is often the case in pivotal moments in history, however, serendipity played its part. There was a temporary change of guard in the Embassy at Berlin caused by Henderson's absence as he was ill and living in London awaiting surgery. This allowed Ogilvie Forbes, the chargé d'affaires and acting Ambassador, to play a much more prominent part in the shaping of the political reaction to the German treatment of the Jews in the following days. Ogilvie Forbes was horrified by what he saw in Berlin. On 13 November he wrote that he could not find strong enough words of condemnation of the treatment of innocent Jews and that the whole world was faced with the appalling sight of 500,000 people about to starve. He and his colleague in Vienna, Donald St Clair Gainer, kept up what was described as a bombardment of dispatches to Whitehall, which would influence the debate in the ensuing days. These messages clearly hit home in certain parts of Whitehall.[32]

The reaction was not restricted to the press and Whitehall. Religious and volunteer organisations likewise did all they could. British and American Quakers were very active in both Vienna and Berlin and sent delegations to report on the conditions of the Jews living there and to make representation to the Nazi authorities. Ben Greene left London for Germany with a delegation of British Quakers and David Yarnell left London for Berlin and Vienna accompanying a group of Quakers who had travelled from the United States.[33]

They wrote detailed reports of what they saw and whom they met. Ben Greene concentrated on visiting Jewish communities in Berlin, Frankfurt and its surrounding areas. This would have been very close to my father's family in Fulda. He reported seeing families in near starvation condition and so desperate that they could only contemplate either leaving or committing suicide. Everyone they spoke to was clear that they had been told that they had a clear choice of leaving the country or being sent to a concentration camp. In one of the more grotesquely ironic stories of this time, Ben Greene reported that the German local authorities in Frankfurt were sufficiently worried about the number of those committing suicide at home, they cut off the gas supply to the Jewish Quarter in the city.

In the meantime, David Yarnell focused on meeting relevant Jewish organisations in both Berlin and Vienna to discuss an orderly programme of Jewish emigration. He also met with Nazi officials to discuss how the Jewish community should be treated in the meantime. He met with Dr Schacht, the head of the Bundesbank, to explore ways in which the emigration of Jews could be facilitated and expedited. On 20 December 1939, David Yarnell was handed by Dr Berliner of the Jewish communal organisation, the *Reichsvertretung der Deutschen Juden*, a table with an estimate of the numbers of Jews left in Germany broken down into different age groups. This estimated that there were about 27,000 children under the age of 15.[34] This was out of a total remaining Jewish population of about 320,000 living in the *Altreich* (Germany before its annexations). About half that number again were living in Vienna, implying a total combined Jewish population in Germany and Austria of about 500,000. This table proved to be important and influential in the next stage of the planned rescue of Jewish children in Austria and Germany, my mother amongst them.

The humanitarian work of the Quakers at this critical time deserves greater attention than it has received. The Jewish communities they visited could not express sufficient gratitude that anyone from outside of world Jewry had taken notice and was really prepared to intervene. The German officials likewise had a lot of respect for the neutrality of the Quaker community. The Quakers had come to Berlin and Vienna and distributed food and clothing in the aftermath of the First World War at their time of need and had also been very critical of the terms of the Versailles Treaty.

The last piece of the puzzle was the need to develop, adopt and implement a new policy which could save meaningful numbers of the 500,000 identified by Ogilvie Forbes. They had to act quickly.

17

Ten Days in November

The ten days in London in November 1938 following Kristallnacht leading to the announcement of the Kindertransport scheme in Parliament do not have the same status of the epic battles of the Second World War and yet it is arguable that this story in some ways has had an equivalent impact on younger generations, as social history has become so central to our study of these events. In the case of the Kindertransport, the story is largely related through pictures of lines of smiling children arriving in this country rescued from fear, hatred and oppression, carrying only an identity card around their necks and a small suitcase. The eventual outcome has to some degree become woven into the fabric of the nation and the notion that we are diminished if we do not stand up for those who cannot stand up for themselves. Britain's part in rescuing children in peril at the hands of the Nazis has become one of the most taught and studied topics of the period. It has also to a considerable extent become profoundly mythologised, which has only served to impede accurate analysis.

This was a very close-run thing, and the outcome could easily have been different right to the very last. There were a number in Cabinet and in the Foreign Office wholly unsympathetic to such plans. There were considerable practical difficulties that had to be overcome by the proponents and time was not on their side. The policy adopted would save the lives of my mother, Judy, and of Ruth, her cousin. It would also allow in practical terms their own mothers to come and live with them in this country working as domestic servants. It would rescue more than ten thousand other children, Jews and non-Jews. No amount of gratitude to the generosity of this country, unmatched elsewhere in Europe, can be sufficient. Yet at the same time the ensuing compromise would be devastating for each of those trapped in Europe who were ineligible to come to England under the adopted scheme and for whom escape to Palestine was the only option. This is the story of those critical days.

Monday 14 November

In mid-afternoon, under leaden skies, the business of Parliament got underway for the week. *The Times* that day reported the aftershock of the previous week's events in the German Reich. There were reports of fire-burnt synagogues in Vienna being pulled down and desperate queues forming outside the British Consulate. The situation in Munich was said to be one of misery, terror and despair.[1] The dominant tone taken was that this was not simply an attack on Jews but an affront to fair thinking citizens of Europe. The subject of the horror felt at these events in Germany was raised in the House of Commons. Four MPs, three on the Labour benches and one independent – Philip Noel Baker, Josiah Wedgwood, George Lansbury and James Maxton – rose in turn. Each of them had consistently led the questioning in previous debates, and now sought clarification from Prime Minister Neville Chamberlain of the government's position and proposed response. The Prime Minister informed the House that sadly it appeared that the reports in the newspapers were substantially correct and had been corroborated in part, at least, by Goebbels himself.

Chamberlain was firm in his condemnation of both the murder of vom Rath and the German response but avoided all questions as to what action would be taken to help those in peril. He likewise avoided questions from these MPs as to whether measures would be adopted to allow Jews to enter either England or Palestine. The response was equally non-committal as regards shelter in some country in the Dominions or British Empire. What was made clear to the House in the course of the questions put to him, however, was that as many as 500,000 Jewish lives were at risk in Germany. Chamberlain in the main responded to the questions by saying he would need to have notice before answering them.

Later that afternoon the Foreign Secretary Lord Halifax convened a special meeting of the Cabinet's Committee on Foreign Policy.[2] No doubt everyone there had been brought up to speed as to the events of the previous Thursday and Friday, particularly what had taken place in Berlin and Vienna, the main centres of Jewish population. The Home Secretary Sir Samuel Hoare raised the question of whether or not any response should be made. Interestingly enough, perhaps by way of reflection on the debate in Parliament or from what he had read in the newspapers, he phrased the question in terms of the danger of matters getting out of control either in the House of Commons or in the country at large unless something were done. Hoare's first suggestion seemed a little unrealistic, that Britain should approach the United States and offer to surrender a part of its own unused quota for British migrants to the United States, which at that time was 60,000. That surrendered quota could then be used to allow increased Jewish migration to the United States. This was rejected in due course by the United States.[3] The quotas were not transferable. Chamberlain made it clear that he was anxious that measures be taken to 'alleviate the terrible fate of the Jews in Germany'. At this time, he anticipated that those measures would be taken in collaboration with the United States.

Tuesday 15 November 1938

At 5pm the next day in the corridors of Westminster, the Prime Minister received a delegation of leading figures from the Anglo-Jewish community to discuss ways in which practical action could be taken to allow the Jews of Germany and Austria to leave. The most senior political figure amongst them was Viscount Samuel, the Liberal peer, former Home Secretary and who as Herbert Samuel had served as former High Commissioner for Palestine 1920-25. Lord Samuel had since 1935 been the somewhat reluctant Chair of the Executive Council for German Jewry,[4] which had oversight of the relief effort undertaken in Germany. As he noted later in his memoirs, when he accepted the appointment, he had made it clear that it was for three months only. In the end, owing to the seriousness of the situation and his unique position both in domestic politics and the Jewish community, he ended up serving in this position for nearly four years.[5] He also led a number of delegations of the Executive Council to the US to discuss what could be done to assist, and in the course of such visits, had the ear of President Roosevelt and met Albert Einstein.[6] He had a good grasp not only of the state of affairs on the ground but also of the then existent relief efforts.

He was also a prominent political supporter of Chamberlain and Halifax's policy of appeasement. He was a supporter of the Munich

Agreement and the attempts made through negotiation to try to avoid war. No doubt this would have meant that some further weight was attached to his views. Chamberlain had also previously offered him a position in his cabinet, which he had declined. This political connection gave him access. As far as Lord Samuel was concerned, the solution to Hitler's aggression needed to be found in the League of Nations and not on the battlefields of Europe. It is not clear at this point whether Lord Samuel still held the view he apparently once confided to Lord Halifax in 1937: that he did not think Hitler, in contrast to Napoleon, would do anything that he knew to be a crime.[7] With Lord Samuel came Viscount Bearsted, Dr Hertz, the then Chief Rabbi, Lionel de Rothschild, Neville Laski and Dr Chaim Weizmann, who was the most prominent Zionist spokesman in the Anglo-Jewish community and went on to become the first President of the State of Israel.[8] This was clearly a heavyweight group.

The scale of the problem was made clear at the outset whilst at the same time the delegation accepted that there was little prospect of diplomatic intervention having any significant effect, something that Chamberlain made clear. They told the Prime Minister that the figure of 500,000 Jews being at risk given in Parliament was accurate and also confirmed the accuracy of the reports given in private papers from the Quakers. They asked the Prime Minister to focus efforts on assisting those who were in a position and of an age readily to leave Germany and Austria. This was estimated to be approximately 300,000 whose lives were in immediate peril.

The specific proposal which had up to that point been considered by the Prime Minister was the admission of German-Jewish orphans of up to five years of age, so long as they had homes found for them by the volunteer organisations and did not receive any support from public funds. Viscount Samuel pushed further and proposed that there be temporary admission for any child or young adult up to the age of 17 who would be provided with temporary shelter, given some re-training and then would be found a home elsewhere in the world. Lord Samuel stressed that the Jewish organisations involved in this effort would give a guarantee that no public funds would be called upon to feed, house or clothe the children.

Dr Weizmann then requested that up to 6,000 men who were held prisoner in terrible conditions in Dachau and Buchenwald concentration camps also be allowed to enter Palestine. The German authorities had told the American Quakers that they would be freed as long as they left Germany immediately. Finally, Lord Bearsted, a distinguished soldier from the First World War and son of the 1st Viscount who had founded Shell Transport and Trading, addressed the finances. Lord Bearsted said that his calculations showed it would cost at least £100 to evacuate one person and so if 300,000 were to leave the Reich as anticipated, then the total cost would be of the order of £30,000,000. Lord Bearstead inquired whether a government loan or even international aid brokered by Britain might be considered.[9] An extremely cold reception was given to the notion of 300,000 immigrants, whether on a temporary basis or not, or indeed any other financial assistance; the Prime Minister also gave no encouragement to the prospect of finding a place to settle such refugees within the British Empire.

According to a report from the Westminster lobby correspondent of the *Jewish Chronicle* 'big rumours' were circulating that the Prime Minister had given a firm commitment that no time would be lost in taking steps to help the Jewish refugees and that the government was willing in principle to agree to admit German-Jewish orphan children up to the age of five. [10] The account given in the newspaper of this confidential meeting was unusual. It might have been leaked deliberately in order to show the Jewish community that decisive action was being taken. Perhaps it was part of a strategy to put pressure on the government. It was in any event not without risk.

Wednesday 16 November
The matters raised had to be taken forward and discussed in Cabinet that afternoon. Much of course would turn on the approach of the Prime Minister, the Foreign Secretary and the Home Secretary. The issue of Jewish refugees was not on the Cabinet Agenda, but nevertheless it was raised early in the discussion as the fifth item by the Foreign Secretary.

Interestingly, his focus initially was on his discussions with the United States Ambassador, at the time Joseph Kennedy. The reaction to these events in the United States was both anti-German and anti-British. The predominant feeling expressed by Joseph Kennedy was that Britain was nearest to the storm, that it had control of Palestine but had not taken effective or sufficient steps to stop the persecution or to assist the Jews. No doubt Halifax's views were also affected by reports of Roosevelt also expressing his outrage at these attacks. Lord Halifax was concerned by this antithetic American reaction and considered that making some locality in the Empire available to Jewish refugees would be important 'from the political point of view'. Having said this, the Foreign Office was against the admission of such refugees. Roger Makins, who would in due course become Ambassador to Washington, had expressed the view in the Foreign Office on 10 November that the measures taken by Germany (confiscating all property) had rendered these people indigent and therefore made the admission of Jewish immigrants, 'from the economic point of view, less acceptable'.[11]

There then followed at Cabinet a fairly extensive survey from the Colonial Secretary Malcolm MacDonald of the possibilities for such a settlement area in Kenya, Northern Rhodesia, Tanganyika. The most promising was said to be in British Guiana, which could offer some prospect for a Jewish agricultural settlement in certain designated areas. This was not a promising sign as British Guiana had previously been rejected as a place of haven for the Christian Assyrian refugees fleeing in the aftermath of the First World War from the brutal and often murderous treatment meted out by the former Ottoman rulers. Chamberlain then informed those present of the meeting the previous day with Lord Samuel's delegation and emphasized the need for immediate action; 'time being of the essence in the matter'.

The last major contribution to the debate came from the Home Secretary who told Cabinet that more than a thousand applications by letter from those seeking permission to come to Britain were being received each day and that at present a central Co-ordinating Committee (of both Jewish and non-Jewish organisations) was processing them. Sir Samuel Hoare suggested to the Cabinet that no one, including the Anglo-Jewish community, was in favour of allowing large numbers of refugees into the country for fear of the process not being properly controlled and giving rise to anti-Semitic attacks. In the end, the Home Secretary felt that it might be possible to admit a limited number of young Jews for the purpose of agricultural training so that they could then be re-settled elsewhere and in addition a number of Jewish maidservants to replace those German nationals who had left the country since the onset of the crisis.

It will be obvious that the Home Secretary's vision of what might be achievable by way of assistance was far distant from what had been outlined in the *Jewish Chronicle* or what would be adopted and become known as the Kindertransport. He clearly needed some help on his road to Damascus. In the end the Cabinet concluded that suggestions for immediate action should be developed by Samuel Hoare, the Home Secretary, Malcolm MacDonald, the Secretary of State for the Colonies and Dominions, and Earl Winterton, the Chancellor of the Duchy of Lancaster.

Thursday 17 November
The next day the Executive Council for German Jewry met in Woburn House near the Euston Road and Lord Samuel reported on the meeting with the Prime Minister two days earlier. The tone of his report to the Committee was more realistic than that which had been leaked to the press. It was clear no specific proposal had been given the green light. Lord Samuel reported that the Prime Minister appreciated the difficulties of the situation and wished to help. He also told the Executive Council that the Government's Evian Conference Committee was already making inquiries as to whether territories in the British Empire could be made available to settle Jews from Germany. According to the Minutes of the Executive Council, the Prime Minister was also reported to have commented that any proposal for the grant of facilities to assist child refugees from Germany would be a matter for the Home Secretary, but that Chamberlain would himself support any such suggestion if it was approved by the Home Office.[12] Lord Bearsted at this meeting once more emphasised that financial assistance of one form or other would be required in order to make any scheme work.

Monday 21 November
The weekend fell between the Cabinet meeting on 16 November and the debate in Parliament on 21 November. There was therefore little time for any substantive change of mind on the part of Sir Samuel Hoare, let alone formulation of a new policy. Nevertheless, this is exactly what did happen.

The speeches given in the House of Commons on 21 November and the conclusion reached repay careful study. Those present in the House of Commons did not just want to grandstand and deliver fine words but rather demanded that specific measures be taken. It is about as good an example as can be found of a legislature working effectively and expeditiously together with charitable organisations. The Prime Minister spoke in the afternoon outlining the efforts which had been taken to date to assist in the refugee crisis.

In the evening Philip Noel Baker proposed a motion calling for a concerted effort amongst the nations including the United States to secure a common policy. Noel Baker spoke for nearly 45 minutes. He was an extraordinary individual, an Olympic athlete and prominent conscientious objector. He was also, like Sir Samuel Hoare, from a Quaker family. His speech spared no detail of the gruesome persecution of the Jews in Germany stretching back to 1933. He carefully exposed the myth of Kristallnacht being a spontaneous popular reaction to the murder of vom Rath. Instead, he informed the House it was a carefully orchestrated State Pogrom starting with the murder of seventy Jews held at the Buchenwald concentration camp a day before the death of vom Rath was even announced. The speech was clear about the need for action to save those Jews left in Germany and Austria. He called for collective action from all those who participated at the Evian Conference in June 1938. He concluded by referring to Goebbels' recent pronouncement that the outside world would soon forget the German Jews. He responded by saying that this conduct would go down in history as a lasting memory of human shame and asked the House; 'Let there go with it another memory, the memory of what the other nations did to wipe away the shame.'[13]

It was after 9.30pm when Sir Samuel Hoare stood to speak. There was little in the opening remarks of the Home Secretary's speech that gave a real indication of any change of policy. He made clear that nothing he said would touch on immigration to Palestine, which would be addressed in the separate debate in Parliament scheduled for 24 November. He also pointed out in some detail the manifold difficulties faced by the British authorities in receiving over a thousand visa applications a day and the need to maintain such a system to prevent chaos and undesirable immigrants. He also noted the strains on staff at the various Consulates, in particular in Vienna. He spoke of the schemes already in place for those who wished to come in with a domestic servant visa and those undertaking training in agricultural work preparing for re-settlement elsewhere. It was only towards the end of his one-hour speech that he came to refer to a meeting that he had held earlier that morning with a joint delegation of Lord Samuel and representatives of Christian organisations. Sir Samuel informed the House that the idea had been put forward at this meeting of the grant of a collective advance visa for 'non-Aryan children' arriving in the country, which would replicate the way in which many Belgian children were admitted during the First World War.

The Home Secretary indicated that he had welcomed this proposal, had profound sympathy with the harsh choice facing the parents of such children and commended that effort to the House. He emphasised first that it would be at no cost to the State and second that it was intended that the entry to the country would be temporary, that those arriving were not allowed to work or take jobs other than as domestics or in agriculture, and importantly that once it was safe for them to do so they would move back to Germany or on to other countries. The scheme he outlined was only temporary shelter and not a scheme for mass permanent migration. So it was, without any legislation being tabled and by a simple practical proposal, that the Kindertransport was born.

It seems at the meeting earlier that day, Lord Samuel had told the Home Secretary that a Co-Ordinating Committee consisting of both Jewish and Christian organisations would be responsible for bringing over such numbers of children whose maintenance could be guaranteed by those with financial means and would therefore not be a burden on the State. First, it would be the responsibility of philanthropists and well-wishers to raise the necessary monies; Lord Bearsted's original proposal that the State provide financial assistance or a loan was not pursued. Second, no limit was to be placed on the number of children. All depended upon the funds raised privately, the resources deployed by the voluntary organisations and of course the untested willingness of parents to part with their children.

In financial terms, this was a major departure from what had been raised with the Prime Minister earlier that week. Nevertheless, Lord Samuel appears to have read the situation well in terms of what was politically acceptable and achievable. In the end, the tabled proposal adopted by Parliament was remarkable, simple and above all a ground-up solution. All would depend upon the willingness and ability of people to come forward and help save the lives of total strangers. The families who took part, such as those of Sir David Attenborough and Lady Margaret Thatcher, would be forever changed.

There has been a good deal of informed speculation as to the precise point of persuasion of Sir Samuel Hoare, who only a few days ago had seemed reluctant to put forward any new scheme at all. Rightly,

much has been written about the role played by the Quakers behind
the scenes. As noted, Philip Noel Baker and Sir Samuel Hoare were
Quakers. Likewise, Bertha Bracey, another leading Quaker, was
involved in marshalling the response of the Christian relief effort and
informing the British Government of the dire situation in Germany.
It is unclear whether Philip Noel Baker himself spoke to Sir Samuel
Hoare proposing the idea of unaccompanied children being allowed
into the country under an organised scheme. Having said all this,
the role played by Lord Samuel himself cannot be understated. He
presented the essence of the scheme at his meeting earlier that day with
Sir Samuel Hoare with clarity and simplicity, he made an important
concession in terms of the scheme's finances, likewise presenting the
scheme as extending to all non-Aryan children irrespective of race
or religion was both important and humanitarian. He must take
enormous credit for his judgment and role in getting this scheme off
the ground.[14]

It is also necessary to refer to another midwife of this iconic moment
in British humanitarian history. This is the role played by Helen
Bentwich, who did not sit on Lord Samuel's Executive Committee on
the Council for German Jewry. Helen Bentwich was the daughter of
Arthur Franklin and so born into a prominent Anglo-Jewish family.
Her politics and social conscience took her in a very particular
direction. University educated, in her mid-twenties she volunteered to
work during the First World War in an armaments factory and was
appalled by the working conditions there, particularly for women.
She tried to form a trades union but was dismissed for her efforts.
This in turn led her to campaign throughout her life both for women's
rights and for the Labour Party. She stood twice unsuccessfully as a
Labour candidate at Westminster and then from 1934 was co-opted
onto what was then the London County Council. Yet Helen Bentwich
did have two very particular connections to the work of the Executive
Committee. First, she was the niece of Viscount Samuel and second,
she was married to Professor Sir Norman Bentwich, the former
Attorney General of Palestine and had accompanied him in Palestine
in the early days of the Mandate, writing a well-observed diary and
excellent memoir of her time there.[15]

At the meeting of the Executive Committee on 17 November, it
would appear from the Minutes that a Memorandum authored by
Helen Bentwich and another, Dennis Cohen, was circulated and

considered by the Executive. The specific proposal which was put forward was to assist in bringing over 5,000 refugee children of all ages and religious denomination from Germany to England, at first placing them in special camps and then ultimately accommodating them with foster parents throughout the country. They presented a convincing case that if the children were brought out of Germany, then homes would be found one way or other. The financial outlay of the scheme was estimated at £3,000 per week.[16] After discussion at the Executive on 17 November, a sub-committee was immediately set up under Lord Samuel to work through the practicality and cost. What seems to have happened is that Lord Samuel considered the proposal and finances carefully, calculated that it could be afforded privately, then presented a version of this plan to Sir Samuel Hoare on the morning of 21 November before the session later that day in Parliament.

There is further important corroboration of this in the records of the Quakers' Germany Emergency Committee, which state that on 21 November Lord Samuel went to see Sir Samuel Hoare with a delegation from the Quakers and presented to him a plan for the admission of 5,000 refugee children up to the age of 17 years of age who would enter the United Kingdom on a special travel document which did not require a visa and would be placed initially in camps and then placed in homes. As was emphasised by the Quakers, the scheme outlined and agreed to by Sir Samuel Hoare was not restricted to Jewish refugees but was open to all.[17] This does appear in all key respects to have been the plan presented by Helen Bentwich on 17 November 1938 and then subsequently accepted by the Home Secretary.

Sadly, my attempts to trace the Memorandum, the foundation document of the Kindertransport scheme, have not succeeded. Helen Bentwich's papers are kept at the LSE but do not detail her efforts in this regard and likewise the Minutes of the Executive Committee do not include the materials tabled at the meeting.

Thursday 24 November

At the previous debate in Parliament on 21 November, Sir Samuel Hoare had made it clear that he would not touch on immigration into Palestine, as this would be the matter for discussion later in the week. This was the province of Malcolm MacDonald, the Colonial

Secretary, who opened the debate that Thursday afternoon. He gave a remarkable speech not just for what it said but what it refused to address. The Colonial Secretary indicated that up until now he had been constrained in making any statement as Parliament as they had to await the Woodhead Commission Report, which had only just been published. There was, however, no recognition in the context of this particular debate of the terms of the League of Nations Mandate, which required Britain as the mandatory power to facilitate Jewish immigration into Palestine.[18] In one section of his address he referred to the numbers of Jews who had previously come to make Palestine their home; in 1933 it was 30,000, in 1934, 42,000 Jews came to Palestine, and in 1935, the number was 61,000.

> The Arabs wonder when a halt is going to be called to this great migration. They wonder whether a halt is ever going to be called to it, and they fear that it is going to be their fate in the land of their birth to be dominated economically, politically, completely. If I were an Arab, I would be alarmed.

Macdonald made no commitment whatever concerning further migration to Palestine even on an emergency basis to alleviate the immediate present peril faced by hundreds of thousands in Germany. He made no attempt to address why saving the lives of Jewish children from the Nazis would imperil or adversely affect the rights or position of any other person living in Palestine at that time. Herbert Morrison, a prominent Labour MP, responded to the speech and noted that there was no proposal to save even one Jewish life from the horrors encountered in Europe through admittance into Palestine. Morrison then directly challenged the Colonial Secretary to allow into Palestine 10,000 Jewish children at risk in Europe whom the Jews of Palestine had made clear they would pay for and support themselves. Morrison then analysed the impracticality of the government's proposal to establish a settlement in British Guiana. The then existing Government policy was to allow migration in accordance with economic absorptive capacity. He pointed out that there was a shortage in Palestine of over 20,000 workers for the forthcoming orange picking season and wondered why such labour could not come from those in fear for their life in Europe.[19] There were important contributions to the debate from others, including Winston Churchill. There were those from the

Conservative benches who indicated that the rise of Zionism was a factor in the rise of anti-Semitism, something sternly rejected by those on the Labour benches.[20]

The outcome of the debate in terms of government policy was in complete contrast to that witnessed on Monday three days earlier. The doors to Palestine would not be opened. Permission for the admission into Palestine of 10,000 children from Germany was refused. Likewise, Dr Weizman's plea for the rescue of 6,000 men being held in Dachau and Bunchenwald concentration camps in Germany was also denied. President Roosevelt had given his strong support for the proposal of the admission of the children into Palestine as a humanitarian gesture.

In this critical week the government's policy had given with one hand but taken away with the other. With the complete lack of progress since the Evian Conference in June, the only place where a significant number of Jews could be taken in those critical months was obviously Palestine. This policy shift and its subsequent rigid enforcement was finally recognized in 2019 as a 'black moment' in British history by Sir Jeremy Hunt as British Foreign Secretary.[21] The effect on the rest of my family trapped in Vienna would all too soon be felt.

18

Safe Shores

There was little time between the announcement of the Kindertransport scheme in the House of Commons on 21 November 1938 and Judy's departure from Vienna. Thousands of names must have been put forward by anxious parents and relatives. Some kind of selection then had to be made for individual transports and once families were informed there was no time to say goodbye.

The first train left Berlin on 2 December. A week later just under 700 children left Vienna, all organised with the help of the irrepressible Quaker volunteer Gertruda Wijsmuller, or Tanta Truus, as she was frequently called. She was the personification of the work undertaken by the Quakers and her extraordinary efforts in rescuing so many before and during the War were recognised when she became amongst the first to be given the distinction of Righteous Gentile by the state of Israel. After that, smaller transports were organised in mid- to end December 1938. My mother was put on the next train out of Vienna with a group of little over fifty girls. In fact, it was rare, contrary to popular imagery, for a whole train to be taken and filled by the Kindertransport. More often than not, a single carriage here and there was booked up and as a rule, particularly in the early days, the children would leave from the inconspicuous surroundings of the suburban station at Hutteldorf and not from the Westbahnhoff station in the centre of Vienna which today houses the memorial to those children who left in such heartrending circumstances.

How did my grandparents reach the almost impossible decision to send their only daughter to a foreign country by herself? How did my mother get onto the list of those lucky to escape and be saved? I tried to find some answers as I trawled through what remained of my grandparents' papers and forms preserved in the archives.

After many hours' scrutiny of the files I had copied so hurriedly in Washington, the first concrete clue was an entry dated 9 November 1938, on the eve of Kristallnacht. It seemed that my grandfather, no doubt after weeks of effort, at long last had made something of a breakthrough for the entire family. There is a record of one Julius Lobl registering himself with the Aktion Gildemeester, or Gildemeester Organisation, for emigration to Shanghai. The opening line refers to 2½ passengers, presumably a reference to a child fare counting as half.

The Gildemeester Organisation was established by a Quaker pastor of that name who had been active in Germany and Austria after the First World War in times of great economic hardship. He was given permission to stay in Vienna by the Nazis to assist in the emigration of the Jewish population and was active in assisting non-orthodox or unaffiliated Jews, many of whom came from marriages of a Jew and a Christian. The particular focus of his work was to assist emigration to certain remote countries or destinations that had not yet placed strict barriers against immigration and as a result saved the lives of many thousands. He charged money to the richer families for their assistance and distributed that money to indigent families. At this time, there were really only two destinations under active consideration: Shanghai and Paraguay. The South American country was one of the few nations to stand up at the Evian Conference and permit the admission of Jews.

Shanghai was at the time under Japanese military occupation, but a small area in the Hongkou District became home to a significant number of Jewish immigrants from 1933 onwards. Today there is a small museum exhibit in the former synagogue of Shanghai dedicated to this almost forgotten piece of history. The largest single source of that migration was Vienna. Following the Anschluss in March 1938, the rumour spread that there was one place on earth where you could go as a Jew without the need for any visa or specific authorization, and that was Shanghai. What is more, there were no relevant age limits or restrictions as to category of immigrant, as was the position under the rules applicable in Britain. More than 20,000 took advantage of this exit route, including members of my wife Denise's family. Although this is twice the number saved under the Kindertransport, very little is remembered of this extraordinary act of generosity. The living conditions there were said to be harsh, but famously it could boast the highest concentration of musical instrument teachers on the planet. After the war, most moved on to other destinations and today only a thousand or so Jews live in Shanghai, hardly any descending from those who arrived during that period. A visit to the old Jewish quarter today in Shanghai is a curious distraction from the art deco splendour of the Bund and glittering high rise buildings which dominate the skyline across the Huangpu River.

Closer examination of the Washington files appeared, however, to show some inexplicable details. The reference to the application made in November 1938 to go to Shanghai was made by Julius Lobl, whose date of birth is given as 1898 and not 1896, the actual year of my grandfather's birth. At first, I thought that this was just a mistake, an understandable error in the recording of his age. On another page, however, Julius Lobl identified his wife as Marie Antoinette and his daughter as Gerda. This was a lot harder to digest and come to terms with. On my return to London from Washington, I found myself sitting round the kitchen table going through this line by line and wondering how on earth this extraordinary family secret could have been kept from me all these years. I had remembered the vague outline of a story that there was a second marriage and second set of children in Julya's family but from what I had been told that was surely Julya's father, not Julya himself.

None of this made any sense. I was frankly quite at a loss to think that Julya had somehow made arrangements to leave Vienna with another woman and child with such exotic sounding names that, let's face it, did not sound Jewish. As far as I knew, Julya and Terci were tightly bound to one another, and Julya was no bigamist. My head was spinning with a series of wild thoughts and for a short while I even played around with the fantasy of having a secret second family and dozens of relatives in Shanghai.

What in fact seems to have happened was a good deal more prosaic. In the confusion of the long line of anxious applicants and the overwhelming quantity of paperwork and demands on the *Israelitsche Kultusgemeinde*, it had simply allowed some of the papers of a man with the same name, with a wife and single daughter, to become mixed up in the file of Julya my grandfather. This second and marginally younger Julius Lobl appears to have been due to board a ship leaving on 7 December 1938. The Gildemeester Organisation agreed to advance 375 RM (about £30) with a balance of 425 RM to be covered presumably by the *Kultusgemeinde*. This Julius' wife, Marie Antoinette Lobl, appears to have gone with him on this journey to safety together with their child Gerda. There is no record of them amongst the victims of the Holocaust. They would appear to have all left together for Shanghai and been saved through the efforts of the Quakers.

In the end, the answer to my original question as to how my mother came to be separated from the family and how she left Vienna was depressingly simple. Following the events of Kristallnacht my grandparents were desperate. They had to find some way of getting my mother out of Austria there and then, even if it meant that she was all alone. No doubt some time from late November to early December 1938, the possibility of emigration to England on the Kindertransport would have become widely publicized in Vienna. It would have been seen by my grandparents as the best option and would at least potentially allow my mother to leave Austria with her cousin, Ruth. Judy and Ruth had grown up together as sisters, both being only children.

Nevertheless, it was of course a tough choice. It would split up each family. It involved sending the two young girls to England without knowing how it would be possible for any of the rest to escape. Rescuing the lives of the young girls would almost certainly involve a price being paid. Julya himself had next to no chance of being allowed into England. The only categories of immigrant that were at this time allowed to enter the country were children under 17 years of age, full-time students, domestic servants or agricultural workers. Although my grandmother Terci could and ultimately did work as a domestic servant, clearly Julya did not fit into any of these categories. Nor did Ruth's father, Jeno. This was the hardest of decisions to make. Nonetheless it was made. As is recorded on his file, in his neat script, my grandfather informed the *Israelitische Kultusgemeinde* that his child, referred to formally as Judith, would leave separately on the Kindertransport and that he and his wife would remain in Vienna under the supervision and care of the community whilst continuing to seek a means to leave. Writing these words, he must have feared that he was also quite possibly sealing his own fate.

How did my mother get to be amongst those selected to be saved? The answer to this is linked with two extraordinary individuals, one living in Vienna and the other in London: Julius Steinfeld and Rabbi

Solomon Schonfeld. By a remarkable quirk of fate, Rabbi Schonfeld not only saved my mother but quite separately my father within a year of one another, the first from Vienna and the second from Germany. Typical of his ingenuity and energy, Rabbi Schonfeld in March 1939 took out an advertisement in a Frankfurt newspaper to seek students to study full time at a yeshiva in Manchester with immediate effect. My father, no doubt scouring the newspapers even at a young age saw this notice, responded and was granted permission to enter England just months before war broke out and borders were closed.

In November 1938, Julius Steinfeld was in his early to mid-fifties, and was the head of the orthodox Agudas Yisroel community to which my mother's family belonged. Julius Steinfeld worked out of offices in the same building that my mother and her parents were living in and so presumably they were able to knock on his door without fuss. Julius Steinfeld was a remarkable man in many ways, steady and brave as you like. Short in stature, he was a businessman but devoted all of his considerable spare energies to the rescue of those caught up in the maelstrom. After the *Anschluss* he had already been arrested and interrogated by Eichmann and so was well acquainted with the dangers involved in his work. Much of his work involved risk, particularly in obtaining entry visas from countries by unorthodox methods.[1] Even after the war began and most exit routes were blocked, he stayed behind in Vienna at enormous personal risk to distribute whatever aid he could. He only left the country in mid-1941 when he had been tipped off that he would be arrested once more. He managed to escape to Cuba where he stayed for two years before emigrating to the United States.[2]

One of the first people Steinfeld wrote to after he heard of the announcement of the Kindertransport operation was an acquaintance of his in London, Rabbi Solomon Schonfeld, whose parents had been born in Central Europe and came from the same strict orthodox tradition.[3] Steinfeld knew that Schonfeld was heavily engaged in the attempts to save those trapped in Nazi Europe and had been raising the desperate plight of the Burgenland Jews since April 1938 with anyone who would listen in Britain. Rabbi Schonfeld was barely half Steinfeld's age. They must have made a strange pair. Schonfeld was in his mid-twenties, a tall, imposing six-footer, ex-British Army. What Schonfeld and Steinfeld shared, however, was that each hated red tape, each had boundless determination to get things done themselves rather than ask others to do the work, and no shortage of ingenuity.[4]

Schonfeld immersed himself in the detail of every aspect of the relief effort, whether it was arrangement of the transportation; or personal guarantees, or the organisation of holding camps or accommodation in foster families. Everyone said of him he never stopped and that it was by no means unusual for people to receive a knock on the door from him after midnight asking for a special favour.[5] Steinfeld did well to get hold of Schonfeld and ask for his help.

Without further thought, Schonfeld, departed London for Vienna as soon as he was asked.[6] Schonfeld may not have seen it this way, but it was a brave thing to do in the immediate aftermath of Kristallnacht to leave the safety of London as a readily identifiable orthodox Rabbi and travel to Nazi-occupied Vienna for the sole purpose of assisting Jews to escape. The Foreign Office advised him not to travel to the Reich.[7] Rabbi Schonfeld and Julius Steinfeld organised the first trains to leave Vienna. Many of those on these first lists would one way or other have been associated with my grandparents' synagogue community, the Schiffshul.

The next thing was to track down the details of the particular transport that took my mother to freedom. This required a little more digging and a return to Vienna. The lists of those who fled Vienna on the Kindertransport are still kept in the archives of the Jewish community in a little office of the *Israelitische Kultusgemeinde* on the second floor of a quiet but well-guarded building at the rear of the Seitenstettengasse synagogue in the First District. I was not sure what I would find in their files but after some email exchanges, I arranged to see the archivists. The only time they could see me was midday and so I killed some time first thing by going to see the Kindertransport bronze at the Westbahnoff train station. The memorial is found in the middle of a busy train station built long after the war and consists of a small boy sitting on a plinth wearing a distinctly non-period pair of trainers and hoodie. I was not at all sure what connection, if any, the many passers-by would make with the events of the past, but no matter. I then made my way to my appointment.

They checked me out first, my bona fides and the relationship to those I was inquiring after, and then gave me a four-page document, suitably anonymised. It was handed to me as if it were an everyday form available at a Post Office counter for some kind of permit. It was the full passenger list of one of the very first of the Kindertransports to leave Vienna. My eyes scanned the pages eagerly, and there it was, my mother's name, address and date of birth.

Judy was part of a transport of girls organised by Agudas Yisroel, leaving Vienna on Sunday 18 December 1938, the day after her birthday. In that moment as I held this piece of paper I suddenly understood and felt some of the vulnerability behind what I had always seen as a very confident exterior. My mother must have associated her birthday with separation. A painful parting from her mother and father in circumstances when it would have been all too obvious that they may never be reunited. I have little doubt now that this would explain the rising tension and anxiety that she felt as her birthday approached each year. It was one of the fundamental features of my mother's personality, that celebration had to be tempered, moderated because of the fear of what lay just around the corner.

Understandably, and for as long as I could remember, my mother never enjoyed her birthdays. For so many years I was convinced that this was part of her not very complex relationship with age and ageing. In essence, she hated both with an equal passion. As with many others of that generation, her age was a closely guarded secret. A matter neither discussed nor disclosed. Big birthdays ending in a zero simply did not get celebrated. They were buried and not mentioned. She propelled herself forward with a vital energy rarely seen in others. She always looked immaculate and would be seen marching at great pace up or down any of the streets of Marylebone in Central London, walking to and from work every day and then off each evening to fulfil a dizzying social calendar. Her most recognisable feature was her magnificently coiffed blonde hair, all held together with a hair spray of industrial strength which had to withstand considerable gravitational force as she sped from here to there. She was a mentor and inspiration to a whole younger generation of women, having herself always combined motherhood and work. I do not think any alternative ever occurred to her.

After my mother passed away, understandably many official records had to be submitted and the large proportion of these required a statement of the deceased's date of birth. Obviously, I knew her birthday was 17 December, but I cannot recall the actual year of her birth being something that was ever openly mentioned. At least not to me. I think this was intricately tied up with her arrival in England on the Kindertransport. The fact that she had come to this country this way was not itself hidden, but it was an awkward discussion for my mother and best avoided. Any person arriving in England as a child in 1938 must have been at least a certain age. So, my mother would when talking about the subject, a rare enough occasion, often emphasise that she was one of the very youngest to arrive in this country on those trains and that as she was so young, she had no real memory of it. This also enabled her to avoid any lengthy discussion of her being born in another country, which she found to be an embarrassing topic. Indeed, a number of her friends had no idea that she was not born in England -- something she was particularly proud of. I was pretty sure that my mother had told me she was born in 1934 or 1935 and so was only three or four when she left Vienna. In fact, as was confirmed on the Kindertransport records shown to me, she was actually born on 17 December 1932. A gentle touch of vanity on her part, disguising her age to the end, even to her own offspring.

So my grandparents would have put on some form of birthday celebration for my mother on 17 December 1938 and then made sure she was ready for her trip to England the very next day. I assume that they would have forced a smile and told Judy how lucky she was to go to England, that she would be with children her own age and that they would all follow shortly. There was a packing list given out to the parents of each child. It identified what was required for the journey and new life awaiting them and consisted of two extensive columns stating each item of clothing from pullovers to coats, from pyjamas and handkerchiefs to socks and shoes. Each mother was required to fill in the form and sign off that they had packed the suitcase for their child and confirmed the contents.

In 2019, marking the 80th Anniversary of the end of the Kindertransport operation, a small but moving exhibition was put on in Vienna. The central theme of the exhibition was focused on the suitcase itself. Each survivor or relative of a survivor was asked to identify an item that had been brought in their suitcase which they had retained. There were only a dozen or so exhibits, but each told its own tale, some with a connection to someone left behind, or with their religion, or with their new life in England. I never asked my mother if she had retained anything from her own suitcase, but I am certain that she had not. Not only were the memories hard for her but there was another reason; a shortage of possessions for her to have kept. Judy was not only a refugee from Vienna, but she was a refugee in Vienna.

She had had the most of her clothes and possessions taken from her before she left Lackenbach. In the weeks after the Anschluss in March 1938, the family house and shop was taken away from them and their possessions confiscated. On 1 July 1938, an inventory was compiled by the authorities in Lackenbach of all the items that had been taken away. I found this amongst the papers held in the archives at Eisenstadt; it includes my mother's dolls. As with everything itemized there, each had a value ascribed to it. The largest doll was said to be worth 40 pfennig, the other two 10 pfennig each.

Each child slated to leave on the Kindertransport had to undergo a test to see if he or she was suitable for the journey and was given two pages of printed instructions for the journey, a long prescription of dos and don'ts. There were definitely more don'ts than dos. The children were told under no circumstances could they open windows or doors, change places with anyone, leave their seat on the train or lean out of the windows. These young girls were strictly forbidden from playing cards or smoking. They were told that the older children should help the younger ones get dressed in the morning and go to bed at night. On arrival in England, they were told they had to carry their red permit around their neck so that it was visible; and above all were told of the need to be quiet and peaceful with all officials at all times.

As it happens, my mother was the very youngest child for that particular transport. Clearly, she would have needed help from an older girl. Immediately below her name on the manifest was that of her cousin, Rosa Lobl, who also came from Lackenbach. She was the daughter of Benno and Elsa Lobl. Benno was a shoemaker in the village. Rosa was about 2½ years older than my mother and the address given for her was the same as my mother, Gross Schiffgasse, 6, Vienna. So, it seems that these two young girls were selected by those in charge to travel together from the same house and no doubt Rosa as the older of the two was tasked with helping my mother, a child of barely six. My mother did talk of the kindness of the older girls who helped her in this traumatic journey, but strangely enough I do not recall her ever mentioning Rosa Lobl by name. Maybe this was yet another example of memory erasure. I found from the records held in Vienna that Rosa emigrated to Canada after spending the war in England. Her older brother who also escaped on the Kindertransport enlisted with the British Army and was killed in action. Like so many others, Rosa did not see her parents again.

I did ask my mother many times about the journey leaving Vienna. Maybe the trauma was too great and the farewell too painful. To say the least, she was not good at looking back and she had been very young. She simply said she could not really remember anything except for the frenetic goodbyes outside the station, the promises that her parents would soon join her. She did add one further detail, the sort of thing perhaps that only a child would remember. Her parents sought to ensure that she would have some emergency funds with her. So my grandmother sewed some money into the lining of her coat and told my mother never to take off her coat or leave it anywhere. Not a bad strategy. There were many stories of Nazi Guards moving up and down the trains taking whatever they felt they could get away with.

There was a further twist in the tale. I am sure that my grandparents would have done everything they could to ensure that Judy and Ruth would be together on the same train. For whatever reason, however, this proved impossible. They had to be separated. My mother was the first to leave, and Ruth left a day or so later. Ruth's train made its way through Germany and then stopped at the Dutch border. As with all the transports, there were inspections at the border and Ruth remembers that the older girl who had been specially designated to look after her on the journey was taken off the train by the German border guards who said she looked too old to qualify for such a transport of children and was not allowed to continue onto England. That girl was not heard of again.

According to the immigration stamp, my mother arrived at Harwich on Christmas Eve 1938. Given that she left Vienna on 18 December, the interval is explained by the fact that groups of passengers generally collected in a holding camp in Holland for a few days before setting out across the English Channel. Her Home Office Permit Number was no. 1818. The immigration stamp stated: 'Leave to land granted at Harwich this day on condition that the holder does not enter any employment paid or unpaid while in the United Kingdom.'

Two images survive of this escape. One was published of Ruth's arrival at Liverpool Street in the *Daily Express* of 24 December 1938 under the strap line; 'Hello England.' Ruth does look mightily relieved at her arrival. She does also seem quite weighed down by a thick coat. I do not know whether Ruth's parents similarly sewed money into the lining, but if they had done, it could have accommodated a fair sum without detection. There is also a photograph of my mother in her file at the National Archives in Kew. It is found tucked away at the very back of one of the many buff-coloured folders found there. In common with many images seen today of exhausted refugees arriving on these shores, it shows a concerned looking young girl staring blankly without emotion at the camera for the purposes of the official documentation. It was distressing to see how far she had changed from the somewhat cheeky face that met the eye in the larger group photograph taken earlier that year. This was quite a loss of innocence in a short period of about six months.

The Kindertransport children were in broad terms divided into two categories, Guaranteed and Non-guaranteed. The first category consisted of those for whom a sponsor family had already been found. This was sometimes a relative or a family connection. More commonly though, it was a family that had responded to the urgent national appeal which Lord Samuel had made on the BBC World Service on 25 November 1938. The Non-guaranteed children had to be found a home and would be supported through the efforts of the Chief Rabbi's Religious Emergency Council, the Central British Fund and the work of the Co-ordinated Committee, principally Jewish and Quaker organisations. Judy fell into this second category. These children were accordingly given temporary shelter, in my mother's case at a Butlins camp at Dovercourt, until foster families could be found. I don't know for certain, but this was probably my mother's only trip to a Butlins Camp. Judy stayed there for just shy of two weeks until 4 January 1939.[8] I tracked down Rabbi Schonfeld's papers recording his work at this time at the archives in Southampton University. A three-page document there tells its own little story. It is a typed list of names of refugees and the addresses of families who had agreed to take them. Except in my mother's case there is no typed entry. When she arrived in England she had nowhere to go. A host family had to be found and until then she had to stay behind at Dovercourt. Rabbi Schonfeld must have succeeded in the end with his great powers of persuasion, as he has written my mother's name in hand in cobalt blue ink with capital letters and next to it the address of the family who had agreed to take in this fragile stranger. This was the Laskey family at 56 Otto Terrace in Sunderland, who agreed to shelter Rosa Lobl as well. Ruth arrived in England just a few days later but did not go with Judy. Instead, she went to live for a while with a family at 11, Tallack Road E.10. Almost certainly the family who had agreed to shelter my mother simply had no space for a third girl.

The children at Dovercourt were looked after and given such medical care as they needed. One of those who saw the children was Mrs Hardistry:

> They had endured over a long period of time and in increasing severity such physical and mental suffering as had stolen their childhood from them. They were often old beyond their years, sometimes dreadfully experienced, always troubled and disturbed. It was not only that at short notice they were torn from the people they loved and trusted, and the places they knew; it was not only that suddenly they were bereft of all sense of security – these blows had been preceded by long periods of unhappiness and fear.[9]

These remarks would no doubt have had most relevance to those children from Germany who had faced persecution since Hitler's rise in 1933. Nevertheless, some part of this I believe applied to all those who arrived in these circumstances. Mrs Hardistry's report continues to refer to the difficulties some encountered when they went to school; many being set apart and deliberately humiliated. I do not know whether my mother experienced anything like this, but I do know that she made a conscious decision not to speak German ever again, to lose all hint of any German accent and to assimilate in the life of her country of adoption, which she loved with an almost obsessive passion.

There is an envelope addressed to my mother from this time that I found amongst her papers. It looked like it had been opened carefully with a paper knife, presumably so as not to damage its contents. The letter was sent by registered post with a Viennese date stamp of 14 March 1939. It was sent by my grandmother from Lilienbrungasse in Vienna's 2nd District. It was sent to my mother care of the Lasky family, at 56, Otto Terrace, Sunderland. My mother kept this envelope for over seventy years. It must have been an extraordinary event when it arrived. Nevertheless, the letter inside the envelope is not there. The letter has been separated from the envelope. Maybe my mother just kept the letter separately somewhere in her papers and I have just never been able to locate it. More likely, the letter has long since been lost, but the envelope itself was precious to her. A reminder of what she received when she was alone and more than a little lost without her parents. The date of the letter would be consistent with my grandmother telling my mother that she hoped she would soon be coming to join her in England.

True to her word, Terci went about getting permission to come to England straight away. On 4 January 1939 she was issued with a German passport No 71309 with all its Nazi insignia and a 'J' identifying her as Jewish. Presumably it was the first passport she had. On 6 April 1939 she was granted permission to come to England on a domestic servant visa. Her application for a permit was strongly supported by the *Israelitische Kultusgemeinde* in Vienna: 'The applicant Theresa is a practising Jew who has been in Vienna for a year and had to leave her business in Lackenbach without any remuneration. The petitioner was also a teacher in needlework in many Jewish schools in the Burgenland.' There would then have been more goodbyes to those she left behind in Vienna. She arrived at Harwich on 14 April 1939 and went straight to Sunderland to be with my mother.

It seems that Ruth and Judy were then reunited in Sunderland in the summer of 1939 after Julci managed to escape Vienna in the very last weeks of July, just before war broke out. She was indeed fortunate to get to Britain just as the shutters were coming down. All four of them were reunited for a short while before the girls were separated once more from their mothers during the Blitz. They were evacuated to a village near to Darlington and lived with a blacksmith and his wife for about a year or so. These arrangements allowed Terci and Julci to find work in Leeds and in due course for all four of them once more to live together in Leeds once it was safe to do so.

There is a note of the Chief Rabbi's Religious Emergency Council recording a visit to my grandmother in January 1944 in Leeds. Terci and Julci were by that time said to be in charge of a kosher boarding house for the orthodox Jewish community at 85, Chapeltown Road, Leeds. My mother and Ruth were with them. The note of the visit records that the girls were doing well at school and were thriving in a happy family atmosphere. By the end of the War, Terci and Julci had moved to Southport and had turned to the only business they really knew, another kosher boarding house.

This was very much a female-run household. This was perhaps the single dominant influence throughout my mother's life. The women lived strong, independent lives, they ran their own show and did not simply provide a support function to men. This was unusual at the time, but the circumstances were also atypical. Husbands were absent, brothers likewise. Max was in Palestine and Oskar who managed to reach England just before war broke out was at first interned as an enemy alien at Kitchener's Camp, Near Sandwich in Kent. He only obtained his release by volunteering to work at the Jaguar plant in Coventry and was lucky to survive its bombing in November 1940. Throughout the war personal news was scarce and received with great trepidation. My mother recalls as a young girl sitting at the top of the stairs and hearing Terci and Julci whispering in German, in the hope that the kids would not understand, about some letter received or snippet of news from overseas.

Terci and Julci ran the enterprise together and the core of the business was their expertise in the kitchen. There would have been many who had heard about but never tasted a full Viennese menu. For all this to have been produced under the strict rules of kashrut would have been unthinkable for many at that time living in England. My mother and Ruth had to help out at peak holiday season such as Passover. This would involve preparing the mixture for and then baking dozens of the traditional wheat-free cakes and biscuits for the festival. Paying guests, mostly orthodox Jews, came from far and wide to discover it for themselves. The hotel itself was frequently full, so others would stay at nearby lodging and come for mealtimes just to taste their legendary cooking. Guests were mainly drawn from Liverpool, Manchester and the nearby towns. They came in eager anticipation and with good appetite.

I can recall as a child the great theatre of Terci and Julci stretching out the pastry dough over the kitchen table in Southport as part of the elaborate preparations for their legendary apple strudel. The smell of their baking throughout the hotel as it was being prepared could drive those of the most equable disposition to distraction. The same was true of their Guglhupf, a round creation with a hole in the middle, the hazelnut and vanilla Kipferl biscuits, the Zwetschgenknoedel (plum dumplings) and their poppy seed cake, made using a more brioche-like dough, which many years later I discovered was called a Pressburger, and no doubt a recipe passed on through many generations. The punters voted with their stomachs and most of them returned regularly for the next twenty-five or so years. When my grandmother died, an elderly Rabbi stood and delivered the eulogy (*hespah*). There were of course scholarly references aplenty as befitting the occasion. What I remember, however, were the tears in his eyes as he recalled her culinary skill.

19

Max's Diary[1]

We are now over 750 on board the *Eli*, 13 November 1938. There are so many of us crammed into the bunk beds below the decks that it is only really bearable when the seas are calm. The bunks are stacked three high and if I get up too quickly, I hit my head on the bed above me. The lowest is barely above the wood plank decking and the top beds are reached by wooden ladders. I am in the middle bunk and feel quite claustrophobic. We are each given a round metal bowl for food and another for water. We have to keep these at all times beside our bed attached to two little hooks. We have been told that there are no spares if we lose them.

14 November
The nights are extremely cold and we only have a thin grey blanket each. If the weather is rough, we hear endless moans and screams from those both above and below us. There is no comfort in the night. It is only when the morning light appears through the heavy tarpaulin covering the top of the cargo space that we all manage to calm ourselves. We have asked the *Madrichim* (group leaders) to try to install a makeshift electric light bulb to make the nights easier for everyone. We will see what happens.

15 November
We pass through the Bosphorus, with Istanbul in the distant shoreline. I was lucky to be on deck at the time, but we were quickly ushered below once more so as not to be seen.

16 November

There are many rules on board. We have a daily assembly in the accommodation hold and Targanksy gives us our orders. He has told us repeatedly that these instructions are not only for our safety, but also for the Captain and his crew who are risking their lives for us on this voyage. The *Betarim* are used to this kind of discipline. It is harder for others. Each section is allocated a specific time to go on deck to wash and take air but only when it is considered safe. We must not be observed from sea or air. We are given a small amount of water to wash ourselves with. We laugh that each day the water seems to get murkier and less suitable for the job of cleaning anything. We have daily activities organised to prepare us for our eventual arrival. We have now all learnt the *Af Al Pi* song. There are Hebrew lessons and also occasional talks about the challenges of the life we can expect in Eretz.[2]

17 November

A wedding on deck, a Chupah on the seas. A big celebration and we all dressed in our *Betar* uniform. As we prepared to go down below again, we think we can see the Island of Rhodes in the distance and then Simi. I was told that there is a Jewish community there, more ancient than any in Europe.

22 November

We are now waiting in an anchorage for a smaller boat to take us on the last part of the journey. The waiting is painful and frustrating. In the early evening we saw another vessel which I think is called the *Kasterborge Caledonia* come towards us with 360 people on board, who had tried but failed to reach Eretz at the first attempt.

23 November

This really is a low moment for us all. We are now 920 people on board the *Eli*. We had to take another 180 of the 360 who had travelled on the *Kasterborge Caledonia*. We have been told that they will only be with us on board for a short time whilst their ship makes a second attempt to land the *Ha'ma'apilim*[3] and then return to us. It is just so crowded and airless. The only good thing is that the weather was much better today.

24 November

We waited. Weather has now turned a bit stormy.

25 November
Friday. Waiting again. In the evening we celebrated Shabbat with a service.

26 November
Shabbat morning. Service with a sermon. In the evening we were told the good news that another ship was coming towards us to help us get to Eretz and land on the shore there.

27 November
Sunday. 210 people taken from the *Eli* onto a smaller ship. Lovely weather. Our turn will come next.

29 November
We are still waiting.

30 November
At 9am the ship we have been waiting for arrives to take us. But we are told there is only room for 214 of us. So no luck for me and many others.

1 December
We moved position to a safer place.

4 December
Very stormy weather. The waiting and the weather are now unbearable.

10 December
Very stormy. Many people are suffering.

12 December
Again, all excitement as a ship arrives to take us off from the *Eli*. But the weather is so bad it could not safely move alongside our ship. Everyone is complaining. Targansky told us that the Captain of the *Eli* is as unhappy as we are. The Captain has to go back to Europe now with or without us.

13 December
Early in the morning another large ship [CSR *Romania?*] came alongside us. This had another 750 people who had come from

Wien and were also going to Eretz under the same organisation. We transferred from the *Eli* to their ship so that we can wait together for the arrival of the smaller craft to take us to Eretz. We say an emotional goodbye to the *Eli* as she sails away from us back to the Black Sea.

15 December

Finally, our ship arrives to take us to Eretz. We transfer to this much smaller boat but it takes a long time in rough seas. Then the weather got worse and so we had to wait yet another night.

16 December

At last, better weather and this has allowed us to set our course for Eretz.

17 December

We are nearing the shore. There is also an almost unbearable excitement on board amongst us. As the sun set we thought we could see land and everyone on board began to sing the *Hatikva*.[4] Then we were told that we had to obey complete silence and that anyway this was our imagination as we were still far from landfall. Targansky's discipline to the end is impressive.

18 December

For once, not one person could feel the cold in the night. Finally, in the early light we really could clearly see land. At exactly 8.45 in the morning I took my first steps on the shore of our beautiful homeland. We had arrived at last. We were hurriedly taken by buses waiting for us in side-streets to a nearby Kibbutz that grows oranges. I could smell the beautiful blossom everywhere. Each bus was sent off to a different Kibbutz and I did not recognize many of the faces who ended up with me on our bus. How strange. We had been together for over 40 days and nights but only really spoke to those immediately next to you or below you in the area of your bunk.

I came into the communal dining room for an early supper at sunset. There on the dining table was a *Menorah* with two candles ready to be lit. The Kibbutz gave me the honour to light the candles and celebrate the first night of the festival of Chanukah. For the first time since I had left Wien, the tears ran down my cheeks, uncontrollably and without stopping.

PART FOUR
LIFE AND DEATH

20

Stripped Bare

In December 1938, Julya faced his own difficult choices. Both options and time were running out and everyone knew that the family would have to be split up. He could not himself get to England. As a forty-year-old village shopkeeper he was not eligible for a visa and his most important priority was to ensure that Terci could rejoin my mother and fulfil the promises made as they said goodbye in Vienna.

As each day went by, the situation became more dangerous. Arrests were made on the slightest pretext and this was accompanied by an endless cycle of rumour. Everyone talked about who was going to be next. It was said those who had fought in the Austrian army in the First World War were liable to be arrested as they might pose some kind of security threat. It was equally speculated that this was an exempt category who would definitely not be arrested, as a gesture of thanks to those who had served. Julya had in fact been enlisted in the First World War, but from what little I was told, his position and rank were modest, relating to logistics, and could hardly have weighed heavily with respect to either proposition.

Then it was whispered that those who owed money to the State were the next to be rounded up. There were also those who expressed the view, perhaps with more than a modicum of justification, that the arrests were just random, in order to sow fear and encourage others to leave more quickly. Nevertheless, the simple fact was that at this moment there was no country that Julya could emigrate to. He had no ticket out, he could not stay put, and he could not be with his own family.

Finally, in late December 1938, Julya was warned by friends that he was about to be arrested and so he resolved to go into hiding and leave Terci in Vienna. She would then pursue her application for a permit to come to England to be with my mother. It is hard now to imagine quite how painful this further separation must have been. The walls were closing in. He would be on his own, without help and unable to protect his wife. His plan was that Terci would move in with her parents who were living around the corner at Lilienbrunngasse, and if the police came to look for him, Terci would explain that she was about to leave for England to join her daughter, but that Julya had already left the Reich for Palestine. This would, he hoped buy him some more time to make arrangements to get on a boat legally or illegally and take matters from there. There was no question, this was a strategy of the highest order of risk. The chances of this working without hitch, either for himself or Terci, were slim. A favourite expression of my grandmother in Hebrew more or less summed up their position at the time; אין ברירה (*ein breira*). This loosely translates as Hobson's choice, or no choice at all.

I have only been able to find out the barest details of his time in hiding. The very last entries in Julya's file kept at the *Israelitische Kultusgemeinde* in Vienna relating to his own circumstances are dated 26 January 1939 and 2 February 1939: two receipts, each containing only one line of writing, which simply refer to him having been advanced RM250 and then RM100. The trail stopped after this and there must be a strong presumption that if Julya had remained in Vienna there would be some mention of him, as he looked entirely to the Jewish communal organisation for financial assistance.

I did discover in the papers preserved in the Eisenstadt archive that Julya was correct to understand that the State Police were on his case. There is a note from Dr Ebner of the Vienna Staatspolizei in Vienna from April 1939, recording that Julius Lobl and the rest of the family had already left the Reich, and despite best efforts could not be found. There is another note from Dr Anton Lang who sat in the liquidator's office in Skodagasse, Vienna, dealing with the property of the Jews from the Burgenland, stating that the 'Jew Lobl' had been reported as having left for Palestine in February 1939.

I do not know the details of where or the circumstances in which Julya was living, but there is a poignant story which my grandmother told me relating to these tense days. It seems that his place of refuge was somewhere outside Vienna. Without being able to find out more, my working assumption is that he was being helped by some work acquaintance or maybe by friends. It was a local train ride away, quite possibly in Wiener Neustadt, about fifty or so kilometres south of Vienna, towards Lackenbach. In any event, each Friday, my grandmother would pack some food provisions in a little bag, then hop on the train and go to see Julya for the Jewish Sabbath (Shabbat), so they could be together and then she would return on the Sunday. Terci also brought the traditional silver candlesticks and silver wine cup so they could make the appropriate Friday night blessings for the day of rest. She did this week in week out until Julya made whatever arrangements he could and moved on. When Terci left Austria herself in April 1939, she took them with her. A tangible connection with the husband she had to leave behind. No doubt these clandestine visits put her in danger, too. Nevertheless, their love for each other was strong and no doubt seeing one another for that short time at the end of the week gave each other comfort.

I have listened to many survivors of the Holocaust at various commemorative events over the years and a strange thing has stuck in my mind. That is the number of times I heard them talk of the peace and beauty of *Shabbat* in their lives before the war. With so much happening and the danger to personal safety, it seems in many ways an extraordinary point of focus but a remarkably powerful memory. The story of my grandmother helped me understand it better. Maybe there was a sense of so much having been taken away in terms of identity and dignity, that this was their ultimate refuge, a sacred space of faith and family to be protected and enjoyed at all costs.

I thought that the story of those months would simply end there, but not for the first time in the course of my research in the archives, there was more to be uncovered. Actually, a lot more. The morning before my dreadful encounter with Herr M in Eistenstadt, I was surprised to receive half a trolley-load of orange-brown files, much of the contents either handwritten or in a Gothic typeface, neither of which was at all easy to decipher. Most of the pages were festooned with the seal of the eagle and swastika. The majority of the communications concluded with '*Heil Hitler.*' Others added the salutation of 'Friendly German Greetings' as well. There were hundreds of pages of records relating to how the State dealt with Julius Lobl and his property. There were many other such files for different members of the family.

Julya was not, I have to stress, a wealthy person. Far from it. He was a modest shopkeeper and property owner. Nevertheless, each and every aspect of the taking of his property was recorded in painstaking detail. The documents came and went from the desk of the Gestapo in Eisenstadt, the Mayor of Lackenbach, the authorities in Oberpullendorf (then the provincial capital of the Burgenland), the Oberpullendorf District Court, the Reich Governor's Office of the Niederdonau Province situated in Vienna, the official liquidator in Vienna, and the State Police in Vienna. Several documents were duplicated, marked as having been sent to half a dozen ministries in Vienna. This was a detailed bureaucratic operation, the transactions concerning just one unfortunate Jew. One of millions.

The Nazi takeover in Lackenbach took place over the weekend of 12 and 13 March 1938. On Sunday 13 March, each head of a household in the Jewish community of Lackenbach had to go to the police station. The local police chief had by this time been replaced by a member of the Eisenstadt Gestapo, over which Tobias Portschy had assumed control. They were all told they would have to leave by 18 April 1938, two days before Hitler's birthday. The Eisenstadt files record that on 13 March each person had to inform the police where they lived and who was living with them. In Julya's case he disclosed that he lived at Berggasse, 18 with his wife, Terci, his daughter, Judy, and his own mother, Johanna. It seems each person must have been told that he or she had to leave their belongings and merchandise behind. Julya appears not to have obeyed this order in its entirety and had some success in selling at least a part of his haberdashery stock, which most likely explains why he was one of the very last to leave Lackenbach on 25 April. It also perhaps explains some of the interest which was taken by the authorities in his case.

In early May, after Lackenbach was declared to be *Judenrein*, free of Jews, an order was then issued by the Eisenstadt Gestapo, confiscating all the real and personal property of the Jews of Lackenbach.[1] The next step was the taking of an inventory. On 8 June 1938, the Mayor of Lackenbach Mathias Scheiber was tasked by the Commercial and Trade Division of Burgenland National Socialist Party in Eisenstadt to take an inventory of the goods and possessions of a number of named Lackenbach Jews. Julya was one of just six names identified on this list. Herr Scheiber was required to send them the report as soon as it was completed.

On 28 July, a further letter was written to Mathias Scheiber from the same Commercial and Trade Division, which noted reports they had heard of locals, including it is said members of the SA and SS, looting these businesses or making private trades for goods. The Mayor was asked to identify each of those involved in this activity. To be fair, the Mayor would have struggled with that particular task. In a letter written some years later by Victor, one of Julya's brothers, he wrote of how in the days after the Anschluss there was a free-for-all, with Jewish shops being broken into and goods taken away. Nevertheless, the Mayor did eventually identify one of the officers supposedly in charge of those engaged in the looting.

The fruits of Herr Scheiber's work are described in detail in a report from Walter Firlich, Chartered Accountant, dated Vienna 13 December 1940, some two years later. Mathias Scheiber appears to have been something of a wheeler dealer. Quite apart from his municipal position, he was described as being a watchmaker, a supplier of kitchen materials and household goods and a coal trader to boot. On 9 June 1938, the very day after Scheiber received his orders to compile an inventory, apparently he went to Julya's house and took away crockery to the value of RM68 in order to settle 'local taxes'. There is no other record on the files of what he took, what he paid, no evidence of the outstanding tax bill or indeed of him applying the payment to settle that amount. The report also recorded that so-called 'worthless items' found were simply handed to members of the SS in town. As far as Julya's shop was concerned, the Mayor was really only left with the bare bones. Either the stock had been looted or Julya had managed to sell some of it before leaving. What little remained was sold off to another town local who was happy to take it away for the sum of RM45. This consisted of shelving and sundry shop fittings.

There is in the file a note from Scheiber dated 12 January 1940 that required the sum of RM45 to be paid to the Postal Savings account at the Eisenstadter Bank. This was the bank account established at the Creditanstalt to pay for the forced emigration of the Jews of the Burgenland. The use of the Creditanstalt with its former association with the Rothschild family was not a coincidence. All told, this was an extraordinarily efficient operation; the basic principle being that the Jews were to pay for their own expulsion through the expropriation of whatever they owned. This was the system that Eichmann followed with such ruthlessness.

In July 1938, Dr Anton Lang came from Vienna and took an inventory of the household goods not just of Julius Lobl but of each of the six named individuals. Dr Anton Lang was nothing if not meticulous. He listed and ascribed a value to each and every item, including my mother's three baby dolls, a toy trumpet, tableware, various flower vases, coffee pots and cups, a double bed, a day bed which presumably Julius's mother slept on, some bed clothes and sixteen hangers. The most valuable piece was a pair of kitchen scissors. The inventory described the very last detail of their everyday life together before disaster struck. It is in some small way similar to the disaster at Pompeii, which allows one to observe the minutiae of ordinary people's lives. A modest existence was revealed. There were never more than six items of crockery and frequently only three pieces were marked down on the list. One exception to this, indicative of Terci's kitchen prowess, was the listing of thirty assorted wooden spoons. In terms of everyday diversions, there was very little to be observed except for a popular Ludo-like board game called, 'Don't Get Angry',[2] which was all the rage at the time and remains so today in Austria. The entire contents of the house came to the princely sum of RM91.60. This was less than £10 at the prevailing rate of exchange. Then came the deductions. Dr Lang first deducted RM15 for his costs including travel; RM40 was said to be payable to the Lackenbach community; RM20 was payable to the SS; and the remaining sum of RM16.60 was owed to Herr Lautner, described as a local business adviser.

There is another handwritten note from September 1938 in Julya's hand, which optimistically gave full power of attorney to his wife Terci to deal with matters relating to his property and to receive any monies. The next and it seems last chapter in the story of their personal possessions took place in January 1941. At this time, Dr Lang came back from Vienna to pay another visit to Lackenbach. He expressed his irritation that monies said to be owed *by* Julius Lobl with respect to the balance of the account from the expropriation of his goods could not be collected. He wrote a report of his trip to Lackenbach, attached a train ticket as part of his expenses and added the cost of writing the report (RM60), a total of RM114.16 – which was to be added to the balance payable by Julius Lobl to the State following the confiscation of all of his possessions.

This then left the family house at Berggasse, 18. In May 1938, all of Julya's property, including the house he lived in together with the shop on the ground floor, was confiscated by the Gestapo. It seems this order was revoked on 24 April 1939 by order of Dr Ebner of the Vienna Staatspolizei, who, quite contrary to the true position, seemed overly keen to maintain the official line that no property had been taken from Julius Lobl who had fled the Reich. Instead, Dr Ebner noted that Julius Lobl's wife, Theresa, had asked the *Israelitische Kultusgemeinde* in Vienna to advance a sum of RM400 in order to help her leave the Reich for England. The report concluded that the property at Berggasse, 18 would be appraised and sold at auction.

The tone of the document is different to many of the others, with a strong emphasis on the fairness of the treatment of the Jews. It seems written with the express purpose of being read by those higher up the bureaucratic chain in order to cover backsides, especially given some of the strange transactions, including personal trading and outright theft already noted.

On 6 June 1940, the house at Berggasse, 18, which included the shop and a garden plot together with a small second dwelling built next to the main house, was sold at auction for RM2400. It was sold to his next-door neighbours, Franz and Maria Weninger, who lived at Berggasse, 20. They had to sign a declaration that they were not Jewish but Aryan.

There was then some considerable to and fro as to how the sale proceeds were to be accounted for. On 24 October 1940, the District Court of Oberpullendorf issued a statement of account of the sale proceeds. There were deductions for taxes, for a mortgage, compulsory payments to the Lackenbach community, health insurance and administrative costs of the process of expropriation. All this left a final credit balance of just RM408. In October 1940 this small sum was said to be available for transfer.

Just days after, an order was issued by the same District Court countermanding the transfer. The reason for this was made clear by a letter dated 7 December 1940 from Dr Haselberger in Vienna addressed to the Reich Governor of the Niederdonau Province, in which Lackenbach was then situated. In this communication it was said that my mother Judy had been seriously ill in the St Anna Children's Hospital in Vienna for 45 days from 26 June to 10 August 1938 and the hospital had calculated that the cost of providing her with hospital meals came to RM270, based on a notional daily charge of RM6 per day. Accordingly, it was directed that the hospital had to be reimbursed RM270 from these funds and a payment authorisation card was enclosed.

I was completely unaware that my mother had been so unwell or that she had to remain in a hospital for so long. I asked Ruth whether my mother had been in hospital at this time, and she likewise had no memory of this at all and thought it unlikely, as she would have remembered. Ruth told me that she herself had been ill in a hospital in Sopron (today in Hungary) prior to 1938 but that was entirely unconnected with the dates or St Anna's Children's Hospital, or the deduction.

Not for the first or last time, these records had the ability to get right under the skin. It was not just the calculating tone of the whole correspondence or the matter of fact reporting of my mother having been so poorly in hospital, or the end result that Julya had all his possessions, shop, stock and house taken from him. It was also not necessarily the fact that the hospital in question appeared to retain a record for two and a half years as regards the notional costs of certain hospital meals. It was not my scepticism that my mother coming from an orthodox community would have been allowed by her parents to eat food prepared and cooked in a hospital kitchen without strict rabbinical supervision. What really struck home was the fact that for each and every single person there was a whole cadre of officials engaged in village after village, town after town, just to ensure that in the end the relevant person was stripped bare and disposed of. These files disclosed the dreadful truth that the persecution of the Jews in the time of the Holocaust involved a titanic administrative effort on the part of tens upon tens of thousands of administrators in every corner of the Reich.

Far too many in this particular region went at it with some relish. The attention to detail was little short of obsessive, the mundane subject matter and polite greetings between officials scarcely papering over the deadly intent. Each detail was followed up, every item recorded right down to a child's doll.

All this raises the question, why would anyone participating in the evisceration of an entire people record all this in writing? The documents themselves perhaps reveal some kind of an answer. The papers display a strange psychosis; a deep-seated hatred combined with a need to record matters so that they would be seen to have been dealt with 'just so', in accordance with all proper procedures, or '*ordentlich*' as the bureaucrats would have said.

The Eisenstadt files regarding Julya's affairs continued throughout the war. There was a lengthy correspondence with regard to Berggasse, 18 and repeated requests made to transfer the name on the title deed from Franz Weninger to his wife's name Maria Grabner. Franz, it seems, had been drafted into the Wehrmacht and was missing in action on the Russian Front. Franz Weninger never returned from the battlefield and the war memorial lists his name amongst the seventy fallen from Lackenbach. In fact, Franz's name is listed twice on the Lackenbach War Memorial, first as having fallen in action in 1943 and then a second time in 1944. Perhaps at first he was presumed dead, missing in action in 1943 but further facts came to light and he was given a revised date of death.

The communications kept flowing. In December 1944, a letter was written by the Reich Governor of the Niederdonau Province to the land registry in Oberpullendorf which raised a query as to whether a mistake had been made on the land registry entry for Berggasse, 18. It apparently showed both Julya's name and his father Moritz Lobl's name as the prior owners. This confusion might have raised a concern as to how to ensure effective title would pass fully to the next-door neighbours as the new owners. These would not be entirely idle thoughts given the state of the war at the time, although the briefest of inquiry would have revealed that Julya's own father had died in January 1937 and was buried in the cemetery at Lackenbach.

The very last entry on the files has a date received stamp of 22 March 1945. This was part of a longstanding but unresolved debate about the consequence of a lien of sorts which had been registered prior to the war on Berggasse, 18. It is hard to follow from the file without seeing the underlying documents identified, but it refers to a security charge created in favour Martin Lobl for the sum of 50 Austrian Shillings. Both Martin Lobl and indeed the Austrian Shilling itself had long since gone, but this did not seem to stop the bureaucratic wheels from grinding on.

One week later, the walls finally crumbled. On 29 March 1945, the Russian army under General Tolbukhin, hero of the Battle for Budapest, crossed the border of Austria at Klostermarienberg in the Burgenland, only a few kilometres from Lackenbach, and in early April 1945 the Austrian participation in the Reich came to an end. Although for the slave labourers billeted at Rechnitz a dozen or so kilometres to the south of Klostermarienberg, this all came too late.

On the night of 24 March 1945, as the German forces were being pushed back kilometre by kilometre, Countess Margit Batthyany held a dinner party for like-minded friends at her schloss in Rechnitz, a last hurrah as the inevitable end approached. Countess Margit was the daughter of Baron Heinrich Thyssen Bornemisza, an extremely wealthy businessman, horse race owner and banker with close connections to Hermann Goering himself. Margit became the Countess after marrying Count Ivan Batthyany, who could offer what remained of the glory associated with this once great aristocratic house which had from the start of this story in the 1680s offered shelter and protection to local Jews, but could contribute no money of his own. Margit was a fervent Nazi sympathiser and several high-ranking officials were present including SS Hauptscharführer Franz Podenz.

Late in the night, Podenz informed those present he had received news there had been an outbreak of typhus fever in the Jewish slave labour gang, which had just finished preparing a final defensive rampart for the Wehrmacht. At this, about a dozen of the guests were handed out weapons from the Schloss armoury and drove off. The wretched Jews had been assembled in separate groups of 30-40, having already been forced in the biting cold to dig a ditch in a field. These guests took it in turns to shoot them one by one. Then after each victim had fallen into their self-dug grave, the guests returned to their dinner party. There is no suggestion that Margit herself took part or shot anyone, but she did certainly cover up this atrocity to the end of her days.[3] Four nights later, the Schloss was set on fire by Russian artillery and was damaged beyond repair.

As for my grandfather's house at Berggasse, 18, with great purpose I marched up and down that street in Lackenbach clutching tightly in my hand the two photographs that Uncle Max had sent my mother decades earlier. Many of the houses on the right side of the road remain as they were before the war; neat, two-storied, well-kept, some draped in flowers. I tried in vain to match up my images with what can be found today. I retraced the steps up the hill that my family could have happily walked along with their eyes firmly shut. I saw each of the dwellings at Berggasse, 20 and 16, but where Julya's house would have stood in between, with its pretty fenced courtyard in which the family had assembled in happier times, is nothing. The ground seems to form part of the garden of the next-door neighbour's house. There is no sign of any one of my relations – or anyone – ever having lived there at all.

21

A Dishonourable Piece of Business

The family must have known that they had taken their leave of Lackenbach for the last time. Julya's thoughts, however, were understandably elsewhere. He was in hiding, aware of the physical danger he faced but ignorant of the machinations of British officials that provided such a powerful coda to those in the Reich who at one and the same time required his departure but prevented his leaving. He had to find a way out and getting to Palestine was his only route to safety. This would mean by whatever means possible getting onto another ship from Europe across the Mediterranean. That last escape route was itself to be much affected by a profound shift in policy in Whitehall that would be revealed in stages from November 1938 to the spring and summer of 1939.

When the Colonial Secretary Malcolm McDonald stood to speak in Parliament, just days after Kristallnacht, to outline his instinctive opposition to continued Jewish immigration into Palestine, it was already apparent that the government's resolve was wavering on fulfilling the obligations it had undertaken in the 1922 League of Nations Mandate. Although misleadingly administered under the purview of the Colonial Office, Palestine was not a British colony. It was not territory Britain had the power or gift to dispose of or indeed rule according to its own self-interest. Instead, it was a protectorate under the ultimate control of the League of Nations and international law – one of fourteen created following the First World War after the defeat of Germany and its Ottoman allies. Each such territory was to be ruled under legal mandate, which established the relevant governing principles and a Mandatory Power entrusted with the responsibility of putting the prescribed terms into effect. In Syria and Lebanon, that power was France. In Palestine it was Britain. Under the terms of the Mandate, Britain had to report to and was responsible to the Permanent Mandates Commission to ensure that the Mandate was fulfilled and not undermined.[1] The consent of the League of Nations was required if there was to be any modification of its terms and nor could it be unilaterally terminated by the Mandatory Power.[2]

There is no question that the Mandate presented problems of an extremely delicate political and legal nature. How could a balance be achieved between on the one hand the requirement to encourage Jewish immigration in Palestine and the duty to create the conditions to secure a Jewish national home there[3] and on the other the obligation to protect the civil and religious rights of all citizens of Palestine?[4] There was also the question of whether or not there was any material distinction, and if so what, between the expression Jewish national home and Jewish State. Indeed, it was not exactly clear what was meant by a Jewish national home *in* Palestine – specifically whether that required a Jewish national home across all of Palestine or rather just in an identified area within the Mandate territory.[5] Jabotinsky and his followers took the maximalist view. Never far from the surface was the tension between the provisions of the Mandate and the emerging principle of self-determination.

In the first years of the Mandate, these tough questions were largely side-stepped, with a significant programme of building of infrastructure and capacity, much of it in Jerusalem, in the vain hope that this would reduce Arab opposition to the establishment of a Jewish national home in any part of Palestine.[6]

Between 1922 and 1938, astonishingly enough, there were more than half a dozen significant reviews conducted of British policy in Palestine.[7] The subject soaked up more than its fair share of time in Parliament and at Cabinet level and seemed to pose endless problems without answers. The most prominent and well-publicised solution was that set out in the Peel Commission, which in July 1937 proposed to the League of Nations the partition of Palestine into a Jewish and an Arab State.[8] A two-state solution. This notion, on which so much of the hopes for peace still rests today, was also eventually at the core of the 1947 Partition Plan adopted by the United Nations, which brought the Mandate to an end, and it was also the ultimate goal of the Oslo Accords of the 1990s.[9]

The immediate trouble, however, was that partition into two states was rejected in the strongest terms by those representing the Palestinian Arabs, the Arab Higher Committee, and the Grand Mufti of Jerusalem, who expressed opposition to any further Jewish immigration into Palestine and stood resolutely against the establishment of any Jewish national home whatever in the territory. The rejection by prominent voices on each side of any part of the national aspiration of the other side has deep roots and is perhaps the single biggest obstacle to finding a pathway to a permanent peace settlement. Sadly, this flourishes today more than ever before in significant elements and perhaps now even with the majority of Israeli and Palestinian politicians (both in Gaza and on the West Bank). One of the consistent demands made by the Arab Higher Command in the 1930s was that Britain should simply revoke the obligations undertaken in the Mandate and immediately takes steps to establish an independent Arab government over the entire territory. Leaving aside all questions of substance, this demand was not in Britain's gift, only the League of Nations could reach that position.

Nevertheless, in the course of nine months from the end of 1938 to the outbreak of war in the late summer of 1939 this outright rejection was given extraordinary encouragement by a British foreign policy which had been shaped to serve its private interest rather than international obligation. Perhaps the most lasting damage of Britain's short period of governance of this region was its all too ready acceptance of the notion that whichever faction considered it had the upper hand or better negotiating position at a particular moment might be encouraged to aspire to obtaining the entire cake and not have to divide it up. Today, this idea has taken deep root in the unlikeliest of political bedfellows: Hamas and Islamic Jihad in Gaza; Hezbollah in Lebanon; large elements of the body politic in the West Bank and the right-wing political parties in Israel. They all harbour the same absolutist objective. Each is well supported and ultimately each only thrives through sowing distrust and encouraging sectarian hatred.

The first tangible sign of Britain's retreat from the terms of the Mandate was the government's reaction in November 1938 to the Woodhead Commission's review of the Peel Commission. Put simply, Whitehall concluded that partition into separate states was not a viable option, as it was so trenchantly opposed by those representing the Palestinian Arabs. The Woodhead Commission had proposed instead of partition a form of federal government, something which MacDonald tellingly did not comment on when he spoke in Parliament on 24 November 1938. Instead, he invited representatives of both the Jewish Agency and the Arab Higher Committee to come to a conference in London on 7 February 1939 to find a solution, with the threat that if nothing could be agreed, Britain would impose its own. Unsurprisingly, the St James Conference closed on 27 March 1939 without agreement. In fact, the Arab Higher Committee and the delegates from Iraq, Egypt and Syria refused even to sit in the same room as the delegates from the Jewish Agency in Palestine.

There was now real urgency in Whitehall to reach some kind of resolution. By this time, the only yardstick was British regional and military concerns and seven weeks after the collapse of the ill-fated talks in London, on 17 May 1939 the British Government published the White Paper which, as previously threatened, imposed its own answer to the problems.[10] The key feature of the proposed policy was the establishment within ten years of an independent Palestine with key administrative functions being handed over at the earliest opportunity to local rule. The state to be established was not constructed on federal lines and no proposals were put forward for legal protection of the minority rights of Jews within it. Critically, no further Jewish immigration would be allowed after a period five years, unless the Arabs leadership in Palestine was prepared to agree (which of course it would not); and that in the meantime immigration would be restricted to 10,000 per year plus a special one-off allowance of 25,000. This was said to be a contribution to the solution of the Jewish refugee problem but was conditional on the High Commissioner of Palestine being satisfied that adequate provision was in place for the maintenance of these refugees.

No one reading the White Paper of May 1939 could have been under any illusion that what was being proposed was the complete abandonment of the establishment of a Jewish national home in Palestine and of the obligation to assist Jewish immigration. Nothing if not bold, it was accepted by the authors that these proposals were not consistent with the Mandate. Instead, it was argued that the Mandate should itself be reinterpreted or changed in the light of the circumstances on the ground. This was the idea that had been raised by the Egyptian Prime Minister in 1937 and now, after the extensive violence against the British in the region, it seems to have taken hold in Whitehall. Yet only the League of Nations could alter the Mandate or terminate it.

Those engaged in the negotiations in the Jewish delegation, such as Dr Weizmann, had long detected that the trend of British policy in Palestine was moving further and further towards the Arab delegates' demands. What was not anticipated, however, was the proposed complete abrogation of the League of Nations Mandate itself. There were mass demonstrations in Haifa, Jerusalem and Tel Aviv when the White Paper was published. On 18 May 1939, a polite march of Jewish protesters in an orderly line paraded through Tel Aviv with a banner demanding that the British, 'Tear up the evil decree'.[11]

David Ben Gurion in Palestine was less polite. In fact, he was incandescent with rage at the betrayal. This operated at two levels. In political terms, Ben Gurion proclaimed that Britain had impermissibly torn up the Mandate. He was also furious with Macdonald himself on a personal level. He had met Macdonald. He had previously written in November 1938 to warn him that after Kristallnacht, 'millions of our people face destruction.'[12] They were both deep thinking politicians of the international labour movement. They had talked through the night on various occasions when Macdonald visited Palestine and Ben Gurion counted him as a good friend. He could not have imagined him signing up to this policy. Ben Gurion wrote in his diary, 'The devil himself could not devise a more crushing and horrible nightmare.' He marvelled at this two-faced betrayal. He recalled Macdonald's 'caresses, promises and extensive dialectic'. Ben Gurion told Dr Weizmann, 'In my view, he is like a member of Hitler's gang, and our friends need to know that no Jew can meet with him.'[13]

Matters soon were to turn uglier and by the beginning of June 1939 Jewish protestors in Palestine took to the streets in violent demonstration and set off bombs in Jerusalem. This was in turn met with increased British military and police presence and stern warnings were given to the editors of the *Palestine Post* not to print anything that might amount to an incitement of violence.[14]

The White Paper was debated in Parliament on 23 May 1939. The Secretary of State received a tough reception. Accusations of duplicity, dishonour, broken promises and betrayal were cast liberally by many on the Labour benches.[15] More than a hundred Conservative MPs abstained including Churchill and near twenty prominent critics of the Government including Amery. Harold Macmillan voted against the White Paper. The Government carried the day, albeit with a sharply reduced majority.[16]

Malcolm MacDonald was then asked to appear before the League of Nations Permanent Mandates Commission at its 36th Session in Geneva in June 1939 to explain himself. Dr Weizmann in correspondence with M. Rappard, the Chair of the Permanent Mandates Commission, was withering in his criticism of the White Paper.[17] The Colonial Secretary made what must be said was a defiant defence of the very difficult position in which Britain found itself.[18] There was, however, only limited sympathy in Geneva for Britain's political dilemma and how the difficulties might adversely affect Britain's international position. The majority of the Commission considered that the international law obligation expressed in the Mandate for a Jewish National Home in Palestine was clear and unaltered by the difficulties encountered in Arab opposition. Britain's argument that the Mandate had to be abandoned, reinterpreted, or altered, largely fell on deaf ears.

On 29 June 1939, at the conclusion of the 36th Session of the Permanent Mandates Commission, a majority of four to three concluded the policy of the White Paper was not in conformity with the Mandate.[19] The majority concluded that the direction of Britain's policy was ruled out by the terms of the Mandate and the fundamental intention of its authors.[20] As a result, Britain was reported to the Council of the League of Nations. The minority three, including Lord Hankey, the British delegate, stated that they were prepared to accept that the existing circumstances would justify the new policy, but only if the Council of the League of Nations did not oppose it.[21] There can be little doubt that but for the four-day intervention and speech making of Lord Hankey, the outcome in terms of votes would have been worse for Britain.[22] Lord Hankey at the time had been appointed as a British director of the Suez Canal Company and was hastily appointed by Britain to the Permanent Mandates Commission to enable him to attend this session and vote in favour of the White Paper. Applying today's standards of requisite independence and impartiality, it is extremely doubtful whether it was appropriate for him to attend and vote in Geneva. Lord Hankey was necessarily concerned with maintaining security in the region, in particular for the Suez Canal and the corporation he was engaged with.[23]

The White Paper had been drawn up in haste and was rejected by the Mandates Commission, yet it is instructive to look further behind the scenes to examine the private discourse between Britain and Palestine's Arab neighbours in the build-up to its publication.

The central go-between in these discussions was the towering Sir Miles Lampson, later Lord Killearn. The six foot five, Eton-educated Sir Miles had spent his whole professional life in the diplomatic service, first serving in Japan and China. In 1934 he became High Commissioner for Egypt. In 1936 after the Anglo-Egypt Treaty, he became ambassador and remained there until 1946. Wendell Wilkie, the Republican nominee for President in 1940 who was to visit Cairo during the war, described Sir Miles as 'for all practical purposes the actual ruler of Egypt'.[24] For all his undoubted closeness to King Farouk, this was, however, vigorously denied by Sir Miles himself.[25] Nevertheless, in the critical months his influential position in Egypt was used to operate a top-secret back channel of communications between the British and the delegates of the neighbouring Arab States. These communications had to be handled delicately. This was not a discussion that the Jewish delegates were to have any say in. He was of course not engaged in finding terms that would be agreeable to the Jewish Agency, or indeed as it happens, what was required by the Palestinian Arabs themselves. His brief was simply to ascertain the price that the Arab delegates required to end the Arab Revolt in Palestine. It is clear from the Cabinet Committee Minutes that no one understood this to be an honourable piece of business.

On 23 March 1939, even before the London Conference had broken up without agreement, in Telegram No 214, marked secret, Sir Miles wrote to the Secretary of State for the Colonies in London stressing the importance of doing everything possible to settle quickly with the Arab delegates.[26] This followed just eight days after proposals had been put forward by the British Government on 15 March which advocated tight restrictions on future immigration of Jews seeking refuge in Palestine, but which had been roundly rejected by both sides.[27] So convinced was Sir Miles of the need to reach agreement with the Arab delegates, according to Malcolm Macdonald, the Secretary of State for the Colonies, he was prepared 'to give the Arabs what they wanted and then rely upon [Britain] one way or other to get out of our pledge if necessary when the time came.'[28]

217

After some discussion, Malcolm Macdonald confidentially authorised Sir Miles to communicate an offer to the Egyptian Prime Minister designed to meet most of the demands of the Arab side. The principal terms of the offer were contained in a telegram sent by Malcolm MacDonald on 6 April 1939.[29] On 11 April Sir Miles informed London by Telegram No 249 marked 'Immediate' of the response from the Egyptian Prime Minister, who said he was authorised by the State representatives to speak on their behalf after meeting with them on 9 April. The Egyptian Prime Minister was playing hardball. He felt he had the upper hand and saw no reason why he should yield. He made significant further demands of the British in terms of the wording of the White Paper and furthermore made it clear that 'Tranquillity could be restored at once in Palestine if immigration were stopped forthwith for a definite period of time.'[30]

The matter now had to be discussed both in Cabinet and in the Cabinet Committee on Palestine, which had met several times already in 1939. A draft of what would become the May 1939 White Paper was circulated in Cabinet on 19 April 1939.[31] The discussion in Cabinet made it clear that the text of the policy was the matter of 'informal discussions with representatives of the neighbouring Arab States' and so would not be released until that process had been completed. In reality, this process had simply become one of concluding a text, which the Arab Palestinian delegates and those from Egypt, Iraq and Saudi Arabia in particular would agree to.

In the meantime, somehow or other word of this back channel reached a number of Members of Parliament, including Tom Williams, who came from a traditional coal mining and trades unions background in the South Yorkshire labour heartlands. On 19 April, Williams raised the subject at Westminster with Malcolm MacDonald. He wanted to know if secret discussions were taking place without the Jewish delegates and if so, why. He asked whether this had led to any variation of government policy as previously set out at the conclusion of the London Conference. MacDonald played down the suggestion and said that he was not aware of any variation to the government proposals being conveyed by or to Egypt, or being agreed.[32] These answers were reported in the news, but frankly look to be wholly unsatisfactory, even misleading, in the light of what was actually taking place in secret, as revealed by the Cabinet and Committee Minutes.[33]

The matter was then taken up once more the next day on 20 April 1939 at the 10th Cabinet Committee on Palestine, chaired by the Prime Minister, Neville Chamberlain. [34] It was at this meeting that the decision was taken in all but name to seek to abandon the establishment of a Jewish national home in Palestine and so walk away from the terms of the Mandate itself. They met in the Prime Minister's room in the House of Commons at 4.30pm in the afternoon. The Minutes record the final stages of this most questionable process and the lengths they went to, to obtain the agreement of the Arab neighbouring states to the British policy on Palestine.

At the outset, the Cabinet Committee addressed the points raised on behalf of the neighbouring Arab States and agreed to alter the text of the draft White Paper to meet the Arab delegates' demands for the handover of key government agencies to Palestinian representatives as soon as peace and order had been sufficiently restored, without reference to any two-year grace period.[35] The next demand made by the Egyptian Prime Minister was to remove any reference to the establishment of a federal state in the text of the draft White Paper (a keystone of the Woodhead Commission and of the discussion at the London Conference), which at a stroke and without discussion was readily acceded to by the Cabinet Committee.

The last question that arose in relation to the wording of the draft White Paper was whether the reduced quota in the White Paper dealing with immigration into Palestine should be maintained or further amended. The wording before the Cabinet already substantially limited Jewish immigration over the next five years followed by a total cessation of further immigration without Arab consent. The Egyptian Prime Minister had hinted to Sir Miles that only an immediate and complete cessation of immigration would end the revolt. This was too much to bear. The Secretary of State already anticipated that this White Paper would be met with a strongly adverse reaction from the Jewish side: 'Our statement of policy (when published) would have dashed to the ground the hopes on which they had been building for many years past. Moderate and extreme Jews would join in the outcry.' After some debate, in this respect the Cabinet Committee stuck to their guns and proposed that they kept to the original text; namely the five-year period of strictly limited immigration followed by a Palestinian Arab veto. The Cabinet Committee resolved that they should inform the

Egyptian Prime Minister that they had given in to all but one of their demands.

Those who sat around the Cabinet Committee table understood the significance of this proposed course of action. The Prime Minister himself was under no illusion as to what was being decided. According to the Minutes on 20 April 1939, he concluded:

> We were now compelled to consider the Palestine problem mainly from the point of view of its effects on the international situation. It was of immense importance as Lord Chatfield [Minister for Co-ordination of Defence] had pointed out, to have the Moslem world with us. If we must offend one side, let us offend the Jews rather than the Arabs.

There were powerful factors underpinning this bleak statement of the *Realpolitik* of the day. An important consideration was the cost and impracticality of the maintenance of a sizable garrison in Palestine with the continued loss of life and casualties suffered, more particularly on the eve of an anticipated war. The Cabinet Committee had already noted in April 1939 that more troops had had to be diverted away from Egypt and Sudan to go Palestine to quell the Arab Revolt. This was becoming increasingly unsustainable. In August 1938, Sir Charles Bateman, a Counsellor in the British Embassy, had written to Sir Lancelot Oliphant, the Deputy Under Secretary of State, making it clear that in his view that each side was as loathsome as the other and noting that there could not be any justification for putting even a single British soldier's life at risk any longer. Sir Lancelot agreed with him.[36]

There was also the real fear of an adverse reaction to the notion of a Jewish national home in Palestine from the wider Muslim world, particularly from the Muslim League in India, which under the leadership of Jinnah had become significantly more vocal. Jinnah had written to the British Government in February 1939 when he was refused a seat at the London Conference to discuss the future of the region, making the point that one third of the troops in Allenby's Palestine campaign had been Muslim. At the meeting on 20 April 1939, Lord Halifax raised his own concerns regarding the Palestinian problem and reported that the notion of a Jewish homeland in Palestine was the only source of trouble between Britain and India's Moslem community. The Marquis of Zetland, the Secretary of State for India, concurred and expressed the view that 'Now was the moment to meet the Arabs as far as we could possibly do so.'[37]

At Cabinet in April 1939, Malcolm MacDonald himself recognised that this policy shift brought to an end any hope of a Jewish national home in Palestine. He then raised the question of seeking to offer a whole colony to the Jews for settlement as compensation. There was no pretence that the idea of a substitute homeland would conform to the terms of the Mandate. The two principal candidates remained those discussed by the Cabinet in November 1938, British Guiana and Honduras. Nothing came of this, although the implausible notion of a Jewish home in British Guiana was raised intermittently at Cabinet in May and June 1939.

By way of a conclusion to the debate on 20 April 1939, the Cabinet Committee agreed that the discussions with the Arab delegates should continue so as to reach an agreed text. Nevertheless, the subterfuge was clear to all. Malcolm MacDonald summarized the situation: 'Our statement of policy should be made as soon as practicable after 28 April 1939. This statement would, of course, be a unilateral declaration by the United Kingdom. The neighbouring Arab States would have no share of responsibility for it, but it would in fact embody our understanding with them.' MacDonald further envisaged that the Arab States would separately issue a statement agreeing with the White Paper and would declare that it met their main demands and that as a result the violence should come to an end. The Secretary of State cautioned that this stage management had to be kept away from the public and had to remain informal, otherwise it would expose Britain to criticism from the League of Nations and the United States.

Ironically, the White Paper was published in the terms that had been secretly brokered with the agreement of neighbouring Arab states and yet the Mufti of Jerusalem would not support it, as it was not sufficiently definitive in terms of abandonment of the Mandate or the complete cessation of all Jewish immigration. At the collapse of the London Conference earlier in 1939, there was jubilation and celebration in the streets of Haifa with shouts of 'Long live the Mufti.'[38] There was apparently disagreement within the ranks of the Arab Higher Committee as to whether to accept the White Paper or not, but the Mufti's rejection was in the end decisive.[39] The Mufti was to be denied a hero's return to Jerusalem. He would not call off the

Revolt and instead drew ever closer to the Axis Powers. Worse still, in Iraq in April 1941, through the Mufti's orchestration, a pro-Axis government briefly came to power following a coup d'état. For Britain this posed the worst nightmare – a threat to the supply of oil to its forces in the Mediterranean from the rear. After all this, the Cabinet had surrendered a good part of its integrity without even getting what it thought it had bargained for in return.

Britain now had incredibly enough sown the seeds of a second rebellion; of the great majority of the moderate and extreme Jewish forces of Palestine who could never put up with the White Paper. That further revolt would, however, not really take hold until after the defeat of Germany and the Axis Powers in 1945.

In the meantime, in the summer of 1939 one third of all Jewish adults in Palestine, men and women, signed consent forms to volunteer to fight the Nazis.[40] Nevertheless, Dr Weizmann is said to have told Neville Chamberlain in 1939 that this was not the last chapter of the story. Chaim Weizmann had previously privately told Sir Miles Lampton that there would be utter chaos if Britain abandoned its obligations under the Mandate, but Sir Miles 'hesitated to believe that the Jews would do anything so foolish or embarrassing to the British Government.'[41] In the end, this was to prove to be a grave miscalculation.

So whilst Julya's plan for escape was set, the British policy was now clear; it was to stop him at all costs.

22

The Rim

By early 1939 there was no question that Julya was in a desperate situation. He had already had to say goodbye to Terci and of course to Judy, and now whatever he had to face he would have to do so on his own. Julya was not someone I was ever able to get to know and yet as I researched and wrote this book, I felt myself drawn to him more and more. The steady gaze looking at the camera and his sunken cheeks revealing perhaps more than he would have wanted us to know of his circumstances. There was, I felt, an extraordinary dignity to his determination always to put others before himself and likewise his steadfastness, however long it took, to bring everyone back together on the other side. Like so many millions in his position, he had been dealt an exceptionally bad hand and it was not possible in my own mind to ignore the faint echoes of his biblical ancestor, Job, tossed around whimsically by a capricious deity.

All that I knew about Julya fleeing Europe had come from my conversations with Max. I was told that in the summer of 1939 Max had managed through his various contacts to get Julya a place on another vessel organised by Willy Perl from Constanza in Romania. In a matter-of-fact tone Max told me, however, that Julya's ship caught fire in the Aegean near to Rhodes and that he was sheltered there for a number of weeks on the island in a football stadium under the fearsome heat of the summer skies, whilst his fate hung in the balance. Max recounted this in the same manner as someone might talk of a frustrating bus journey to a remote destination. Looking back on this now, I think this reflected a time when the extraordinary was commonplace. Every voyage involved danger and the only imperative was survival. As ever, I probed Max for more details, but without success on this occasion. So in the first instance, in order to unlock the story, I had to discover the name of the ship that Julya had boarded.

I thought that the best place to start would be on Rhodes itself. I went there one late autumn not knowing if I would be able to find anything of the Jewish community or whether I could trace the narrative of this ill-fated voyage. In the old city, tucked away in one of the narrow alleys of the former Jewish Quarter (*la Juderia*), some distance away from the tourist trail, there still stands a synagogue with its black and white chevron mosaic floor, elaborate wooden carved bench seating and a central archway at the back leading to a tranquil courtyard with a fountain, where the priestly *cohanim* have their feet washed before blessing the congregation. It is of course considerably more modest in scale than the renowned attractions of Rhodes built by the Knights of St John in Crusader times but is certainly no less beautiful for it. The Kahal Shalom Synagogue dates from 1577. It has brought the community together there for over four hundred years and is one of the oldest serving places of Jewish worship in the world.

Only a handful remain of the nearly two thousand Jews who had lived on the island, some of whom could, with considerable pride, trace their roots back before the exile from Judea at the hands of the Romans at the time of the fall of the Second Temple in 70 AD. Jews all over the world are seen largely as a dispersed people, who originally came from somewhere else. A significant exception to this is Rhodes, where the community in large part since biblical times had always been from Rhodes and were not refugees from another land.

Attached to the synagogue there is a very small museum exhibition telling the story of the island's Jewish community, which was all but wiped out by the Holocaust. There were a number of grainy black and white pictures from before the war in the museum which encouraged me to think that they might well hold records relevant to Julya's journey.

I was able to speak to the curator and caretaker who looked as though perhaps he had been born within a handful of years of the events in question. I told him what I knew of my grandfather on Rhodes just before the outbreak of the Second World War and asked how I could learn more. His response was a little disconcerting. He asked me which ship my grandfather had been on. That was, however, precisely my question for him. It seems that more than one vessel had been forced to offload its unfortunate human cargo at Rhodes. I then explained further what I knew of Julya's odyssey, his rescue and his stay at the football stadium. At this his eyes lit up and he said knew exactly what I was referring to. This all took place in July 1939. Scratching his sun-kissed head, he told me that he believed a small number who were swept up onto the island that summer did not survive and were buried in the Jewish cemetery. I cross-checked the date with a list of illegal immigration transports that I had been able to secure from my visit to the Washington archives. It was *The Rim* which had left Constanza on the Black Sea coast of Romania in late June 1939 and had sunk off Rhodes in early July 1939. It was also listed as having been organised by Willy Perl. I was sure I had found what I was looking for.

From the very start, the voyage of *The Rim* was a troubled operation. By early 1939, Willy Perl had it seems been removed as organiser in chief of this sea route from Vienna.[1] This was the result of successive failures in his various attempts to take Jews out of Europe. In response, Perl decided to establish his own independent operation, but this was as yet not exactly tried and tested and he certainly lacked financial resources or back-up. In order to progress the arrangements, Perl joined forces with others who had useful connections in Romania. The problems, however, continued to multiply, due to the continual tightening of the screws of British control of immigration in the course of 1938 and 1939.

As a result, a number of vessels had been forced to return to Constanza by British naval patrols after trying without success to make it all the way to Palestine.[2] The upshot of all this was that Constanza, normally a bustling city on the shores of the Black Sea with elegant villas and boulevards was simply overrun with refugees looking for a ticket on any boat. The scene must have shared more than a passing resemblance with that witnessed more recently on our televisions of transit camps filled with those fleeing today's many conflicts.

To make matters worse, there was then an outbreak of scarlet fever amongst some of a group of a hundred and fifty passengers who had arranged though Perl to get to Palestine. They were referred to as 'the China Group', having left Vienna in February 1939 with false papers stating that they had tickets to go to Shanghai, not Palestine. The China Group arrived in Constanza after a long and tortuous voyage, but some weeks after they reached the Black Sea the spread of this highly infectious disease, meant they had to be quarantined, leading to further delay and considerable protest from the port authorities.

The stakes could not have been higher, as reports circulated that the Nazis had changed their policy of encouraging Jews to emigrate and would now just deal with those that remained. People knew what this would entail and what the consequences would be if their ship sailed without them, or if they were sent back to the Reich from Romania. People were quite literally dying to get on *The Rim*. In the end, they would be just as eager to get off it.

Julya would have considered himself indeed fortunate to hold a ticket in his hand. In my mother's papers my brother, Theo, found a photograph of him amongst some of his fellow travellers at the dockside, each looking mightily relieved to have made it that far. There were smiles aplenty and a discernible relaxed air. Behind them can be seen the busy traffic of the port and a windsock almost horizontal, indicating a stiff breeze. Julya on the far right of the group of ten is wearing what looked to be suit trousers, shirt and tie, a Homburg hat, city shoes and an overcoat. He looks like he is part of a work conference, not a group of penniless refugees. A Jew originating from Austria or Germany is sometimes referred to as a *yekke*, this being a bastardisation of the German for jacket (*jacke*). It is a gently chiding nickname referring to the reputation for punctilious formality and fondness for suits and ties. This group certainly conformed to their stereotype.

Most likely Julya and his friends posed for the camera wearing all of their worldly possessions and he sent the photograph to Terci for reassurance. What an extraordinary image for her to have received. She would not have seen Julya for several months, she had not known if he was alive or dead, or whether he had any realistic means of escape. No doubt, though, knowing my grandmother, she would have been relieved to see that Julya's dress standards had not slipped. In her eyes, he would have looked more than ready for a challenging sea crossing.

It took some months before each of the sick had recovered and the all-clear was given to board. *The Rim* was due to leave on 26 June 1939, but at this stage it became apparent that there would be insufficient space for all those with a ticket and some had to be left behind. What had happened was this. As the vessel had waited at Constanza for the end of quarantine, the costs continued to mount, and Willy Perl had to raise further funds, or *The Rim* would have simply sailed off. He concluded that it was not possible to raise any sums from those who already had a ticket, as each had had all their money and possessions taken from them by the Nazis. Perl then came up with the idea of selling about three hundred and fifty more tickets to Jews on Rhodes, who themselves in the summer of 1939 had been given expulsion orders by the Italian authorities there.[3] In essence, he was selling the berths twice over. The money raised in this fashion would then pay for the additional outlay and he concluded that the vessel could easily stop at Rhodes *en route* to Palestine.

As was typical of Perl, the plan was to say the very least unorthodox, even unscrupulous. It is unclear how the selection was made, but the China Group seems to have been allowed to board. There were extraordinary scenes of anger and frustration amongst those told they could not now leave, even though they had a ticket. Fights broke out at the quayside and in the chaos a large number managed to smuggle themselves onto the ship without being noticed. For many, this was the very last hope of salvation.

The Rim weighed anchor and forty desperate people leapt into the sea. They tried without success to scramble on board, only to drown in the attempt as the vessel left the harbour. The press report of this dreadful scene makes for disturbing reading, although Perl would no doubt have argued that the terrible means justified the ultimate end of saving lives.[4]

The problems just continued. *The Rim* could not pass Constantinople and through the Bosphorus without the permission of the Turkish coast guard. They asked to board the vessel and sought proof that those on board indeed had valid permits to reach their end destination.[5] This of course was somewhat delicate. Some of those on board had forged papers for Shanghai, others would have had valid permits for Palestine, but it must be assumed that the large majority had nothing at all. It is a fair bet that money changed hands to allow the voyage to progress. The next port of call was Rhodes, where the passengers to whom Perl had oversold places then boarded.

It would have been prudent for the owners of *The Rim* to have taken advantage of the lengthy delay at Constanza to make sure the vessel was seaworthy. She was built in the 1880s, in her twilight years. *The Rim* had scarcely left Rhodes when a fire broke out in the engine room, and the Captain sent a distress signal, 'We are on fire.' Soon after he gave the order to abandon ship off the coast of the Dodecanese Island of Simi.[6]

I doubt very much whether Julya had ever swum in the open sea before that day, but even if he had done so, the conditions would have tested him to the limit. Those on board were extremely lucky. The Captain of *The Rim* was able to beach the vessel on Simi. As she approached the shallow waters the passengers were able to jump into the sea and wade to dry land. Ten hours later they were rescued by an Italian vessel, the *Fiume,* which took them to Rhodes.[7] In his papers now in Washington, Perl kept photographs of *The Rim* at Simi, which did look to be in a sorry state. In Perl's memoirs he blamed the shipwreck on arson by the crew. There is no evidence to support this.[8] Perhaps he felt his reputation had taken a further beating and so sought to deflect some of the blame.

The British Admiralty was following the faltering progress of *The Rim*, which it suspected correctly of carrying illegal migrants under a false Panamanian flag.[9] The British policy was to put pressure on any state or authority on the shores of either the Black Sea or the Mediterranean not to aid such vessels. The news of *The Rim's* shipwreck was broadcast by an Arabic service from Germany on 7 July 1939: 'Fire broke out in a ship flying the Panama flag with 814 Jews on board. Unfortunately, these errant Jews were rescued from the death that they deserved by nearby boats.'[10]

On Rhodes, Julya and the rest of *The Rim's* passengers, including those who were themselves from Rhodes, were accommodated in tents in a local football stadium. They were closely guarded there by Italian police, forbidden to leave the camp and any infringement of these rules was met with severe collective punishment in the form of beatings.[11] They sweltered in the July heat as they waited for news and had nothing by way of clothes other than what they arrived in. Insufficient food and lice infestation were constant problems. The survivors were reduced to rags. One recalled that they did little by day except eat figs and hunt for lice. The local community showed incredible compassion and generosity. Each day they brought food and where possible arranged for new clothing, even though they had little for themselves.[12]

If any of them in the stadium had managed to source a radio and listen to the news in English, they would not have been reassured. On 13 July 1939 Malcolm Macdonald gave notice of a temporary suspension of all further Jewish immigration to Palestine with or without permits for a six-month period starting in October 1939.[13] In August, further amendments were made to the Palestine Immigration Ordinance, which now provided for a maximum prison sentence of eight years for anyone convicted of assisting illegal migration, including the ships' crews, and allowed the authorities to confiscate any vessel or craft involved irrespective of size.[14] Those who understood the local news would have been equally dispirited, as a large proportion of the Jews of Rhodes were now classified as foreigners and had been given a final deadline to leave the island by Governor De Vecchi.

As soon as he heard the news Willie Perl travelled to Rhodes to try to sort out matters as best as he could. On his arrival, however, he was kept under house arrest. His papers were taken away and he was told that he would only be released once he had made arrangements for all *The Rim*'s original passengers, together with three hundred and fifty Rhodes Jews, to leave.

Perl had to be at his most resourceful. He turned to the owners of a larger Greek steamship, the *Aghios Nikolaos*.[15] They agreed not only to provide that ship but three smaller landing craft as well. The ship's Captain must have been an extraordinarily brave soul. Quite apart from the risk of confiscation of his vessel and imprisonment, there was considerable physical danger. He had already undertaken a voyage to Palestine from Tulcea in Romania in April 1939 and the *Aghios Nikolaos* had been fired at by British naval patrol vessels, with three on board killed,[16] a shameful incident which had been raised in Parliament by Colonel Wedgwood on 5 June 1939.[17] Nevertheless, the Greek Captain agreed to return once more in August 1939, this time from Rhodes to Palestine, albeit with a slightly modified plan of operation for disembarkation.

In early to mid-August 1939, Julya was one of about 800 passengers crammed into whatever space could be found on the Greek steamer. This was now their Noah's Ark, although there would have been many more than two of each kind on board. The orthodox and the assimilated all crammed together. There were Zionist activists, socialists, those who had ran businesses in Vienna and Prague, teachers, doctors, young mothers and children, Ashkenazim of Central Europe and the Sephardim of Rhodes. They also took with them on this further exodus a gift from the Rhodes community, a torah scroll with a richly decorated cover. The Jews on Rhodes who did eventually leave through Willie Perl's efforts were amongst the very few from the island to survive the Holocaust. In September 1943, Rhodes was occupied by the German Army after a four-day battle with Italian soldiers. Nine months later, the Germans began to deport the Jews of Rhodes to Auschwitz and all but two hundred of this ancient community were murdered.

The *Aghios Nikolaos* was loaded to the gunnels but no doubt it was felt that the five-hundred-mile voyage would most likely only take a few days. They took such provisions with them as they could find. One survivor recalled that the diet on board largely consisted of sardines, presumably another gift from Rhodes and that she would have an anxiety attack at the very sight of them for years after. The *Aghios Nikolaos* left accompanied by the three other smaller craft. The idea was to transfer the passengers into the three small ships when they got near to the territorial waters of Palestine. This way they could attempt to land ashore on different beaches, stretching the British patrol boats and enable the *Aghios Nikolaos* to escape and fight another day.

Their plan, however, was anticipated by British naval intelligence and as a result they were shadowed at all times as they neared their destination. Various stratagems were deployed to try to outwit the pursuers, but as might be expected they were to no avail. All this took time, a luxury they did not have. As planned, the *Aghios Nikolaos* transferred everyone onto the smaller vessels and then sailed away to evade confiscation. The flotilla could not keep the passengers on board for any length of time. For a good while they remained thirty miles off the shores of Palestine and so beyond its territorial waters and the legal reach of those who sought to arrest them. But since all food and water had run out, a decision was taken on the Friday evening 18 August to try to make for the shore and just hope for the best.

Early next morning the British caught up with them. Shots were again fired and one refugee was killed before even stepping ashore.[18] The scene was described in graphic detail on the front page of the *Palestine Post* of 20 August 1939. The eyewitness account recorded a bedraggled procession reaching the shore in torn rags whilst those who had come to enjoy a quiet swim on a Saturday morning at the coastal resort of Netanya looked on. As the refugees were arrested and taken off to the Sarafand and Atlit Detention Camps, crowds of people gathered at the waiting buses and starting chanting, 'Free Immigration Now' and singing the *Hatikva*.

Julya was amongst the exhausted group that Saturday morning. He was arrested and taken to prison. He thereby achieved the questionable distinction of being the first person recorded in the family to do time. Sarafand, about 20km to the south of Tel Aviv, was one of two detention camps run by the British military in Palestine. The other was Atlit (with its ancient links to a Crusader castle built on the site) to the north, between Tel Aviv and Haifa.

My heart ached when I saw a copy of the front-page coverage by the *Palestine Post* of my grandfather's arrival. I just felt his helplessness, his exhaustion and complete lack of control over his own destiny. He was it seems literally washed up. I needed to know for certain what had happened to him. The Sarafand Camp has long since disappeared, but there is a museum at Atlit, which according to its website does show in some detail how prisoners were kept at that time. The visitor page stated that a number of prison barracks had been preserved, as well as a disinfection unit and the railway spur that took the prisoners straight from the boats to prison. There is also an important archive kept there which records as far as possible those who arrived ship by ship in Palestine at this time and those who were then put in prison.

So the next stop was Atlit to try to retrieve my grandfather's records. At the Atlit Camp Museum, I was told that I was exceptionally unlucky with my timing, as the archivist had gone away on a trip for a few days. I protested that I had come a long way to get this information and wondered if anyone could help me. After some frantic explanation and desperate gesticulation, an army volunteer who had been sitting quietly in the corner came forward speaking excellent English and saved me. After I told her what I was looking for, we went off together to try our luck with the computerised archives housed in a very dark auditorium no doubt used for much more important gatherings. It was equipped with a hard-drive and a very large screen on which the results were projected.

After a few keystrokes, there it was in giant Hebrew lettering; the original passenger list of *The Rim* from 1939 setting out the names of those who were part of that transport who then transferred onto the *Aghios Nikolaos*, arriving in August 1939. Josef Lobl (his Hebrew name) was listed as passenger no. 157, aged 43 born in 1896 from Austria, and his status was given as married with a wife and daughter in England. Others identified on the same page were listed as having come from Germany, Czechoslovakia, Romania, and of course Rhodes. The database showed that he had then been taken to Sarafand. There was very little further information on the file there, apart from him having been processed and entered in the prison records in August 1939. I thanked the soldier profusely and seeing that I wanted some time to reflect, she left me in the room only illuminated by Julya's name in an over-sized font with the cursor blinking beside it. First of all, I felt so conflicted as a proud British citizen to see how my country had treated my grandfather, weakened, in ill health and frightened for his life. The message was simple, Julya was not an individual but simply yet another part of a much larger age-old problem – the Jewish Question. A people wanted neither here nor there. Then my thoughts wandered to my own journey. Was this it? I could not help thinking that the lack of any other details meant that I had reached the end of the road as far as his records were concerned.

In trial work you often need, but more rarely get, that bit of luck. Sometimes it is the unanticipated favourable answer to a question in cross examination, or that crucial document which turns up in the discovery process. There is a special pleasure in these little triumphs, which of course at the time you attribute without any possible justification to your own genius. So it has been on occasion with my pursuit of this family tale. After this visit I went back to my hotel room and once more looked at the online archives of the United States Holocaust Museum in the light of what I had just discovered. I entered various word search requests which I thought I had previously looked at a fair few times, changed them round a bit to reflect my new-found knowledge and there it was staring back at me. Remarkably, I had found the records kept by the Palestine Police Force processing those arrested and detained at Sarafand from *The Rim*.

There are two mug shots of Julya holding up a piece of paper with the number 146 written on it stapled to an official document. It looks like the photographs were taken inside a tent. They are attached to a form which was completed by a member of the Palestine Police Force, FPC 1338, dated 21 August 1939.[19] It recorded his height at 1.80 metres, his mouth and nose were said to be 'normal' and that he had eight false teeth in his upper jaw. His place of birth was stated as Lackenbach, Burgenland, said to be in Germany, not Austria, which had to all intents and purposes ceased to exist. His last address was given as Grosse Schiffgasse, 6 in Vienna. It stated he had left the country of origin in February 1939 with a German passport, Number 71308. Amongst those passengers who had started their journey on *The Rim* there were a fair few who also stated that they had left Vienna in February 1939. This would almost certainly indicate that he had left Vienna with the China Group. It also matches precisely the frustrated reports of the Vienna State Police who came looking for Julya at that time.

The form itself is a P252, Application for an Order of Deportation. On 17 August 1939, just days before Julya's arrival, a further change in law in Palestine was announced in the *Palestine Gazette*. Illegal entry into Palestine would now be treated as a criminal offence under the Emergency Regulations as well as under the Immigration Ordinance.[20] This allowed for summary trial and imprisonment. Deportation, however, it seems was the principal measure used, but this required a special procedure and application. Illegal immigrants were either to be deported back to the country of origin and when that was impractical, they were to be sent to detention centres in Mauritius and Cyprus.[21] Today, an extended stay in either Mauritius or Cyprus would not excite strong adverse reaction, but this was not so at the time; the perils of the sea journey alone, with the risk of interception by enemy ships, were not to be dismissed lightly.[22]

War with Germany broke out only days after Julya's arrival. A decision to deport would have been recorded in a P254 Order. The records of the time have not been preserved in the archives by reference to individual ships on which the refugees arrived, instead, there are a number of such P254 Orders available for review in the Washington records in alphabetical order. Many thousands of such orders were made, including younger members of Julya's wider family who had made the journey from Lackenbach to Vienna and then to Palestine. There is no record of any order having been made for Julya's deportation and so mercifully he was at least spared this. There is also no date specified in the records on file for his release. Where no deportation order was made, a typical length of imprisonment for this offence would have been anything from one to six months for more 'serious' cases. It would seem that Julya was not imprisoned for any great length of time.

There would not have been much space in the camp for all these new inmates. There is a short news report from the end of August 1939 indicating the release of about 300 of those recently sent to Sarafand.[23] This would match with Julya's arrival in Palestine and at the age of forty-three he would have been a promising candidate for early release.

Make no mistake, the British policy of prevention of all immigration was enforced with deadly earnest. The conditions at both Atlit and Sarafand were extremely harsh. There had been a hunger strike by seventy-three Jewish prisoners at Sarafand just days before Julya's arrival. Correspondence passed between Malcom Macdonald and Sir Harold MacMichael, the High Commissioner, as to how to break the protest. In the end forced feeding was recommended and carried out, although the Colonial Office stopped short of whipping, which was used in such circumstances in India.[24] In another stomach-churning moment during my researches I came across reports of prisoners at Atlit who had been taunted on their arrival by the British soldiers saying, 'Here is your Dachau.'[25] Since over a hundred and fifty passengers on the *Aghios Nikolaos* had been released from Dachau only weeks before boarding *The Rim* at Constanza, this was dark indeed.

The British determination to stop the refugees at all costs was firm and fixed. The first people shot and killed by British soldiers on 1 September 1939, the day war broke out, were two unarmed refugees on SS *Tiger Hill*, which was the next vessel to arrive after the *Aghios Nikolaos* laden with those fleeing the Nazis.[26] This is to say the least an extremely uncomfortable page of British history.

Indeed, it had seemed so at the time to a number of the soldiers who were stationed there. By the oddest coincidence I was able to hear the account of one of the soldiers who would have been on the beaches tasked with the job of preventing those like Julya from landing. In all places I came to hear of this on an early morning walk with Oscar, our dog. Amidst the small crowd of regulars on Primrose Hill was Howard, just shy of his hundredth birthday with the wonderful bearing and straight back of a former British army officer. He had initially served with the paratroops and was then recruited into the SAS during the Second World War, undergoing gruelling training in Scotland. Today in all weathers, sometimes in a fetching yellow sou'wester with a matching hat, he can be seen with his four-legged troops struggling to keep pace.

One morning, as we walked around together with our canine charges, he greeted an Israeli member of our little group with a cheerful salutation in fluent Hebrew. I was suitably astonished, and he told me the following. In the war he had served as an officer in the British special forces behind enemy lines in the build-up to the Normandy landings (his principal task being to survey the list of target beaches and collect sand samples for further analysis). He was then sent on a quite different mission to Palestine to repel all those who tried to enter the country and deal with any local disturbance. He could still recall vividly standing on a vantage point, only yards away from where Julya had landed, overlooking the beach at dawn seeing a group of bedraggled immigrants arrive by sea, wading onto the shoreline. One of his fellow junior officers questioned why they were not firing warning shots or at the very least arresting them. Howard responded that it just did not seem right to hound these wretched people and that they had suffered enough. Shortly after this incident he was reported for this conduct to his superiors by the junior officer who had witnessed Howard's reluctance. His card was marked as 'PZ' – Pro Zionist – and he was transferred out of Palestine and stationed elsewhere.[27]

The British policy with regard to immigration had an unintended consequence. It united, at least temporarily, the many warring factions of the Zionist movement. Each was as determined as the other that those who could be saved from Europe had to be, and by whatever means. In August 1939, Berl Katznelson, one of Ben Gurion's closest advisers and a leading socialist figure in the Zionist movement, spoke up at the Twenty-First Zionist Congress in Geneva. What he said applied to Julya and in part to a whole generation in his position:

> We do not determine the course of history, and neither can foresee what it will bring. We may ask why it is that history did not choose free, wealthy and well-behaved Jews to be the bearers if its mission, but preferred instead the Jewish refugee, the most wretched of all humankind, cast adrift on the seas. But this is a fact we cannot change. This is what history has determined and it is left to us to accept its choice and to follow the refugee.[28]

This powerful image was an uncomfortable one and was seen as such by those who survived and had suffered in doing so. There is a natural reluctance for any people to be seen as being on its knees and this was, I believe, a key factor in the silence that followed for years after the war. The notion of the pitiable refugee or survivor touched on emotions too difficult to process and certainly too awkward to display before another, younger generation. Many felt it was simply better to close up and say nothing. Others made a distinct virtue of consigning the past to the dustbin. As one survivor Eliezer Adler put it: 'Forgetfulness is a great thing. A person forgets, because if they couldn't forget they couldn't build a new life.'[29]

Dwelling on the past certainly did not fit the mood of the society into which Julya had landed. There was even a little embarrassment.

Those who, like Julya, survived, also knew how slender the margin was. Some could never overcome the guilt they felt about those who did not make it or were left behind. For many others it would loosen or even destroy their previous tight bonds of faith. Frequently, orthodox Jews will invoke divine providence (*Beshert*) if they find themselves the beneficiary of some unexpected upturn in fortune. It must have been hard for anyone who had escaped the horrors to do this when logic would imply that this same divinity had determined so many blameless innocents would suffer and die.

In spite of everything, Julya did survive his ordeal, but the price was a high one. His health was broken and he had caught encephalitis in the waters off Simi, or maybe in the camp at Rhodes. He became thin, almost gaunt. He can be seen at this time with his suit ill-fitting and falling off his slender frame. Gone was the confident expression at the quayside in Romania. It was not just his health that suffered. His sprit was a little shaken, too. He was separated from all he loved, his wife and daughter. I am not sure how exactly they maintained any kind of relationship, I do know, however, that they corresponded regularly and he sent photographs whenever he could. Now that he had landed in what would become Israel, he adopted his Hebrew name, Josef, and discarded any reminder of his Austro-Hungarian past. As a proud man and head of the family it must have really hurt that he was not able to protect them but instead was largely reliant on handouts. He was not a provider but a burden. It must have been emasculating in the extreme. Julya spent the Second World War in Palestine, first on a kibbutz and then for some years living in Tel Aviv with Max. Apparently, on occasion he helped his younger brother-in-law in his tailoring business. After all, Julya knew all about cloth from his haberdashery store in Lackenbach, but this was modest work and would hardly achieve his object of allowing himself to settle down and perhaps bring his family over to join him.

Terci hung onto all of Julya's letters from Palestine together with the silver candlesticks she had taken to him each week in her secret visits before she left Vienna. She kept them in a compact weekend travel case when she moved to her flat in North London's Golders Green from Southport. There they remained until they were stolen in a burglary in the early 1970s. At the time of the break- in, at the tender age of ten or so, I remember how upset she was but never fully understood why. These were some of her very last relics of her stoical husband.

23

The Kladovo Transport

There was a lively atmosphere at the quayside on the Danube at Bratislava that crisp morning in late November 1939. Over a thousand had gathered from all parts of Austria, Slovakia, Bohemia, Moravia, and Germany, to start their journey to Palestine, first by river and then by sea. Many others had come to see them off. This was the largest such group to date to leave Central Europe. The transport was devised and funded exclusively by and for members of Zionist youth organisations. These were teenagers led by group leaders and activists like Ehud Nahir in their twenties looking to fulfil their dreams of starting a new life in a Jewish homeland. So it was not just an escape from the terrors of Europe but also freedom from all parental restriction and control and with the potential to build something quite new. The atmosphere was akin to an oversized university jamboree travelling to take part in youth games in foreign parts. At the centre of the project were those involved in *Hashomer Hatzair*, a socialist youth organisation that encouraged emigration of those who sought to live on a kibbutz and do agricultural work. There were many others, including *Hehalutz* pioneers and Zionist religious groups. This kaleidoscopic assembly became known as the Kladovo Transport.

Two of the excited passengers were Heinrich and Karoline's eighteen-year-old twins, their daughters, Wilma and Gina. It must have been next to impossible for the parents to see them off and say goodbye, even though Heinrich had always said that if he were younger, he would himself go to Palestine and no doubt some of that infectious enthusiasm had been passed on to them. The girls would have felt the separation keenly. Each would have understood that from that moment Heinrich and Karoline would have been alone in Vienna.

The passage by sea to Palestine had been tried and tested and no doubt everyone was anxious to ensure that if they could leave, they should do so and quickly. What is more, now that war had been declared between Britain and Germany, the wider political landscape was uncertain to say the least, and it was unclear to everyone how long even this perilous route on the Danube would be open.

They left Bratislava on a luxurious river steamboat of the Danube Steamship Company called the *Uranus,* which had been used in better times by tourists plying up and down the river. At the border of Hungary and Serbia near to Bezdan, they were transferred onto smaller and much more modest river boats that had been hired for the rest of the journey. Three such boats were hired for the purpose: The *Tszar Nicholas II,* the *Tszar Dusan* and the *Queen Maria* – their flotilla was referred to as the two Emperors and their Queen. Wilma and Gina were placed on board the *Tszar Nicholas II,* which took most of the younger women. Two of the leaders accompanying the group were the brothers Emil and Jozi Schechter. Emil was a businessman and responsible for much of the logistics on board. Jozi Schechter, the younger brother, was more mechanically minded, an electrician and with experience as a carpenter. As matters tuned out, the skills of each would be needed for the journey ahead.

As I grew up any mention of the twins to Terci and Julci required extreme care. They were indivisible, joined at the hip. They were referred to simply as 'the twins'. They can be seen standing in the middle of the back row of the family photograph wearing identical floral dresses. They were clearly not, however, identical. One looked very much like her mother, my great grandmother, Karoline, with darker hair and a pretty smile. The other, perhaps a little more like her elder sisters, had a more rounded and slightly more serious face. As I grew up, I never even asked their names to identify each of them separately. It is only some ninety years after the events in question that I have been able to source a photograph of Wilma labelled as such.

If all those years ago I pressed for any details or stories about them, Terci would sigh, tell me how beautiful they were, and that was it. Even making allowance for all the usual sensitivities surrounding the past, I learned pretty quickly that this was a subject best left alone. So, the story told here has had to be sourced primarily from the long-forgotten records held in dusty archives, the surviving accounts of those within the group and remarkably enough, what I have discovered of the twins' own words.

The two Emperors and their Queen made their way through Czechoslovakia, Hungary and Serbia down the Danube, travelling at a suitably stately pace for royalty. By December 1939 they had travelled nearly eight hundred kilometres and reached Kladovo, a small town on the right bank of the river, situated at the border of what was then Yugoslavia and Romania (across the river from Kladovo, could be seen the non-descript Romanian industrial town of Severin). The twins were now more than halfway to the Black Sea and freedom. In the meantime, three weddings had taken place amongst the group of passengers, with the Captain of each boat taking turns to surrender his cabin for the wedding night, after which the newly-weds had to return to their very basic slatted bunks with minimal room and no heating.

The first sign of trouble was encountered when they reached Kladovo. The news was relayed to the boat Captains that they had to wait at the border of Romania because the organisers had not yet been able to secure a ship and crew to take them from the Black Sea port of Sulina to Palestine. Each effort came to naught. The initial arrangements collapsed when an attempt was made to purchase a vessel for US$42,000 from Turkish owners, only for Turkey to pass a law prohibiting the sale of Turkish vessels to foreigners.[1] Then attention shifted to another vessel the SS *Hilda,* but that, too, came to nothing when a crew could not be secured for the voyage.

Their situation was taken up in both the British Parliament and in the press. On 7 February 1940, Vernon Bartlett MP raised the matter in the Commons with the Colonial Secretary and asked whether the British Government would address the humanitarian disaster on the Danube by allowing these refugees to proceed to Palestine, thereby also removing the threat of imprisonment which faced the shipowners. Addressing the few MPs present in the chamber sufficiently interested to hear of the position, Malcom Macdonald said he knew of those stranded on the Danube but declined to adopt the proposed suggestion. He cited the heightened concern in times of war of the dangers posed by supposed enemy agents travelling to Palestine by such means.[2] This line had been taken in a Foreign Office report from January 1940, but Macdonald did not really have his heart in the notion. On 20 February 1940, the Colonial Secretary wrote to the Foreign Office questioning whether it would really be practical for the Germans to introduce agents in this way. But Macdonald lacked the will or courage to take any stand and he simply bowed to the views of the Foreign Office mandarins.[3]

The matter did not stop there. British intelligence interrogated prisoners to find evidence of infiltration from those who arrived in Palestine on such ships, unsurprisingly without success. The Foreign Office as a result had to report; 'No proof yet regarding suspicions sending enemy agents amongst passengers.'[4] Without any scruple, Whitehall agitated where it could in order to impede the journey of such refugees. Some of this effort clearly bore fruit, such that on 17 January 1940 the Foreign Office reported in an internal telegram:

> The harbour authorities at Constanza have forbidden seamen registered in Romania to sign on with ships bringing Jewish emigrants to Palestine... This is good news... The agitation is probably an echo of our BBC Foreign News items. We should ask Mr Downie to give us whenever possible material for BBC. SS *Hilda* case [which as a result could not find a crew] should provide excellent material.[5]

Wilma, Gina and the rest of the group were all trapped on the Yugoslav side of the border. The winter of 1939-1940 was exceptionally severe. The Danube froze over and was impassable until about March 1940. Temperatures dropped to more than twenty below freezing. Drinking water had to be obtained by drilling through the ice. Many came down with dysentery or scurvy. Perhaps unsurprisingly, none of the passengers was allowed to leave the boats or go into Kladovo itself.

The Jewish community of Belgrade, nearly four hundred kilometres away, came to the rescue at a cost that it could ill afford to bear. They provided food, winter clothing and schnapps, which could be added to the tea in order to give some respite from the cold. Every piece of available fabric material was used for additional clothing and the boats were stripped of any spare wood for fuel.

The British Foreign Office continued to monitor the position closely and stepped up its obstructive response. Incredibly enough, this extended to making efforts to stop humanitarian aid reaching the group freezing in the bitter conditions. Word had reached London that the American Joint Distribution Committee (a Jewish charitable organisation) was seeking to provide financial assistance to the Jews of Belgrade so that they could continue providing their help. A telegram on 20 January 1940 from the Foreign Office stated dryly that 'an effort should be made to prevent the assistance being given.'[6] After confirmation of the report of what was intended from America had been received from the British Consul in Belgrade, Sir Harold Emerson, a former Governor of the Punjab who in September 1938 had been appointed as the League of Nations High Commissioner for Refugees, reported that he had tried to prevent those in America from giving any aid.[7] Remarkably, given his job title, he did not consider that his role extended actually to providing assistance to Jewish refugees.

The spring of 1940 turned to summer, and the military situation in Europe had of course sharply deteriorated. Germany had invaded Belgium and France. The British forces were surrounded and in full retreat towards Dunkirk. Kladovo was a long way away from that theatre of war and those stuck there were now largely forgotten. Nevertheless, after the harsh winter receded, there was a material improvement in the conditions of the group. Permission was received for accommodation to be set up in tents on the shoreline of the river, allowing people to leave the boats at long last. Others were put up in local houses, which were rented. A coal barge was even converted with bunks to alleviate some of the crowded conditions on the three original boats. Romances blossomed. A number of babies were born and arrangements were made to circumcise the male babies in these makeshift conditions. There was considerable surprise when a group of about thirty young Jews who had come all the way from Poland on foot appeared from nowhere to join those at Kladovo.

With the warmer weather, it was possible to swim in the Danube and pass the time with sport. There was even a mini football league contested by the different youth organisations. One photograph shows a half a dozen young men wearing not that much to cover their modesty forming a human pyramid.

I have scoured through the many pictures which have been collected in both the archives of the United States Holocaust Museum and at Yad Vashem in Israel, looking for some sign of the twins. My starting assumption was that if they were to be found in these images, then it would be amongst one of the more religious of the organisations at Kladovo. I then spotted something in an image of a group of about fifty standing in front of a house, apparently at Kladovo. Two flags are being waved, each with Hebrew writing. On the right, the flag identifies the group as *Brit Hanoar Hamizrachi*. The flag on the left displays the Star of David and the slogan *Torah ve avodah* (Bible and Work.) This was the first picture I had seen of a religious Zionist youth group at Kladovo and so potentially looked promising.

In the fourth row, standing fifth and sixth from the right and just below the man bearing the *Hanoar Hamizrachi* flag are two young women wearing identical plain white blouses next to one another and smiling. Are these two Wilma and Gina? The strong resemblance is undoubtedly there. Of course, nothing can be known with any certainty except that they were there in Kladovo, together with a religious youth group of this size. It would be comforting to think that they were at this time living with a tight group of friends, each looking after one another. They look contented, and not overwhelmed by concern as to what might happen to them. There would no doubt have been close friendships, unbreakable bonds, crushes, passions and liaisons. They were all living together in such close quarters for too long for anything else to be realistic. No one was watching. They were marooned and not at liberty, but they were more or less free amongst themselves. A small number of their letters have survived from this time written small so that as much as possible could be crammed onto the page.

From Gina and Wilma Grunsfeld c/o No 918 Adjancia, Kladovo, Yugoslavia

2 August 1940

Dear Hugo

I am sure you'll be very surprised to hear from us after such a long interval and to get a sign of life from us from Kladovo. Yes, unfortunately, and perhaps thank God, we are still here, and who knows when will get away. At the moment that isn't the most important thing. Most important is that we are all well and that we can assure you of this. Now we have a big request to ask you. We can't get in touch with Julci and Terci. I would ask you to pass on to them from us our very best greetings. We have heard that we can get in touch with them through you. We haven't heard anything for a long time from our dear parents. We would dearly like to have a sign of life from them. We used to get post quite regularly from our parents. They were apparently well and had enough to eat. Of course, they would like to leave there as soon as possible. As for us we could write you a whole novel of what has happened and what we had lived though in the last eight months. The long winter in the boats. That was no small thing. We have now been here three months, we're quite well accommodated with fifty young people in one house. It's often very merry but sometimes too loud and I'd rather be alone. When the weather's nice, we go swimming in the Danube. It is very beautiful there.

We have got sufficient to eat but the food is not very good. It's very difficult to be without any money but we have to trust our fate into the hands of God and hope there our circumstances will change for finally one day [sic] and the time will come when we will be able to leave here. There was talk here that we will get certificates to travel to our destination but we no longer believe it. I won't really believe it until I see it. We have been promised so many things, so many times and nothing happened so that in the end we have stopped believing in anything. Sad enough for young people. We have suffered so much and had some disappointments.

But enough of that, how are you and how are both your parents, Monica, Elsa and her husband? Please write to us in detail. It is a Yom Tov (a holiday) for us when we get any post. Please write whether you have heard from Julci and Terci and if you know anything about them? Is there any point in writing to the Red Cross?

I remain with many greetings and kisses from your ever grateful Gina.

My dears,
I too would be very grateful to you if you could send our best wishes to Julci and Terci tell them that they should please write to us. I would be very happy as we know nothing about what has happened to them. We are quite well. We have what we need. How are you all?

I remain with many, many greetings your ever grateful Wilma.

The Hugo addressed was a cousin, Hugo Sussman, who lived in Zurich. He was used as a postal intermediary benefitting from an address in neutral Switzerland and so able to forward their news to the rest of the family. Hugo was an extremely kindly man. Some years after the war ended, he opened his house to Judy and Ruth as they undertook their first independent travel through Europe by train. He was always at hand to provide help, support, send food and ensure as far as possible the letters reached their ultimate destination. It seems he even once visited the twins whilst they were marooned and delivered food and provisions. By no means all the twins' letters reached their intended destination, however, and even fewer such communications reached them at Kladovo.

In September 1940 the whole group was told that they could no longer stay at Kladovo and they were to be transferred to a more permanent camp at Sabac, about two hundred kilometres back towards Slovakia, further away from the hoped-for freedom on the Romanian coast. Sabac was situated on the banks of the Sava River, one of the tributaries of the Danube. Psychologically, this must have been a bitter blow. The obstacles were mounting higher each day. It seems a tussle was taking place behind the scenes between the Yugoslav and Slovakian governments, each telling the other that they could not remain on their territory.[8] The uniform position adopted at this time across Europe was that Jews were simply a problem. They were rejected by all, accepted by none – and this was not limited to the Reich.

To make matters worse, a large river boat was seen passing them towards Romania carrying another multitude of refugees at the same time as the Kladovo group retreated into the heartland of Central Europe. People cried out as they thought they saw faces they recognised. There was near panic as some attempted to jump ship and take the passage going in the other direction towards the Black Sea.

At least the living conditions in Sabac were at first by and large bearable, before winter set in. People were allowed for the first time to go into the small town, walk around. Relatives and friends were allowed to visit them if they could get that far. If they had been sent or given money they could buy food, or even go to see a film at the local cinema which apparently showed a number of popular German films. A large amount of time was spent writing letters to loved ones and those that might be able to assist in obtaining visas or permits for Palestine.

Whilst the twins waited first at Kladovo and then at Sabac, the search for a vessel to take this growing group by sea to Palestine continued.

In the early summer of 1940, it seemed for a moment there was a breakthrough – the raising of funds with the assistance of the American Joint Distribution Committee to buy a vessel which could then be used to save those stuck at Kladovo and for subsequent journeys. This was the *Darien II*. The purchase was completed by June 1940 and it was then to be refitted to take the Kladovo refugees.[9] At this point, some sort of informal understanding appears to have been reached between Mossad (the intelligence division of the Jewish Agency in Palestine and forerunner to the Israeli secret service today) and the British authorities. The true nature of the arrangement has been kept under lock and key for more than eighty years, but at its core it appears to have involved an agreement to shelve plans to utilise the *Darien II* that summer to try take the Kaldovo group to Palestine. Mossad agreed to provide some assistance to the British war effort as part of a wider plan to persuade Whitehall to loosen the restrictions on immigration. The precise form of assistance that would be provided by Mossad has itself been the subject of some speculation. One account has it that *Darien II* was not to be used as a passenger ship at all but fitted with high explosives and sunk at 'the Iron Gate,' a strategic location in a narrow gorge on the Danube, to block the river to German shipping.[10]

These somewhat fanciful plans came to nothing. British intelligence and Mossad quickly realised that if the Danube was to be blocked effectively, a very large number of vessels would have to be used and this required a scale of operation that was simply beyond reach. By late November 1940, the original plan to use *Darien II* to take the Kladovo refugees to Palestine was revived. The *Darien II* reached Sulina, but there was no sign of the luckless refugees who by this time were stuck at Sabac. In the meantime, Wilma and Gina had been told that their departure date from Sabac was fixed for 3 December 1940 and they were to pack their bags. Once more they were disappointed, this time on the very day fixed for them to leave, as the Yugoslav shipping company due to take them on the river to Sulina simply refused, for fear of not being able to return before the river froze.

22 December 1940, Sabac Yugoslavia

Dear Hugo

You will surely be very surprised to hear from us again after such a long time. You probably think that we would have arrived in Eretz [Palestine, 'the land'] a long time ago, but despite all efforts, we are still here and so I hardly need to tell you how we are, since there are so many emigrant camps near you. However, I don't want to complain. We should be pleased that thus far we are well and everything else is in God's hands. All we need is patience, but it is such a shame that we're spending the best years of our lives here doing nothing while a new future waits for us in Eretz.

I have a request: we have been attempting to contact our dear ones in England for some time and to an extent we have been successful, since we have received news from them via Switzerland. I would be very grateful if you could use the enclosed postal coupon to forward this letter to the address below. Please let me know if they can go by airmail, in which case I know if they can go back and how, in which case I shall send you more coupons to cover the cost.

You can well imagine how we are yearning for all of our loved ones. They are all now in many different locations and the only pleasure and joy we have in when we receive post from them. Life here is extremely monotonous although we are busy learning Hebrew and studying other subjects.

All this is not really a help, however, when it comes to our daily worries. For instance our dear parents were supposed to visit us, but when we were told we would be leaving here we put them off coming. Indeed, we had already packed all our belongings as the date had been fixed and the luggage sent to Belgrade but suddenly the trip was called off due to the icy conditions. By that time it was too late for our parents to undertake the arduous journey as the frosty conditions had already set in. And so we have to bide our time and wait until our luck changes. We simply have to keep on reminding ourselves that we trust in the Almighty and who knows what will happen.

However, I don't wish to burden you with our problems since you have also have your own. How are you and your loved ones? In particular. How are your dear parents? How often I think of the lovely times we enjoyed when you were here with us, but they are long past and we children have had to grow up fast and attain adulthood prematurely.

And so enough for today in the hope you're well and that you dear Hugo will be able to arrange to fulfil my request to forward the letter, with every good wish, your thankful Gina.

Please answer us soon

PS The address is Mrs Gerwurtz, and Mrs Lobl 24 Moorland Drive, Leeds 7

By 29 December 1940, the *Darien II* had left Sulina for Constanza and then for Palestine without the Kladovo refugees.[11] By then the group had become more or less resigned to their fate. Both the Danube and Sava Rivers froze over and it would have been widely understood that there would then be no chance of any exodus until the spring of 1941. By this time hope was all but gone.

Undated

Dear Hugo,

I do not wish to miss the opportunity of writing a few lines to you. We left home more than a year ago. Our apprehension knows no bounds. You know all too well how we all live together and that we were practically never apart and now we are spread all over the place, separated from each other and none of us know when we shall be reunited. It is in the hands of God: we are still young. We are not giving up the struggle and we only hope a better future awaits us. We have already suffered much and so we have not had much joy in our youth but nevertheless... [illegible]

How are you? Please write and let us know how you, the children, your parents and all of you are. How is Elsa? How is her father and the children? Please write. You can't know how we long to receive post from our loved ones. I thank you in anticipation for your kindness. I hope it isn't too much trouble for you and send best wishes to you and your loved ones

Your
[illegible]
Wilma.

24

Journey's End

What did the other letters say that have not survived? No doubt they would have described their wholly inadequate accommodation in an abandoned old corn mill at Janka Veselinovic in Sabac, with only broken windows to keep out the northerly wind and drifting snow. They would have added their thanks for the help provided by those who lived in the town, including a small Jewish community, who distributed food supplies out of a makeshift store. They might also have spoken of the occasional postcards received by the group from some of the lucky ones who had managed to get to Palestine. It is possible that those in the group who had come from Poland would have heard news of the Nazi occupation of Poland and the rounding up of their families into ghettos. Others wrote ever more desperate letters seeking to obtain by hook or by crook a permit to land in Palestine. The suffering caused many to lose all hope. Those who had no religious faith were hardest hit.

At the end of March 1941 there was bittersweet news. Finally, the British Government relented in part and agreed to provide permits to enter Palestine for about two hundred refugees, but only for those between the ages of fifteen and seventeen. Once more, Wilma and Gina were out of luck and ineligible. They were eighteen at the start of this fated odyssey and now had just turned twenty. There would presumably have been an emotional farewell for those who at long last left Sabac.

As for those who escaped, in the absence of any vessel they travelled by train. First there was a short hop to Belgrade, then a train to Greece, and onward through Turkey, Syria and Lebanon before finally making it to Palestine two weeks later.[1] Even at this stage, the only real impediment for those left behind was the British immigration policy in Palestine, which had in the summer of 1939 been determined to be unlawful by the Permanent Mandates Commission. Worse still, the policy adopted involved a refusal even to allow entry for the numbers provided for in the White Paper of May 1939. The Anglo-American Committee of Inquiry prepared in 1945-46 concluded that for the five-year period from 1939 to 1944, even allowing for those like Julya and Max who had arrived without a permit, a total of 51,186 Jews had been allowed into Palestine, compared with the promised figure of 75,000 set out in May 1939 before Parliament.[2] There was and should have been room for Wilma and Gina, indeed the whole Kladovo group and many more besides.

On 6 April 1941 air raid sirens could be heard in the early afternoon in Sabac. German bombers were seen overhead on the way to Belgrade. German, Hungarian and Bulgarian forces had combined to invade and dismantle Yugoslavia. Within days, German troops arrived at the Janka Veselinovic mill and ordered everyone out. They were moved to a nearby former military barracks, and it was gleefully announced that this took another 1000 'vermin' off the streets. The group was divided into six huts, each with about 150 prisoners. They were given harsh work details, but even at this stage there was no indication of their fate from the German soldiers guarding them.[3]

In late September 1941 the German army units at Sabac found themselves surrounded by a well-armed and disciplined Serb partisan group. For a few days the Germans feared the worst. They had been outfought and outmanoeuvred. In a nearby related action, many German troops were taken prisoner by the partisans.[4] At the very last gasp, German reinforcements arrived and beat them back. The *Daily Mirror* reported the fighting and that in consequence the German army rounded up and shot 73 partisans and those suspected of helping them.[5]

In the wake of these events, fresh terror descended on the military barracks. On 11 October 1941 at 6pm in the evening, an Einsatzgruppe unit arrived and ordered all the men to line up in the yard in alphabetical order. The order was then given for them to march.

In the archives of Yad Vashem is a photocopy of Report No 108 sent on 9 October 1941 by Wilhelm Fuchs, the Chief of the Belgrade Office of Einsatzgruppe Serbia, to RSHA Director Eichmann in Berlin. It records that following the recent operation, 22,000 had been captured and held in a makeshift warehouse and were to be kept there under the command of an SS unit and the Belgrade Police. The report continued that after it was found that twenty-one German soldiers had been shot in an attack near Topola, 2,100 Jews and Roma were to be executed; 805 from the Jews and Roma held at the Sabac camp and the rest from the Jewish community in Belgrade.

The document bears on its front page the stamp 'Office of the Chief Counsel of War Crimes Document No 3156'. It was part of evidence used against twenty-two defendants for their involvement in the crimes of the Einsatzgruppen across Nazi-occupied Europe. This became known as the Einsatzgruppen Trial. In April 1948, they were found guilty and fourteen were sentenced to death by hanging for their direct involvement in murdering an estimated two million, including Jews, Roma, Ukrainians, Russians, Serbs and many others.[6] That last sentence forces the mind to pause. Included in the overall figure of six million Jews killed in the Holocaust were the estimated 1.3 million murdered by bloodletting on an unimaginable scale by the Einsatzgruppen who marauded over the conquered territories of Central and Eastern Europe from May 1941 until 1943.[7] This figure exceeds, by some margin, even the horrors of Auschwitz-Birkenau.[8]

The Einsatzgruppen Trial judgment started out with two important observations. That the number of dead itself could not be grasped, being too big, and for it to be mentally assimilated it had to be broken down into separate incidents. It had to be looked at in terms of individuals or family groups in order to be understood. It was also noted that this was not killing at a distance from an office desk but in the field by those 'superintending controlling, directing and taking an active part in the bloody harvest'. It has been called the Holocaust by bullets.[9]

The judgment recorded that the principal and often sole evidence for the prosecution was found in the daily reports sent by the Einsatzgruppe Chiefs to Berlin of what they were about to do and what they had done. These reports were extraordinarily explicit. This was a body of evidence created between 1941 and 1943 before it would have seemed likely to any of the authors that Germany would lose the war. Hence the candour. Jews and Roma were referred to as being 'executed'; 'shot'; 'liquidated', 'disposed of', 'killed', and 'done away with'. Only rarely would there be some kind of dissimulation, referring to Jews having been 'appropriately treated'. Nevertheless, all room for ambiguity would be dispelled when after a series of such actions an area or region would be declared to be, 'Free of Jews'. Throughout, there was a commoditization of treatment. For hundreds of years in Europe, Jews had not been treated as individuals but as a collective problem. Now the victims were simply referred to by number, location and final outcome.

In other reports, the murder of a number of Jews was said to be justified because of an outbreak of typhus or similar. Jews were an infection to be removed from society. It is sometimes asked, when did the Holocaust begin? It is not clear if the question serves a useful purpose or whether any answer can be given, but it can be said that it could not have happened but for the generic treatment of Jews as an indivisible people supposedly exhibiting all the negative characteristics marshalled and developed over centuries that could then be held accountable collectively for punishment. Equally, it is frequently debated whether mankind has forever banished these horrors or whether they are lurking beneath. The same response must be given: however many memorials are built to the past and however much is taught in schools, the danger persists today so long as this collective identification and treatment exists and flourishes.

As is recorded in the Einsatzgruppen Trial judgment with regard to Report no 108,[10] there was no attempt to suggest that the 2,100 Jews and Roma to be murdered were in any way involved in the recent military action or responsible for the deaths of the twenty-one soldiers and the collective punishment formed part of the evidence leading to the conviction of those involved. The 22,000 suspected of being partisans who were rounded up appear to have been kept in some form of camp. It was also pointed out in the judgment that the figure of 2,100 was obviously a hundred times the number of the killed German soldiers and intended to instil a sense of terror in the local populace.

There is also at Yad Vashem a list of all those killed in October 1941 at Sabac, with their names, ages and where they came from. Some were fractionally above the seventeen-year-old threshold and so ineligible for a permit to get to Palestine. One or two were younger than that, but for whatever reason did not receive a permit or just did not leave in March that year. A partisan hiding in the nearby woods told of their fate. German troops fixed staves into the ground and in groups of fifty at a time they were shot. Two soldiers for each prisoner. A detachment of prisoners then had to dig graves. Before anyone was buried, they searched the bodies for valuables and had to hand them over to the watching troops.

The role of Eichmann in the murder of the Jews of Belgrade alongside those at Sabac surfaced in the course of his trial in 1961. The matter was exposed in this way. On 8 September 1941, a representative of the German Foreign Ministry in Belgrade sent a message to Berlin with regard to the Jews of Belgrade and proposed that they be rounded up and deported to one of the islands on the Danube delta. Another proposal was to send them to Russia. On 13 September 1941, Franz Rademacher, who worked in Berlin at the Foreign Ministry as Advisor on Jewish Affairs, noted in a typed memorandum in his name that in response to these proposals, 'According to Eichmann there is no possibility of sending them to Russia. Eichmann proposes to kill them by shooting.' Rademacher was examined on this document at the Einsatzgruppen Trial. He gave evidence that he spoke to Eichmann on the telephone and recorded Eichmann's conclusion and decision in the memorandum. Rademacher said 'Eichmann repeated, kill them by shooting, *Erschussen*.' At his own trial, Eichmann denied this and instead argued that the document was simply a forgery. No evidence to support such a defence was advanced and it was rejected.[11] This was typical of Eichmann, to assert forgery when faced with damning documentary evidence giving the lie to his denials.

After the murder of all the men, the women and children remained at the barracks. By this time Wilma and Gina would have been required to wear a yellow star on their clothing. In fact, two yellow stars. One on the left breast and one on the right shoulder. Then on 26 January 1942, all those who remained were taken from Sabac and transported about sixty kilometres to a concentration camp at Staro Sajmište on the outskirts of Belgrade. It was built on the site of Belgrade's old fairground. For the twins, who before they left Vienna had been living just around the corner from the Prater fairground, this must have been a grim irony.

Anna Hecht who had lost her husband in the mass shooting at Sabac wrote that the conditions there were harsh. In the bleak winter of 1942 work details cleared the snow at the nearby airport to enable planes to land. Wearing torn, inadequate clothing they were given brushes to sweep the snow from the runway, only for it to be blown back immediately by the biting wind. After several hours of this work, each was ordered back to the camp and given a bowl of soup. The camp at Staro Sajmište held both Jewish and Roma prisoners. Anna Hecht wrote that she felt particularly sorry for the Roma, who were treated even more harshly and given worse food rations. It is estimated that over a third of the Roma of Serbia were murdered or died of disease and starvation at Sajmište.

Wilma and Gina must have known that time had run out. I have for some time hesitated as to whether to write these next paragraphs. I have had to ask myself what purpose is served by providing the last grim details. I could simply record that from the documents I have seen Wilma and Gina Grunsfeld were murdered at Sajmište near Belgrade in 1942. Two of the six million. Nevertheless, I have in the end come to the conclusion I must set down the rest. There should be no averting of our gaze so that we can understand better the consequences of action and inaction.

On 20 January 1942, at the invitation of SS Obergruppenführer Reinhard Heydrich, fifteen senior Nazi government ministers, including the Minister of Justice, the Interior Minister, and the Under Secretary at the Foreign Ministry, met at Wannsee in order to endorse and set in motion the Final Solution for the rounding up and extermination of the Jews of Europe. Heydrich was the director of the RSHA in Berlin at which Eichmann worked. Eichmann reported to Heydrich through Heinrich Muller. The purpose of the Wannsee Conference was better to co-ordinate the effort of a large number of different ministries in order to implement a centrally organised plan for mass murder, which would then be directed and carried out by the RSHA. Since May 1941, the Einsatzgruppen had already been carrying out the infamous Führer Order for the murder of Jews. In July 1941 Heydrich had issued a decree to the SS that all Jewish males between 15 and 45 were to be deemed partisans and shot.

Nevertheless, the Nazi leadership could not see systematic shooting even on this unimaginable scale as fulfilling their objective. The matter had to be approached methodically. As part of the preparation, Eichmann provided a list of the numbers of Jews said to be present in different territories. Eichmann estimated that 11 million Jews lived in Europe at the time. It also required discussion of which categories of person, if any, was to be spared. Specifically, Jews over the age of 65 and those who had fought in the First World War and either been severely wounded or received an Iron Cross were not to be killed.

Likewise, those needed for particular areas of war work. Not for the first time in this story, age mattered. The exemption of those over 65 years of age would apply to Heinrich Grunsfeld, the twins' father. Karoline, their mother, however, would not be so lucky. The plan also needed clear identification of those responsible to carry it out. The Wannsee Conference was principally concerned with methodology and hierarchical structure. It was not the formulation of a new policy that Jews in the Reich and occupied territory were to be killed. This was more the who and the where. The Wannsee Conference did not it seems discuss how the Jews were to be killed. These were granular operational details, which would not be suitable for such a large meeting.

The methods used for mass killing of Jews developed over time. It is said that in August 1941 Himmler attended a mass shooting of Jews in Minsk and vomited. He is reported as saying that other ways of killing the Jews had to be found. It was also recorded in the Judgment of the Military Tribunal that when the Führer Order for the shooting of Jews was extended to women and children there was a degree of sympathy amongst the soldiers for the victims. It was necessary therefore, if the killing were to continue, to find other means of carrying out these orders which did not disturb (to the point of inefficiency) those carrying out the orders. Mass industrial-scale murder was designed as a balm for the perpetrators.

The first major alternative that was put into operation was the gas van; a sealed van which gassed to death through carbon monoxide poisoning those imprisoned inside, developed by the SS under the watchful eye of two notorious henchmen of the Nazi regime; Reinhard Heydrich and Walter Rauff.[12] The specially modified vehicle was used extensively by the Einsatzgruppen in the conquered territories in the East and also in Yugoslavia, where it was called the *Dusegupka*, the soul killer. Each gas van was fitted out in Berlin with a gas pipe and then driven to wherever it was needed.

In March 1942 the *Dusegupka* arrived at Sajmiste and was put into operation. As was frequently the case with the Nazi Holocaust, deception was used in order to set the wheels in motion. So the Austrian camp concentration commander, SS Untersturmführer Herbert Andorfer, told the women and children that it had been determined that the Sajmište Camp was too crowded and they were to be taken by transport to another camp.[13] As each group was led to the gas van they were methodically stripped of their valuables, money and sometimes clothes. Emanuel Schäfer of the Einsatzgruppe Serbia oversaw the operation. A little over 7,000 Jews at that time imprisoned at Sajmiste were murdered in these gas vans. They were killed fifty at a time, including Wilma and Gina, whilst the sealed van with no windows was driven round the streets of Belgrade as people went about their daily business. Amongst those killed were also the Jews of Belgrade whom Eichmann had said should be killed. There were many Roma who suffered the same fate. Serbian prisoners in work details then had to bury the dead in mass graves in Jalinici. The *Dusegupka* had finished its work by 10 May 1942. Only a handful escaped and were able to tell the tale.[14] Schäfer then wrote to the RSHA in Berlin declaring with considerable pride that 'Belgrade is the only great city of Europe to be free of Jews.'[15]

Schäfer's work was nothing if not thorough. Of the total population of 75,000 Jews in Serbia before the war, only about 11,000 survived. Unlike Jews elsewhere in Europe, they were killed in situ and not deported to concentration camps in Poland.

In the records of the Kladovo Transport held at Yad Vashem in Jerusalem, Wilma and Gina are recorded as victim numbers 316 and 317 of a total number of 1037. They died between March and May 1942. Their fate, however, had been sealed some time prior. Emanuel Schäfer was tried after the war in Germany and sentenced to six and half years in prison. He died in Germany a free man in his own home just short of his 75th birthday in 1974.

25

Eichmann

In mid-May 1960, David Ben Gurion, Prime Minister of Israel, received word from Harel Isser, the Director of Mossad, that Eichmann had been captured in the suburbs of Buenos Aires in Argentina and would be put on a plane to Israel. A fifteen-year search for one of the protagonists of each phase of the Holocaust had come to an end.

At the very end of the war, when German defeat was imminent, Eichmann took to the Blaa-Alm lodge in a secluded valley north of Altaussee in the Salzkammergut, the beautiful Austrian lake district a hundred or so kilometres from Linz where he had grown up and gone to school; incidentally, the same high school that Hitler had attended some years prior. Initially, he disappeared with a small cadre of trusted soldiers but then he found himself holed up with amongst others SS-Obersturmführer Anton Burger, his good friend and former commandant of Theresienstadt concentration camp. After a somewhat heated discussion, the view was expressed that the Allies were looking for Eichmann and not them, and so he should sling his hook, which Eichmann did and headed for Saxony.[1]

In May and again in June 1945 Eichmann was arrested and held briefly by the United States Army but gave a false name and was released on each occasion. Both his SS blood group tattoo near the arm pit and his stated name, Eckmann, ought to have given rise to more detailed inquiry but in the confusion of the immediate aftermath of war he slipped through the coarsely woven net. For nearly five years he was sheltered in Lower Saxony in Germany until he was able to reach Argentina through a network of former brothers in arms, where he was then assisted by a substantial group of like-minded friends and acquaintances, including the notorious Auschwitz torturer Dr Mengele with whom he would share the occasional drink at the Café ABC in Buenos Aires, and Eberhardt Fritsch, the editor of the openly Nazi monthly journal, *Der Weg*.[2]

Each attempt to track him down led nowhere. In 1952, his wife who had been living in Bad Aussee in Austria and had unsuccessfully tried to register Eichmann as deceased, then joined him in Argentina. There they raised their three children. Eichmann, now in his mid-forties, managed to get by taking a variety of jobs for which his past record did not particularly equip him. Amongst other things, he worked in a laundry, on an Angora rabbit farm, as a car mechanic and posed in a photograph working as a gaucho replete with poncho.[3] Then chance or fate intervened.

His son Nicholas Eichmann met and had a date with the Jewish daughter of a curious blind retiree who lived alone in Coronel Suarez, a few kilometres from Buenos Aires. The blind man had been born in Germany and his parents had been murdered in the Holocaust. When the father and daughter caught up, he asked about her new boyfriend and the name Eichmann rang a bell. He encouraged the daughter to find out more and eventually after she gave a few further details which seemed to fit, she arranged one day to meet him at his house. Nicholas answered the door and Adolf Eichmann stood immediately behind him wearing his distinctive black-rimmed glasses. She gave this description to her father who was now certain he was on the trail. He wrote to Fritz Bauer, the Public Prosecutor in Essen, Germany. He in turn informed Israel's Mossad who sent a team to identify and capture Eichmann.

After an elaborate operation, on 11 May 1960 he was bundled into a car and taken to a safe house on the outskirts of Buenos Aires. There was at first a brief moment of denial, and then he solemnly said, 'Ich Bin Adolf Eichmann SS number 45326.'[4]

Ben Gurion quickly saw the advantage of an open trial – the State of Israel vs Adolf Eichmann. The ends of justice had to be met and properly served, nevertheless this was also a unique opportunity to inform the whole society of the course of the Holocaust from start to finish.

In this context it is important to understand that between 1948 and 1951, over a quarter of a million Jews had been forced out of Iraq, Yemen and Libya by hostile government action as a result of the creation of this new country in 1948 and had come to live in Israel without any real experience of the catastrophe that had befallen Europe's Jews. By the time of the trial in 1961, the number of enforced exiles from Arab lands had substantially increased and so constituted approximately half of Israel's total population (today less than a third of Israelis are of European descent). Whilst many had indeed felt the full force of the murderous destruction, the shame of survival was such that in Israel a silence had fallen over this whole period of history.

On 17 April 1961, the Attorney General, Gideon Hausner, who led the prosecution, rose to his feet. He delivered over the course of two days one of the most famous trial opening statements of all time. Hausner had only finished his final tweaks to the opening lines with his wife's approval in the small hours of the morning before. Shimon Peres many years later said that the whole country shivered when he spoke these words;[5]

When I stand before you here, Judges of Israel, to lead the prosecution of Adolf Eichmann, I am not standing alone. With me are six million accusers. But they cannot rise to their feet and point an accusing finger towards him who sits in the dock and cry: 'I accuse.' For their ashes are piled up on the hills of Auschwitz and the fields of Treblinka, and are strewn in the forests of Poland. Their graves are scattered throughout the length and breadth of Europe. Their blood cries out, but their voice is not heard. Therefore, I will be their spokesman and in their name I will unfold the awesome indictment.

There are certain aspects of this trial which distinguished it so memorably from the Nuremburg hearings. Eichmann was being tried in Jerusalem in Israel by a national court and not an international tribunal. He was being prosecuted and judged by the very people he stood accused of seeking to exterminate. This led to the accusation that the trial amounted to the victim's justice. [6] This was unfair, as Nuremburg could always be said to be the victor's justice. It also lacked any sense of reality, as Eichmann had to be tried by some court other than the courts of Nazi Germany. What really mattered was the process itself. Eichmann was afforded the opportunity to present his defence and cross examine witnesses through his chosen attorney, whose fees were paid for by the State, and tell his own story through eight days of testimony in chief. It was also the first war crimes trial to be televised and broadcast to viewers across the world and could be followed live on the radio across Israel.

So when Eichmann was sworn in, blinking behind his thick glasses, this was captured live on television. Likewise when he pleaded that he was not guilty of what he had been charged with and some in the public gallery fainted and had to be carried out of the courtroom. Further, unlike at Nuremburg, a policy decision was taken to bring evidence that engaged as far as possible the full chronology of the destruction of European Jewry. At certain times this led to evidence being adduced irrespective of a direct link to Eichmann himself. This is a fair criticism, nevertheless such evidence was the exception and was dealt with swiftly by the Court and did not form any part of the ultimate judgment. As a result, witnesses were called covering the forced expulsion of the Jews of Vienna in 1938, and the devising and implementation of each aspect of the Final Solution right up until the closing days of the war.

Professor Vered Vinitzky-Seroussi has written extensively about how palaces of collective memory are built in society.[7] In some ways the Eichmann trial was itself a palace of memory, albeit one built with the assistance of the technology of television. Wherever you were in the world, you could hear Eichmann's emotionless voice and clipped Austrian accent attempting to deny, explain away or defend his conduct. You could see his snarling, upturned lip – his condescending expression indicating his bemusement that he could be questioned in this way by a Jewish prosecutor in a trial taking place in Israel.

It is something of a curiosity that even though Eichmann was one of the principal architects and implementors of the destruction of Europe's Jews, his name had been mentioned only rarely in the course of the evidence before the International Military Tribunal at Nuremburg in 1945-46. This was perhaps understandable as he escaped arrest after the war and the prosecution clearly had enough to contend with concerning the defendants before them. There was no doubt, however, as to his importance, being head of the Office for Jewish Questions in the Reich's Security Main Office, the dreaded RHSA. Eichmann was identified in the main Nuremburg Trial judgment as having told one of his deputies, Dr Wilhelm Hoettl, that he, Eichmann, in a private conversation in the autumn of 1944, had estimated that Nazi policy had led to the extermination of about six million Jews in Europe, four million in the extermination camps and approximately two million murdered by the Einsatzgruppen. This evidence was more directed at giving a sense of the scale of the crimes than anything else and Hoettl would in the course of the Eichmann trial add a further chilling detail with regard to that evidence. When Eichmann told his deputy of his estimation of six million dead, Hoettl said Eichmann expressed concern. Eichmann misunderstood Hoettl's reaction as being one of disappointment and explained that this was a conservative estimate and sought to reassure him by adding that Himmler had thought the number was higher than that.[8]

Eichmann's overall perspective on these events was perhaps best captured by the evidence of what he said to a fellow officer in the last days of the war in 1945: 'I will leap into my grave laughing, because the feeling that I have five million human beings on my conscience is for me a source of extraordinary satisfaction.' In the course of evidence at the trial in Jerusalem, as had become his trademark, he tried to explain away this evidence as referring not the Holocaust but to events at the Russian front, but Judge Yitzhak Raveh referred him to a separate record where Eichmann had expressly referred to five million Jews, which Eichmann then accepted was a faithful reflection of his views in 1945.[9] When talking freely in Argentina amongst his cadre of wartime colleagues his principal regret was that 'We had not done our work correctly.'[10]

Prior to the commencement of his trial in Jerusalem, Eichmann was interviewed over a period of eight months by Chief Inspector Avner Less, born in Berlin before he emigrated to Palestine in 1936. The questioning which started on 29 May 1960 was conducted in German over multiple sessions lasting in total for more than 275 hours and continued until February 1961. As Less explained in his evidence at the trial, Eichmann was asked before the questioning began only to talk of his activities during the Third Reich between 1933-1945. Given this opportunity, Eichmann clearly had plenty to say. The full transcript filled 3,500 pages and when finalised it was approved and signed off by Eichmann, who acknowledged its accuracy. After this formality was completed, a photograph was taken of Eichmann and Less in the room which they had used each day. Eichmann even wrote to his brother praising the mode of procedure of the Israeli police.[11]

Avner Less formed the impression that Eichmann was often pleased with his answers and considered he had given a satisfactory account of his wartime record. Eichmann in setting out a defence of his conduct appeared to demonstrate good knowledge of the lines of argument deployed at Nuremburg. It is said that he spent a good deal of time in hiding in Germany reading the transcripts and judgment of that process. Quite apart from jurisdictional objections, he would consistently deny knowledge of events until a document was presented. When confronted with a document in his hand or addressed to him, he would try to play down his involvement as being merely an insignificant part of a much larger machine. When shown orders he himself had given, he would fall back on the well-worn defence that he was merely obeying orders.

Avner Less had prepared his groundwork meticulously. He had been given considerable help by H. G. Adler the Holocaust historian, and by the archivists at Yad Vashem who provided Less with a mass of contemporaneous records needed to unpick Eichmann's story. For each aspect of the case, he would show Eichmann one document after another rendering impossible any sensible form of denial of involvement. Parts of the interview have been translated into English. It is both a compelling record of the history of the Holocaust and a remarkable example of what might be described loosely as an 'open cross examination'. This is one of the hardest feats to accomplish for any advocate, let alone a police officer. It requires complete mastery of the record, good documentary support, and above all endless patience. Frequently it involves giving the witness enough rope to do the work for the questioner.

Time after time, Avner Less would show Eichmann a document and simply let him talk and provide an explanation without interruption. Eichmann would give lengthy, often rambling answers in a somewhat hard to understand German. At one point, Eichmann apologised and asked the police chief if his German was really that poor. Eichmann would try to work his way through the document and draw up a line of plausible deniability, only then to be confronted with the next document and the process started all over again. At the end of this marathon process, Eichmann seemed to have developed a grudging respect for his questioner, even though he must have known that this material alone would be enough to see him hanged.

Less was called himself to identify and authenticate the full interview tape and transcript.[12] When the policeman took to the stand and was sworn in, the cameras focussed not on him but on Eichmann, who knew exactly what was coming. He took out a pair of glasses from his suit pocket and began a lengthy process of cleaning then examining them whilst the witness took the oath. None of this would have been of particular note except for the fact that Eichmann was already wearing his black-rimmed spectacles. Less was cross-examined for under ten minutes by Dr Servatius, Eichmann's counsel, who no doubt sensed that there would be no advantage in extending his presence in the witness box. Extensive passages of the answers set out in the transcript were put to Eichmann in cross examination and referred to in the Court's judgement.

As for Eichmann's nemesis, many years later Less remarked that throughout the process he found himself fighting against his own hate, which he said did not achieve anything but only caused more problems. As with his biblical ancestor Job, Less seemed to appreciate that anger itself could kill a righteous man. Far better to follow the words of the Deuteronomist: 'Justice, justice shall you pursue.'

So much has been written about Eichmann and the trial that it is hard to focus on specific aspects which have not already been analysed repeatedly. Yet still, certain details in the course of Avner Less's questioning and the trial evidence do demand attention, illustrating perhaps Eichmann's most striking feature: his unswerving obsession with regard to the wider policy of extermination of an entire people, alongside his attention to specific details about the individual. This is of more than passing relevance to my family's story.

There is a passage in his interrogation which concerns a visit that Eichmann made to Auschwitz. Eichmann had been asked by Avner Less about some correspondence that had come across Eichmann's desk in December 1943 concerning an Italian Jew called Bernardo Tauber. Avner Less asked Eichmann why he was so concerned about the life of one single Jew. A wonderfully simple and elegant question. Eichmann gave the following answer. He said he was neither a Jew hater nor an anti-Semite and that he had repeatedly said the same to all of the Jewish leadership with whom he had dealt with when he was working in Vienna in 1938. 'I never had any trouble with the Jewish functionaries. And I don't think any of them would complain about me.' Eichmann then continued to recount the story of his dealings with Berthold Storfer.

Storfer's involvement at Evian and in the early attempts in 1938 and 1939 to find safe haven for the Jews of Vienna has already been recounted. Eichmann found that he could turn to Storfer when he needed results. So in October 1939, Eichmann summoned Storfer together with leaders of the Jewish community of Vienna and ordered them to draw up a list of 1,000 healthy Jews for resettlement in

Nisko in Poland. They duly complied. This was to be one of many forced deportations. By May 1940 Eichmann had appointed Storfer as the sole intermediary for all overseas transport affairs for the Jews of Vienna, Berlin and Prague. From this point on, any organisation seeking to make arrangements for Jews to leave Vienna had to work with Storfer and through Storfer with Eichmann.[13] This made Storfer a target of constant attack and many viewed him as a traitor. There cannot be any real doubt, however, that he would have had a hand in arranging the ships that took Max and others in the family away from Vienna. Storfer once protested to Eichmann about forced expulsion of those who were clearly sick and not in a position to leave. Eichmann responded, 'Let me be clear, these Jews will either leave in the Danube or on the Danube.'

In 1942, Storfer, along with many tens of thousands of others, was deported from Vienna to Theresienstadt, a concentration camp in the present-day Czech Republic. Despite his baptism he was still classified as a Jew under the Nuremberg laws. In May 1944 he was then taken from Theresienstadt to Auschwitz. Eichmann was the head of Section IV.B.4 of the RSHA (the Reich Security Main Office) which had overall responsibility for Jewish affairs, the deportation to the extermination camps, for the establishment of Auschwitz as a death camp and for the implementation of the Final Solution. The German railways transported many millions to their death, but this was organised and paid for by Eichmann's unit.

Some time after Storfer's arrival at Auschwitz, Eichmann received a communication from Rudolf Höss, the notorious Auschwitz camp commandant with regard to Storfer. It seems that Storfer had pleaded with Höss that his having been sent to Auschwitz was a huge mistake as he was not himself Jewish and had worked closely with no less than Eichmann himself. Accordingly, Höss wrote to Eichmann asking what he should do. Höss was subordinate to Eichmann in the chain of command and had written to him seeking guidance. Eichmann did not respond to the telegram. Instead, in mid-1944 as Eichmann explained to Avner Less, he undertook the journey of nearly 600 kilometres from Berlin to Auschwitz in person. As Rudolf Höss detailed in his memoirs, he had met Eichmann on more than one occasion at Auschwitz who from time to time would come in person to discuss the minutiae of the operations of the extermination of the Jews, which in Höss's words he was obsessed with.[14] By all accounts this was a very different trip.

Eichmann's version of events as told to Avner Less was that after his arrival at Auschwitz, Storfer was brought to him and Eichmann explained to him, 'What rotten luck we have had. Ah my dear good Storfer.' He explained, 'I really cannot help you.' He said he would speak to Höss the camp commander so that he would be given special treatment, allocated menial duties with no excessive hardship.

What Eichmann actually said to Höss cannot be known. In the trial transcript Eichmann then said he went from there back to Hungary but added that after he finally returned for the last time from Hungary to Germany in late 1944, he spoke to Höss who told him that Storfer had been shot. The records in the Austrian archives indeed show that Storfer was deported to Auschwitz in May 1944 and murdered in November that year, about two months before the liberation of Auschwitz by the Russian army and shortly after the time when the gassing of Jews there had ceased.[15]

A few months before these events, it should also be noted that Eichmann had told Hoettl in Berlin in August 1944 at the same meeting in which he referred to the extermination of six million Jews that it was unlikely that he and Hoettl would meet again. Hoettl asked why that was, and Eichmann replied that he had learned that he was on the Allies' most wanted list of war criminals.[16] So at this time Eichmann did have one eye as to what might happen after the war ended.

There are so many questions raised by this specific aspect of Eichmann's story. These have less to do with his wider guilt or involvement than his dealings with this one person. How could Eichmann say he could do nothing for Storfer when he was one of those directing the entire project, of which Auschwitz formed a part, a key part? If in truth he could not do anything, then why would Eichmann actually go all the way to Auschwitz to see him? Was his real purpose to make sure that if this was indeed Herr Storfer, that he would not survive the war and give evidence against him? Why was it that Eichmann, who went on to Hungary personally to oversee the murder of so many in such a short time, wanted to learn the fate of this one person? And why would Höss feel the need to inform Eichmann of this? What can be said is that those who encountered Eichmann up close had every reason to fear for their lives. It was for good reason that he was already known by the Jews of Vienna in 1938 as *Das Teufels Stellverterer* (the Devil's Deputy).

Some days after the opening statements had been completed in the trial, a transcript of evidence recorded twenty-five years previously was read into the record from SS Captain Dieter Wisliceny who had worked as one of Eichmann's closest cadre in Berlin and been tried in 1946.[17] Eichmann and Dieter Wisliceny were once so close in the war that Eichmann named his middle son after him. Wisliceny gave evidence that Eichmann had once said to him; 'We are all sitting in the same boat, no one is allowed to step out.' Given the state of the war in November 1944, Storfer, who had worked with Eichmann, knew too much of the details of Eichmann's operations in Vienna and could not be allowed to step out the of boat.

Another passage of Eichmann's interrogation also stands out – and sadly is still very relevant today. One part of Eichmann's defence was to assert that he held no animus towards the Jews, and that he was in favour of Jews being allowed to settle in Palestine.[18] When Eichmann had been captured by Mossad in Argentina he floated this story to see how well it played and claimed that he had been a great admirer of Israel, that he had Jewish friends and that if he were a Jew he would be a Zionist himself.[19] Once again, this was not an effective or remotely truthful line and was contradicted by the documentary record. Eichmann went further with Avner Less and suggested that before the war he had visited Palestine at the invitation of Jewish leadership and had expressed his sympathies towards the Jews' position there. Eichmann said he was knowledgeable about the Jews' struggle to establish a homeland and had read Theodor Herzl's *The Jewish State*.

Remarkably enough, he had indeed studied and learnt some basics of Hebrew and had even created a false myth that he was born in the German Templar Colony in Sarona in Palestine.[20] Avner Less then showed him a copy of the report of his short trip to Palestine that was written up in November 1937. The following summary is from the report:

> Seen from the economic angle, Palestine represents a deplorable picture. We were told that most payments are made by bills of exchange, which no one redeems, but which nevertheless, though completely devaluated [sic], are passed from hand to hand.... Drafts on the German Templar banks are regarded as the safest means of payment, once those are the only solvent banks. This

financial chaos is attributed to the fact that the Jews swindle one another and are unable to conclude their business dealings with Aryans because there are not enough of them. Typical of the total incapacity of Jews to maintain an orderly economy is the fact that in Jerusalem alone there are said to be forty Jewish banks which live by cheating their fellow Jews.

Eichmann was tackled on these conclusions and asked if they presented a picture of someone favourably disposed towards the Jews in Palestine. His response that it was drafted by another, Hagen, who accompanied him on the trip, and that he only looked through to correct it before signing it. He was also asked about another passage in the report of Eichmann's trip which concluded that the German Jews in Palestine would be better off if they were to 'go back to Germany and be sent to a re-education camp'. When he was asked whether by this it was meant concentration camp, Eichmann confirmed that this was indeed clearly what was being said, because there wasn't any other type of camp.

Further on, comment was made in the report on the British mandatory authority proposal for the immigration of 50,000 Jews from Europe into Palestine. 'This [plan] was out of the question in view of the fact it is the policy of the Reich to avoid the creation of an independent Jewish State in Palestine.'[21]

There was a repeated refrain in Nazi slogans and posters in the 1930s of statements such as, 'Out with the Jews. Pack them up for Palestine,' or 'One way to Palestine.' These were of course not statements in support of Jewish self-determination in Palestine. They were hateful racist slogans. Indeed, the Israeli author Amos Oz noted that when his father grew up in Vilna, Lithuania, in the 1930s he saw many such posters demanding that he leave for Palestine. He did so and set up a family there. Fifty years later he went on a short visit to Vilna and saw that once more the walls were filled with posters, this time demanding that the Jews immediately leave Palestine. According to this racist doctrine this is a people eternally without a home.

What was Eichmann actually doing in Palestine in 1937? One of the objectives of Eichmann's visit was to meet the members of the inner circle of the Grand Mufti of Jerusalem, Haj Amin Al Husseini, the chief Sunni cleric who was also de facto the leader of the Palestinian nationalist movement, President of the Aran Higher Committee and from the outset a vocal supporter of the Nazi regime.[22] It was estimated in 1940 and again in 1941 that about 60 per cent of Palestinian Arabs were of the same view.[23] Hitler's *Mein Kampf* had been serialised in numerous Arab newspapers at the time and the book was a bestseller. All this served to increase the popularity of the stance taken by the Grand Mufti. British intelligence, however, got wind of Eichmann's impending trip and informed him that he had to leave Palestine within 48 hours to prevent any such meeting. Eichmann complied and went on to Cairo instead, where he had discussions with close associates of the Grand Mufti.[24]

As is well documented, the Grand Mufti was expelled from Palestine by the British in the late autumn of 1937 and fled to Baghdad. He spent a large part of the Second World War in Berlin on the Nazi payroll broadcasting on a propagandist radio station and amongst other things seeking to encourage recruits for the Waffen SS in Bosnia. For these services the Grand Mufti was paid today's equivalent of US$12 million a year, which was raised by the selling of gold confiscated from Jews in the Reich.[25] He would leave Europe in 1945 for Cairo in order to avoid prosecution for war crimes.

On 28 November 1941, the Grand Mufti met Hitler in Berlin together with Dr Fritz Grobba, the German Ambassador to Baghdad. Grobba prepared a briefing for the meeting stressing that the ideological and strategic interests of the Mufti and Hitler appeared to be to some extent aligned.[26] A photograph shows Hitler and the Grand Mufti that day in animated conversation, but this seems to have been highly staged, in fact the meeting did not get off to a good start as the germophobic and racist Hitler refused to shake the Mufti's hand or drink tea with his guest, saying (untruthfully) he did not do so with anyone. Grobba appears to have had the role of ensuring accurate Minutes were taken and they have survived.[27] The Grand Mufti explained to Hitler that Germany and the Arabs were natural friends as each had the same enemies; the English, Jews and Communists. The Grand Mufti referred to a letter which Hitler had sent him explaining Germany's policy of elimination of the Jewish National Home in Palestine but nevertheless wanted a public statement to this effect. According to the Minutes, Hitler told the Grand Mufti that first the Reich would complete the total destruction of the Judeo-Communist empire in Europe and that once the German armies secured the southern exit from the Caucusus, the hour of liberation for the Arab would arrive and Germany's objective would be solely the destruction of the Jewish element living in the Arab sphere under the protection of the British. The Grand Mufti thanked Hitler and said he was satisfied with these assurances.[28]

At around the same time, the Grand Mufti also met Eichmann in the Reich Security Main Office on the Kurfuerstenstrasse, Berlin. There was some disagreement in the trial evidence as to where exactly the meeting took place, but the fact of the meeting was admitted by Eichmann, although he suggested that it was only brief.[29] One detail is worth noting. Eichmann told Wisliceny that he had met the Grand Mufti and taken him to his famous Map Room, briefed him as to numbers of Jews living in different European countries under Nazi rule and also gave his thoughts on the planned solution to what he referred to as the Jewish Question.[30] The Grand Mufti was apparently impressed and asked Eichmann to send one of his trusted advisors to Palestine to work with him after the Axis Powers achieved victory in Europe. That comment ought to be understood in the light of the meeting that the Grand Mufti had earlier held with Hitler. Eichmann asked Dieter Wisliceny if he would be interested in performing this role, but Wisliceny politely declined.

In the months following the decisions taken regarding the Final Solution at the Wannsee Conference in January 1942, enormous effort was expended to perfect some means of mass extermination. At the most dreaded Sachenshauen Concentration Camp, a special area, Section Z (denoting the last stage of a prisoner's journey) was built and by May 1942 the designers were confident that their sealed gas chamber could be used to murder Jews *en masse*. In late May Himmler ordered a trial run of the murder of 250 Jews to test the system. It succeeded beyond anything that could have been expected.[31] Amongst the very first who then expressed a wish to inspect the camp's new technology were four officials from Germany's Arab allies. Once again, Fritz Grobba acted as the organiser in chief.[32] The most senior representative was Rashid al Gaylani who had led the attempted coup against the British in Iraq in 1941 and then fled to Germany. He was accompanied that day by three others in the Iraqi and Palestinian Arab political leadership.[33] It does not seem that the Grand Mufti attended himself but rather sent a deputy. Nevertheless, it is apparent that the aspiration of the Nazis and their allies in attendance were at this time closely aligned.

In the meantime in May 1942, Walter Rauff, an SS Officer close to Heydrich and one of the inventors of the mobile gas van in late 1941 that was used in the murder of Wilma and Gina in Belgrade, was despatched to North Africa to put into effect the first stages of the solution to the Jewish question in the Middle East.[34] Rauff's orders from RSHA were to carry out what was euphemistically called 'executive measures' against the 75,000 Jews living in Egypt. This practically unknown project of genocide in the Middle East led to the rounding up and murder of thousands of Jews living in North Africa under German occupation.[35] According to US intelligence reports Rommel was disgusted when Rauff in June 1942 explained his plans to round up Cairo's Jews and gas them in his vans. The General threw Rauff out and tried to have him sent straight back to Germany.[36] Rommel did not get his way until 9 May 1943 when Rauff and his unit were surrounded by Montgomery's forces in a small enclave in Tunis.[37] He was flown out just days before the city was liberated.

By this time, far from Rommel's HQ, Rauff had managed to establish a local branch of the Gestapo in Tunis with the help of a hundred Arab soldiers. He rounded up and killed over 5,000 Jews in Tunis, Libya and Morocco.[38] Rauff survived the war and ended up working first for Syrian intelligence, recruiting at least forty-seven Nazis in a complete overhaul of its operations and then for President Suharto in Indonesia.[39] He lived out his days in Chile and never stood trial.

At the same time as Rauff's evacuation from Tunis, the Grand Mufti and Eichmann once more came to deal with one another. A plan had been agreed in principle between Eichmann and Himmler that up to 10,000 Jewish children would be allowed to leave Europe on boats via Romania and the Black Sea for Palestine, if in return an equivalent number of German civilians would be released by the Allies. The plan was ambitious and no doubt extremely hard to bring about, the British would probably not agree to it. The Grand Mufti learnt of the plans and protested loudly to Himmler, explaining that in due course these children would become adults and strengthen the Jewish population in Palestine. The proposal was abandoned.[40] It is not possible to draw any conclusion as to whether the Grand Mufti's objections had any causative impact. The fact of his reaction and objection, is, however, clear.

All this is set out because of the view occasionally stated by some on the extremes of politics that somehow or other Nazi policy was supportive of a Jewish homeland in Palestine and that Zionism and Nazism are natural political bedfellows. These are hateful racist slurs. Nazi policy and that of their close supporters was as firmly opposed to the establishment of a Jewish homeland as it was homicidally opposed to Jews wherever they were in the world. Many of the leaders of Arab nationalism, be it the Mufti himself, the Muslim Brotherhood or their allies in Iraq, had aligned themselves to the Nazi cause and ideology. Eichmann and his cadre were more than content to receive this support.

In the course of the Attorney General's opening statement, he referred to Eichmann as part of a new breed of killer, someone who exercised his craft behind a desk.[41] Hannah Arendt who reported on the trial for the *New Yorker* is sometimes credited with coining the phrase 'desk murderer' by reference to Eichmann.[42] In one sense this is of course true. Eichmann did occupy a grand office, first at the Rothschild Palais in Vienna and then in Berlin, and he did give orders which were carried out by hundreds if not thousands of others. Nevertheless, he was not by any means remote from those he arranged to have killed. He was as fully engaged with the fate of one individual such as Storfer, or the entire group of a thousand held in Sabac including Wilma and Gina, as that of European Jewry as a whole.

Rudolf Höss noted that at this time Eichmann was a man in his thirties, full of life and energy. He would keep endless files with him annotated with personal notes for urgent action. When Eichmann established his Central Office for Jewish Emigration in Vienna, he could be seen frequently at his desk, at the end of what has been described as an administrative conveyor belt of human suffering. He would be looking up and down whoever was standing before him, ready either to apply or withhold the relevant stamp permitting the person in question to leave or not. At his whim those he wished to mark for special treatment were sent to Dachau. There is no doubt that Max, like all in his position, had every reason to tremble when he was brought to stand before Eichmann in November 1938. Equally, Max had every incentive, along with a multitude of others, to queue up outside the courtroom in Jerusalem in the heat of that summer of 1961 to try to catch one last glimpse of his tormentor.

26

Jeno

Und morgen wird die Sonne wieder scheinen
... Wird uns, die Glücklichen, sie wieder einen[1]

As I wrote this book, I was fortunate indeed to have Ruth, my wonderful Aunt and quasi-sister to my mother, as one of my principal readers. I would go to her for Sunday tea to hand over the latest instalment for her to look at in draft. She patiently corrected any factual errors that she came across, made the occasional wry observation on an inadvertent spelling mistake, was extremely generous with her praise and only occasionally paused to mutter quietly, 'damn those ....' as she reflected on the history as it unfolded. She encouraged me to continue. Nevertheless, as I wrote these next chapters I hesitated for a long time and wondered whether I could really show them to her for comment. Maybe I had too become infected by the family code of silence, waiting for a better time to speak of these matters. In the end I decided that it would be best for her to see this for the first time in print. Sadly, she died before that plan could be realised. So, this is her father's story, that she almost certainly knew but never saw written down.

Amidst all the turmoil and desperate struggle to flee from Eichmann's tyranny in Vienna, there were tens of thousands who remained rooted to the spot, unable to leave or having to look after others who could not. One of these was Jeno, Ruth's father and Heinrich and Karoline's son-in-law. For most of 1939, Jeno was Heinrich and Karoline's entire support network. He can be seen in the back of the family photograph on the very far right standing behind his wife, Julci, and young daughter Ruth. Up to that point he had been unable to get a visa to come to England and was still exploring a means of getting out to join the family or to get to Palestine.

Jeno was born in 1896 in a small town in Northern Transylvania, at that time on the Hungarian side of the border of Hungary and Romania, called Beszterce in German and Bistrita in Romanian, and which in his childhood had achieved some fame amongst lovers of gothic fantasy.[2] In Bram Stoker's *Dracula*, Jonathan Harker went to stay in Beszterce at the Golden Crown Hotel before meeting the Count. Today, tourists follow in Harker's footsteps. Beszterce was home to a Jewish community several thousand strong. It boasted an impressive synagogue and a strong Hassidic presence that had become established in the region since 1848 when Jews were first allowed to settle there. It is not clear why or exactly when Jeno left Beszterce, but after the First World War he moved first to Vienna seeking work and then to Lackenbach, married Julci in 1931 and pursued his life there. Jeno stated on the various forms he had to fill in that he spoke Hungarian and Romanian as well as German. Although when he referred to place names in the letters he wrote, he largely used the Hungarian spelling, perhaps indicating his natural affiliation.

At some point in early 1940, Jeno considered it too risky to remain in Vienna. The Gestapo were rounding up all able-bodied men, sending them to Dachau and Buchenwald concentration camps. He returned to his parents and place of birth to try to escape the ever-widening net of the Reich. But in November 1940 Hungary and Romania, within three days of one another, joined the Axis powers. The life of Jews there became increasingly harsh and in due course Admiral Horthy, the Regent of Hungary, forced many to join work battalions. Those who refused were liable to deportation to the ghettos in Ukraine without any advance notice.

Once Jeno had left Vienna, Heinrich and Karoline's isolation would have been almost complete. And Jeno was cut off from his wife and daughter and felt this keenly. As the war progressed, he seems to have understood the seriousness of the situation that he found himself in and the real possibility that there was no way out. Yet still he organised food and other provisions to be sent to Heinrich and Karoline in Vienna. He wrote frequently, both to give reassurance and air his most deepfelt fears and longings. The destructive effect of the enforced separation seeped into every line of his letters and postcards.

Fragments of a largely one-sided correspondence have been kept for over eighty years. Jeno was a diligent writer. He wrote to his wife in England, to Karoline, and to Wilma and Gina, the twin girls marooned in Sabac. As time passed, the letters and postcards became shorter and more desperate in tone. It is clear from the surviving letters that many others were written which did not get through to the intended recipient or have been lost since.

Jeno passed relatively freely at this time between Romania and Hungary to try to find work. He wrote in German in a very fine hand with minuscule lettering. He also seems to have understood that what he wrote would be read by more than one censor. Often the letters passed through Hugo Sussmann in Zurich, who had given so much help to Wilma and Gina. He referred mostly to each person's Hungarian diminutive or affectionate pet name. These have been retained where possible.

12 April 1940, Romania

My dearest Julci

I received your letters of 27 March and 10 April 1940 together. It is just before Shabbat but I do want to write to you and if possible in some detail. I write quickly as my thoughts come and you will have to excuse me if this letter is a little disjointed. In addition, you probably don't want any high-flown phrases from me, surely you just want to know what comes from the heart? You will appreciate that all I can do is write in plain words.

I hope you are now convinced that it is not my fault that you had to wait so long for the post. The same applies to me when I await impatiently for news from you. Of course, my impatience is double, as I await news from two of my dear ones, but I know that this is not because they are too lazy to write, but the postal service is so poor. You know my dearest that in the past few weeks I have been plagued by such thoughts as: How are my dear ones really doing? Are they really well? Yes, we are certainly in anguish and torment and I am wondering when there will be an encouraging sign that we may be reunited. These thoughts plague me day and night and threatened to overwhelm me. I should really be convincing myself that given the circumstances you are still the more sensible and insightful one and that you are doing everything possible to ensure the well-being of our child and that you are not allowing the situation to get you down. These thoughts calm me down. You should know that I carry you constantly in my heart. I know my duty. I am also convinced that you have done everything possible in all directions, and that you must be aware that I'm doing the same. I shall not cease in my efforts until I have achieved the desired result. I'm ashamed of myself and I can also be angry with you if you keep on asking me to repeat time and again what is self-evident.

My dearest you have asked me to give you details of my situation, of my income and what food I am eating. I have tried to depict the situation exactly as it is, but it seems that you have not really understood me. I have no income, but next week, God willing, I will seek any form of position which will provide some wages. I will work anywhere in the country and then try to ensure the family is reunited. I am also told by many people that I should be happy that my wife and child are where they are. The main thing is that my wife and child can enjoy life.

Regarding money, let me tell you once and for all time, if you don't want me to be cross with you, don't mention the subject again. It is painful enough for me, that I cannot provide for you.

I would have written some more, but I've already been called to go to synagogue and so I must close. Dear Magda [his step-sister] will be writing soon.

In the constant hope of good news, hugs and kisses,

Your ever faithful Jeno

15 April 1940, Romania

My Dearest Julci

I wrote you a long letter on Friday, but I have the need to write to you again because I want to come back to one of the things that you have written about. I am well aware and convinced that you are preoccupied with constant thoughts of how we can be reunited, so that together we can work towards our goal.

If this were not the case, then the smouldering fire in my heart, which is the yearning for my wife and child, would not serve as a source of strength to continue the fight, but would become a destructive hellfire consuming my body and soul. My reply was in no way a denial of this eventuality, because I too have been thinking along the same lines as you and in the absence of a better solution, I'm working in the same direction as you. Only we must not lose ourselves in dreams and we must have no illusions. We have to be cold and clear in confronting our fate, so that in the event of a solution in one or other direction, we do not simply buckle under the pressure, but can carry on uncowed. I only hope, my dearest, and this is my deepest wish, that you and the children are all together and are well and enjoying life's pleasures. You would make me very happy, if you could enclose the promised photograph with your next letter.

I send you hugs and kisses,

Your loving Jeno

26 April 1940, Romania

My Dearest

I read your card with great pleasure. This time, I shall once again have to be content with just sending you a postcard, even though I have plenty of time and the wish to write you a letter, but I have to concede to my father's wishes not to write long letters on a *yom tov* [a Jewish festival day on which writing is not permitted in Orthodox Judaism]. Well my dearest, I shall briefly report that I have taken on a job as a commercial salesman and shortly after the holidays, I shall travel directly to Bukovina. The company makes schnapps, not exactly my cup of tea, but I do want to earn some money. Last week as I have already told you I went to Cluj to try to obtain a permit to trade but that is virtually impossible at the moment. I have also sent your dear parents several small packages and a 10 kg parcel for Passover. I hope and pray that they have received all of them. At last, I received a postcard from dear Max and he wrote and he and Julya are both in Tel Aviv. He thinks that there should be room for me there too.

I hope that you are all well and I send you hugs and kisses,

Your loving Jeno

10 May 1940 postcard from Romania passed by the UK censor

Dearest Julci

I have been away from Besztrece Naszod since Monday and will
be arriving in Mures just before Shabbat. I am staying with my
dear sister Rosa and I don't need to tell you how pleased we
were to see each other again. She has four boys and two girls.
Not bad eh? One sweeter than the next. Her husband is also
a very pleasant man. They could also be quite well off, if only
times would improve. Not much to say concerning my work at
the moment. The general situation is also greatly affecting my
business. I have just received your letter, which was sent to me
from Besztrece Naszod. It was high time that I heard because I
had been worrying, as you can imagine. It is already late and there
is I would also like to write a few words and so enough for today.

With my love and kisses,
Your faithful Jeno

PS: [In a different hand] We send our love and kisses too. Yours
Rosa and family.

26 May 1940 postcard from Romania passed by the UK censor

My Dearest Julci
You cannot imagine my great joy receiving the photograph of our
darling child, for which I thank you with all my heart. Why did
you not complete my joy by sending a photograph of yourself,
so that at least that way I could see you too? I am worrying
about this now and feeling that perhaps you are not well, or that
worry, sadness and work has so changed you that you did not
dare to have yourself photographed? Please reassure me but also
do tell me the truth. From the picture I can see that our little
mother [Ruth, his daughter] looks good and I am hoping that
she is healthy. You write very little about yourself and you must
know that I'm interested to hear all about what you are doing.
For myself well, all I can say is that with every beat of my heart,
I am thinking of you all. And if God should grant that all goes
well with me and I can earn enough, then I will not only be with

you in thought and with every heartbeat, but I shall be physically there and with you at last.

I have not yet heard from your dear parents. Have you heard anything? How are you doing with learning the language? My case [for permission to come to England] is being processed and I hope it will be settled next month. I haven't contacted your lady yet, but I've been promised an English book and then I shall write to her. My dearest, do you know what? Write me a card, who knows – I may still be here when it arrives.

In the hope you are all well, I embrace you with my heart and soul,

Your faithful Jeno

15 June 1940 postcard from Romania

My Dearest Julci

I regret to report that out of the letters and cards you mention, to date I have only received one letter, although I'm sure that you have written. Of course, I am with you constantly in my thoughts and that has helped and is still helping me to cope with this horrible torture. My dearest, I am pleased that you are able to look after, care for and protect our dear child but my pain at the fact that you have to do this on your own without me is very great. I am only living for you and in the hope that the Almighty will grant that I shall be able to join you and then I can show you in person my infinite thanks for your loyal maternal heart. I am earning a pittance at the moment, but perhaps the situation will change. I have to tell you that just before Easter I managed to earn something but then I received a letter from your dear parents who told me that their situation was dire and so I bought a little food and sent it to them. You certainly don't have to ask me to write to your dear parents more often, because I do this every week also unbidden anyway. I received a letter from them about a week ago in which they reported that they are well and thank God have more or less everything they need. I also had a letter from Wilma and Gina and they also seem to be well. I shall try to send them something. I have not heard anything from Max or Julya in Palestine.

I send you hugs and my undying devotion,

Your Jeno

27 January 1941, Beszterce-Naszod, Hungary

I read your letter with great joy and sent it directly to your dear parents. You write just a brief few words about what you are up to, but I know how hard you are working to maintain yourself and look after our dearest child. I am powerless to support you at the moment and I am suffering because of this. I cannot repeat often enough, my own fervent hope is that the Almighty will help me make this up to you. Every day and every second, yes every second of the day, I regret that we are so far apart and the feeling that we belong together is becoming more and more powerful. No fraction of a second passes without my thinking of you. These are not empty words when I say that, with the Almighty's help, I shall make all this up to my dearest, most brave woman, like no one has ever done before. I don't have much to report about myself, only that I am well. The prospect of any change is negligible. However, I am always making efforts to enable me to keep sending our parents food parcels, and I have also contributed to the savings box for our dearest girls, but I have not had confirmation yet that it has been sent and I'm hoping it will be soon. I receive post from our dear parents nearly every week. Thank God they are well and the girls are also, in Sabac. I am in constant correspondence with them. My most dear one, I just have one wish and that is the Almighty will keep you in good health and that we should be reunited again. With the help of God and in the hope that this letter finds you well, I send you my fondest eternal love, Jeno.

Cable and Wireless telegram 20 June 1942 from Hugo Sussmann in Zurich via Red Cross Office in Leeds

Mother healthy, father ill. No news from Wilma and Gina. Always giving Jeno your news. Parents moved. Jeno sent money. Letter will follow. Sussmann.

Telegram 7 July 1942 from Hugo Sussmann via Red Cross Office

Received news from mother. Father in hospital having asthmatic treatment. Hoping for improvement. They live at the same place. Kind regards and kisses to all relations, Hugo Sussmann.

Jeno

Red Cross Message sent from Leeds, 10 July 1942

Dearest Jeno. Hugo wrote our father is ill. Terribly worried. I beg
you to help. Where are the girls? Are you well? All our love Julci,
Terci, children.

Telegram 9 October 1942, Jeno to Julci

I can only repeat what I said before about parents and that from
their handwriting and what they write, they seem to be well.
Hope to hear re girls soonest. All my love Jeno

Postcard 21 May 1943, delivered 18 June 1943, Jeno to Julci

Dearest, parents in Theresienstadt, girls transferred somewhere.
Direct contact and girls address may be possible through Hugo
Sussman or the Red Cross there. So far, I have had no success in
making contact. Hugs

*Red Cross Message from Leeds, Ruth to Jeno in Hungary dated
12 August 1943, delivered 31 August*

Dearest Papa, I'm well. Been on summer holiday with Mammi. It
was lovely. How are you? Are you well? We had news from Uncle
Simon [this could be a code name]. Kisses Ruth, Mammi

Postcard from Hugo Sussmann to Julci and Terci, 29 August 1943

My dear ones,
We have not received any news from you for some time
and I hoping that you are well, as we are here. I received a
card from Theresienstadt from dear Karoline, date-stamped
17 November 1942 to the effect that sadly, dear Heinrich died
on 15 November 1942, on 6 Kislev [Jewish calendar month]. It
grieves me to have to tell you this news. My serious condolence
to you. I hope that the dear departed will be at peace and with
the Almighty. I am sure you only have good memories of him.
I have sent Karoline a package and hope it arrives. Until now,

I've not heard from her. I hope to be able to send you some good news soon. How are you? The children are surely well settled now.

Fondest love and kisses to all of you, including Karoline.

Yours Hugo

Red Cross Message from Julci to Jeno dated 2 November, delivered 1 December 1943

Dearest Jeno. No news from you and also deeply sad about father's death. Otherwise, everything is alright. Children are doing well at school. Have you heard from Mama? Longing for your news, Julci, Terci, and children.

Undated

Dearest Julci

I cannot understand why you haven't heard from me. I write every month. I shall be [censorship redaction] with Mama and will report to you immediately.

All my love, Jeno

9 December 1943, Jeno to Ruth in Leeds

My dearest Little Mother, grateful thanks for your lovely news. Am well. Pray to the Almighty that he keeps you in good health and joy. A big hug, Papa

The correspondence ends here.

27

Time Runs Out

In the space of a few months no further correspondence would have got in or out of Besztrice. By mid- March 1944, Berlin had put intolerable pressure on Hungary and effected a change of government headed up by its puppet, Döme Sztójay. The new government was to lend its full support and assistance to the Nazi's planned deportation of Hungary's Jews to Auschwitz.

In order to carry out such a plan, Himmler turned once more to Eichmann. On 19 March 1944, Eichmann arrived in Budapest and installed himself in a villa at Rosa Hill that he had confiscated from a Jewish owner.[1] He also took over the Majestic Hotel and installed his trusted cadre there, those who had previously operated with deadly effect in Poland and the Ukraine. Amongst them was Captain Dieter Wisliceny of the SS, whose evidence was admitted at the Eichmann Trial. Lists of the leaders of the Hungarian Jewish community had already been prepared, following the well tested methodology used six years previously in Vienna and Prague. Eichmann's deputies summoned the community's leaders to a meeting in Budapest within days of their arrival and told them that nothing would happen to the 600,000 or so Jews of Hungary as long as they complied fully with all the orders and regulations. This deception was designed to buy some time whilst the arrangements for deportation were put in place.

On 7 April 1944, Decree 6163 of 1944 was passed by the newly installed government calling for the immediate eradication of the Jews of Hungary. This operation was to be overseen by László Endre,[2] Under Secretary of State in the Ministry of Interior, together with Eichmann's specially formed *Eichmann-Kommando*. That same day,

Endre and Lieutenant Colonel Ferenczy who commanded Hungary's 20,000-strong 'De-Jewification Unit' of the gendarmerie, met with Eichmann's men to plan how to carry out the decree. They agreed to divide the country into different zones or regions. Besztrice in Northern Transylvania was in Zone II. It seems that speed was essential. As throughout so much of Jewish history, Passover was to be the focal point. The rounding up began on 16 April 1944, on the first day of the festival.[3] Systematically, region by region, the Jews of Hungary were herded into ghettos. Despite the overwhelming documentary evidence, at his trial Eichmann contended that as regards the events in Hungary he was only involved marginally in the preparation of timetables and no more.[4] As was noted in the Court's judgement, it did sound incredible, because there was no truth in it.[5]

Once the news of the roundups reached Budapest, three Hungarian Jews, Yoel Brand, Rudolf Kastner and Sam Springmann, formed and led the Hungarian Rescue Committee. They decided that they would do whatever it took to negotiate a deal with Eichmann to save the Jews of Hungary, or at least as many as they could. Jeno's life and the lives of many hundreds of thousands like him depended on their success.

The first step in the plan was to obtain a face-to-face meeting with Captain Wisliceny in April 1944, who was thought to be somewhat less ideologically fixed upon the pursuit of racial purity. It was understood that he was prepared to consider the rumoured Europa Plan, which involved an exchange of payment in dollars for the lives of Jews. The Rescue Committee paid a bribe of US$24,000 just to hold this meeting with Wisliceny. They outlined their proposal to pay US$2,000,000, payable in ten monthly instalments to save the Jews of Hungary. The significance of the ten monthly instalments was the open assumption held on both sides that the war would be over by then and the Germans were insistent on obtaining full payment before such an eventuality.

The Rescue Committee's proposal was that the Jews would be allowed to live untouched, not held in ghettos, or subjected to any form control or punishment, and permitted if they wished to emigrate to Palestine. Wisliceny listened carefully but said it was impossible to consent to Jews being allowed to leave for Palestine because of the agreement reached between the Reich and the Grand Mufti, which prohibited any such deal. This policy appears to have been quite rigidly enforced. Only a few days before this meeting took place, the

Tari was ready to depart Constanza with 1500 Jewish refugees for Haifa, but the Germans refused to allow the vessel to leave by way of a firm nod to their commitment to the Grand Mufti.[6] The discussion with Wisliceny was amicable, but at this point the matter had to be raised with Eichmann himself.[7]

Brand met Eichmann for the first time on 25 April 1944. Three meetings would take place, each held at the Majestic Hotel headquarters. Brand complained of the rounding up of the Jews in provincial towns and villages, including his elderly mother, which had contradicted the earlier assurances. Eichmann listened to Brand's opening salvo and responded, 'Do you know who I am? I am in charge of the deportation operation. You know what happened to the Jews of Austria, Czechoslovakia and Poland. Now it is Hungary's turn.'

With this threat hanging in the air, Eichmann came straight to the point and said he was open to agree a bargain of one million Jews in return for goods. When Eichmann gave evidence at his trial in Jerusalem, he explained that he came up with the idea of a trade for a million souls on the basis that it was such a large number that it could not be ignored or dismissed.[8] Brand was stunned by Eichmann's bluntness and said nothing at first. Eichmann barked back; 'What do you want, merchandise or blood?' Brand told Eichmann he had no merchandise to offer because as Eichmann well knew, all possessions had been confiscated by the Nazis. He offered dollars instead, but Eichmann refused.[9]

They met a second time a few days later and Eichmann set out his position and named the ransom price. He said he would trade a million Jews for 10,000 army trucks. Eichmann continued as if he had wandered into a motor show to place a big order, 'That is a bargain for you. But the trucks must be new from the factory, with accessories, trailers and equipped for winter operation.' Eichmann could see that Brand had serious misgivings about any proposal involving the supply of military equipment but Eichmann then gave his assurance that the trucks would only be used on the Eastern Front and not against the Allies. Furthermore, according to Brand, Eichmann insisted he would blow up the installations at Auschwitz if the goods were delivered. This was one of the very few points of Brand's story that Eichmann contested, otherwise he described it as being 'a very truthful account'.[10]

Eichmann then came up with another idea, what he described as a 'ten per cent clause'. He offered to release ten per cent of the total numbers as a gesture of good faith, if Brand was able to persuade the Allies to co-operate with the scheme.[11] Eichmann ended with the flourish of a back alley black marketeer, saying that if Brand was able to load the trucks with a few tons of chocolate, coffee, tea and soap, he would be able to reciprocate in kind. Brand looked at him with complete amazement and stammered; 'Who will believe me? Who will give me 10,000 trucks?' Eichmann responded, 'A German officer keeps his word.' That currency had been somewhat debased over recent years and Eichmann conveniently put to one side that only a few weeks earlier this had been shown to be false, when Wisliceny had promised that the Jews would remain unharmed if they fully complied with orders. Brand was struck dumb and said he would have to discuss it with his committee.[12]

Kastner and Springmann were waiting for him around the corner when he emerged from the Majestic. History does not record his opening line to his colleagues, but it was presumably filled with some choice language. After only a brief discussion, they all agreed that they had no alternative but to try to make something of this proposal. The potential prize was too big, although each recognised that it would be next to impossible to deliver what was being demanded. Still, they all agreed that the possibility of just securing the safety of the ten per cent referred to and the blowing up of Auschwitz, if the Allies were simply willing to agree to engage in talks, was too valuable not to explore. Since Brand was the main contact for these discussions, it was agreed that the job of progressing the offer would rest with him. This was a burden that Brand recorded he regretted taking on each day and night for the rest of his life.

A third and last rendezvous was then organised on 14 May 1944. Eichmann questioned why Brand was still in Hungary and warned him that time was running out as he would soon start the deportations to Auschwitz. Eichmann was quite specific, he said this would be at the rate of 12,000 a day. They discussed modalities and arrangements to get Brand to Turkey so he could contact the British authorities. Brand would be accompanied to Turkey by a Gestapo officer. Eichmann then dropped in a strong hint of menace that his wife Hansi Brand and their children would have to remain under his watchful eye in Budapest and report to him each day until he returned.

On 16 May 1944, Yoel Brand was flown to Turkey from Vienna on a German military transport. He crossed the border into Syria and after he made contact with the British authorities was taken into custody near Aleppo. He was taken ultimately to Cairo where he was thoroughly interrogated for up to eight hours a day for months on end.

Brand's appearance in Syria gave rise to a frantic high-level diplomatic discussion from June to September 1944. The British Government did not know how to respond. At first, perhaps understandably, they doubted Brand's story and bona fides, particularly as he was understood to have arrived in Turkey accompanied by a Gestapo officer, but extensive covert inquiries confirmed the essentials of his story. What should or could be done? It also should be said that Yoel Brand in questioning did change his story more than once, mentioning several different numbers that might be saved under the proposed plan. Brand explained this at the trial of Eichmann by saying that no one believed him when he mentioned the figure of a million men and women and so he then referred to the lower number of 100,000 (which he derived from the so called ten per cent clause) He also on occasion referred simply to a number of Jews for each truck supplied, which he thought might be more palatable (a hundred Jews per vehicle), but this really did not help his cause.[13]

It would seem that instinctively the British wanted to do something but agreeing on a course of action would prove impossible. They thought of trying to string the Germans along, but no one could agree on how best even to do that. The Americans appeared to have been more inclined to act, subject to manifold legal obstacles, but the Russians would have to sign off on any plan. Nothing, however, was finalised, no response was formulated and more delay ensued.

The fate of the Hungarian Jews was not simply being discussed in the corridors of Whitehall, at Capitol Hill and in top-secret telegrams. It was out in the open in the press. On 10 May 1944, the *New York Times* carried an article stating that the rounding up of the Jews of Hungary for deportation had begun. It was made clear that the same fate awaited them as the rest of European Jewry, namely, to be put death in 'gas chamber baths'.[14] On 18 May 1944, the same newspaper carried a report that 80,000 Jews in the Carpathian provinces had already disappeared.[15]

A not infrequent but serious misunderstanding about the Holocaust is the notion that the Allies and indeed the press both in America and Britain did not know either the scale or the details of the Nazi killing machine until the very end of the war and the liberation of the camps such as Auschwitz-Birkenau in January 1945 and Belsen in April 1945. This is not correct.[16] The mass murder of Jews by the *Einsatzgruppen* had been known about from intelligence signal interception since 1941 and was directly raised by Churchill in a radio broadcast on 14 August 1941. Ed Murrow of the CBS network in December 1942 told listeners from what was then known that the many concentration camps established could no longer be understood to be anything other than extermination camps in which Jews were being murdered *en masse*. This followed a report carried in the *New York Times* at the end of November of Jewish adults and children being burned in mass crematoria at Auschwitz, near Cracow.[17] Less than two weeks later, the Allies issued a Joint Declaration Regarding Atrocities Against the Jews in Occupied German Countries and it was taken up in Parliament by Sir Anthony Eden in a speech on 17 December 1942, who made it clear that those participating in these crimes would be prosecuted after the war.[18]

The degree of certitude reached another level largely as a result of the Vrba-Wetzler Report completed at the end of April 1944, after the escape of Rudolf Vrba and Alfred Wetzler from Auschwitz. They described in pellucid detail the systematic extermination of Jews at Auschwitz-Birkenau in gas chambers and crematoria, they presented hand drawings of the layout of the crematoria, the detail of the deception right up to the moment of death and detailed each transportation of Jews to arrive over this period of time, occasionally providing details of particular families. They estimated that 1,765,000 Jews had been killed in that one location alone between 15 April 1942 and 15 April 1944.[19]

This report was then re-packaged by The Very Reverend Paul Vogt, Head of the Refugee Relief Committee in Zurich, supposedly giving it a greater sense of dispassion and objectivity. His 9,000-word exposé was released nearly a year prior to the liberation of Belsen. Its shocking content was carried prominently in the *New York Times* which added that up to a third of Hungary's Jews most likely had to be added to the tally at Auschwitz-Birkenau. The story also ran in Britain in provincial and Jewish newspapers during these critical months when the fate of the Hungarian Jews hung in the balance – but not in the mainstream press.[20] This was not because the account was dismissed by those with ministerial responsibility, far from it. In 1944, Brendan Bracken, the Minister of Information, estimated the number of Jews murdered in 'abattoirs' at more than 3 million with what he described as 'characteristic Prussian efficiency'; admittedly his acceptance of this data was more a stick to beat the Germans with than anything else.[21] All told, there was no room for ambiguity in the summer of 1944. The actual or threatened deportation of Hungary's Jews to Auschwitz was understood, by all who were faced with making a decision, to equate with a death sentence.

Faced with these dreadful reports, Dr Chaim Weizmann turned to Winston Churchill on 6 July 1944 and implored him to bomb Auschwitz-Birkenau or the railway lines leading to the camp to save the Hungarian Jews from a certain fate. Similar requests were made to the United States. Churchill responded to Anthony Eden, the Foreign Secretary the next day: 'Get anything you can out of the Air Force and invoke me if you can.'[22] Nearly two months later, on 1 September 1944, Richard Law, Permanent Under Secretary of State at the Foreign Office wrote to Dr Weizmann informing him that Eden had asked the Air Ministry to consider the proposal but the response was that 'in view of the great technical difficulties involved, we have no option but to refrain from pursuing the proposal in present circumstances.'[23]

Eichmann trial judge Halevi asked Gideon Hausner, the Prosecuting Attorney General, whether these difficulties were explained in another document on the record, and the Attorney General replied that they were not.[24] It is not possible fully to understand what these technical difficulties were, especially when it was reported in the *New York Times* in December 1944, that Fortress and Liberator bombers from the US 15th Air Force did indeed bomb Auschwitz, but not the death camp or the railways leading to it. Instead, the target was a neighbouring oil facility.[25] The desire of the Allies to bring the war to an end remained the paramount concern throughout. Nonetheless, those at the top of the chain who made this choice of target could not then be surprised to learn of the terrible cost in human life of failing to act as requested by the Prime Minister.

In the meantime, Brand remained under a sort of house arrest in Cairo and was beside himself with anxiety, both for the Jews of Hungary in general and of course in particular for his wife and children. After many days of pleading to be released to go back to Budapest to try to do something to help save lives there, he went on hunger strike. He kept on repeating Eichmann's offer to exchange lives for trucks and was occasionally brought back for further questioning. One evening this led to an exchange that has evoked controversy. There is a dispute as to who spoke to the beleaguered prisoner and indeed also the precise location (Brand placed this particular event at the Anglo Cairo Club where he had been taken to be questioned) but no serious challenge to what was uttered by a tall, slim man, who according to Brand was in a position of authority. The British official said to him, 'What shall I do with a million Jews – where shall I put them?' Brand responded: 'If there was nowhere on this planet for us, then there is no alternative to the gas-chamber for our people.'[26] He then asked to be excused and be taken back to rest. According to the evidence Brand gave at the Eichmann trial, on the way out, Brand said he asked a British soldier who who he had been talking to and was told it was Lord Moyne, the Secretary of State for the Middle East in Cairo.[27] There is considerable doubt as to whether Lord Moyne spoke to Brand. In this regard it is important to note that in his autobiography published in 1958, Brand said that he learned some time afterwards that the person who spoke these words was not Lord Moyne but another who could not be identified.[28]

Nevertheless, the British policy at this time and indeed after the war remained resolutely opposed to the admission of any material number of Jews into Palestine or anywhere else. What can be said for certain was that by the time Brand was released in October 1944, Eichmann had all but completed his work in Hungary. On 6 November 1944, Lord Moyne was assassinated in Cairo by two Jewish gunmen[29] of the Stern Gang or Lehi (the acronym by which it was known to its members),[30] a self-proclaimed terror organisation of the far-right which Brand himself had joined as soon as he was freed.

It is unlikely that any significant part of this extraordinary bargain with the devil could ever have succeeded. Nevertheless, it must be understood as yet another pivotal moment. At this time, the principal actors knew both what was at stake and the consequence of failure, and yet nothing was actually done. There is some speculation as to what exactly Hitler and Himmler knew of this proposal. It seems likely that Himmler at least knew of and approved the terms. What can be said of the underlying motive? If it was to examine the solidarity of the British and Americans with Russia, the Allied powers passed the test. If it was to test their collective humanitarian conscience as regards the fate of Europe's remaining Jews, the Allies manifestly failed.

Only one transport was organised by the Rescue Committee. This was chiefly the work of Rudolf Kastner who had remained in Budapest and by this time was having an affair with Hansi Brand, Yoel Brand's wife. He did manage to raise the ransom money of US$1,000 a head for what became known as the Kastner train. It left Hungary in June 1944 with 1,684 Jews on board, including a fair number of Kastner's family. This transport did arrive in Switzerland in December 1944, but only after a terrifying detour to Bergen-Belsen where they had to wait in a siding for days. Perhaps this was just to prove the power still held by the Nazi command.

This rescue proved to be so controversial in the new-born State of Israel that it led to Kastner being accused in the press of being a Nazi collaborator and responsible indirectly for the deaths of Hungarian Jews by failing as one of the community leaders to warn them of their impending doom but instead peddling misleading information to an ignorant population. A defamation trial followed in 1954 and Kastner was assassinated after the Judge Halevi found against him. The judgment was reversed on appeal by the Supreme Court, although that was cold comfort for Rudolf Kastner.[31] The Eichmann trial in Israel had many demons to slay, both internal and external, and it was of considerable moment to Halevi, who sat in judgment of both Kastner and Eichmann.

Meanwhile, in mid- to late April 1944, the Jews of Beszterce were imprisoned in a ghetto at Stamboli Farm by Mayor Norbert Kuales and local police chief Miklós Debreczeni. In the surrounding villages of the county, the roundup was guided by László Smolenszki, the deputy prefect, and Lt Col. Ernö Pasztai of the gendarmerie. The conditions for the thousands imprisoned there were wholly degrading. They were held in farm outbuildings and pigsties, no doubt to the sadistic amusement of Heinrich Smolka, who was in charge. On 6 June 1944, D-Day in Normandy, the 5,981 Jews from Beszterce were deported. They were sent on a three-day train journey to Auschwitz via Kosice to be murdered in the gas chambers on arrival.[32] Jeno was amongst them.

In total 434,351 Hungarian Jews were sent on 147 separate train transports to be gassed at Auschwitz from May to July 1944.[33] The reason that such a precise figure can be given is because of the records kept of each and every trainload by those who organised them.[34] The scale and speed of this murderous operation exceeded anything in the whole of the Holocaust. It led to complaints from the camp commander of Auschwitz that the gas chambers could not cope with the numbers being sent. [35]

Six weeks later on 14 July, Admiral Horthy, after being pressured by President Roosevelt and the Pope, ordered the deportations to Auschwitz be stopped. The outcome of the war by this time was really no longer in doubt and this act did at least save the last 120,000 Jews of Budapest from being murdered. It came a few weeks too late for Jeno.

28

Heinrich and Karoline

Whilst Jeno scrambled back and forth between Hungary and Romania looking for meagre work and seeking to escape his fate, Heinrich and Karoline remained in Vienna awaiting the inevitable. In the morning of 10 July 1942 at precisely 7.08am, Heinrich and Karoline's train pulled out of the nearby Aspangbahnhoff in Vienna's Third District. They left Vienna together with 960 Jews under the armed guard of six Schutpolizei and did not return. The two of them were taken on Transport No 30 under the command of First Lieutenant Josef Tremer,[1] which was made up of those over the age of 65 or who had served in the First World War and who were to be spared deportation to the camps in Poland. Although Heinrich served in the war in a hospital and not on the front line, he ticked both these boxes and Karoline as his wife was allowed to accompany him. The average age of those taken that day was 73. One of the ruses deployed by the Nazi regime was to describe this move for older people simply as 'a change of residence'. Those deported were required in advance to transfer all their property, money and household possessions over to a State fund, in return for which they would be looked after, housed and fed. Eichmann accepted when pressed that the term residence 'was probably coined to gild the old people's ghetto'.[2]

Their journey in the summer heat without food or water took them at a crawl three hundred or so kilometres northwest via Floridsdorf, the site of the last resistance of the armed socialist struggle in February 1934 against Austro-fascism, past the beautiful medieval town of Stockerau, on to Gmund, then Prague and finally Bohušovice, halfway between Prague and Dresden. There they disembarked and were forced to march by foot, reaching Theresienstadt Concentration Camp in the afternoon on 11 July 1942.[3] On arrival, Heinrich and Karoline were relieved of all their luggage. This was the result of a new order which had only been issued the day before and completed the systematic process that had stripped them of their life, home, possessions and dignity.[4]

Although the end of Heinrich and Karoline's love story is sadly all too well documented, its beginning some forty-five years earlier is somewhat less clear. Karoline's maiden name was Wellisch and she is recorded as having been born not in Lackenbach but in the nearby town of Turnitz, in Lower Austria.[5] In orthodox Jewish circles at the close of the nineteenth century, a bride would normally have only moved away from her family and birthplace as the result of an arranged marriage. Intriguingly, a significant number of those living in Lackenbach before 1938 are recorded with the family name Wellisch and so it is a fair guess that some cousin of hers living there would have made the match and Heinrich was the fortunate beneficiary.

They were an extremely handsome couple. Heinrich clearly looked after his appearance and unusually for a religious man seemed to have an interest in the fashions of the day. At the time of their marriage, Lackenbach was in Hungary and the two of them celebrated in the nearby Hungarian town of Sopron, a few kilometres to the north-east of Lackenbach. A photograph of them in the late 1890s was taken by a professional photographer in Sopron, Heinrich resplendent in white tie and with a waxed moustache, Karoline, who would have been about sixteen or seventeen, wears a high-necked top and formal long sleeved woollen jacket. This is the last time that Karoline would have left her hair uncovered in public.

As the head of the family, Heinrich and Karoline had been used to living in the close company of their six sons and daughters and three grandchildren. They were both looked up to, and after, by all. Heinrich's kindly, reassuring expression reminded me so much of his eldest son, Uncle Oskar, who I remembered from my own childhood. Oskar lived in Manchester but would magically appear for short visits to London on a Sunday afternoon bearing packets stuffed full of Brazil nuts, which seemed almost impossibly exotic to my young mind. I suspect that Oskar inherited a lot of Heinrich's natural charm.

As 1939 passed into 1940 and each of their offspring scrambled in their varied ways to leave the Reich, for the better part of two and a half years prior to their deportation Heinrich and Karoline had lived mostly by themselves without any tangible means of support. It would have been hard for them simply to find food to put on the table and Jeno's modest food parcels sent from Romania would no doubt have been of the utmost importance. From September 1941, there was the humiliation of having to wear a yellow star on their coat as they went about the streets of Vienna's Second District.

Theresienstadt was not built or organised as an extermination camp. It had long been a garrison town and was of some strategic importance in the Austro-Prussian War of 1866, standing between the Prussian army and a further advance on Vienna. Theresienstadt's role during the Second World War was different. It was expressly mentioned in Heydrich's Protocol presented at the Wannsee Conference of 20 January 1942 as being the likely destination for the elderly and those who had certain specified war service or decorations. In fact, Eichmann busied himself with a 600km round trip to Theresienstadt the day before the Wannsee Conference in Berlin. He went there to inspect the potential for expanding the existing camp, which up until that time had held only a few thousand Jews from Prague. The timing of that visit could hardly have been coincidental. It was linked to the presentation he would make the following day.[6]

No set of numbers can describe adequately the conditions of those who spent time there at the mercy of the sadistic Austrian camp commander Hauptsturmführer Anton Burger, who had also served at Auschwitz but was brought back by Eichmann to Theresienstadt in mid-1943. This was a disease-ridden ghetto prison filled with semi-starved inhabitants, a large number of whom came all too quickly to the end of their strength. An overview, however, gives something of the picture. Between 1942 and 1944 approximately 141,000 arrived at the camp. Of these, 33,456 died largely as a result of a combination of infection and lack of food and another 88,196 were deported onwards to the Nazi death camps in Poland. At the height of its occupation, an average of a hundred and fifty burials were held a day. On some days this reached three hundred.[7] On 9 May 1945, there were just 16,832 who remained of those who entered the gates.[8] This was a transient population, a revolving door. People came and either died of disease or were in due course deported and murdered.

Despite this, the International Committee of the Red Cross (the ICRC) visited Theresienstadt on more than one occasion and each time gave it a clean bill of health. For the prisoners there this must have been like a familiar scene from a bad movie, when police pass by a house where people are being held captive, shine a torch at the window but see nothing and leave. The ICRC in fact commented favourably on the conditions. Those in charge of the camp went so far as to forge letters in the name of Jewish Council of Elders stating that there was so much medicine there that the ICRC should stop supplying it.

There was an inspection of the camp in June 1944 at the express request of the Danish government, which has achieved some notoriety. Maurice Rossel was in charge that day and spent several hours there. Many years after the war, in a documentary made by Clause Lanzmann, Rossel complained of the Jews' 'passivity' and 'sterility'. He understood the prisoners there to be 'rich and privileged' and that if they had had any complaint about their conditions they should have said something to him.[9] The ICRC was shown various unused packages of medicines heaped up in a pile which they noted positively, albeit with a measure of surprise.[10] The June 1944 ICRC report stated; 'The SS Police at the camp gives the Jews the freedom to administer themselves as they see fit... We were convinced that its population did not suffer undernourishment.' The Nazi propaganda machine made full use of this report and described Theresienstadt as a 'model village'. No sooner had the ICRC visit finished, work was started on a propaganda film with the grotesque title; *The Führer Gives a City to the Jews*. The filming was completed in September 1944, although it was not ready for release until March 1945, by which time almost all of the 'city's' population had been either deliberately starved to death or deported.

A key element of the promotion of Theresienstadt to the outside observer was its cultural life, which seems today to be completely incompatible with our conceptions of a ghetto or a concentration camp. It is perhaps this aspect that has garnered most attention. It needs to be made clear that this was not invented by the Nazi cameramen. A significant number of those held there were intellectuals, university lecturers, authors, composers, a significant cross-section of the Vienna Philharmonic and actors who had graced the Burgtheater of Vienna. There were regular performances covering the entire classical music repertoire. One opera, *The Bartered Bride*, a popular comedy by the Czech composer Smetana, was performed over forty times in two years. Many other plays, operas and operettas were staged. In the cold winter nights of December 1943, over four hundred attended a popular series of lectures on moral philosophy.[11] Incomprehensible though it might seem, this cultural programme served as the only diversion from the misery of the conditions.

The poet and songwriter Ilse Weber was at Theresienstadt and wrote some of her most famous lieder there, including the beautiful but haunting lullaby for children, *Weigela*. The Czech Pavel Haas was there, too. Viktor Ullmann, a well-known composer in the Schönberg school who had converted to Catholicism, was also a prisoner. Apart from organising concerts, he composed a chamber opera in the camp, entitled *Der Kaiser von Atlantis, The Master of Atlantis*. It was not approved for performance by the censor at Theresienstadt, said to be a parody of authoritarian rule, and he was soon after deported to Auschwitz.

It is not possible to detail what Heinrich and Karoline made of all this and how they managed from day to day. The unsanitary accommodation, shortage of food and medicines would have been extremely hard for the elderly or those not enjoying good health. Heinrich had not been well even prior to his arrival at Theresienstadt. He had been in hospital in Vienna suffering from asthma and breathing difficulties in June and July 1942. He was almost certainly in no fit state to travel at all. On 15 November 1942, Heinrich died of typhus at Theresienstadt, although this news took the better part of a year to reach the outside world. Karoline remained at Theresienstadt; she was now alone.

The transportations out of Theresienstadt to the extermination camps in Poland began in January 1942 and ended on 28 October 1944. The last train load being just a matter of days before the gas chambers of Auschwitz were finally decommissioned in November 1944. In Theresienstadt, there was sufficient knowledge of the fate that awaited those at Auschwitz (indeed the Camp Commandant had first-hand experience of what took place there) that it was considered desirable by the Nazi camp administrators to engage in complex schemes of deception to obtain the maximum degree of co-operation from the prisoners. Those first selected were not told that they were going to Auschwitz. They were told instead that their destination was a labour camp in Upper Silesia, which is where Auschwitz is situated. On other occasions they were simply told that they were being sent to 'Reich territory'. As rumour upon rumour circulated, even this was insufficient.

Then the practice of post-dated postcards began. Prisoners selected for subsequent deportation were forced to write postcards, which were post-dated often by a period of up to six months and sent back to Theresienstadt as a form of proof to those left behind that their loved ones were still alive. In September 1943, the disinformation was taken to another level by the creation of what was referred to as 'a family camp' at Auschwitz-Birkenau. Those selected for deportation were told that they were the lucky ones, as they would all be kept together in a family encampment, far away from the other prisoners. They were tattooed with a special reference 6SB, which they were told meant that they were to be quarantined and separated from the other parts of the camp for at least six months. In fact, it was code for execution after exactly six months.

Even with all these twisted lies, the fate of those at Theresienstadt was widely understood to be a desperate one. As the war dragged on into 1943 and then 1944, Max was in Tel Aviv and he knew of his father's death; he also knew that he had to act speedily in order to try to save his mother. He reached out repeatedly to a former colleague of his at the Jewish Agency in Geneva. This was someone he had worked with when he was back in Vienna working at the Jewish Agency for Palestine, although Max never told me his name. Max asked him over and over if there was anything that could be done. Anything at all. After a number of these requests and several months of waiting, Max was amazed to hear that there might indeed be something. Max was told in extremely vague terms that a plan was being formulated, which if it succeeded would lead to thousands of Jews being released from Theresienstadt and sent to safety in Switzerland. Max did not know the details but begged and pleaded that his mother somehow or other be added to this list of those who might be released and so saved. His contact said he would do his very best and asked that Max leave it to him.

In early 1945, Max received word from Geneva of extraordinary news. Karoline had been saved. She was one of a transport of about 1,200 released from the camp and it was hoped she would arrive shortly in Switzerland. Max was beside himself with joy, it was nothing less than a miraculous salvation. How could this have come about?

As with so many of the stories from these times, truth was stranger than fiction. Although Max did not know any of this at the time, the rescue operation came about largely as a result of the work of one woman, Recha Sternbuch, and the connection she made with a far-right leaning politician in Switzerland, Jean Marie Musy.

Recha Sternbuch, was born in 1905 in Krakow into a strictly orthodox family and had spent her early years in Antwerp. Before the war, she married and went to live in Montreux, Switzerland. With the discovery of each new chapter of horror during the war, Recha became entirely focussed on the effort to rescue of the Jews of Europe. She became a key member of the *Va'ad Hatzalah* (the Rescue Committee).

In September 1944, Recha heard the intriguing story of a Jewish couple who had been rescued from a concentration camp by the payment of a ransom fee of 10,000 Francs. To her astonishment, the go-between for this negotiation had been none other than Jean Marie Musy, a former President of the Swiss Confederation, publisher of the far-right weekly *La Jeune Suisse* and an erstwhile vocal supporter of Hitler.[12] Recha obtained an introduction to Jean Marie Musy through a mutual friend. Recha's thinking was that if this could work for one couple, why not on a much bigger scale? [13]

It then turned out that Jean Marie Musy's childhood friend and school companion was none other than Heinrich Himmler, the number two in the Nazi chain of command. The 10,000 Franc ransom had been negotiated by Musy through channels established by his connection with Himmler. Just how far could they take this connection? In October 1944, Recha obtained a new Mercedes for Jean Marie Musy and filled it with petrol obtained on the black market. It was agreed Jean Marie Musy would go to Berlin to see Himmler and ask what it would take to free 300,000 Jews, which was thought to be all that remained in the various concentration camps. Musy's pitch to Himmler was that he should open such a dialogue now, as it was clear that the war had more or less run its course and that Germany's defeat was inevitable.

A meeting took place between Jean Musy, Himmler and General Schellenberg on 19 November 1944. The price discussed was 20 million Swiss Francs, equivalent then to US$5 million. As it seemed to Musy, Himmler's main focus was not so much the money as the purchase of goodwill. Himmler wanted assurances from Musy that the release of Jews held in camps would receive a positive press.[14] A number of details were discussed and on 21 November 1944, the following extraordinary cable was sent to the Rescue Committee in New York

> After finishing negotiations with H, our delegate informed us about the possibility to evacuate 300,000 Jews for the amount of 20,000,000 Swiss Francs to neutral states. Such evacuations could be accomplished in groups of 15,000 persons monthly, the money to be deposited in a Swiss bank in proportionate rates of one million francs after arranging the evacuation of each group.[15]

The identity of the bank account in which the money would be held and the release of funds in tranches as each batch of prisoners were set free were negotiated.[16] There was also some discussion of placing the 300,000 under the protection of the ICRC until the time of release.[17]

By the end of 1944, the plan hit what seemed to be an insuperable problem. The Rescue Committee could not raise the money in time, they were still some way short. Nevertheless, Recha wanted to keep the negotiations alive and so asked Musy to buy more time by holding a further meeting, raising the possibility of offering something other than money; namely supplies of the antibiotic Cibazol manufactured in Switzerland by Ciba AG.[18] In late December 1944, Musy and Schellenberg met again. Himmler was not present, as he was otherwise occupied with the last-ditch Ardennes offensive. These discussions did not progress far because Schellenberg was mainly focussed on the idea of opening some kind of secret back-channel peace negotiations with the Allies.

There was another meeting between Himmler and Musy at the beginning of the new year. Musy had been summoned to a meeting in Bern at the German legation on 12 January 1945. Himmler was not in Switzerland, but again Schellenberg was there to meet him. Schellenberg said that they would have to travel to meet Himmler, who was near Bad Wildbad in the Black Forest in Germany. The three of them met at a hotel on 15 January 1945, but this time the meeting was more confrontational. Himmler was angered that the press attacks on Germany and its treatment of the Jews continued unabated. He also wanted assurances that any Jews released would not remain in the Reich and launched into an anti-Semitic rant about the poison of Jews in Germany after the First World War. He was also upset that there was still no proof of the money.

On it went. After further discussion, Himmler said he would agree to a transport of about 1200 Jews from Theresienstadt to cross the border into Switzerland, without payment of any price except favourable press coverage. This was agreed. In the meantime, a massive fund-raising effort gathered pace in the United States with an overwhelming response. However implausible at the outset, it looked like this plan could actually work.[19]

On 7 February 1945, a trainload of precisely 1,210 Jews left Theresienstadt for Switzerland. When they arrived at the Swiss border town of Kreuzlingen many wept, others kissed the ground before they were sent off to a quarantine camp in nearby St Gallen. Amongst the group were 58 children, most of whom had been born in the camp and had never enjoyed a day of freedom in their lives. The newspapers did cover the story in Switzerland, although in the United States it did not attract headlines in the major dailies.[20] *The Times* in London did not cover the story but the *Jewish Chronicle*, which Himmler almost certainly did not subscribe to, did.[21]

On 19 February 1945, Musy and Himmler held their last meeting. At this stage, the wheels of the wagon had begun to loosen and would then fall off altogether. First, there were apparently internal divisions at the highest level of the Nazi command structure between Kaltenbrunner and Himmler. There were also rumours circulating that this escape route to Switzerland had been negotiated for both Jews and a number of high-ranking SS officers, although there was no hard evidence of this.

Himmler was furious that the coverage in America was so muted. Kaltenbrunner it seems had shown Hitler some newspapers covering the story in a negative light and made much of the suggestion in the coverage that a series of weekly releases of Jews had been agreed in secret. Hitler ordered that no further train transports should be allowed to leave Germany for Switzerland.[22] The first transport of 1210 Jews turned out to be last organised by Musy. In the meantime, gas chambers were being built and prepared at Theresienstadt to liquidate the very last surviving prisoners and a few who had been marched there from Auschwitz. In a dark ironic twist, the workmanship turned out to be faulty, as the gas chamber doors were not airtight so not fit for their deadly purpose. They had to be re-ordered three times, by which time the camp had been liberated.[23]

Max meanwhile in Tel Aviv waited impatiently for more news from Montreux but for several months did not hear anything. The war ended in May 1945 and still there was no update. Half of Europe was looking frantically for the other half and confusion reigned. He was about to get married to his fiancée Hilda. Then on 19 June 1945, the day of his wedding, he received the dreadful news that there had been an awful mistake.

Karoline was not amongst the 1,210 released prisoners. They had looked in vain for her in Theresienstadt, but she had already been deported to Auschwitz in May 1944 and had perished with so many others. Poor Max. The shock, his dashed hopes. That morning he went to his bride's apartment in Tel Aviv (which in orthodox Judaism is itself strictly prohibited before the wedding ceremony) his deep blue eyes were reddened with tears. When Hilda answered the door, she looked at him, afraid of what he might say. She asked him softly whether Max did not want to go ahead, whether he had changed his mind. He reassured her and told her instead what had happened. They observed the traditional seven days of blessing that follow a wedding and then he sat *shiva* (seven days of mourning).

For many years, I hesitated to go Auschwitz. Whilst my parents were alive, I had always thought that I would go there with them. After they both passed away, my brother Theo and I talked about going together, but for a long time I felt I just might not be up to it. Finally, I booked on a series of group trips to go there and each time something came up that prevented me from going: a trial which overran; a hearing abroad that simply refused to settle; a family illness. By that time, I had started writing this book and I realised that there was something else, something more fundamental that stood in the way, and it was simply this.

The connection between Karoline and Auschwitz was so slender. This was just where the Nazi machine had decided to send her and the millions like her. On another day it could have been Treblinka, Bergen-Belsen or Buchenwald. She had no sooner entered through the dreadful gate promising her freedom through work than she perished. She never lived there and her soul did not really die there either. Likewise, Heinrich at Theresienstadt. Lackenbach was their birthplace, their home town where they (as generations before them had done) grew up, laughed, fell in love, worked, prayed and had a family. This was where they were torn from and this was where some memorial to their name, however small, should be laid.

PART FIVE
TAKING ACCOUNT

29

Lackenbach Revisited

'Proceed thence to the ruins, the split walls reach,
Where wider grows the hollow, and greater grows the breach'[1]

For years after the war, Vienna was not just divided into demarcated zones but the ubiquitous rubble and bomb debris served as a constant reminder of a past that most thought was best forgotten. Nevertheless, on 5 November 1955, the Vienna State Opera, which ten years previously had been set alight in an American bombing raid, was able once more to open its doors after a meticulous restoration. The choice for the first night on re-opening was Beethoven's *Fidelio*. Sixty-five years later, a recording of Karl Bohm's luminous performance from that night still holds the listener from the first to last note. At the start of the second act, Florestan – political prisoner and victim of political tyranny – is alone on the stage, bound in chains, without hope and very near the end of his strength. As the curtain rises and the heartbeat of the cellos fades away, Florestan cries out in one long howl of pain, '*Gott! Welch Dunkel Hier,*' (God! What darkness here)'. That night in November 1955, there must have been many members of the audience who were simply overwhelmed by what they saw and heard.

Beethoven had composed this work in 1805, when Vienna was being freed by Napoleon's invading forces from what he considered to be Austrian Hapsburg tyranny. On most levels Beethoven was no lover of Viennese society. Leaving aside that often forgotten irony, this opera, perhaps more than any other, has become a part of Vienna's DNA. It is a symbol of what became the newly imagined post-Second World War narrative; Florestan represented Austria's suffering as the victim of Nazi rule, its resistance to fascism and Leonore his wife as the symbol of loyalty, selfless bravery and a quiet but determined fight to overthrow the oppressor.

The other searing visual image of this time was that of the great multi-coloured roof of St Stephansdom ablaze, the result of the work of Allied bombers in April 1945. Across all of Austria, no one could read the newspapers without seeing this splashed on the front pages. The pictures told the story of Austria not just wiped out by the invading Nazis but by the liberators, too. When the cathedral was rebuilt some years later, the highly symbolic graffiti 'O5' engraved on the wall by the front entrance remained visible to all. O5 was a reference to the wartime resistance group of that name, the O referring to the first letter of 'österreich' and 5 to 'e', the fifth letter of the alphabet, in order more accurately to replicate the pronunciation of the umlaut accent in German.[2] The imagery was clear, this was to be understood as a nation that freed itself from its unwelcome invaders.

The timing of this performance of *Fidelio* was propitious. In May 1955 the Austrian State Treaty had been signed, re-establishing Austria as a free sovereign state. At the end of October 1955, the four Allied powers finally left Austrian soil making it possible for an independent state to be built on the well-established foundation of recognition of Austria's victim status. Since 1945, the country had been divided up into different military zones controlled by the Americans, French British and Russians. South of Vienna, Lackenbach and all of Burgenland fell within the Russian sector and suffered considerable hardship under its occupation.

It should not come as a shock to discover that the origin of Austria's 'first victim status' was entirely political. Winston Churchill was one of the first to coin the phrase in a speech in February 1942, accompanied by the somewhat grand sounding promise never to desert the Austrian's cause of establishing freedom from the Prussian yoke. The recognition of Austria's position in the war was then embedded in what became known as the Moscow Declaration in 1943, designed by the Allies to try to cement Austria's position as a bulwark against German expansionism. Soon it would also serve a fresh purpose: Austria was to be kept out of the Soviet sphere of influence. As a result, Stalin's qualification in the Moscow Declaration that 'Austria has a responsibility, which she cannot evade, for participation in the war on the side of Hitlerite Germany' would soon be forgotten.

By April 1945, when the Second Republic was formed, Austria's victim status was not just accepted as fact, but hardwired into the constitutional documentation.

The truth was simply not a convenient one for the Allies and Austrians to face in the aftermath of the Second World War. There were of course considerable numbers of Austrians who were the victims of Nazi terror. This can be seen in the meticulous work of dedicated organisations such as the Documentation Centre for Austrian Resistance, DÖW, in Vienna, detailing the arrest, torture and murder of the many thousands who fought fascism and others who were simply killed on the grounds of their race or religion. Some of this has already been described here. On the other hand, the first victim status accorded to Austria, for far too long allowed a veil to be drawn by the Austrians themselves over the acts of those who volunteered to serve in the SS, or other elite units, or stood by and lent support here and there. Worse still, it has enabled a silence to descend over those who actively participated in these horrors, which included many of the most notorious camp commandants. Indeed, around 70 per cent of Adolf Eichmann's staff were Austrian, and likewise 300 or so soldiers and officers who participated in Operation Reinhart under the direction of the Austrian Nazi Otto Globocnik, during which over 1.8 million Jews were murdered.[3] The story of Lackenbach both during and after the war perhaps illustrates these historical tensions better than most.

The swift expulsion of the Jews of Lackenbach was complete by the end of April 1938, but there was always a third element of the local community in that part of Austria. Besides Jews and Catholics, there was a significant number of Roma, referred to by the Austrians, in a derogatory fashion, as *Ziegeuner*, or gypsies. The Roma did not in the main run shops or own farms or local hostelries but were at least in part an itinerant population. They were said to have emigrated from northern India over a thousand years before and their distinctive Romani dialect is generally thought to be derived from Sanskrit.[4]

Ruth remembered as a child seeing Roma in the streets of Lackenbach with their distinctive clothes, some with a darker skin complexion. She recalled that many lived in wagons in an informal encampment besides the river on the outskirts of the village. The men often travelled for days to smaller nearby local communities selling cloth or other goods they had been advanced on credit terms by shop owners in Lackenbach such as my great grandfather, Heinrich. At the risk of reinforcement of stereotypes, many were renowned for their skill as craftsmen, horse traders and above all for their marvellous musicianship. The weddings of Terci and Julya and then Julci and Jeno in the early 1930s were celebrated not with traditional klezmer music or mock Cossack style dancing familiar to many today, but by Roma playing Strauss's Radetzky March outside the synagogue and people dancing the Polka in a round. Perhaps this performance was by way of repayment for a debt owed to Heinrich at his shop, which could not otherwise be paid off. More likely it was simply because a wedding would not be complete without some Roma musicians and joyful dancing.

Contrary to the absurdly romanticised depiction by Strauss in his operetta, *Die Ziegeunerbaron* ('The Gypsy Baron'), the Roma were not well loved in the Burgenland, where like the Jews they had settled for a considerable amount of time. Again, in common with the Jews, their distinctive appearance, separate Romany language and strong identity made them easy targets. They were distrusted, and their particular lifestyle allowed many tropes to propagate, identifying Roma as being simply street beggars and responsible for any theft in the area (in the English language 'to Jew' and 'to gyp' are each offensive terms meaning to steal or take without asking). Once the Jews had been expelled, it was not long before attention turned to the Roma.

As was noted so poignantly by the Lutheran priest Martin Niemöller, hatred and persecution often follow a hierarchy and when one community has been dealt with, attention falls on the next in line. Nevertheless, those lower down on the list still dare to believe that the axe will not fall on themselves.

Tobias Portschy, the Austrian Nazi and self-appointed gauleiter of the Burgenland, made the position clear. In a major speech in Eisenstadt on 11 March 1938, the day after the Anschluss he proclaimed that 'The gypsies and the Jews have been intolerable since the founding of the Third Reich. Believe us, we will solve this question with National Socialist consistency.'[5] Portschy acted to prohibit Roma from practising their traditional trade of travelling salesmen. As this caused increased financial hardship, anyone caught begging would then be threatened with deportation. In August 1938, Portschy published an influential memorandum entitled *The Gypsy Question*, which set out step by step his own suggested policy roadmap for the elimination of the Roma population. Much has been written about this publication which achieved wide readership in Berlin. Tempting as it might be to attribute the writing to Portschy himself, much of it was re-hashed or simply plagiarised from others who had written in the far-right press in the 1920s and 1930s.[6] According to Portschy, sexual intercourse between gypsies and German Arians should be prohibited, as was already the case with regard to Jews. Enforced sterilisation was recommended. He also advocated labour camps being established to ensure that the Roma were put to 'useful work' and kept away from the general population.[7]

Although this started as just a policy paper, Portschy, insofar as he was able to, piece by piece attempted to implement as much of this as he could between 1938 and 1940. There is also little doubt that Portschy tapped into popular sentiment, there was a growing chorus in the Burgenland which demanded the immediate removal of Roma communities. It was only necessary for a small amendment to be made to the old slogan calling for the removal of Jews: '*Das Burgenland Ziegeunfrei*' ('Free the Burgenland of Gypsies').[8] Enforced work gangs were established with strict punishment for those considered not to be pulling their weight. At this point, as with so much of the treatment of the Roma, Austrian leadership showed the way.

Then to the dismay of provincial Burgenland government, in October 1940 the Reich Interior Ministry in Berlin issued a decree announcing that the relocation of the Ostmark Roma to what was referred to as the *Generalgouvernement*, occupied Poland, would be postponed until further notice. This unanticipated change of policy simply would not do. Several provincial leaders in the Burgenland, notably those in Eisenstadt and Oberpullendorf, decided that they would establish and finance themselves an internment camp for Roma in the Burgenland. This was perhaps the only Nazi concentration camp directed and run by local leadership and not central command.[9] The thinking was that if Berlin would not take care of the Roma, surely the Burgenlanders should do so themselves.

They moved quickly and in less than a month, the Schafflerhof Estate outside Lackenbach was expropriated from the Esterházy family and chosen as the intended site.[10] On 23 November 1940 the Lackenbach Camp was opened in a disused barn and a sheepfold.[11] As a result of its extraordinary origins, the Lackenbach Camp was not under the control and command of Berlin or the SS but rather under the direction of Reich Commissar Kapphengst of Department II.B of the Vienna Criminal Police.[12] It was not accorded the status of concentration camp but instead was classified as a crime detention centre, a local measure to prevent the inmates from travelling around committing criminal offences.[13]

Conditions at the Lackenbach Camp for the first two years in particular were horrendous. There was practically no heating, only straw bedding, and the food and sanitary conditions were unspeakable. It was a little better for those who arrived in and slept in their own wagons parked up on the site. Lackenbach Camp was initially established to house about two hundred Roma, local to the village and its surroundings. After successive roundups by the local police, in November 1941 over two thousand were imprisoned there, 40 per cent of them children under the age of 15, somewhat belying the paper-thin pretext of this being a crime prevention centre as opposed to an instrument of local genocide. The unsanitary conditions caused outbreak of typhus fever which killed between two and three hundred Roma prisoners held there and then did for Hans Kolross, the first camp commandant.

In January 1942, Franz Langmuller the deputy commandant succeeded to the post. Franz Langmuller was born in 1909 near to Bratislava. After the First World War, like many others he moved in search of work. He came to the Burgenland, joined the police service, was assigned first to the criminal police burglary department and then worked as a police dog handler in Lackenbach. Langmuller's sadism appeared to know no bounds. For the nine months in which he was in charge of Lackenbach Camp he instituted a vicious system under which Roma camp kapos were instructed to beat other prisoners.[14] This, did not seem to satisfy his blood lust and he would frequently be seen himself administering the punishments. According to eyewitness testimony, Langmuller himself was said to be responsible for the death of 287 inmates by his own hands.[15] In September 1942, Langmuller was transferred to the Waffen SS and was sent to Poland to continue his war work there. He was succeeded by Julius Brunner of the Vienna Police, who attempted to restore some semblance of order to the conditions in the camp, which in turn enabled him with greater efficiency to commence the deportations to the death camps in Poland.

Until the prisoners were taken away to their death, this being a work camp, gangs would be sent into Lackenbach as well as the neighbouring villages in full view of the local population. One key aspect of the work they were forced to undertake was the construction of a road to the nearby hilltop at Hornstein, the site of a top-secret radar station used to help shoot down US bombers form the 15th US Air Fleet.[16] #

In late 1942, the synagogue in Lackenbach which previously had been ransacked of its valuables in March 1938, then set ablaze in

November 1938, was finally blown up and razed. The Roma were ordered to march into Lackenbach and break up the masonry so that it could be re-used for building or repairing roads. Some of it was purchased or simply taken by the villagers themselves. There is today no sign of the synagogue in Lackenbach. Templegasse, where the synagogue stood, has simply disappeared from the map.

Between 1941 and 1944, approximately 4,000 prisoners were kept at the Lackenbach Camp. From 1943 the Roma were systematically taken to Auschwitz following Himmler's notorious Auschwitz Order of December 1942, which was originally intended to cover Roma and Sinti living in Poland but was then extended to the whole Reich.[17] At Auschwitz they were generally kept in a special encampment away from others, and the conditions there according to Rudolf Höss the Camp Commandant, lacked even the most basic requirements if the intention was to keep them alive.[18] In January 1945 when the Russians liberated the camp, only about 300 prisoners remained. It is estimated that under Nazi rule up to 500,000 Roma and Sinti were murdered.[19] As far Austria itself was concerned, it is estimated that between 60-70,000 of its Jews and 6,000 of its Roma had been killed.[20]

In 1945 post-war, it was time for the newly established Second Republic to consider bringing charges against those with responsibility for these crimes. The Allied Powers established a denazification programme under which Austrians had to register their Nazi affiliations. Over half a million Austrians registered their affiliation to the Nazi Party, the SS or other criminal organisations. Of these, 41,906 were labelled major offenders. Portschy and Langmuller were amongst them.[21]

As has already been described, Tobias Portschy as the first Gauleiter of the Burgenland had been one of the chief instigators of the murderous and sadistic policies towards both Jews and Roma in this region, having seized the opportunity to take the reins of power in March 1938. He was also cited in eyewitness accounts as having been responsible for the killing of Hungarian Jews forced onto so-called Death Marches in the spring of 1945 at the very end of the war. In his own words, he described himself as the principal preacher of National Socialism in the Burgenland.

Portschy was put on trial in 1949 in the *Volksgerichte*, the People's Court established to prosecute Austrian Nazi war criminals. Portschy was not prosecuted for his criminal acts against Jews or the Roma or indeed for any specific individual offence, despite the comprehensive detail and eyewitness accounts in the papers before the Prosecutors' Office.[22] Instead he was found guilty in March 1949 of what might be described as the more political offence of seizing power as Gauleiter in the Burgenland in 1938 without legal authority. He was sentenced to fifteen years of hard labour and stripped of his law degree.

Within a year of his conviction, Portschy filed a plea for clemency to the Austrian Federal President. It was supported by the new Governor of the Burgenland, together with his old hometown Mayor and a lengthy list of notables who felt that whatever had happened had to be re-cast and re-written. The *leitmotif* of the plea was that Portschy did whatever he did in furtherance of his undying love of the homeland and so could not really be guilty of any offence.[23]

Less than two years into his fifteen-year sentence, in February 1951 Portschy was pardoned by Austrian Social Democratic Party President Theodor Korner. In doing so the President noted that Portschy had already suffered much from being stripped of his degree and his ability to work and further that, in stark contrast to Portschy's own testimony, he had really not played any significant part in the Nazi Party.[24] All this served further to amplify his victim status. In his eyes, he was a politician who continued to suffer for acts for which he had been formally pardoned. In 1957 the conviction itself was annulled as part of a wider Austrian Nazi Amnesty. There was now no stain on his name. This allowed him to advance the notion that too many good Austrians had had to suffer the avenger's false sense of justice.

Porstchy went back to lead his life in the town of Rechnitz which as has already been recounted had had its own horrific war story, which was to remain buried by a dreadful vow of silence alongside its innocent victims. In any event, Portschy appears to have selected Rechnitz as a suitable place for his later life. He sat on the board of a local savings bank and with no apparent sense of irony served as chairman of its tourist association.[25] He became active in the right-wing Freedom Party and lived to the ripe old age of 91. Four years before his death in 1996, he gave a number of interviews, including for Egon Humer's film, *Guilt and Memory*. He railed against the injustice of his conviction, insisting that he had only been following Nazi laws, which he described as being amongst the most humane in the world.[26] He then once more returned to the theme of his visceral hatred of the Roma, referring to them as parasites and refusing to utter any denunciation of his past ideology or a word of regret.[27] This led to a re-opening of a criminal investigation against him, which had not been completed at the time of his death.

Langmuller was also put on trial in 1948 before the People's Court. The witness testimony of those who passed through the Lackenbach Camp whilst it was under his command spoke of his sadistic abuse leading to the death of hundreds. Taking into account the classification of the Lackenbach Camp as a crime prevention centre, Langmuller was convicted of handing out 'too drastic a means of education contradicting the natural concepts of humanity and dignity'.[28] Even taking account of Austrian sensitivity this was a bizarre euphemism. He was given one year in prison on 15 October 1948 but was released after only two and a half months as his detention pre-trial counted towards the fulfilment of his punishment. With some minor exception, each of those responsible for the genocidal programme against the Roma and Sinti escaped meaningful punishment.[29]

A variant of this theme played out in the trial of those responsible for the cold-blooded murder of 180 Jews at Rechnitz. Shortly after the commencement of the trial of those charged, two of the key witnesses were murdered, one being Karl Muhr who had handed out the weapons at the Schloss and was therefore able to provide incriminating evidence. After this it was near to impossible to get anyone to talk of these events, and Franz Podenz, the chief instigator, died in 1995 in his mid-eighties.[30] These were not isolated instances. Anton Burger, the notorious Austrian Camp Commandant of Theresienstadt who briefly holed up with Eichmann after the war, was tried and sentenced to death in 1947, but managed to escape not once but twice from prison. He lived out his days dying of natural causes on Christmas Day in 1991 under an assumed name, Wilhelm Bauer. Obscenely enough, Wilhelm Bauer was a Jewish prisoner in Theresienstadt whom he had personally murdered.[31]

Pál Esterházy, the last great Prince of the dynasty which had for so long given shelter to the Jews of this region and on whose expropriated land the Lackenbach Camp was built, fared considerably worse than either Portschy or Langmuller. He spent most of the War in Budapest. An internal Nazi intelligence report compiled by Karl Werkmeister, the German chargé d'affaires in Budapest, voiced suspicion that he was a Jewish sympathiser.[32] The Prince in the main kept his head down and tried to live quietly in Budapest in one of the twenty-eight palaces owned by the family. In March 1944 the Germans occupied Budapest and started the round-up of the Jews of Hungary. Esterházy was disgusted and reached out to The Sisters of Mercy, a Catholic organisation and donated a very large sum from his private fortune to aid the rescue of Jewish children, many of whom were hidden in a convent school building in the 11th District of Budapest.[33] Although he could have fled, Esterházy remained in Budapest after the war ended.

By this time the Hungarian and Austrian governments were trying to find ways to expropriate the vast family estates which were to be found in both countries. In February 1949 Esterházy became caught up in one of the most notorious of the post-war communist political show-trials, that of Cardinal Mindszenty. The two of them on separate occasions had been followed to the same bank in Budapest and were said to have taken part in an illegal foreign currency exchange. The two had nothing to do with one another and the evidence itself was to say the least thin, but each defendant was highly symbolic, Esterházy being the most prominent name of the old aristocracy and the Cardinal the leader of the Church. They were inevitably both found guilty and each sentenced to fifteen years in prison. Esterházy was offered the opportunity of release if he surrendered all his lands to the State, but he refused.[34] He was freed only in 1956 as a result of the all too brief Hungarian Revolution and lived the rest of his days in Switzerland. The Cardinal was also freed at this time, but before he could escape the new regime fell and Soviet control was reimposed. He was holed up in the United States Embassy in Budapest until 1971.

The Lackenbach Camp itself was destroyed shortly after the war with the exception of the administration building, which was left in a derelict state until the late 1970s. Remarkably enough, before it was also demolished a cache of records was found there which has enabled historians and researchers to recreate much of the detail of the daily conditions, including the food rations, punishments and work rotas. Today, with the exception of a few photographs, these records and survivors' testimonies, nothing remains.

As for the victims themselves, no Jews have returned to the Burgenland but the synagogue in Eisenstadt remains open to the public as a museum. That life and community has gone forever. When I visited in the course of writing this book, there was no memorial to the Jews of Lackenbach, no sign or word of their long history in this part of Austria. The Roma have not really fared any better. Some did survive the war and try to build new lives for themselves but found that they still faced significant prejudice and discrimination. In 1984, on the initiative of the Cultural Association of Austrian Roma, a memorial created by the architect Matthias Szauer was put up at the site of the former camp in

Lackenbach. After explaining the significance of the memorial and the location, it bears a simple inscription: 'They had to suffer and die just because they were different.' It was not until 1988 that Lackenbach Camp was officially recognised as a concentration camp, but its establishment by local leadership and money is still not acknowledged.

The post-war history of the steps taken by Austria to come to terms with the past and the conduct of so many of its citizens between 1938 and 1945 is a long and tortuous one. Following the establishment of the Second Republic, it was felt that a little encouragement had to be given to the creation of a new moral foundation for the country. In 1946 the Austrian Ministry of Foreign Affairs published the Red White Red Book (the colours of the Austrian flag), which bedded down certain key aspects of the mythology. Originally it was intended to be published in two volumes, the second being dedicated to the story of the Austrian resistance, but it seems not enough material was found to fill the proposed second volume. Instead, contrary to the substantial body of evidence, in the only volume published the authors declared that in 1938 70 per cent of all Austrians had not just opposed the Anschluss but felt a fanatical animosity against it.[35]

At the end of the war about 750,000 Austrian Wehrmacht soldiers were released from Allied POW camps and returned home. This was celebrated widely across the whole of Austria. In these exhausted and relieved homes, there was it seems no room for contemplation of what had happened in the war or responsibility.[36] In due course, these ex-soldiers formed veteran associations up and down the country and themselves became a powerful political force on the far right.

Opinion polls were conducted from time to time in the late 1960s up to the mid-1980s to find out if people agreed with the proposition that the Jews during the period 1938 to 1945 had got what was coming to them and were in part responsible for their own fate. In 1969, 55 per cent of supporters of the far-right Freedom Party answered in the affirmative. Amongst those supporting the centre right Austrian People's Party, 30 per cent concurred. Even 18 per cent of those supporting the SPO, the Social Democratic Party, agreed. By 1985 these percentages had dropped but were still at 45, 25 and 16 per cent respectively.[37] Clearly, the views of Herr M encountered earlier in this book were not completely divergent from opinion across the political spectrum in Austria after the war.

So complete was the victim myth that in Austria there was a measure of disbelief, at least for those on the right or centre right of Austrian politics, when international outrage met the election of Kurt Waldheim as President of Austria in 1986. Waldheim was a former Nazi intelligence officer, from 1971 to 1982 was UN Secretary General and then stood as the candidate of the Austrian People's Party. It is beyond the scope of these pages to examine the claims or independent committee's findings with regard to his war record. Nevertheless, such was the force of international reaction, that it proved to be something of a catalyst for change. It was a turning point as regards the Austrian State's own acceptance of responsibility. It was simply no longer possible to stick to the old recital that had served so well for forty years, and the result was dramatic.

In 1991 Chancellor Vranitsky delivered a public apology for the conduct of Austria in the war and made an official visit to Israel in 1993, during which further acceptance of responsibility was made clear. There followed an extension of the terms of existing compensation to the victims of Nazi terror, and this was made not just to Jews but to Roma as well.

For the very first time, difficult conversations could take place. It was during the period of Waldheim's presidency that I went to Vienna with my father-in-law, Henry, for the first time. Denise and I were just married, and this was a sort of get-to-know-your-family trip. He took me to a number of the places he remembered from his childhood, including his old school in the Second District. We were standing outside in a public courtyard when Henry decided simply to walk in the school and show us his old classroom. There was no time to consider whether this was sensible or indeed allowed. We just found ourselves at the foot of a grand staircase with a giant portrait of Waldheim looking down on us. At this point the head teacher popped out of her study and asked us what we were doing. Henry answered politely in perfect German that he was born in Vienna and that this was his old school and that he apologised for causing any interruption. The head teacher was bowled over.

She took Henry by the arm and guided him into a classroom of some of the older children, aged from about 10 to 12. She explained to the class teacher what had happened and that the class was indeed fortunate to have Henry there, who could describe to them his schooldays. Henry spoke without any further prompting. He explained that the school was situated then in the vibrant Jewish Quarter of Vienna and his class was at least fifty per cent Jewish. He spoke of the Anschluss, the rise of Hitler youth in Vienna and in the school itself, and how he was chased home every night by schoolchildren looking to beat him up.

He then explained the events of Kristallnacht in November 1938 and how he was forced to leave the country. It is almost impossible nearly thirty-five years after this incident to describe the astonishment on every child's face, and those of the two teachers. The head teacher was trying to find a point in the story when she could thank their special visitor for dropping by and bring this impromptu lesson to an end. Denise and I looked on in embarrassment, the kind specifically reserved for the acts of a parent, or in this case my father-in-law.

I think that moment taught me how difficult this whole subject was in Austria and that it was and still is a topic that many would like if at all possible to avoid. During my research I visited Austria a number of times and those undertaking any form academic research or working at the relevant archives could not have been more engaged and empathetic. Nothing was too much trouble. Every detail was chased down, and the book could not have written without their encouragement, professionalism and kindness. In the main, this is a younger generation of Austrians determined to forge a new image and redress the wrongs of those who preceded them. The most striking illustration of the extent to which the conversation has moved on is the legislation passed in August 2020 allowing thousands of descendants of those forced to flee Austria after the Anschluss in March 1938 to apply for Austrian citizenship. This would be remarkable enough by itself, but the prime mover behind this was Sebastian Kurz, then the young dynamic Chancellor of Austria and member of the centre-right Austrian People's Party. Anyone hearing his words after a recent terror outrage in Vienna could see that he is a standard bearer for a very different kind of Austria.

Despite all this, I was quite unsure of the reaction that I would receive when I made contact with the Mayor of Lackenbach. There was a very specific reason to get in touch with him. It was to obtain his support to lay *stolpersteine* memorial plaques outside the houses on Berggasse in Lackenbach from which my mother, grandfather, and the generation before them were deported in 1938.

Stolpersteine, literally translated as stumbling stones, are the brainchild of Gunter Demnig, an artist from Berlin. His idea was that the family of those affected can apply to local authorities to lay a small brass square in the shape of a cobble stone which is then cut into the pavement outside the last known address where victims of Nazi terror had lived before the war. Once permission is given Gunter Demnig then himself casts and lays the brass cobble stone shape with the names of those remembered. The address should be last place where the person or family had lived in freedom, it was not to commemorate a place of imprisonment. The concept applies equally to those killed in the concentration camps, those who fled and others who committed suicide. *Stolpersteine* are not limited to Jews but to all victims. Once laid on the pavement, the idea is that those who walk by will pause or stumble and reflect. Stones have been laid by Gunter Demnig in more than 2,000 locations in Germany, Austria and right across Western and Central Europe. There are now more than 90,000 *stolpersteine* in twenty-one countries.

As soon as I came across the *stolpersteine* project it seemed to me to be an entirely appropriate way to honour the memory of those in my mother's family whose fate has been described. Those who were murdered in the war have no grave to mark their death. Those who survived have no remembrance of their life before deportation. Each was taken from a place where they had contributed much, lived peaceably in a community for so many generations and yet practically all trace of their past or what happened to them has been removed. Lackenbach's own website sought to proclaim ignorance of their fate and certainly a lack of responsibility for what happened.

This therefore provided some of the background to my thinking when I approached the Mayor of Lackenbach specifically to ask for his support to lay such *stolpersteine*. I emailed the Mayor on several occasions over a number of months including on International Holocaust Remembrance Day and on the anniversary date of the end of the Second World War in Europe. I gave the details of my family who had lived in his village, the street name, the house numbers and what happened to each of them.

For a long time, I received no answer, making me wonder whether the emails had not reached him. Then one Monday afternoon whilst I was packing up at work and heading off for home, a response from the Mayor flashed up. He thanked me politely for getting in touch with him, told me that some of the facts that I had recited with regard to my family in Lackenbach were 'unclear' and some of the details of the house numbers were 'inaccurate', then outlined a number of steps that were under consideration for a communal memorial to honour the 800-year history of the Jews of Lackenbach (this being done in conjunction with the Viennese Jewish community), but he did not address the question of the *stolpersteine*.

The response did at least answer the question as to whether the Mayor had received my communications but in every other respect it was not what I had expected and was not an answer to my request. I have since repeatedly asked him for a direct response and to identify what he meant by a lack of clarity or inaccuracies. I also pointed out that the neighbouring town of Mödling (the Mayor wanted the precise spelling complete with an umlaut for accurate identification) had already allowed such *stolpersteine* to be laid, so there was a useful precedent. In addition, I identified from the Eisenstadt archives another house on Berggasse at which my great grandfather had conducted his business. I told the Mayor that the information I had given him came directly from the records I had inspected and copied. I have also asked him more than once to share any information with me that might lead to different conclusions. That single response is all I have received and although at present the position does not seem to be promising, I have not abandoned hope of honouring my family in this small but appropriate way.

The Mayor is an elected figure. He came from the left of centre in Austrian politics which today dominates the political landscape of the Burgenland and which had in the past been at the forefront of the movement to acknowledge Austria's role in the Nazi horrors. I think that his political instincts were sound and I have no reason to doubt his moral conscience. Nevertheless, I have of course also thought at length what different version of events he might have been referring to, without producing anything in support. I then looked once more at the name he signed off at the foot of the email. Of course, his family name might be popular and common in Lackenbach and so I did not want to leap to any conclusions. But it is a very small village, and his is the same family name of those who ended up, through the expropriatory auctions, as the owners of my grandfather Julya's house at Berggasse, 18. Who knows? Was this just an irrelevant coincidence? Or maybe the emails that I had sent him had raised a concern in certain quarters as to where these inquiries might ultimately end up and so had to be pushed back. As I had witnessed on numerous occasions, the war casts a very long shadow in this part of the world.

30

Open and Shut

Ich bin der Welt abohnden gekommen[1]

The specially reserved table at the National Archives in Kew had a metal trolley beside it, holding a handful of files scattered across its two dark green shelves. I placed them on my table with care. Each was tied with white ribbon that had been in place for nearly seventy years. I took up the first folder, marked 'Aliens Department – Home Office – Closed Until 2053' and paused. Clearly my closest relations were not meant to see what was inside, realistically the same applied to me and I hesitated for a good while. What would be found inside? Anything I read in here could not be unread. This was, however, the last step after the Freedom of Information Act request had been made and granted. If I was not prepared to finish the task, why start at all? Maybe the truth was simply that after this lengthy and emotional journey, I was not quite ready for the conclusion; not prepared to say my own goodbyes to those who had lived through all this and yet were not here with me to guide me through the contents. Ever so gently, as if it might disintegrate at my touch, I opened the first page and was soon entirely immersed, lost to my surroundings.

Each file had a brown cover page on which many officials would record with a comment or simple cross their reaction to a particular piece of correspondence or application. Inside each file was found all manner of different writing to and from officialdom, handwritten supplication and terse typed response.

After the war had ended, it was clear Terci had only one thought on her mind: how to reunite the family. Terci had settled in England. Together with her sister Julci, she was running a kosher boarding house in Southport and my mother was doing well at school. Julya was still in Palestine, which at that time remained under the British Mandate. The obvious step was for Julya to apply to come to Britain to join his wife and daughter, whom he had not seen for nearly seven years.

It might have been thought, particularly in the light of the horrific images of the Holocaust seen at that time in newspapers and cinema newsreels, that there would have been a flood of sympathy displayed towards those who had suffered so much or been separated by this terrible persecution. These papers did not reveal any such wellspring.

In the first two years post-war, Julya applied repeatedly for permission to come to Britain, even if only to visit his wife and daughter, but he was refused on each occasion. Julya had written directly to the Home Office and so attempted to by-pass the Director of Migration and Statistics in Jerusalem. This received short shrift. The Home Office noted tartly that after all this time and so many applications, he should know the drill. The position taken was that Julya had made his decision to go to Palestine and so if the family were to be reunited, the solution was for Terci and my mother to apply through the appropriate channels join him there. In their eyes there were no exceptional circumstances. The Home Office also noted Terci had herself only been given permission temporarily to land in the United Kingdom in 1939 with strict limitation on her freedom to work. So a considerable degree of pressure was brought to bear in June 1945 by refusing her permission to carry on the business of a boarding house or taking in paying guests. She was reminded that this contravened the confines of the work permission she had been granted on arrival, which was restricted to working as a domestic servant. These restrictions made little sense in post-war Britain as it was a country desperately short of labour. In 1946 the British Cabinet Manpower Working Party estimated that there was a need for approximately a million additional pairs of hands.[2] The unstated assumption was that without any means of supporting herself in England, Terci would simply pack up her bags and admit defeat.

Julya and Terci nevertheless stuck to their task. Julya applied once more in 1947 for a visa to make a short family visit, this time on the basis that he only intended to stop in England *en route* from Palestine to America. I have no idea if this was indeed the case. It sounded more than a little unrealistic, but the outcome was the same as before. Julya described himself as able to support himself and as being a restaurant owner in Tel Aviv. I had never heard anyone speak of this and even though I have asked as many questions as I can of those who might know, there does not appear to have been any truth in that piece of self-aggrandisement. No doubt Julya had been advised by others to give as good impression of himself as he could, but it worked decisively against him and only reinforced the decision that the family should be reunited, if at all, in Palestine.

The attitude adopted by Britain to the question of the million or so Jewish refugees in Europe who had survived the Holocaust was encapsulated in the announcements made to the House of Commons on 13 November 1945. James Chuter Eade was the Home Secretary and Ernest Bevin the Foreign Secretary in Clement Attlee's post-war Labour Government.

Two different aspects were addressed in the Commons in the course of that afternoon. The first was the Distressed Relatives in Europe Scheme. Chuter Eade's starting point was to recognise the scale of the suffering, but however meritorious that might be in general terms, it was not possible for Britain to accept further immigration except within tightly restricted categories.[3] A basic principle was that a wife could join a husband already in Britain but not a husband join his wife. The major exception to this would be to enable a man to join his wife or family if he was incapacitated or too old to support his wife and family abroad.[4] Julya's bit of puffery as a man of business in Tel Aviv made him ineligible to rejoin his wife and daughter in England, as he had asserted his own economic independence.

The second aspect concerned the continued and vexed question of Jewish immigration to Palestine. The United States and indeed many of the democracies in the free world joined in the chorus to allow those who had survived the slaughter and were currently being held in temporary shelter in Displaced Persons (DP) camps, often under armed guard and behind barbed wire,[5] to go to Palestine if they wished. Britain stood firm in opposition. The ringleader of those opposed to any such permission being granted was Ernest Bevin. The result was a call in the strongest terms from the United States to allow in the first instance 100,000 of those living in camps across Europe to emigrate to Palestine if they wished. Bevin would not agree to this in the knowledge that the Palestinian Arab community had remained firmly opposed to any further immigration.[6] Bevin's starting point was to refuse to accept that those displaced Jews had no future life where they had come from in Europe.[7] Nevertheless, on 13 November 1945, Ernest Bevin under considerable pressure from across the Atlantic, announced the creation of the joint Anglo-American Committee of Inquiry on Palestine, which was established not only to make recommendations on the question of immigration but wider proposals to be submitted to the United Nations. Whatever Bevin's own views on the subject were, the truth was that Britain was not in any position to resist the American demand for an inquiry. At this point, Bevin was seeking the advance of a very considerable loan at low interest from the United States and the balance of power between the two nations had already irreversibly shifted. This radical new initiative held out the promise of wider international engagement and co-operation and was welcomed in the mainstream press.[8] The Anglo-American Committee reported in April 1946 and recommended amongst other things the immediate admission of up to 100,000 Jewish refugees. Britain remained opposed.[9]

The logical consequence of the twin aspects of the policy adopted by the government was that Julya could not join his wife and daughter in England as, in his own words, he was neither incapacitated or unable to support himself. And it was not possible for the family to be reunited in Palestine, because the government line was to deny or at any rate severely limit Jews permission to enter from Europe.

Bevin's belief as expressed in November 1945 that the survivors of the concentration camps could or should go back to live in their original communities in Europe was utterly unrealistic. By July 1946, it was quite simply untenable. On 4 July 1946, slaughter returned to Kielce, a hundred or so miles from Warsaw. About two hundred Jews, a tiny remnant of the tens of thousands who had once lived there and who had survived the ghettos and concentration camps after the war, had returned to their home town. They could not go back to their old houses which had been taken from them by locals and so they were mostly accommodated in a single communal building in Planty Street.[10] Such incidents traditionally started with the disappearance of a Christian boy. Nevertheless, this time the conspiracy theorists went large and accused the Jewish community of kidnapping and murdering no fewer than twelve Christian children for ritualistic purposes and of course at a time of year which had nothing to do with Passover or indeed any festival. The blood libel was as strident as ever. A murderous mob swept through the streets and thirty-six Jews were killed in an orgy of violence. Another fifty or so were seriously wounded.[11] Ultimately, nine were arrested, charged with the murder of these innocents and sentenced to death. What is still not clear is the extent to which this was a spontaneous outpouring of violence or whether it was encouraged by political forces.[12] One of the main instigators of the story was a nine-year-old boy who when arrested told the police that he had been told by local leaders to identify certain members of the Jewish communal organisations as responsible for the supposed ritual killings.[13]

As a result, approximately a hundred and fifty thousand of the remaining Jews in Poland packed up whatever they could and walked for over 650 miles to Germany in order to join the many others in the DP Camps waiting to go to Palestine. Such was their desperation they joined the many millions of German refugees expelled from Central and Eastern Europe after the Potsdam Conference. It was described as 'the world on foot'.[14] They marched from the place of their birth in Poland, where they were still hunted down as child killers, to DP Camps. Many of them ended up in a camp in Munich of all places, the birthplace of Nazism.[15] Still the British Government refused to change its position.

At this point the situation deteriorated rapidly. Not only was there increasing international pressure to let the refugees into Palestine but the British faced an ever-greater military threat from Jewish underground paramilitary forces in Palestine operating independently of and against the wishes of the central command of David Ben Gurion. This culminated on 22 July 1946 with the most infamous and deadly of all attacks; the bombing by the Irgun of the British administrative headquarters in Jerusalem, the King David Hotel, in which 91 were killed, many of whom were Jews and Arabs at work there.[16] The attack was roundly condemned by the Jewish Agency in Palestine as well as by all communal leaders in Britain.[17] Nevertheless, the effect on Jews living in Britain was severe.

I had occasionally talked to my mother about this period of her life after the war. She was a young teenager trying to enjoy all the things any young girl would, albeit in the wider context of the austerity that Britain faced. As with so many others of her age, her abiding memories of those years were of the easy new friendships formed at school and the first time she tasted a fresh and not dried banana. I am not sure to what extent at this time she was following the politics of the day as she would do with considerable passion in university and in later life. Nevertheless, there was one name, the mere mention of which would be sure to be met with pointed displeasure. That was Ernest Bevin. The point that my mother made was that you could agree or not agree with a particular policy of the government of the day, but that in his case she felt there was a nastiness, an animus against Jews in Britain and abroad, which at that time in particular was both worrying and deeply hurtful. It also allowed an atmosphere to develop which many took advantage of.

In his biography of Ernest Bevin, Lord Adonis set out a body of relevant material which could be deployed in any indictment of his attitude towards the Jews. My mother had no doubt sensed all this in his tone, if not in his words and deeds. In 1931, Bevin explained to the TUC conference that the financial crash was 'a game of Shylock versus the people, with Shylock getting the pound of flesh every time.' In December 1946 Bevin returned from a trip to New York and was much vexed by the strength of the Zionist feeling in America. Prime Minister Attlee in correspondence with his brother said that when he returned from New York Bevin told him that 'A Zionist is defined as a Jew who collects money from another Jew to send to another Jew in Palestine, with the collector taking a good percentage.' According to Bevin, Jews were at least in part responsible for anti-Semitic behaviour. Too often they did not behave well enough or with sufficient gratitude. In saying this he made clear he was not referring to 'the working Jew' but chiefly the 'nouveau riche or moneyed person'.[18] Those who were near to Bevin in Whitehall knew his position. Christopher Mayhew, a junior Foreign Office Minister, wrote in his diary in May 1948:

> There is no doubt in my mind that Ernest Bevin detests Jews... He says they taught Hitler the techniques of terror and were now paralleling the Nazis in Palestine. They were the preachers of violence and war. He says, 'what can you expect when people are brought up from the cradle on the Old Testament.'[19]

Money, power, influence, responsibility for the global financial crisis, behaving like Nazis, vengefulness, un-Christian behaviour, disloyal and a lack of proper assimilation meant that they were responsible for their own victimhood.

In the meantime, Terci clearly thought, or perhaps had been advised by others, that the repeated rejection received by Julya was due to a lack of appreciation in the Home Office of the hardship that he had had to face over the last few years. Accordingly, as was clear from a handwritten letter in the second of the files, on 30 April 1947 she wrote a lengthy plea to the Secretary of State for the Home Office, Aliens Department at 10, Old Bailey, London EC4 in support of a special request for Julya to be allowed to come to Britain. Terci always had a fine hand and her plea was concise and well-pitched. She described how Julya had been hounded out of Austria by the Nazis, had all his possessions taken and spent seven months on the road before he was able to sail for Palestine, albeit omitting the fact that he did so without permit. She then added a missing detail that I had never understood before; that before Julya left Austria, he had been arrested and imprisoned by the Gestapo and was only released on the condition that he would immediately leave the Reich. This perhaps explained the particular interest taken by the police in Vienna as to whether Julya had indeed left the country. She spoke movingly of the hardship of having to bring up my mother without her husband at her side, that nevertheless my mother had excelled at school and won a scholarship. She added, without giving any details, that she was of independent financial means and that Julya would be no burden on the country. This last point was no doubt extremely delicate because the source of her independence logically must have been the kosher boarding house in Southport that the authorities had earlier refused permission for her to run. The application was once more unsuccessful.

The atmosphere faced by Jews in Britain in 1947 continued to spiral downward. On 5 January 1947, *The Sunday Times* carried an editorial questioning the loyalty of the Jews of Britain, as the violence in Palestine continued unabated. In May 1947, the United Nations Special Committee on Palestine (UNSCOP) was formed to make recommendations as to the future governance of Palestine. To most it looked inevitable that some form of partition of Palestine would result – a Jewish and an Arab State, even though this was met with fierce opposition from the Arab League. Meanwhile, Ernest Bevin remained fixed in his determination to prevent further Jewish immigration into Palestine and this led in July 1947 to the turning back from Haifa of *The Exodus*, perhaps the most famous of the post-Second World War migrant vessels. Whilst UNSCOP carried out its work, both the insurgency and counter- insurgency in Palestine raged. Then in July 1947 practically every British newspaper covered the truly dreadful story of the hanging by the Irgun underground of two British sergeants, Clifford and Paice, supposedly as a macabre response to the hanging of three of their members in the aftermath of a mass break-out at the Acre Military Prison earlier in the spring. The *Daily Express* printed the shocking photograph of the two soldiers suspended from the branches of a eucalyptus tree.[20]

The military position in Palestine was fast spinning out of control and very soon this spilt over to an outpouring of violence up and down the country against Jews living in Britain[21] Over the first weekend in August 1947 it was reported that 150 violent attacks on Jews, synagogues and Jewish property took place, with over a hundred of these in Liverpool alone, where supposedly Jewish-owned factories were set alight and shop windows smashed.[22] There was also widespread damage and destruction in Bristol, Hull, Glasgow, and Warrington. On Sunday 24 August 1947 over the August Bank Holiday weekend, a Jewish wedding was being celebrated at the Assembly Room on Cheetham Hill Road, the heart of the Jewish community of Manchester. A large crowd were inside with music playing and traditional dancing, when a mob descended smashing windows, hurling abuse and besieging the building until one in the morning. At the end of these riots, the windows of practically all the houses owned by Jews in the street were smashed.[23] This was not far from Southport and certainly too close for comfort for those like my mother and grandmother who had fled from Kristallnacht. In Eccles, a former sergeant major was arrested and fined for telling a crowd of several hundred that had gathered: 'Hitler was right. Exterminate every Jew – every man, woman and child.'[24] Variants of these sentiments are frequently encountered today on social media. During the 2014 Gaza conflict, the most prominent rallying cry was '#HitlerWasRight.'

Perhaps the most symbolic long-running battles were reserved for London where Jeff Hamm and the British Union of Fascists held a series of rallies and demonstrations each weekend for two or three months in the summer of 1947 at Ridley Road, Dalston, with its large Jewish community. The crowds grew in number and excitement as the return of Oswald Mosley to the streets of London was rumoured to be imminent. According to a somewhat quaint practice, the police took the view that whichever of the fascists or counter-demonstrators arrived first would have the protected 'pitch' for the weekend. It was first come first served and as a result, these displays of tribal force increased in length and ferocity.

What happened next, however, was unexpected. A number of Jewish ex-servicemen organised themselves as the 43 Group, to meet force with force.[25] Many had been discharged from the armed services without regular employment. If a job could not be found, a good cause might well do. One of these was Howard, the former SAS officer and my wonderful nonagenarian dog-walking companion. He had heard talk of Mosley's intention to hold a rally in the East End over of the August Bank Holiday in 1947. He contacted a number of his fellow soldiers and set out his views, that they had not fought Hitler only for Mosley to be allowed back on the streets of London. It was time to stand up and fight. Howard told me that there were about two hundred like-minded men in the crowds that day and on a signal, they surged forward and despite the best efforts of the police to separate the two sides, 'gave the Blackshirts a good kicking'. Ironically enough, if the idea of the fascists' orchestrated violence was to obtain increased support for attacks against the Jews elsewhere, the effect was at least in part the precise opposite. Many, including Howard, then volunteered to fight in Palestine on the side of the Jews. They were simply sickened by what they had seen.

At around this time, Terci concluded that it was time to change tack– if Julya could not come to England, she would go to him. Whether she was also affected by this violence and these demonstrations, I don't know. My mother and Terci applied for special travel permits as registered Aliens. My mother's travel permit was neatly tucked away in a brown envelope within one of the sealed Home Office files. There was a standard black and white passport photograph. The permit had been issued in London on 15 October 1948 and was valid until 10 April 1949.

The timing of this trip to Israel was certainly not without complication. On 3 September 1947, UNSCOP had, as many predicted, recommended that the British Mandate be brought to an end and a majority recommended that the Mandate Territory be divided into two states, a Jewish and Arab State. On 29 November 1947, the United Nations passed Resolution 181 adopting the majority UNSCOP recommendation and stipulated that the British should withdraw before 1 August 1948. On 14 May 1948, as the thirty-year-old British Mandate was coming to an end, Israel declared independence, but was immediately invaded by its five Arab neighbours. A bitter fight for survival ensued.

Terci and my mother arrived in Israel on 3 December 1948 under visa number 0433 issued in London by way of a bright blue stamp on behalf of the newly formed State of Israel. It was valid until 1 February 1949. The two of them had flown from what was recorded as London Airport on 2 December 1948 to Belgium and then to Tel Aviv. It was the first time either of them had ever flown. The number sequence on the visa indicated that they were amongst the first visitors to the Jewish State. They arrived shortly after Leonard Bernstein had come to

Israel to conduct the Israel Philharmonic. His concerts were repeatedly interrupted by air raids and a collective rush for the shelter.

When my mother arrived, Israel was still very much at war.[26] The Grand Mufti had three months earlier been elected as President of the All Palestine Government. From its base in Gaza it was resolved on the destruction of the Jewish state (not much change there then). The fighting was everywhere and extensive bomb damage, the result of the work of Egypt's air force and naval shelling, was visible on the streets of Tel Aviv. It could not have been an easy time, or safe. My mother had spoken to me on various occasions about this trip, but her recollection was notable as much for what she did not say as anything else. She described seeing the young soldiers in uniform, many only a year or so older than her, and a fair few caught her eye. She spoke also of the rubble in the street and at the site of the Central Bus Station, where many had been killed by an Egyptian bomb raid. She was also shocked by the dreadful accounts of those who had been besieged and noticed the ragged clothes that ordinary people were dressed in. What she did not talk about, however, was Julya, her father, my grandfather.

Maybe they had been away from one another too long. Perhaps she was embarrassed that she had no real recollection of him after all this time apart. It was also quite apparent by this time that he was really not well, suffering from the onset of Parkinson's Disease. It is also likely that my mother was scared that she would have to up sticks and move country once more, Austria to England and then to Israel. More upheaval, another strange language, a new way of life.

Terci and Julya had to do some serious thinking. It looked very much like the Home Office would just not allow him to come to England and the question then was whether they could all live together in Israel. By this time Terci had established a business in England, my mother was at long last settled and doing well at school. There just was no obvious solution and 1 February 1949 came round all too quickly. Nothing had been decided. Terci applied to extend their visa until 10 March 1949, another five weeks or so to work out if they could start over in Israel. Whatever happened, if they were to return they had to be back in England by April 1949 in accordance with the terms of their travel permits. I cannot be sure what was discussed and whether they even asked my mother, although I suspect that they did. The decision was then taken. According to the neat stamps on the travel permits, on 3 March 1949 Terci and my mother left Israel. They returned to England via Rome without Julya. There must have been a strong sense of guilt on their part. It was unclear whether this would be the end of their road as a family, but that must have been a strong possibility.

Julya, however, had not himself given up hope. In my mind's eye he appears to have transformed from Job to Odysseus, striving against all odds to get back to his wife and family. He applied for the fourth and fifth time in December 1949 and March 1950 for a visa to come to Britain but each time was once more pushed back. The reason given on the file was that Terci herself had only been granted a temporary residence in the country and that it was almost certain that he intended to come on a permanent basis. Then it seems that sixth time around the track, he got lucky. Julya had been repeatedly reminded to apply to the British consulate authorities in Israel rather than London. In August 1950, he did exactly that and to the dismay of the Home Office, they granted him a two-month visa without reference to the Aliens Department, whose address on the file was given as the Old Bailey. As a result, Julya arrived in England at long last with a valid permit. The Home Office recorded its considerable irritation and noted tartly in my grandfather's file: 'We must insist on alien leaving the country at once. The fact that he and his wife have been separated for 11 years appears to be the choice of his wife rather than force of circumstances.'

Nevertheless, Julya had a toe hold. He was required to leave the country at the end of his two month visa and did so. He decided to go to Antwerp to set himself up there and continue to make his case to be reunited with his family. In the correspondence on the Home Office file, Julya, with the exaggerated ease of a gentleman on a European tour of old, gave his address as the Café des Sports in Antwerp. It is unlikely in the extreme that that this was his regular watering hole, but more probably served as a *poste restante*. By December 1950 it looked like things had turned an important corner; the Board of Deputies of British Jews became involved in advocating his case and a lively debate ensued between the hawks and doves in the Home Office as to whether Julya should be allowed into the country on a permanent basis. In January 1951, the doves prevailed and Julya was given permission to come over from Antwerp at long last.

Before he could make the journey, the files showed that inquiries were made by both MI5 and the police in Southport. The reports were it seems favourable as regards both Terci and my mother. The authorities wrote to the kind Mr Laskey at Otto Terrace who had looked after my mother in Sunderland when she had arrived in England in 1938. Mr Laskey ran a tobacconist shop in Sunderland. It was recorded he not only put a roof over my mother's head but then agreed to stand surety for Terci so that she could come to this country and be with her daughter, and also agreed to employ Terci as a cook. He spoke movingly of both of them.

By the end of 1950, permission had been granted for Terci and her sister Julci to run the Sandhurst Hotel, their kosher boarding house. Their establishment was referred to openly in the reports, noting that it was 'properly run'. Terci provided the Home Office with up-to-date tax returns and the business accounts. She also noted that she did not yet have a bank account as all the proceeds had been ploughed back into running the boarding house. The people contacted by the police and MI5 attested that life in Southport without the Sandhurst Hotel was simply unthinkable as the entire orthodox Jewish community ate there, including the local Rabbi.

Julya did not live long enough for me to have any particular memory of him, as he died in the early 1960s when I was very young. The last of a long list of strokes of fortune that I have enjoyed on this journey took place as I had all but finished my writing, when a history of the Jews of Southport was published, which mentioned the Sandhurst Hotel.[27] I wrote to the author and after exchanging reminiscences he sent me a wonderful photograph of Julya in his later years at the Sandhurst Hotel, smiling and perfectly content, even though his suit still looked several sizes too big for his slender frame.

The very last entry on the files at Kew records that the processing fee for Julya's permission to enter had been increased to £13, that this sum was still overdue and had to be paid in full or the registration would be annulled. For want of £13 the whole project that they had been striving to achieve for years might have collapsed. No doubt, although not recorded, one way or another the money was found and paid. With that I shut these files, tied them up once more and put them back onto the metal trolley so that they could be placed back on the shelf where they had been for so many years.

To my considerable relief there was no dark family secret in these files, no life-changing revelation. Just the constant droning sound of officialdom at work and a strong whiff of bureaucratic anti-Semitism. The endless barriers and hoops did seem heartless, but the bark was in the end worse than the bite and of course my family, in comparison with refugee families across the centuries, was of one of the very lucky ones; something that my mother frequently acknowledged.

After the events described in these Home Office files, my mother finished her studies in Manchester and then moved to London to work in the forerunner of the Export Credit Guarantee Department. She was almost obsessively loyal to anything manufactured in Britain. For years she would only ever buy a British-made car or home appliance. Her determination would never falter and I remember as a schoolboy on many a cold winter's morning she could be heard imploring her Vauxhall Viva simply to start up whilst the neighbours effortlessly cruised off, cosseted in luxury in some German vehicle or other.

In a short time after the Home Office file was closed, she was introduced to my father, a handsome young penniless doctor who had fled from Nazi Germany and was also making his way in this country after enjoying a spell working as an obstetrician in a hospital in Israel. He was not just a healer of the sick but had endless charm and was an accomplished musician with a beautiful baritone voice that he would deploy to great effect. In my own childhood he passed through the great body of German lieder to sing me to sleep. Theirs was a great love story, with many shared passions. The two of them were a formidable team, not just strong for one another but I can now see they were also able to shield my brother and me from some of the harder edges of this story.

I remained at the desk for a while longer and my mind wandered back to the spring of 2011. I had been working away in London. It was a Wednesday evening, four days before the Passover festival. I got a phone call from my mother. She had been on holiday in America but had changed her return flight plans because, in her words, she had not felt that magnificent and in fact uncharacteristically had paid a fleeting visit to a hospital in Florida. I was concerned and told her without fail to check it out. She played it all down and asked whether I was free for supper.

I was and we had a wide-ranging conversation that carried on long into the night. It is not all that often in life that two people quite separately read the same book at exactly the same time without having previously discussed it at all. We had both just finished Edmund de Waal's magnificent and beautifully crafted *The Hare with Amber Eyes*, which traced the story of the Ephrussi family and a collection of Japanese netsuke over a century and a half. I wanted to hear what she thought, though I knew that any account involving looking back over such family history was difficult territory. I cannot now remember her exact words, but we covered a lot of ground. She talked freely of her past in a way I had not heard her do before. In short, she said that the Ephrussis were in large part discriminated against because of their wealth, supposed influence, and their intense desire to assimilate.

By contrast, she said the Jews from Lackenbach, after centuries of imperfect dissimulation on the part of their close neighbours, had been despised and hated because they were largely poor, defenceless, of a different religion and wished to live a separate life from majority society under their own rules. For century after century anti-Semites had invoked many so-called justifications for this ancient prejudice. It was a multi-headed Hydra with malignant variants both on the far right and left of the political spectrum that almost certainly could never be eradicated but had to be managed with careful watchfulness.

Ultimately, she concluded that there were two lessons she had learnt; first, that a people without a state is inherently vulnerable and that statehood had changed fundamentally the course of Jewish history. It had for the first time in nearly two thousand years given the Jewish people both inside and outside Israel a small measure of agency. The second was that whilst detailed examination of those who had lived before us had its own value to teach us the lessons of the past, we do not spend so long on this earth and each of us had to take responsibility to take forward as best as we can the work started by others before us. In the end she agreed with the conclusion in Edmund de Waal's book, that the time had come to cease chasing those elusive shadows, the last missing detail and instead to focus on the here and now – the urgent job in hand. We had dinner that Friday with the whole family and it was a noisy and lively affair, filled with humour and banter. The next day my mother was in her flat, on her own, getting ready to go out with her friends on a Saturday evening when she collapsed suddenly and died, the day before Passover.

At the National Archive, I thought once more of her last advice. As I put those long-forgotten files away, it was so different to that time in Washington at the archives of the Holocaust Museum a few years earlier, when I was ushered out of the building at the end of the afternoon with frantic drama and my research was in its infancy. I sat motionless for what seemed like an eternity, it was as though the many voices that had filled my head had become one perfect, quiet note, like the last bars of Mahler's Third Rückert-Lieder where the mezzo-soprano's voice merges with the receding sound of the clarinet and oboe, allowing the listener gently to move from one world into another. I gathered my bags and drove off to be with the family for the Jewish New Year. As I headed home, I felt a wide array of emotions, which clearly needed to be put into some kind of order, but above all, I felt a small but distinctly discernible sense of peace.

Notes

Preface

1. *A Bintel Brief, Sixty Years of Letters from The Lower East Side to the Jewish Daily Forward*, Isaac Metzker and Harry Golden (1971).

2. The Times, '*Anti-semitic attacks scar British cities*' 27 July 2014; *Jews Don't Count*, David Baddiel, TLS 2020; and placards seen at a mass rally in Central London 22 May 2021.

3. An interview with Luciana Berger MP, The Times 2 March 2019; The Jewish Chronicle 4 July 2021, '*Bus Passenger Threatened, I Will Slit Your Throat for Palestine*'; BBC Online 21 August 2021, '*Stamford Hill attack: Man punched in alleged anti-Semitic incident*'.

3 Esterházy's Jews

1. This was not the first Ottoman siege of Vienna, but it was the longest. In 1529 under Suleiman the Magnificent the Ottomans famously reached the gates of Vienna but the siege was brief and unsuccessful.

2. From a pamphlet in the Bodleian Library, Oxford entitled 'A True and Exact Relation of the Raising of the Siege of Vienna and the Victory Obtained over the Ottoman Army, 12 September 1683' published in translation in *The Hapsburg and Hohenzollern Dynasties in the Seventeenth and Eighteenth Centuries*, C.A. Macartney pp 59-66.

3. The Letters of Rabbi Joseph Halevi of Livorno to Jacob Sasportas of Hamburg, 1666-1667 published in *Shabbatai Tsvi, Testimonies to a Fallen Messiah*, David Helperin, Littman, 2007.

4. *The Making of Western Jewry, 1600-1819*, Lionel Kochan, p 110.

5. Portrait by unknown artist at the Austrian State Jewish Museum.

6. Quoted in *The Making of Western Jewry, 1600-1819*, Lionel Kochan p 104 and cites S Berger (ed) *The Desire to Travel, A Note on Abraham Levy's Yiddish Itinerary 1719-1723* Ashkenas VI (1997) pp 497-506.

7. *The Court Jew, A Contribution to the History of the Period of Absolutism, in Central Europe*, Selma Stern Chapter3; Encyclopedia Judaica 1906 Edition on Samson Wertheimer by Isidore Singer and S Mannheimer; and *The Making of Western Jewry, 1600-1819*, Lionel Kochan, p 110.

8. *The Court Jew: A Contribution to the History of the Period of Absolutism in Central Europe*, Selma Stern, Chapter3.

9. *The Landed Estates of the Esterházy Princes*, Gates-Coon, p 115.

10. *The Hapsburg and Hohenzollern Dynasties in the Seventeenth and Eighteenth Centuries*, C.A. Macartney, p 258.

11. *The Landed Estates of the Esterházy Princes*, Gates-Coon, p 118.

12. *The Landed Estates of the Esterházy Princes*, Gates-Coon, p 117.

13. First, Second and Eleventh Articles.

14. *Nationalsozialismus im Burgenland, Eine Judische Familie im Burgenland*, Max Grunsfeld p 318.

15. *Schutzbrief*, Fourth Article.

16. Contrast the Brandenburg decree of 1671, which restricted the re-entry of Jews to 50 families in the Electorate and prohibited the building of a synagogue.

17. Referred to in German as a *teuch* (literally a pond) but more commonly known in Hebrew as a *mikveh*.

18. *Schutzbrief*, Second Article.

19. *The Landed Estates of the Esterházy Princes*, Gates-Coon, Chapter 5, and Fourth Article of *Schutzbrief*.

20. *Schutzbrief*, Fifth and Seventh Articles.

21. *Eighteenth Century Schutzherren, Esterházy Patronage of the Jews*, Rebecca Gates-Coon, Jewish Social Studies (1985) Vol 47 no 1 p 193 and Esterházy Archives p 150, 8 March 1769.

22. *The Landed Estates of the Esterházy Princes*, Gates-Coon, Chapter 5; and *Eighteenth Century Schutzherren, Esterházy Patronage of the Jews*, Rebbecca Gates, Jewish Social Studies (1985) Vol 47 no 1 p 192. And see the *Schutzbrief* Second Article.

23. *The Court Jew, A Contribution to the History of the Period of Absolutism, in Central Europe*, Selma Stern Chapter 3.
24. *The Court Jew, A Contribution to the History of the Period of Absolutism, in Central Europe*, Selma Stern Chapters 3 and 10.
25. *The Landed Estates of the Esterházy Princes*, Gates-Coon, p 126.
26. *The Landed Estates of the Esterházy Princes*, Gates-Coon, p 130.

4 The Blood Libel of Orkuta

1. One of the first surviving records of the accusation of the consumption of blood is the Fulda Blood Libel of 1235. After a tragic household fire in which five children died whilst the parents were at Church, the accusation rose up against the Jews of the small town of Fulda that they had killed the children and drunk their blood for their own remedy. Retreating soldiers from the Sixth Crusade passed through a few days after the fire and slaughtered thirty-four Jews there. My father's family came from Fulda, Germany.
2. *The History of Anti- Semitism Volume 1*, Leon Poliakov, pp 240-241; *The Origins of the Ritual Murder Accusation and Blood Libel*, Albert Ehrman, A Journal of Orthodox Jewish Thought (1976) Vol 15 no 4 pp 83-90.
3. Matthew 27.25 and Bach's Matthew's Passion Recitative and Chorus no. 59.
4. David Nirenberg, *The Rhineland Massacres of the Jews in the First Crusade*, in Gerd Althoff Memories Medieval & Modern, Cambridge 2001 pp 279-310. For nearly a thousand years, orthodox communities in the Ashkenaz tradition in Europe at the festival of Shavuot have recited a special memorial prayer for those martyred, *El Malei Rachamim*, which dates from the massacres in the First Crusade.
5. See in particular the blood libel accusations in Sandomierz (1710), Zaslow (1747), Zytomierz (1751), Zhytomir (1753), Yampol (1756).
6. Report of Cardinal Ganganelli with Introduction by Cecil Roth 1934. Cardinal Ganganelli became Pope Clement XIV in 1769. His report was not widely published or circulated. In 1913, Lord Rothschild sought its reaffirmation and publication by the then incumbent Pope in response to the international scandal of the last blood libel trial in Europe, which was held in Kyiv; the trial of Mendel Beilis, a 39-year-old man accused of killing

a 13-year-old boy to use his blood for Passover matzo. His trial lasted for 34 days. The jury found him guilty of the act of ritual draining of his blood for religious purposes but not of murder. The case attracted wide international attention and the name of the accused, somewhat like Dreyfus, passed into folk memory but with dramatically different effect. The Nazi press, *Der Volkischer Beobachter*, and *Der Sturmer* took up this cause as well-established fact and the soap made from human remains at Auschwitz was widely referred to locally as 'Beilis' soap'.

7. Pressburg was one of a number of capital cities in Central Europe in the eighteenth and nineteenth centuries dominated by a majority ethnically German population with significant Jewish populations; others included Prague (Bohemia), Konigsberg (Eastern Prussia) and Lemberg (Galicia). For further examination of the extensive reach of these now vanished German communities see Neil MacGregor, *Germany, Memories of a Nation* (2014) Allen Lane and *Central European Crossroads, Social Democracy and National Revolution in Bratislava (Pressburg) 1867-1921*, Pieter C. van Duin Ch 3.

8. *The Jews of Hungary*, Raphael Patai Ch 21, The Theben Story.

9. *An Economic history of Nineteenth Century Europe*, Ivan Berend p 184.

10. *The Making of Western Jewry, 1600-1819*, p 170.

11. This was said to have cost the Empress over two million florins – see Derek Beales, *Joseph II Vol 1, In the Shadow of Maria Theresa* p 116.

12. With thanks to Nicole Placz Schuller at the Austrian National Archives; this document can be seen at https://www.archivinformationssystem.at/bild.aspx.

13. *The Jews of Hungary*, Raphael Patai Ch 19, pp 203-204.

14. *Absent Jews and Invisible Antisemitism in Postwar Vienna: Der Prozess (1948) and The Third Man (1949)*, Lisa Silverman, Journal of Contemporary History 2017 Vol 52(2) 211-228.

15. *Meet Europe's New Fascists*, James Kirchick, 12 April 2012 Tablet Magazine.

5 Beards and Bayonets

1. *The life of Koppel Theben (Leader of Israel)* Joshua Levinson, Warsaw 1898 p 22.

2. *Jüdische Familienforschung* (March 1926).

3. *The Origins of Totalitarianism* (1951), Hannah Arendt pp 18-20.

4. *The Life of Koppel Theben (Leader of Israel)*, Joshua Levinson, Warsaw 1898 pp 31-32.

5. *The Life of Koppel Theben (Leader of Israel)*, Joshua Levinson, Warsaw 1898 pp 27-30.

6. *Joseph II, Volume 2, 1780-1790, Against the World*, Derek Beales pp 196-213 pp 603; J Karniel *Die Toleranzpolitik Kaiser Joseph II*; and C.A. Macartney ed. *The Hapsburg and Hohenzollern Dynasties in the Seventeenth and Eighteenth Centuries* (New York 1970). The legislation outlined here only constituted one small part of the overall Josephinian reforms, consisting of a staggering 6,000 edicts and 11,000 new laws.

7. *The Landed Estates of the Esterházy Princes*, Rebecca Gates-Coon p 120.

8. *The Landed Estates of the Esterházy Princes*, Rebecca Gates-Coon p 119.

9. The policy statement is quoted in full in Derek Beales (op cit), p 201: 'In order to make the very numerous members of the Jewish nation in my hereditary lands more useful to the state, which up to now they could not be because of the limited range of employments permitted to them and because of the means of their enlightenment were lacking and were considered by them superfluous, the first useful step will be quietly to displace their national language – except in their worship where they may retain it – by requiring that all their contracts, engagements, will, bill, ledgers, witness statements, in short everything that is to be binding in judicial or extra judicial proceedings, should be treated as null and void and disregarded by the authorities.'

10. J Karniel *Die Toleranzpolitik Kaiser Joseph II* pp 567-585.

11. J Karniel *Die Toleranzpolitik Kaiser Joseph II* pp 430-431.

12. Patent of 31 March 1783 Articles 3-9. As with most such measures, there was carrot and stick. No Jew could enter a trade craft for ten years unless he or she produced a certificate of attendance at a state-approved school.

13. *Hungary Before 1918*, Michael K Silber, The YIVO Encyclopaedia of Jews of Eastern Europe, Yale University Press p 781.

14. Patent of 31 March 1783 Article 10.

15. Patent of 31 March 1783 Article 13.

16. *The Life of Koppel Theben (Leader of Israel)* Joshua Levinson, Warsaw 1898 pp 32-35.

17. *Habsburg Jewry in the Long Eighteenth Century*, Michael K. Silber, p 783

18. *Jüdische Familienforschung* (March 1926).

19. *Der Judenrichter Beim Kaiser, Die Stimme 1932*, Georg Patai.

20. *Der Judenrichter Beim Kaiser, Die Stimme 1932*, Georg Patai.

21. Article 24 of Toleration Edict of Lower Austria 2 January 1782.

22. Über *die bürgerliche Verbesserung der Juden,* On the Civil Improvement of Jews (1781), and see more generally Michel Silber, *From Tolerated Aliens to Citizen Soldiers, Jewish Military Service in the Era of Joseph II.*

23. *The Life of Koppel Theben (Leader of Israel)* Joshua Levinson, Warsaw 1898 pp 39-40.

24. *Der Judenrichter Beim Kaiser, Die Stimme 1932*, Georg Patai.

25. *Ibid*

26. Selma Stern, *The Court Jew, A Contribution to the History of the Period of Absolutism* Chapters 3 and 7.

27. *The Life of Koppel Theben (Leader of Israel)* Joshua Levinson, Warsaw 1898 pp 78-79.

28. *City Under Siege*, Chatam Sofer.

29. Peter Salner and Martin Kvasnica, *The Chatam Sofer Memorial.*

6 Emancipation to World War

1. The opening words of the song from the 4th Movement of Mahler's 3rd Symphony – 'O *Man Take Heed! What does the deep midnight say? I was asleep, asleep.*' – Friedrich Nietsche.

2. *On the Jewish Question ('Zur Judenfrage')*, Karl Marx, February 1844.

3. Marx's views on race and his supposed link between Jews and black people are essentially unpublishable. This was biological racism of the worst kind seeking to de-humanise Jews and black Africans alike.

4. Nicholas II Esterházy, A Hungarian Prince Collector, Catalogue of exhibition at Compiègne (2007) p 88 in an essay by Orsolya Radvanyi, *The Art Collection of the Esterházy Family in the C18 and C19 and the Birth of the National Gallery.*

5. There is a direct connection between the blood libel and the accusation of Jewish businessmen as bloodsuckers. Each accusation has the

same root, that Jews serve no proper or useful function but merely leach off others.

6. The *Encyclopaedia Judaica* of 1906 noted the rise of Lueger as part of the rise of anti-Semitism and that the ramifications had not yet been worked through.

7. Poliakov, *The History of anti-Semitism Vol 2*.

8. Pulzer, *The Rise of Political Anti- Semitism in Germany and Austria* pp 168-169.

9. *Austria From Hapsburg to Hitler*, Volume 1, p 28, Gulick.

10. In *Mein Kampf* Hitler stated that the scales dropped from his eyes when he understood that it was the Jews who led the movement of social democracy.

11. Poliakov, *Suicidal Europe 1870-1933*, Volume 4 of *The History of Anti-Semitism*, pp 24-25.

12. *Antisemitism in Austria,* Dirk van Arkel (1966) p 73, doctoral thesis University of Leiden.

13. *Hitler's Vienna*, Briggitte Hamann, p 279

14. '*Wer Jude ist, bestimme ich.*'

15. Poliakov, *Suicidal Europe 1870-1933*, Volume 4 of *The History of Anti-Semitism*, p 25.

16. 'Alack, what heinous sin it is in me/To be ashamed to be my father's child!/But though I am a daughter to his blood/I am not to his manners.' Merchant of Venice Act II Scene 3 ,14-16.

17. *Mein Kampf* p 99 and 180 quoted in *Hitler's Vienna*, Briggitte Hamann, p 285.

18. *Austria From Hapsburg to Hitler*, Volume 1, p 26, Gulick.

19. '*Ein hypermoderner Dirigent*', *Mahler and Anti-Semitism in fin de siècle Vienna*, 19th Century Music (1994-1995) pp 257-76, and *Mahler, Victim of the 'New' Anti- Semitism*, Edward F Kravitt, Journal of the Royal Musical Association (2002) p 72.

20. *Mahler, A Musical Physiognomy*, Adorno, University of Chicago Press 2013; *Jewish Intellectuals and the University*, M. Morris pp 58-59.

21. *Paul Esterházy, 1901-1989 Ein Leben im Zeitalter der Extreme*, Stefan Lutgenau, pp 17-21 and Mordechai Grunsfeld *Die Juden in Lackenbach*, Tonbandufnahme 20 June 1986, Yad Vashem Archives Jerusalem, PKA/E-53.

22. *Paul Esterházy, 1901-1989 Ein Leben im Zeitalter der Extreme*, Stefan Lutgenau, p 19 and Rafelsberger, *Vermogensverkehrsstelle an Reichwirtschaftsministerium*, 17 July 1939 RK 145 (2160/6).

23. Die Wiener Morgenzeitung, 16 February 1927.
24. With thanks to Rabbi Amram Binyamin Wieder of Bnei Brak, Israel, Chairman of the Lackenbach Institute. He also sent me details of the family who lived in Lackenbach in the mid- to late nineteenth century. Their gravestones are preserved in the Jewish cemetery today alongside nearly 1700 buried there over a period of about three hundred years.
25. *Hungary Before 1918*, Michael K Silber, *The YIVO Encyclopaedia of Jews in Eastern Europe*, Yale University Press, 2008 p 771.
26. *Eine Judische Familie im Burgenland*, Max Grunsfeld from *Nationalsozialismus im Burgenland*, ed. Herbert Brettl.

7 12ᵗʰ February Battalion

1. 'We only wanted paradise on earth,' Prive Friedjung, Memoirs of a Jewish Communist, Vienna, 1995.
2. In the collection of the Jewish Museum of Vienna.
3. *Before the Fall, German and Austrian Art of the 1930s*, catalogue of an exhibition at the Neue Galerie, New York.
4. *Austria from Hapsburg to Hitler Vol 1*, Gulick p 718.
5. *Ein Weiter Weg* pp 153-154, Julius Deutsch.
6. *The Jewish Vote in Vienna*, Walter B Simon, Jewish Social Studies Vol 23 no 1.
7. *The Jewish Vote in Vienna*, Walter B Simon, Jewish Social Studies Vol 23 no 1. It is also noted that in the 1949 elections the Social Democrat vote in Vienna markedly declined after the total destruction of the Jewish community, lending further credence to the conclusion that the Jewish vote was heavily directed to the Social Democratic Party.
8. Eva Blau, *The Architecture of Red Vienna* (Cambridge MIT Press 1997).
9. *Austria from Hapsburg to Hitler Vol 1*, Gulick p 728.
10. Yad Vashem Archive 03/1203, cited in *The Anschluss and the Tragedy of Austrian Jewry*, Herbert Rosenkranz.
11. E. J. Hobsbawn in *The Age of Extremity* described the 12 February uprising as 'the glorious memory of resistance to fascism by arms and not by speeches'.
12. *Austrian Requiem*, Kurt Schuschnnigg (The Left Book Club, 1947) p 13.
13. *The Sunday Times* 18 February 1934.

14. Alexander Clifford, *Fighting for Spain, The International Brigades in the Civil War 1936-1939*, p 151. The XI and XV Brigades largely consisted of international volunteer officers and Spanish troops.
15. *Jews Who Served in the Spanish Civil War*, Sugarman, Assistant Archivist at AJEX.
16. Available at *Dokumentationsarchiv des Osterreichischsen Wilderstandes* amongst its Spanish Civil War archives (the'DOW').
17. https://Sidbrint.ub.edu/es/content/lobel-martin
18. *La Guerra Civil en Cordoba*, Gomez, p 505.
19. Le Soldat de la République, *Fussballspiel hinter der front*, Martin Lobl.
20. Giles Tremlett, *The International Brigades: Fascism, Freedom and the Spanish Civil War*, Chapter 42.
21. *Foreign Volunteers in the Spanish Civil War 1936-1939*, Bruno Mugnai.
22. *Germans against Hitler, The Thaelmann Brigade*, Arnold Krammer, Journal of Contemporary History (1969) pp 65-83.
23. Giles Tremlett, *The International Brigades: Fascism, Freedom and the Spanish Civil War*, Chapter 11.
24. The New Republic 12 January 1938, Hemingway, Reports from Spain p 275.
25. Giles Tremlett, *The International Brigades: Fascism, Freedom and the Spanish Civil War*, Chapter 42 and Landis, Lincoln Brigade p 350.
26. Hugh Thomas, *The Spanish Civil War* Ch 44 (50th Anniversary Edition) and more generally see Henry Buckley and Herbert Matthews, *Two Wars and More to Come* (1938) for a contemporary account of the battle.
27. The New Republic 12 January 1938, Hemingway, Reports from Spain p 275.
28. Cortada, *Modern Warfare in Spain, American Military Observations on the Spanish Civil War* p 188, also cited in Alexander Clifford, *Fighting for Spain, The international Brigades in the Civil War 1936- 1939*, p 160.
29. Giles Tremlett, *The International Brigades: Fascism, Freedom and the Spanish Civil War*, Chapter 42.
30. Giles Tremlett, *The International Brigades: Fascism, Freedom and the Spanish Civil War*, Chapter 42 and Landis, Lincoln Brigade p736.
31. Hugh Thomas, *The Spanish Civil War* Ch 44.

32. Hemingway, *On the American Dead in Spain*, February 1939.

33. Alexander Clifford, *Fighting for Spain, The International Brigades in the Civil War 1936-1939*, p 164.

9 White Flags

1. 'I came a stranger/and a stranger I depart' – *Gute Nacht, Der Wintereise*, Schubert/Wilhelm Muller.

2. The Book of Esther Ch 3 verse 8. Adolf Hitler, in *Mein Kampf*, covered very similar territory when he recounted the apocryphal story from his early adulthood in Vienna of seeing an orthodox Chassid walking towards him dressed in a long caftan and sporting flowing black side locks, and he asked himself, 'Is this a Jew?' Hitler then said that he almost immediately found himself asking a different question, 'Is this is a German?' The reader did not need to be told the answer.

3. *The Order of the Day*, p26 Eric Vuillard, Picador.

4. *Austrian Requiem*, Kurt Schuschnnigg, pp 27-29.

5. *Austrian Requiem*, Kurt Schuschnnigg, p 32.

6. Otto Fritsche, '*Die NSDAP im Burgenland 1933-1938*' (Ph.D. dissertation, University of Vienna, 1993), p. 211.

7. Forced Emigration of the Burgenland Jews, Milka Zalmon, 1999 PhD thesis Bar Ilan University.

8. *Austria from Hapsburg to Hitler*, Gulick, p 1847 (Vol II).

9. *Berlin Diary*, William Shirer, Alfred A Knopf 1941, pp 95-103.

10. *Fallen Bastions*, GER Gedye, 1939, p 350.

11. *Austria from Hapsburg to Hitler*, Gulick, p 1854 (Vol II).

12. Library of Congress Lot no 2732 (confiscated from Dr Frick at the time of his prosecution at Nuremburg).

13. *Interview with Johann Kriszan*, United States Holocaust Memorial Museum, Accession Number 2018.342.16

14. Interview of Max Grunsfeld with Milka Zalmon.

15. Jewish Telegraphic Agency newswire for 25 April 1938.

16. *Interview with Johann Kriszan*, United States Holocaust Memorial Museum, Accession Number 2018.342.16.

17. *The Rise and Fall of the Third Reich*, William L. Shirer, p 350.

11 Vienna's Spring Pogrom

1. Lamentations Ch 1 verse 1, written about Jerusalem after the fall of the first Temple in 586BC. 'How she sits alone, the city once great

with people.' The rest of the verse reads: 'She has become like a widow. Great among nations, mistress among provinces, reduced to forced labour.'

2. The Jewish population of Vienna in 1860 was said to be less than 10,000 and 200,000 in 1938.

3. Hugo Gold, *Gesichte der Juden in Wien*, 1966 Tel Aviv.

4. The traditional leather tefillin used by orthodox Jews as an essential part of the morning prayer ritual.

5. G.E.R. Gedye *Fallen Bastions* (1939) p 18.

6. Jewish Chronicle 25 March 1938.

7. *The Jews of Nazi Vienna 1938-1945*, Ilana Fritz Offenberger, Chapter 2.

8. Hugo Gold, *Gesichte der Juden in Wien*, 1966 Tel Aviv.

9. The Manchester Guardian, August 1938 reporting on conditions at Buchenwald, and accounts written in *Germany Reports,* a monthly publication of the German Social Democratic Party and see pages 341-44 of *Fallen Bastions*, 1939 (supra).

10. See the comprehensive and groundbreaking research in *Backing Hitler: Consent and Coercion in Nazi Germany*, Robert Gellately (2001).

11. The Times of London 17 July 1938.

12. The Times of London 18 June 1938.

13. Audiotape of Eichmann speaking to Nazi friends in Argentina in 1957, transcribed by Bettina Stangneth and translated by Ruth Martin, published in *Eichmann Before Jerusalem: The Unexamined Life of a Mass Murderer* by Bettina Stangneth (2015).

14. Gainer to A.B. Hutcheon 9 August 1938 PRO FO 372/3284 T10774/3272/378 cited in Louise London, *Whitehall and the Jew 1933-1948* p 66.

15. *Fallen Bastions* (supra) at pp 352-353.

12 Shuttered Gates

1. *Whitehall and the Jews,* Louise London, p 42.

2. ibid p 42.

3. M.D. Peterson 18 February 1935, FO 371/19676 cited in *Whitehall and the Jews* (supra) p 42.

4. *Why We Watched, Europe America and the Holocaust*, Theodore S Hamerow p 104, WW Norton & Co (2008).

5. Hansard 14 March 1938 and Cabinet Meeting of 16 March 1938 no 14 of 1938.

6. *Why We Watched, Europe America and the Holocaust*, Theodore S Hamerow p 110, WW Norton & Co (2008).

7. Home Office Meeting with a Jewish delegation, 1 April 1938 HO 213/42 and *Whitehall and the Jews*, p 61.

8. *Why We Watched, Europe America and the Holocaust*, Theodore S Hamerow p 110, WW Norton & Co (2008).

9. *The Road to September 1939*, Yehuda Reinharz and Yaacov Shavit, Chapter 3 and *The Nazi Holocaust*, Ronnie Landau (2006) pp 137-140.

10. Germany was not invited but it seems unofficially sent an SS officer to attend who subsequently sent a report to Richard Heydrich.

11. *The Evian Conference on Political Refugees*, Social Service Review, Chicago University Press September 1938 pp 514-p 518.

12. *Escaping The Holocauast*, Daliah Ofer pp 104-105, Jewish Telegraph Agency, 9 July 1938.

13. *The Anschluss and the Tragedy of Austrian Jewry – 1938 to 1945*, *The Jews of Austria* (Collected Essays) pp 479ff, Herbert Rosenkranz.

14. For a more praiseworthy and perhaps realistic assessment see *9096 Leben, Der Unbekannte Judenretter, Berthold Storfer, The Forgotten Rescuer of Thousands of Jews*, Gabriel Anderl (2012) Goethe Institut.

15. *The Evian Conference*, Bulletin of International News (16 July 1938) pp 16-18.

16. *The Road to September 1939*, Yehuda Reinharz and Yaacov Shavit, Chapter 3,

17. *The Evian Conference on Jewish Refugees*, Royal Institute International Affairs, 30 July 1938 pp 8-10.

18. For a comprehensive account of the July 1938 conference and its outcome see *The Evian Conference of 1938 and the Jewish Refugee Crisis*, Paul R. Bartop (Palgrave 2017).

19. *Palestine Post* 6-15 July 1938 and Jewish Telegraph Agency 6-15 July.

13 Af Al Pi

1. *Jews On Route to Palestine 1934-1944*, Artur Patek p 52.

2. *Becoming Eichmann*, David Cesarani pp 61 3. It seems that Eichmann had been told in Berlin at the start of 1938 to prepare

for the installation of a Nazi regime in Austria and so was ready at the moment of the Anschluss.

3. *The Jews of Austria, Illegale Transporte*, Wolfgang von Weisl, pp 165-169 , *The Four Fronted War*, Willy Perl p 21 and more generally Willy Perl's interview recorded by the United States Holocaust Memorial Museum, 7 October 1996, RG 50.030-0443.

4. *The Four Fronted War* p 23.

5. *The Four Fronted War* pp 25-45.

6. *Illegale Transporte*, Wolfgang von Weisl, essay in Jews of Austria pp 165-176.

7. *The Four Fronted War* p 97.

8. The numbers on board the Draga vary according to source anywhere from 220 to 380; see *Before The Curtain Fell*, Ludmilla Epstein.

14 The Next Boat Out

1. *Eichmann's Jews: The Jewish Administration of Holocaust Vienna 1938-1945*, Doron Rabinovici p 54.

2. *The Rise and Fall of the Third Reich*, William Shirer, p 351. Shirer was living around the corner in an apartment in Plosslgasse and saw SS officers carting off the valuables from the Palais Rothschild after its requisition.

3. On 20 August 1938 a decree was passed establishing the Central Office.

4. *Eichmann's Jews*, Rabinovici p53.

5. Evidence at Eichmann Trial Session 17 p 269 and Eichmann Judgment paragraph 63.

6. Eichmann Trial Judgment paragraph 63.

7. The Danube from Ulm to the sea was declared an international waterway under the terms of the 1919 peace treaties – see *The Danube River*, Anton Florian Zeilinger, Max Plank Encyclopaedia of International Law.

8. *The Four Fronted War*, William Perl p 115.

9. Von Weisl, *Illegale Transporte* p 173.

10. Perl (op cit) pp 120-121.

16 Kristallnacht/Kristalltag

1. 'Whenever men burns books, in the end they will burn human beings too' – Heinrich Heine, the German poet and playwright from his play *Almansar* written in 1821 about the persecution of

Muslims in Spain at the time of the Reconquest. Heine's books were publicly burned by the Nazis at every opportunity.

2. By contrast in Berlin the main destruction took place from 2am until the early hours of the morning.

3. Fifth Statutory Regulation under the Reich Citizenship Law 1938.

4. 'An Aryan Englishman', *The Spectator* 19 August 1938

5. Henry's letter to his grandchildren (undated *c* 2000).

6. The details of these attacks are taken from *Hitler*, by Hugo Gold, *Gesichte der Juden in Wien*, 1966 (Tel Aviv).

7. The Times 1 November 1938.

8. *Two Unequal Tempers; Sir George Ogilvie Forbes and Sir Nevile Henderson and British Foreign Policy 1938-1939*, Bruce Strang, Diplomacy and Statecraft (2007) pp 107-137 and note of R.M. Makins dated 10 November 1938 in TNA – PREM1/326 p 88 marked as seen by Prime Minister.

9. *Hitler*, by Hugo Gold, *Gesichte der Juden in Wien*, 1966 (Tel Aviv) and see *The Jews of Austria, The Destruction of the Jewish Community in Austria 1938-1942*, Norman Bentwich p472.

10. The Times report from Vienna on 11 November 1938, p 14.

11. Note of R.M. Makins dated 10 November 1938 in TNA – PREM1/326.

12. Ruth Maier's Diary for 10 November as cited by David Cesarani (op cit) p 191.

13. Henry's letter to his grandchildren (undated *c* 2000).

14. *Refugees Crawl Over Frontier*, Daily Telegraph, 12 November 1938.

15. Jewish Chronicle 18 November 1938.

16. Note from A.R. Boyle for attention of the Prime Minister November 1938, TNA – PREM1/326 at pp 61-62 marked Top Secret.

17. *Verordnung zur Wiederherstellung das Strassenbildes* (12 November 1938)

18. Cesarani (op cit) pp 203-205 and *Allianz and the German Insurance Business*, Feldman (2001) Cambridge University Press.

19. *Kristallnacht*, Martin Gilbert p 146.

20. David Yarnell's Factual Notes on German Trip 7 December 1938, p 3 at Quaker Archives, Friends House, Euston Road London.

21. *Whitehall and The Jews 1933-1948*, Louise London, p98.

22. Minutes of Friends Service Council, Germany and Holland Committee, 16 November 1938.
23. Articles condemning the brutality of the Nazis' attacks were to be found in The Times, The Manchester Guardian, The Daily Telegraph, The Daily Herald, and The Daily Express.
24. *Reporting on Hitler*, Will Wainewright (2017) Chapter 16.
25. *Der Novemberpogrom 1938* (1988 Historisches Museum der Stadt Wien) essay by Johnny Moser - *'Kristallnacht Ein Wenderpunkt der Europaischesn Gesichte?'* (A Turning Point of the European story?).
26. *Resistance and Persecution in Austria 1938-1945* (1988) Siegwald Ganglmair p 35.
27. Cesarani (op cit) p 187.
28. *Two Unequal Tempers; Sir George Ogilvie Forbes and Sir Nevile Henderson and British Foreign Policy 1938- 1939*, Bruce Strang, Diplomacy and Statecraft (2007) pp 107-137.
29. *The Holy Fox, A Biography of Lord Halifax*, A. Roberts p 128, and *Appeasement, the Diplomacy of Sir Nevile Henderson*, Peter Neville p 127
30. *Appeasement, the Diplomacy of Sir Nevile Henderson*, Peter Neville p 126.
31. *Munich Why?* Oliver Popplewell, p 189.
32. *Kristallnacht*, Martin Gilbert p 153.
33. British Quaker Archives at Friends House, Report of visit to Germany by Ben Greene dated 12 December 1938 and Report of visit of David Yarnell to Berlin and Vienna 7-25 December 1938.
34. David Yarnell Report of Berlin trip to Germany Emergency Committee, Quaker Archives, Friends House, London.

17 Ten Days in November

1. The Times, 15 November p 14.
2. PRO CAB 27/ 624
3. The quotas were not transferable at the option of the named country. Nevertheless, there was some flexibility in that the United States in the course of 1938 did combine the quota allocated to each of Germany and Austria after the Anschluss to reflect the new state of affairs.
4. This later became known as the Central British Fund, but here is referred to by its name at the time.
5. Viscount Samuels Memoirs p 254.

6. Ibid p 255.

7. *British Jewry and the Holocaust*, Bolchover, pp 88-89.

8. TNA-PREM 1/326, Minute of meeting dated 15 November 1938 in Prime Ministers' Office Correspondence and papers 1919-1940. There are also a number of references to what transpired not only in the Jewish Chronicle of 18 November 1938 but also in Lord Samuel's memoirs and in contemporaneous records in the Quaker archives.

9. *Island Refuge*, A.J. Sherman pp 171-172.

10. The Jewish Chronicle 18 November 1938.

11. Makins minute, 10 November 1938 FO 371/21636, C13661/1667/62.

12. The Weiner Library, MF Doc 27/1/2/, Council for German Jewry Executive Committee Minutes 17 November 1938.

13. Hansard 21 November 1938 vol 341 cc 1428-83.

14. Viscount Samuel's *Memoirs* p 255. His whole involvement in this crucial meeting and the organisation of the Kindertransport occupies just ten lines of his memoirs.

15. See more generally *Mandate Memoirs 1918-1948*, Norman and Helen Bentwich, Hogarth Press and *They Found Refuge*, Chapter 5, Norman Bentwich.

16. Wiener Library MF Doc 27/1/2, Minutes of Executive Meeting 17 November 1938 p 5.

17. Minutes of Meeting of Quaker Germany Emergency Committee 28 November 1938, archives of Friends House, Euston Road.

18. Article 6 of the Palestine Mandate stated: 'The Administration of Palestine, while ensuring that the rights and position of other sections of the population are not prejudiced, shall facilitate Jewish immigration under suitable conditions and shall encourage, in co-operation with the Jewish agency referred to in Article 4, close settlement by Jews on the land, including State lands and waste lands not required for public purposes.'

19. See also the Jewish Chronicle, 2 December 1938 which pointed out that there was at a minimum a need for an additional 50,000 labourers in Palestine. There was zero unemployment in the Jewish yishuv and apart from the temporary employment requirements for the orange picking season there were major industrial and construction projects that would employ additional people. Principal amongst these projects was new refinery plant in Haifa.

20. See in particular speech from Sir Archibald Sinclair.
21. Sir Jeremy Hunt, 29 January 2019.

18 Safe Shores

1. *Holocaust Hero*, Solomon Schonfeld, David Kranzler p 8.
2. *They Called Him Mike*, Yonason Rosenblum p 236.
3. Ibid p8-9.
4. Ibid p9.
5. Solomon Schonfeld, *A Purpose in Life*, Derek Taylor p 60 and conversation with Rabbi Schonfeld's son Jeremy Schonfeld and with Susanna Perlman, his first cousin.
6. *Resisting the Holocaust*, Paul R. Bartrop p 254; *Holocaust Hero, The Untold Story of Solomon Schonfeld*, David Kranzler p 56.
7. Solomon Schonfeld, *A Purpose in Life*, Derek Taylor pp 59-60.
8. There are records of a girls' hostel in Sunderland which was used to house refugees who came on the Kindertansport from Germany and Austria. This also came under the supervision of Dr Schonfeld. It is not clear whether this hostel was open by this time, but nevertheless the extent of Dr Schonfeld's work and reach in Sunderland is demonstrated by my mother being accommodated there from January 1939.
9. *They Found Refuge*, Norman Bentwich p 68.

19 Max's Diary

1. What is set out here follows Max's handwritten diary kept in the archives of the Jabotinsky Museum. It was written in German in the faintest pencil and on thin lined paper which has become fragile to touch. Max's writing at the best of times was hard to read and this proved to be an additional challenge. Some of the words written are now so faint that I have had to guess the meaning or sense. Max appears to have been fastidious in recording numbers of people, location, weather and other such matters, almost like a ship's log. Presumably these details were provided in daily briefings. In the longer entries I have added to this a few details which he spoke of and wrote down in his life story.
2. Literally translated from Hebrew as 'the Land'.
3. *Ha ma'apilim* was the Hebrew word used at first in the *Af Al Pi* movement to connote an illegal immigrant to Palestine. It then

passed into general vocabulary. They were named after one of the first illegal boats which was named *Ha'm'apilim*.

4. *Hatikva* was the emblematic song of freedom sung by the Yishuv in Palestinae and today is the national anthem of Israel and literally translated means 'The Hope'.

20 Stripped Bare

1. Interview Max Grunsfeld.
2. *Mensch Argere Dich Nicht.*
3. *A Crime in the Family*, Sacha Batthyany.

21 A Dishonourable Piece of Business

1. Article 24 of the Mandate.
2. Article 27 and 28 of the Mandate.
3. Article 6 of the Mandate.
4. Articles 2, 13 and 14 of the Mandate.
5. The Preamble to the Mandate referred to 'the establishment in Palestine of a national home for the Jewish people' and Article 2 referred to the establishment of such a national home.
6. The Peel Commission Report, 1937 Cmnd No 5479 at Chapters III and V. Visitors to West Jerusalem today can walk up King David Street and wonder at the architectural optimism of the YMCA built as a shrine to the vision of a shared future for the three Abrahamic faiths with Christianity at the apex.
7. See in particular, Haycraft Commission1922 Cmnd No 1540; Churchill 1922 White Paper Cmnd No 1700; Shaw Commission March 1930 Cmnd No 3530; Passfield White Paper Cmnd 3692; Sir John Hope Simpson Report 1930 Cmnd No 3 686; Peel Commission July 1937 Cmnd No 5479; Woodhead Commission Cmnd No 5854 and Government Policy Statement on Woodhead, 9 November 1938 Cmnd No 5893.
8. Peel Commission July 1937 Cmnd No 5479.
9. UN Resolution 181, 29 November 1947.
10. Cmnd No 6019.
11. *The Guardians, The League of Nations and the Crisis of Empire* (2015), Susan Pedersen p 387.
12. *Ben Gurion and the Holocaust*, Shabtai Teveth, xxxvi.
13. *A State at Any Cost, The Life of David Ben Gurion*, Tom Segev, pp 285-287.

14. Report of the state of affairs to the 36th Session of the Permanent Mandate Commission on 13 June 1939 p1, www.unispal.un.org

15. HC Debate 23 May 1939 Vol 347 cc 2129-97.

16. HC Debate (ibid) record of the division on the question 'This House approves the policy of His Majesty's Government relating to Palestine as set out in Command Paper No 6019.' See The Manchester Guardian, 24 May 1939 p 11.

17. Weizmann to Rappard, 9 June 1939.

18. Minutes of the 36th Session of the Permanent Mandates Commission pp 95-102.

19. Paragraph 14 of the Report of the Permanent Mandates Commission to the Council dated 29 June 1939.

20. Minutes of the 36th Session of the Permanent Mandates Commission, and A Line in the Sand, (supra) p 196.

21. Minutes of the 36th Session of the Permanent Mandates Commission pp 274-275.

22. For an account of the success of Lord Hankey's intervention, see *The Guardians* pp 387-390. Lord Hankey, previously as Sir Maurice Hankey, was Secretary to the Cabinet. He was not a supporter of the League of Nations, noting that the British Empire was worth a thousand Leagues. He was after the Second World War a prominent critic of the Nuremburg War Crimes Trials.

23. Indeed, Philip Noel Baker at the time questioned in Parliament whether it was appropriate for Lord Hankey to be appointed to attend and vote.

24. *One World*, Wendell Wilkie (1943) p 15.

25. *The Killearn Diaries*, ed. Trefor Evans, January 1972, p 313.

26. The secret telegram is referred to in the minutes of the 10th Cabinet Committee on Palestine 20 April 1938, p 97.

27. Letter from Dr Chaim Weizmann to Malcolm MacDonald dated 10 March 1938, publication of the British proposal on 15 March as reported in the Palestine Post of 16 March 1938, Dr Weizmann's rejection of the proposals on 17 March 1938 and Dr Weizmann's letter to PM Neville Chamberlain, dated 24 March 1938 – *see* Volume 19 of *The Collected Letters and Papers of Dr Weizmann*, Israel Universities Press, 1979.

28. Minutes of 10th Cabinet Committee dated 20 April 1938.

29. Telegram No 274

30. Paragraph 3 of Telegram No 249 11 April 1939.

31. PRO Cab 21 of 39.
32. Hansard 19 April 1939, Vol 346 cc 346-8.
33. See for example Jewish Telegraph Agency, 20 April 1939.
34. 10th Meeting of Cabinet Committee on Palestine, 20 April 1939.
35. Ibid
36. *One Palestine Complete, Jews and Arabs Under the British Mandate*, Tom Segev p 436.
37. 10th Meeting of Cabinet Committee on Palestine, 20 April 1939, p 10 of Minutes.
38. *Nazi Palestine*, Martin Cuppers, p 42.
39. *Enemies and Neighbours, Arabs and Jews in Palestine and Israel 1917-2017*, Ian Black p 90.
40. *A State at Any Cost, The Life of David Ben Gurion*, Tom Segev, p 288.
41. *Killearn Diaries*, 7 February 1938, p 94.

22 The Rim
1. *Before the Curtain Fell*, Ludmila Epstein p 30.
2. *The Sandu* and *Assimi* were both turned back by British patrols at Haifa and escorted to Constanza in March and April 1939; *Jews on Route to Palestine 1934-1944*, Artur Patek p 89 and Hansard 23 April 1939.
3. *The Four Front War*, Willie Perl p 220.
4. The Jewish Telegraph Agency 27 June and 7 July 1939.
5. News report from *Haboker*, 7 July 1939. The report in this newspaper indicated that the Romanian authorities issued permits to those on board who lacked them, but this appears to be unreliable as only the British authorities could issue permits to enter Palestine.
6. *The Road to September 1939, Polish Jews, Zionists and the Yishuv on the Eve of the Second World War*, Jaacov Shavit, p 248.
7. *The Four Front War*, Willie Perl pp 220-221.
8. *The Four Front War* p 220.
9. Admiralty telegram 23 June 1939 to Foreign Office ADM 116/431 and *Jews On Route to Palestine*, Artur Patek p 88.
10. *Jewish Telegraph Agency* 16 July 1939 reporting that the story had also been carried in The Times on 14 July. The number of passengers reported on *The Rim* would appear to have

been inaccurate. It is understood that only about 450-500 left Constantza.

11. Anonymous testimony of one of those shipwrecked, Jabotbinsky Archives, Tel Aviv.
12. *A History of Jewish Rhodes*, Esther Fintz Menasce, pp 155-156.
13. *Palestine Post* 13 July 1939
14. Amendments to the 1933 Palestine Immigration Ordinance of August 1939.
15. The vessels engaged in this work usually flew the Panamanian flag, particularly since changes in Greek law imposed fines and made it an offence to carry Jewish refugees to Palestine without proper certification.
16. The risk of imprisonment was tangible. Captain Pagolitis of the *Assimi* was arrested and sentenced to nine months in prison. The vessel itself was escorted back to Constanza by a naval patrol in April 1939, JTA 21 April 1939.
17. Hansard, 5 June 1939 Vol 348 cc 171-177.
18. *Before the Curtain Fell*, Ludmila Epstein pp 38 and 80.
19. USHMM – 0344700958/59 jpg.
20. Jewish Telegraphic Agency, 17 August 1939.
21. *The Mauritian Shekel, The Story of Jewish Detainees in Mauritius*, Genevieve Pitot.
22. A year later in October 1940, an attempt was made to enforce a mass deportation order for those arriving on three ships from Romania by transferring the immigrants onto *The Patria*, which was then due to sail for Mauritius and detain them there. The Hagannah was determined to prevent this deportation and planted explosives on the vessel. The resulting explosion killed 200 Jewish migrants and 50 British soldiers. One of the worst terror attacks against the British.
23. Jewish Telegraph Agency, 31 August 1939.
24. 31 July 1939 TNA – CO733/405/75759/1.
25. *Jews On Route to Palestine*, Artur Patek p 92.
26. Report by US Consul at Jerusalem to the Secretary of State 21 September 1939, 867.N.55/196.
27. Interview with Captain H, 2017.
28. *Escaping the Holocaust, Illegal Immigration to the Land of Israel, 1939- 994*, Dalia Ofer p 19.

29. www.yadvashem.org – The Return to Life 1945-1956, A Visual Retrospective.

23 *The Kladovo Transport*
1. *Jews on Route to Palestine*, Artur Patek, p132.
2. Hansard 7 February 1940, Col 236 and *Jews on Route to Palestine*, Artur Patek, p 132.
3. FO 371/25240/8510 cited in *Escaping the Holocaust*, Dalia Ofer p 129.
4. CO 733/429/76021/1/40 cited in *Escaping the Holocaust*, Dalia Ofer p 129.
5. W 1082/38/48/ no 311 and *Four Front War*, Perl p 188.
6. FO 341/35238/1809 cited in Dalia Ofer, *Escaping the Holocaust* p 129.
7. W 10038/1369/48.
8. Jewish Telegraph Agency, 5 June 1940.
9. *Escaping the Holocaust*, Dalia Ofer p 55.
10. *Escaping the Holocaust*, Dalia Ofer p 57.
11. The British tried to persuade Turkey to stop the vessel at the Bosphorus without success. Eventually the *Darien II* arrived at Haifa in March 1941. The vessel was impounded, the 878 passengers were ordered to be deported to Mauritius but no vessel was available for this purpose and so they were imprisoned for eighteen months at Atlit.

24 *Journey's End*
1. They left Sabac on 16 March 1941, reached Thesaloniki on 18 March, then Istanbul by 27 March, Beirut by 30 March and Haifa on 31 March 1941.
2. A Survey of Palestine for the Anglo-American Committee of Inquiry, Chapter VII, paragraph 38.
3. Letters from Hertha Reich, one of the Kladovo group.
4. Birmingham Daily Gazette 11 October 1941.
5. Daily Mirror 14 October 1941.
6. The International Military Tribunal by its Decision rendered on 1 October 1946 determined that the Einsatzgruppen had been responsible for the murder of approximately two million.
7. Judgment of Military Tribunal in United States of America v Otto Ohlendorf and others, the Einsatzgruppen Trial Judgment p 412.

8. The United States Holocaust Memorial Museum estimates that approximately a million were murdered at Auschwitz-Birkenau, 925,000 at Treblinka and 435,000 at Belzec.

9. For a more detailed discussion of this aspect of the Holocaust see essay by Peter Black, senior historian at the USHMM in *The Holocaust: Memories and History*, 'Holocaust by Bullets: Hitler's Hidden Holocaust?'

10. Judgment of Military Tribunal in United States of America v Otto Ohlendorf and others, the Einsatzgruppen Trial Judgment p 420.

11. Eichmann Trial Judgment paragraph 106.

12. Heydrich was assassinated in Prague by Czech resistance in May 1942. Rauff was sent to North Africa in 1942 and placed in charge of a relatively unstudied plan to extend the systematic round up and murder of Jews in Europe to North Africa, see *War of Shadows*, Gershon Gorenberg. Rauff survived the war. He escaped to Chile and avoided extradition and trial in the 1970s on the grounds that the alleged offences were time barred under Chilean law.

13. *Kladovo Eine Flucht nach Palestina* , Alisa Douer, p 21.

14. Including Herta Reich and Ernst Pollatschek who escaped to Italy and Fanny Wiener to Bulgaria and then Palestine; see *Zwei Tage Zeit, Die Flucht einer Murzzuschlager Judin* (1988) and *Kladovo Eine Flucht nach Palestina* , Alisa Douer, p 22.

15. *The Origins of the Final Solution*, Christopher Browning pp 422-423.

25 Eichmann

1. *Hunting Evil, How the Nazi War Criminals Escaped and the Hunt to Bring Them to Justice*, Guy Walters, Bantam Press (2009) p 11.

2. *Eichmann in my Hands*, Peter Z. Malkin and Harry Stein, pp 51-72.

3. *Eichmann in my Hands*, Peter Z. Malkin and Harry Stein, pp 73-74, and Der Spiegel 1 April 2011, A Nazi War Criminal's Life in Argentina.

4. *Eichmann in my Hands*, Peter Z. Malkin and Harry Stein, pp 172.

5. *Justice in Jerusalem*, Gideon Hausner, with Introduction by Shimon Peres.

6. This is taken up in Hannah Arendt's *Eichmann in Jerusalem* p 252ff.

7. *Silence and Memory*, Oxford (2019), Vinitzky Seroussi and Chana Teeger.

8. Evidence of Hoettl admitted on 26 May 1961 at the Eichmann Trial by way of request for assistance to the Austrian courts.

9. *Becoming Eichmann*, Cesarani p 300 and Trial ref Vol 4 pp 1802-1812

10. Der Spiegel 1 April 2011, A Nazi War Criminal's Life in Argentina.

11. *Becoming Eichmann*, Cesarani p 243.

12. Eichmann Trial Session 12.

13. *Eichmann's Jews*, Doron Rabinovici pp 83-89.

14. Memoir of Rudolf Höss November 1946, as admitted into the trial of Eichmann in 1961 (Session 16).

15. Eichmann Judgment paragraph 116. Gassing ceased at Auschwitz on 2 November 1944.

16. Evidence of Hoettl at Eichmann Trial on 26 May 1961.

17. Transcript 16th Session, 26 April 1961 following Decision 7 on its admissibility.

18. This theme was taken up once more in the course of Eichmann's lengthy examination in chief.

19. *Eichmann In My Hands* (supra) pp 192-193

20. Trial Judgment paragraph 61.

21. Trial Judgment paragraph 155.

22. In 1933, the Grand Mufti went to the German Consulate in Jerusalem to offer his co-operation; *Nazis, Islamists and the Making of the Modern Middle East*, p 4, Barry Rubin and Wolfgang G. Schwanitz (Rubin and Schwanitz).

23. *One Palestine Complete, Jews and Arabs Under the British Mandate*, Tom Segev, p 462.

24. Trial Judgment paragraph 61 and statement of SS Captain Dieter Wisliceny dated 26 July 1946, whilst he awaited trial in Czechoslovakia after the war. He had been tasked by Eichmann with responsibility for deportations from Slovakia. He was found guilty and hanged in 1948. His evidence was admitted into evidence at the Eichmann Trial pursuant to Decision no 9 – Session 16.

25. Office of Chief of Counsel for War Crimes Doc No NG 5462-5570, Sworn Statement of Carl Rekowski, Bremen 5 October 1947 pp 1-10 cited in Rubin and Schwanitz p 5.

26. *Nazis, Islamists and the Making of the Modern Middle East* p 6, Rubin and Schwanitz, citing US National Archives, College Park Maryland, T120, R63571, R50682 '*Der Grossmufti von Jerusalem*' Berlin 28/11/41.

27. *Nazi Palestine* p 89, Klaus-Michael Mallmann and Martin Cuppers (2009).

28. Documents on German Foreign Policy, Series D Vol XIII (London 1964).

29. Trial Judgment paragraph 156.

30. Eichmann Trial Session 16.

31. Rubin and Schwanitz, pp 1-2.

32. PArchAA, R100702, F1784-85 – Fritz Grobba on 26 June 1942 wrote to the Ministry of Foreign Affairs that the Kalainis wished to visit a concentration camp and when questioned by the foreign Ministry, he wrote that there should not be any concerns about their participation in this inspection (which took place at Sachenshausen) – see Rubin and Schwanitz, p 2.

33. Rubin and Schwanitz, pp 1-2.

34. *War of Shadows* (2021) p 199 and p 312, Gershon Gorenburg.

35. Rubin and Schwanitz pp 9 and 139, and *War of Shadows* (2021) Gershon Gorenburg.

36. Rubin and Schwanitz, pp 138.

37. *War of Shadows* (2021) p347-348, Gershon Gorenburg.

38. Rubin and Schwanitz, p 138.

39. Rubin and Schwanitz, pp 223-224.

40. Eichmann Trial Session 16.

41. 'In this trial, we shall also encounter a new kind of killer, the kind that exercises his bloody craft behind a desk, and only occasionally does the deed with his own hands.' - Hauser's Opening.

42. *Eichmann in Jerusalem*, Hannah Arendt.

26 Jeno

1. 'And tomorrow the sun will shine again ... it will reunite us, the lucky ones.' From Morgen, Op 27 No 4 (1897), Richard Strauss setting to music a poem by John Henry Mackay.

2. This part of Hungary passed to Romania at the end of the First World War, and then was ceded back to Hungary as part of the Second Vienna Accord in July 1940, and today is part of Romania.

27 Time Runs Out

1. *The Final Solution*, David Cesarani, p704, and *The Record, The Trial of Adolf Eichmann*, Lord Russell of Liverpool, p 171.

2. Laszlo Endre was tried in Budapest in December 1945 and sentenced to death by hanging in March 1946.

3. *The Final Solution*, David Cesarani, p 707

4. Eichmann Trial, Eichmann's evidence in Session 86, 5 July 1961.

5. *Eichmann Trial Judgment* paragraph 117.

6. Chapter 9 of *Buried by The Times, The Holocaust and America's Most Important Newspaper*, Laurel Leff.

7. Eichmann Trial Evidence of Yoel Brand, Session 56.

8. Eichmann Trial, Evidence of Eichmann, Session 86.

9. Eichmann Trial Evidence of Yoel Brand, Session 56.

10. Eichmann Trial, Evidence of Eichmann, Session 86.

11. Eichmann Trial, Evidence of Eichmann, Session 86.

12. Eichmann Trial Evidence of Yoel Brand, Session 56.

13. New York Times 1 June 1961, coverage of the Eichmann Trial. One of the three Judges was particularly insistent in exploring this line of questioning.

14. New York Times, 10 May 1944, p 5 Levy and see Chapter 9 of *Buried by The Times, The Holocaust and America's Most Important Newspaper*, Laurel Leff.

15. New York Times 18 May 1944.

16. For two full accounts see *Beyond Belief, The American Press and the Coming of the Holocaust 1933-1945*, Deborah Lipstadt (1993); and *Auschwitz, the Allies and Censorship of the Holocaust*, Michael Flemming (2021).

17. The New York Times, 25 November 1942 p 10.

18. The United Nations Review (III) No 1 (1943).

19. For a brilliant account of their escape and report see *The Escape Artist* (2022), Jonathan Friedland.

20. See for example, The New York Times 4 July 1944, the Belfast Newsletter 4 July 1944, the Jewish Telegraph Agency 7 July 1944, and the Jewish Chronicle 14, July 1944 and 1 September 1944. The Times did not cover what had happened at Auschwitz until after the conclusion of the war at the trial of the guards in September 1945. The Telegraph did carry an article on the estimated murder of 2,000,000 Jews in Auschwitz in November 1944 but did not cover the Vogt Report in July 1944.

21. Manchester Evening News, 3 August 1944. It should be recalled that a year earlier on 26 May 1943 the view had been expressed in a detailed report by Cyril Radcliffe (who would later be instrumental

in drawing up the partition boundary between India and Pakistan), then Director General of the Ministry of Information, to Minister Brendan Bracken, that the behaviour of a large number of the Jews of Britain was itself largely responsible for the marked rise of anti-Semitism on these shores – see The Times, 23 August 2018.

22. *Churchill and The Jews*, Martin Gilbert, p 212 and Premier Papers 4/51/10.

23. Evidence admitted into Eichmann Trial, Session 57 and quoted in full.

24. According to *Auschwitz*, Martin Gilbert p 285, Sir Archibald Sinclair (leader of the Liberal Party and Secretary of State for Air) had suggested at the time that bombing Auschwitz could only be done in the daylight and that this would be a matter solely for US bombers and not the RAF; see further *The Escape Artist* (supra) p 234.

25. In addition, on 13 September 1944 US bombers bombed the main camp by accident as several bombers on their way to Monowitz went astray. Fifteen SS guards and twenty-three Jews were killed and there was some minor damage to the railway sidings; see *Auschwitz*, Martin Gilbert, p 315.

26. *Advocate for the Dead*, Yoel Brand's Story as told to Alex Weissberg p 130.

27. Report of Brand's testimony in the New York Times of 1 June 1961.

28. *Advocate for the Dead*, Yoel Brand's Story as told to Alex Weissberg p 130.

29. The two gunmen were Eliahu Bet Zouri and Eliahu Hakim. They were tried and executed in 1945.

30. The acronym was taken from the Hebrew לח״י – לוחמי חרות ישראל *Lohamei Herut Israel – Lehi*, 'Fighters for the Freedom of Israel – Lehi'. David Ben Gurion was steadfastly opposed to this terror group and all it stood for. In May 1948, Lehi was forcibly disbanded and a number of its former member were put on trial by the nascent State. Nevertheless, by January 1949 a general amnesty was granted to its former fighters, including Yitzhak Shamir who became Prime Minister of Israel in 1983.

31. *Kastner's Crime*, Paul Bogdanor, and *The Escape Artist* (supra) pp 235-241 make the case against Kastner. The chief charges against him were his failure to warn the Hungarian Jewish community of their fate impending deportation to Auschwitz and Kastner instead giving out misleading information about the so-called arrival of an earlier deportation of Hungarians at a fictitious destination,

Waldsee. The charge against him was that Kastner did all this as a part of a deal with the Nazis to save members of his own family.

32. *The Holocaust in Northern Transylvania,* www.Yadvashem.org and Eichmann Trial evidence, Session 53, Vol. III, pp. 971-972, Mr Ze'ev Sapir.

33. Even this number itself does not represent the totality of Hungarian Jewish victims of the Holocaust. As is detailed in the Yad Vashem archives, a further 130,000 Hungarian Jews lost their lives independently of these deportations as a result of the acts and policy of the fascist government in Hungary.

34. The aggregate number was provided in a report prepared by the Hungarian authorities in July 1944 together with an accompanying schedule analysing the overall outcome of the operation – see Eichmann Trial Judgment paragraph 111, and Ferenczy's Report on 9 July 1944, which lists each transport by date, location and with precise numbers. The Report also noted that the Auschwitz gas chambers were working at full capacity and could hardly cope with the pace of the transports.

35. *The Final Solution,* David Cesarani p 710.

28 Heinrich and Karoline

1. DOEW Records. This was one of 47 sequentially numbered transports that left this station and took 50,000 Viennese Jews to Theresienstadt. Records are preserved for each transport detailing each person taken. From 1943 deportations from Vienna were made directly to the death camps in Poland and left the Nordbahnhoff.

2. *Eichmann Interrogated,* ed. Avner Less, p 178.

3. DOEW Records.

4. *Theresienstadt, 1941-1945, The Face of a Coerced Community,* H.G. Adler p 608.

5. DOEW Records for Karoline Grunsfeld.

6. *Theresienstadt, 1941- 945, The Face of a Coerced Community,* H.G. Adler p 20.

7. The Times 21 June 1945 quoting from a letter written in May 1945 by a camp survivor.

8. *Theresienstadt, 1941-1945, The Face of a Coerced Community,* H.G. Adler p 41.

9. *A Visitor from the Living,* a documentary made by Claude Lanzmann consisting of a single conversation with Maurice Rossel.

10. *Theresienstadt, 1941-1945; The Face of a Coerced Community,* H.G. Adler pp 739-740.
11. *Theresienstadt, 1941-1945, The Face of a Coerced Community,* H.G. Adler pp 517-553.
12. *The Final Solution,* David Cesarani, p759-760.
13. *Heroine of Rescue,* Joseph Friedenson, David Kranzler Chapter 12.
14. Ibid
15. Archives of Vaad Hatzalah, Yeshiva University New York.
16. *In The Name of Humanity, The Secret Deal to End the Holocaust,* Max Wallace p 281.
17. *The Final Solution,* David Cesarani, pp 759-760.
18. *In The Name of Humanity, The Secret Deal to End The Holocaust,* Max Wallace p 283.
19. *In The Name of Humanity, The Secret Deal to End The Holocaust,* Max Wallace pp 284-291.
20. The New York Times of 8 February 1945 only carried the story in a few lines tucked away on p 8, although it did mention Himmler's part.
21. The news was mentioned briefly on p 8 of the 16 February 1945 issue.
22. *The Final Solution,* David Cesarani, pp 759-760.
23. The Times 21 June 1945 quoting from a letter written in May 1945 by a camp survivor and *Theresienstadt, 1941-1945, The Face of a Coerced Community,* H.G. Adler p 618.

29 Lackenbach Revisited

1. From *In The City of Slaughter,* Chaim Nahman Bialik.
2. *Austrian Victims and Austria as Victim in the Short 1940s,* Ina Markova, from collected essays in Austrian Federalism in Comparative Perspective, New Orleans Press (Markova) p 183. This graffiti can also be seen on the walls of the underground Weinkanal in the chase at the end of *The Third Man,* shot in 1949.
3. *War Crimes Trials in Austria,* Winifred Garscha and Klaudia Kuretsidis-Haider, in a paper presented at 21st Annual Conference of the German Studies Association, 1997, and Winifred Garscha, *An Attempt at Justice, NS-War Crime Trials in Austria after 1945.*
4. *Forgotten Victims, The Nazi Genocide of the Roma and Sinti,* Barbara Warnock, Wiener Holocaust Library, 2019, p 7.

5. Herbert Brettl, *Portschy's Denkscrift – Ein Plagiat*, Essays in *Schiksalsjahr 1938, Burgenland* pp 150-151.

6. Herbert Brettl, *Portschy's Denkscrift – Ein Plagiat*, Essays in *Schiksalsjahr 1938, Burgenland*.

7. Portschy, *Die Ziegeunerfrage*, Eisenstadt, August 1938.

8. Guenter Lewy, *The Nazi Persecution of the Gypsies*, p 58.

9. The private financing of the building of Auschwitz has also been the subject of considerable attention in the last twenty years. Credit lines from major German banks have been disclosed and in the course of the settlement of victims' claims for compensation.

10. *Österreichisches Staatsarchiv, Archiv der Republik (ÖStA, AdR), BMI file: Zl. 47.558-2/53*, and the United States Holocaust Memorial Museum, Holocaust Encylopaedia.

11. Karola Fings et al, *The Gypsies During the Second World War, From Race Science to the Camps*, 1997.

12. Erika Thurner, *National Socialism and the Gypsies in Austria*, Chapter 5 Camp Lackenbach, p 44.

13. Documentation Centre of the Austrian Resistance, DOW, *Ahndung von NS Verbrechen an Roma und Sinti*.

14. Two Kapos were released from another concentration camp to fulfil this function – Guenter Lewy, *The Nazi Persecution of the Gypsies*, p 111.

15. Guenter Lewy, *The Nazi Persecution of the Gypsies*, p 110.

16. Austrian State Archives; AT-OeStA/KA NL, 2359 (B).

17. Karola Fings et al, *The Gypsies During the Second World War, From Race Science to the Camps*, 1997, pp 94-95. The Order referred to the deportation to Auschwitz of 'mixed gypsies' meaning those with even a portion of gypsy blood. Certain exemptions from deportation were set out, although in practice this saved few people.

18. Karola Fings et al, *The Gypsies During the Second World War, From Race Science to the Camps*, 1997, pp 97-98.

19. *Forgotten Victims, The Nazi Genocide of the Roma and Sinti*, Barbara Warnock, Wiener Holocaust Library, 2019, p 5.

20. Markova, p 173.

21. Markova p 174.

22. Marcus Wagner, Tobias Portschy – *Ein Leben fur die volkischdeutschnationale Idee, Sozialisation under Reintegration eines ewig Gestrgen* (Vienna 2013) Chapter 6.

23. (ibid) Chapter 6.

24. (ibid) Chapter 6.

25. Ernst Klee; *Das Personelexikon zum Third Reich*, Frankfurt am Main, p470.

26. Wagner, Chapter 6 (supra).

27. Herbert Brettl, *Portschy's Denkscrift – Ein Plagiat*, Essays in *Schiksalsjahr 1938, Burgenland*, p 155.

28. Documentation Centre of the Austrian Resistance, DOW, *Ahndung von NS Verbrechen an Roma und Sinti*.

29. *From Race to Science to the Camps, The Gypsies During the Second World War* – Postscript of Gilad Margalit.

30. *A Crime in The Family*, Sacha Batthyany.

31. *A Daughter's Search for Her Own Father*, Bruce Eekma.

32. *Paul Esterházy 1901-1989, Ein Leben im Zeitalter der Extreme*, ed. Stefan August Lütgenau, p 25. The Werkmeister Report called Esterházy 'Jewish,' but it was used in the sense of being a sympathiser of the Jews.

33. *Paul Esterházy 1901-1989, Ein Leben im Zeitalter der Extreme*, Laszlo Karsai, pp 69-70.

34. *Paul Esterházy 1901-1989, Ein Leben im Zeitalter der Extreme*, Jeno Gergely, Chapter 6 pp 85ff.

35. Utgaard, *Remembering and Forgetting the Holocaust in Austrian Schools 1955-1996*, pp 201-215.

36. Markova, p 186.

37. Anton Pelinka, *SPO, OVP – Isolation or Integration*, p 255 in a collection of essays, *Conquering the Past, Austria Nazism Yesterday and Today* (1989).

30 Open and Shut

1. '*I have become lost to the world*' – the opening line of Mahler's third song in the Rückert-Lieder cycle. It was composed in the summer of 1901. There is a close affinity between this composition and the adagietto in Mahler's Fifth Symphony composed later that year, immortalised in Visconti's *Death in Venice*.

2. *Black and British*, David Olusoga, p 491.

3. By contrast the United States made its own statement of intent by passing the Displaced Persons Act in June 194,8 which in due course allowed approximately 400,000 survivors of the Holocaust to emigrate to America. Even so, President Truman who passed

the bill into law was critical of it as it was too restrictive in its scope, shutting out those who had survived the war but had entered a displaced persons camp after December 1945, a somewhat arbitrary cut-off in his view.

4. Hansard 13 November, Vol 415 col 1923.

5. Earl Harrison's Report issued in August 1945 laid bare the extremely poor conditions of the Jewish survivors in these camps. Harrison was President Truman's emissary and he visited 30 of the camps in order to report on the treatment of the Jews held there. There was quite widespread coverage and concern at the findings and it led to material improvement.

6. Hansard 13 November, Vol 415 col 1928-1929.

7. Ibid

8. The Times, 14 November 1945 p 5.

9. In October 1946, the British Government proposed instead that 1,500 per month be admitted into Palestine up to a limit of 96,000.

10. *Reflections on the Kielce Pogrom*, eds Kaminski and Zaryn, p 57.

11. The Times, 6 July 1946 p4.

12. *Reflections on the Kielce Pogrom*, eds Kaminski and Zaryn, pp 26-78.

13. The Times, 6 July 1946 p 4.

14. *Off Limits*, Hans Habe (London 1956 in translation) pp 32-33 cited in *Aftermath, Life in the Fallout of the Third Reich*, Harald Jahner p 44. It has been estimated that in 1945-1946 approximately twelve million ethnic Germans who had lived across Central and Eastern Europe were forcibly expelled from their homes and marched towards Germany. It has been described as the largest ever single movement of people in Europe. Most of them accompanied by whatever possessions could be squeezed into a wooden handcart which was pulled along. *Germany, Memories of a Nation, The Germans Expelled*, Neil McGregor (2014).

15. *Aftermath, Life in the Fallout of the Third Reich*, Harald Jahner, p 53.

16. The Times, 23 July 1946 p 4.

17. Ibid

18. Adonis, *Ernest Bevin, Labour's Churchill*, pp 282-283.

19. Ibid, p 285.

20. Daily Express, 1 August 1947.

21. *1947, Where Now Begins*, pp 155-158, Elisabeth Asbrink.

22. Jewish Telegraph Agency 5 August 1947.

23. *Jerusalem Is Called Liberty*, Walter Lever, (1953).

24. Ha'aretz, 2 August 2018, Rosie Whitehouse.

25. For an account of the 43 Group see, *We Fight Fascists, The 43 Group and their Forgotten Battle for Post-war Britain*, Daniel Sonabend.

26. An Armistice Agreement was only signed with Egypt on 24 February 1949.

27. *Philanthropy, Consensus and Broiges, A History of the Jewish Community of Southport*, John Cowell, 2019.

Acknowledgements

This story could not have been written without considerable help from many quarters. Much more than that, however, what I found as I progressed my research over the years was that the project was embraced with heart and soul by those who gave me the encouragement I needed to get to the finishing line. It seemed that the quest had touched a lot of people in ways that I could not have imagined.

This might be because of the somewhat particular starting point of Max's idiosyncratic life story. I suspect that he would have smiled at me with his piercing blue eyes if he had lived to see the outturn as set out in these pages. I can also imagine him puffing out his chest to his fellow residents as if to say, 'You see this is what I had been telling you.'

A great deal of the material is derived from multiple archival sources across the world. In every case I was met with unbelievable kindness, exceptional diligence and true professionalism. There was no request which was too much or too tiresome. Every piece of paper, image, reference, and file was chased down. Accordingly, I wanted to start with heartfelt thanks to the respective teams at the Burgenland Regional Archives, which were held at the time of my research in Eisenstadt, until their recent move to Mattersburg, the *Israelitische Kultusgemeinde* (IKG) in Vienna, the Documentation Centre of Austrian Resistance, the Austrian National Archives, the Hungarian National Archive, Yad Vashem, Jerusalem, the Jabotinsky Institute, Tel Aviv, the National Archive of the History of the Jewish People, Jerusalem, the National Archive of Israel, the Atlit Museum in Israel, the United States Holocaust Memorial Museum, Washington, the Wiener Library, London, the Library of the Society of Friends, London, the National Archives, Kew, the Kahal Shalom Synagogue in Rhodes, the National Archive of Spain, and the curators of the papers of Rabbi Schonfeld at Southampton University. It is invidious to mention specific names, but without the help I received from Dr Evelyn Fertl in Eisenstadt who unearthed the full family files in Lackenbach and from Amira Stern at the Jabotinsky Institute who found for me Max's diary of his escape from Europe, key parts of this book could not have been written.

I also need specifically to mention the role that serendipity has played throughout. When I was struggling to access the most relevant materials from the Spanish Civil War, this led to a fascinating dialogue with a group of my youngest son Joe's Spanish friends from Imperial College. It started with Isa and then her father Diego, who left no stone unturned in their moving search for Martin at the Battle of Teruel. What was particularly remarkable for me, was to learn that this history is still so raw in Spain that the majority will not learn about it at school or university.

At the other end of the age spectrum, a chance placement at a dinner party led to a wonderful conversation with one of Rabbi Schonfeld's last surviving cousins, Susanna Perlman, then well over ninety years old, who sadly has also since passed away. Equally, chance led me to the discovery of the extraordinary war history of Howard Halprin in Palestine, Howard my wonderful nonagenarian dog-walking companion who somehow embodies much of the spirit of that incredibly brave, no-nonsense generation. Throughout, I have never been shy of asking anyone and everyone for help and more often than not it has paid rich dividends, as with the researchers at the United States Holocaust Museum, likewise Martin Paisner who holds in his private collection one of the rare full editions of the Complete Letters of Chaim Weizmann and with the somewhat beleaguered caretaker at the Chatam Sofer Memorial in Bratislava.

I have also been fortunate in the assistance I have received in translation of original materials, whether from German, Hebrew, Spanish or Hungarian. I cannot mention all those who assisted but I must mention the special help given to me by Andrew Kaufman in the translation of the Eisenstadt papers from a difficult and somewhat archaic German often written in stiff gothic script. Andrew's work so perfectly demonstrated that this is more an art than a science and when the exact correct sense was arrived at, I could see the satisfaction on Andrew's face. Likewise, I must acknowledge the great skill of Marion Godfrey who translated the letters of Gina and Wilma and of Jeno with such sensitivity.

I have been extremely fortunate to have had inciteful and caring readers of the manuscript. Chief amongst these was my wonderful and much missed Auntie Ruth, who also discussed a great deal of this book's subject matter with me over lengthy Sunday teas and gave me considerable precious insight. Thanks also to my special goddaughter Kitty Walker who has spent many a year in the publishing industry, my exceptional and exceptionally well-read friend Stephen Hermer and of course above all my extraordinary wife Denise. I also need to thank my birthday twin, Stephen Walker. We were each of us writing quite different books at the time. We would go for lengthy walks on Hampstead Heath with my ever-faithful dog, Oscar, and take turns to explain a difficult part of the narrative that needed resolution. I am not sure how much we listened one to the other, but it was nonetheless excellent therapy.

A good deal of time was spent not just researching the primary materials but also interpreting them. On many an occasion this would involve lengthy discussion with my brother Theo who would spare no effort in turning over the details in order to make sure that every angle was squared off. Theo has shared this life story with me from the earliest memories in Southport to the present. I can only say no one could ask for a more considerate brother or a better friend. Alongside Theo I must also mention Jeremy Smilg, Ruth's son and my cousin. Jeremy has been at all times beyond generous with his time and sharing original materials in the possession of his side of the family, including in particular the letters I have already mentioned. Thank you.

At this stage, however, the book was still a fair distance from being where it is today. For this I must start with a very special thanks to Shan Vahidy whose brilliant skill in editing was of inestimable value to me and I think to the reader too. I also must thank Catherine Hanley, Tom and Daniel Lobl, Irina Berdan and Olga Gekhman at the Jabotinsky Institute for all the help with the many moving photographs and images that accompany the book, my sister-in-law Charlotte for her great skill and patience with the all-important maps, and once more to Denise for the family tree which reproduces in graphic form what Max had told me about and then set out in writing in Tel Aviv.

Huge thanks to Jonathan (Jay) Marks who not only believed in the story but spent time introducing me to those who counted. Thanks also to Alexander Fyjis Walker, my good friend from Cambridge days for introducing me to Kate Horden of Kate Hordern Literary Agency, my wonderful agent, who has guided me with great calm and expertise throughout the whole process. Above all, I am hugely indebted to my long-standing friend and former work colleague Sara Cockerill (aka Mrs Justice Cockerill) who introduced me to Amberley who then took this book up with such enthusiasm.

Connor Stait and the whole team at Amberley, I want to thank each of you from the bottom of my heart, you have been superb throughout. It has been so important to me to have publishers who have had such a deep sensitivity and understanding of this story.

Finally, I must say a very particular and special thank you to my family. First to Denise my wife, who has not only accompanied me on life's journey but on this somewhat special quest over a number of years. You have been there with me throughout as we travelled through Central Europe, often having to face difficult material and shocking revelation. As we have a shared history, you knew instinctively how much this project has meant to me and quite simply, without you there is no book at all. Thank you for your endless love, your wisdom, and much needed humour. In return, I now promise to archive the many hundreds of books I have collected along the way and which now occupy most of my study floor. I must also mention the wonderful, remarkable and much missed Henry Bass, my father-in-law, who appears on these pages with great spirit. Last but not least, I also want to thank our three wonderful grown-up sons, Sam, Ben and Joe. Each of you have helped me tell this story in so many ways, but I have also learned from you that some of this material is perhaps over-familiar to me but needs to be explained from first base to another generation. I hope that in some small measure I have succeeded so that we can learn the right lessons from history and not repeat it.

Bibliography

Archives Consulted

Anglo American Committee of Inquiry in Palestine 1945- 1946
Atlit Museum, Israel
Austrian National Archives
Burgenland Regional Archives
Cabinet Papers
Central British Fund for World Jewish Relief
Colonial Office Papers
Documentation Centre of Austrian Resistance (www.doew.at)
Eisenstadt Jewish Museum
Esterhazy Archives
Hansard
Hebrew University Law Library
Home Office Papers
Hungarian National Archive
Israelit Kultusgemeinde (IKG), Vienna
Jabotinsky Institute, Tel Aviv
Jewish Geneology, Kehila Links (https://kehilalinks.jewishgen.org)
Kahal Shalom Synagogue, Rhodes
Lackenbach Institute, B'nei Barak, Israel
Law Reports of Palestine, 1919- 1947
Library of Congress
Middle Temple Library
National Archive of the History of the Jewish People, Jerusalem
National Archive of Israel
National Archive of Spain
National Archives, Kew
Quaker Library Archives, Friends House, London
Peel Commission
Palestine Royal Commission
Shanghai Jewish Refugees Museum

Southampton University, Papers of Rabbi Schonfeld, (MS 183)

Transcripts and Judgment of the Nuremberg Major War Criminals' Trial (1946-1946) (www.avalon.law.yale.edu)

Transcripts and Judgment of the Trial of Adolf Eichmann (www.nizkor.com)

Transcripts and Judgment of the Einsatzgruppen Trial (www.archives.soton.ac.uk)

United Nations Archives of the Permanent Mandates Commission for Palestine

United Nations Special Committee on Palestine, 1947

United States Holocaust Memorial Museum, Washington

Wiener Holocaust Library, London

Yad Vashem, Jerusalem

Yale Law School, The Avalon Project, Documents in Law History and Diplomacy

Secondary Works

Achcar, Gilbert, *The Arabs and the Holocaust: The Arab–Israeli War of Narratives* (Picador, 2011)

Adler, H.G., *Theresienstadt, 1941–1945: The Face of a Coerced Community* (Cambridge University Press, 2017; originally published in German in 1955)

Adonis, Andrew, *Ernest Bevin, Labour's Churchill* (Biteback, 2021)

Adorno, Theodore, *Mahler, A Musical Physiognomy* (University of Chicago Press, 1996; originally published in German in 1960)

Alter, Robert, *The Hebrew Bible: A Translation With Commentary* (Norton, 2019)

Anderl, Gabriel, *9096 Leben, Der Unbekannte Judenretter, Berthold Storfer, The Forgotten Rescuer of Thousands of Jews* (Goethe Institut, 2012)

Andics, Hellmut, *Die Juden In Wien* (Kremayr & Scheriau, 1988)

Apsler, Alfred, *The Court Factor, The Story of Samson Wertheimer* (Covenant Books, 1964)

Arendt, Hannah, *The Origins of Totalitarianism* (Schocken Books, 1951)

----- *Eichmann in Jerusalem* (Viking, 1963)

van Arkel, Dirk, *Antisemitism in Austria,* PhD thesis, University of Leiden, 1966

Aronson, Shlomo, *Hitler, the Allies and the Jews,* (Cambridge University Press, 2004)

Asbrink, Elisabeth, *1947, Where Now Begins* (Scribe, 2016)

Avineri, Shlomo, *Herzl and the Foundation of the Jewish State* (Weidenfeld & Nicolson, 2013)

Baddiel, David, *Jews Don't Count* (Harper Collins, 2021)

Baedeker, Karl, *Austria together with Budapest, Prague, Karlsbad, Marienbad* (12th Ed, Baedeker, 1929)

Barr, James, *A Line in the Sand* (Simon & Schuster, 2011)

----- *Lords of the Desert* (Simon & Schuster, 2018)

Bartrop, Paul R., *Resisting the Holocaust* (ABC-CLIO, 2016)

----- *The Evian Conference of 1938 and the Jewish Refugee Crisis* (Holocaust in Context Series, 2018)

Batthyany, Sacha, *A Crime in the Family* (Quercus, 2017)

Bayer, Pia, Szorger Dieter, *Schicksalsjahr 1938, NS-Herrschaft Im Burgenland* (Eisenstadt Landesmuseum, 2018)

Beales, Derek, *Joseph II, Volume 1: In The Shadow of Maria Theresa, 1741–1780* (Cambridge University Press, 1987)

----- *Joseph II, Volume 2: Against the World, 1780–1790* (Cambridge University Press, 1987)

Before the Fall, German and Austrian Art of the 1930s, catalogue of an exhibition at the Neue Galerie, New York (2018)

Bentwich, Norman, *England in Palestine* (Kegan Paul, 1932)

----- *They Found Refuge* (Cresset Press, 1956)

----- 'The Destruction of the Jewish Community in Austria, 1938–1942', in *The Jews of Austria: Essays on their Life, History and Destruction*, ed. Josef Fraenkel (Valentine Mitchell, 1967)

Bentwich, Norman and Helen, *Mandate Memoirs 1918–1948* (Hogarth Press, 1965)

Berend, Ivan, *An Economic History of Nineteenth-Century Europe* (Cambridge University Press, 2012)

Berger, Shlomo, 'The Desire to Travel: A Note on Abraham Levy's Yiddish Itinerary 1719–1723', *Aschkenas*, 6 (1996), 497–506

Bierman, John, *Odyssey, The Last Great Escape, The Story of The Pentcho* (Simon & Schuster, 1984)

Black, Ian, *Enemies and Neighbours: Arabs and Jews in Palestine and Israel 1917–2017* (Penguin, 2018)

Black, Peter, 'Holocaust by Bullets: Hitler's Hidden Holocaust?', in *The Holocaust: Memories and History*, ed. Victoria Khiterer (Cambridge Scholars Publishing, 2014), pp. 2–42

Blau, Eva, *The Architecture of Red Vienna* (MIT Press, 2018)

Bogdanor, Paul, *Kastner's Crime* (Routledge, 2016)

Bolchover, Richard, *British Jewry and the Holocaust* (Cambridge University Press, 1993)

Brettl, Herbert (ed.), *Nationalsozialismus im Burgenland* (Studien Verlag, 2013)

Browning, Christopher, *The Origins of the Final Solution* (University of Nebraska Press, 2004)

Buckley, Henry, *The Life and Death of the Spanish Republic* (Bloomsbury, 2021; originally published in 1940)

Cesarani, David, *Becoming Eichmann* (Little Brown, 2007)

----- *The Final Solution* (Macmillan, 2016)

Channon, Henry ("Chips"), *Diaries Volumes 1 and 2*, Edited by Simon Heffer, (Hutchinson, 2021)

Clifford, Alexander, *Fighting for Spain: The International Brigades In the Civil War 1936– 1939* (Pen & Sword Military, 2020)

Cortada, James, *Modern Warfare in Spain: American Military Observations on the Spanish Civil War* (Potomac Books, 2011)

Cowell, John, *Philanthropy, Consensus and Broiges: A History of the Jewish Community of Southport* (John Cowell, 2019)

Darman, Peter, *Heroic Voices of the Spanish Civil War, Memories of the International Brigades,* (New Holland, 2009)

Das Rotes Wien 1919–1934, catalogue of exhibition of the same name at Wien Museum (Birkhauser, 2019)

Delaney, Paul, 'Land, Money and Jews in Later Trollope', *Studies in English Literature*, 32 (1992), 765–87

Deutsch, Julius, *Ein Weiter Weg* (Austria: Amalthea, 1960)

----- *Antifascism, Sports, Sobriety: Forging A Militant Working Class Culture* (PM Press, 2017)

Douer, Alisa, *Kladovo: Eine Flucht nach Palestina* (Mandelbaum, 2002) van Duin, Pieter C., *Central European Crossroads: Social Democracy and National Revolution in Bratislava 1867–1921* (Berghahn Books, 2009)

Eekma, Bruce, *A Daughter's Search for Her Own Father* (Universe, 2011)

Ehrman, Albert, 'The Origins of the Ritual Murder Accusation and Blood Libel', *A Journal of Orthodox Jewish Thought*, 15 (1976), 83–90

Epstein, Ludmilla, *Before The Curtain Fell* (Misdar Jaobtinsky, 1990)

Evans, Trefor (ed.), *The Killearn Diaries* (Sidgwick & Jackson, 1972)

Feldman, Gerald, *Allianz and the German Insurance Business* (Cambridge University Press, 2001)

Fings, Karola, *The Gypsies During the Second World War: From Race Science to the Camps* (University of Hertfordshire Press, 1997)

Flemming, Michael, *Auschwitz, the Allies and Censorship of the Holocaust* (Cambridge University Press, 2014)

Frankopan, Peter, *The Silk roads, A New History of the World* (Vintage, 2017)

Faenkel, Josef, *Robert Stricker* (Claridge, Lewis & Jordan, 1950)

Freidenreich, Harriet, *Jewish Politics in Vienna, 1918-1938* (Indiana University Press, 1991)

Friedenson, Joseph and David Kranzler, *Heroine of Rescue* (Artscroll Mesorah Publications, 1984)

Freedland, Jonathan, *The Escape Artist* (John Murray, 2022)

Fritsche, Otto, *Die NSDAP im Burgenland 1933–1938*, PhD dissertation, University of Vienna, 1993

Ganglmair, Siegwald, *Resistance and Persecution in Austria 1938–1945* (Federal Press Service, 1988)

Gates-Coon, Rebecca, 'Eighteenth-Century "Schutzherren", Esterhazy Patronage of the Jews', *Jewish Social Studies*, 47 (1985), 189–208

----- *The Landed Estates of the Esterhazy Princes* (Johns Hopkins University Press, 1994)

Gedye, G.E.R, *A Wayfarer in Austria* (Houghton Mifflin, 1931)

----- *Fallen Bastions* (Faber & Faber, 2009; originally published in 1939)

Gellately, Robert, *Backing Hitler: Consent and Coercion in Nazi Germany* (Oxford University Press, 2002)

Genosse Jude, Wir Wolten nur das Paradis auf Erden, catalogue of exhibition of same name at Jewish Museum Vienna (Amalthea, 2017)

Gilbert, Martin, *Auschwitz* (Pimlico, 2001)

----- *Kristallnacht* (Harper Press, 2006)

----- *Churchill and the Jews* (Simon & Schuster, 2007)

Gold, Hugo, *Gesichte der Juden in Wien* (Olamenu, 1966)

Gomez, Francisco, *La Guerra Civil en Cordoba* (Editorial Alpuerto, 1985)

Gorenberg, Gershon, *War of Shadows* (Public Affairs, 2021)

Genville, Anthony *Stimmen der Flucht Osterreichische Emigration nach Grossbrittannien ab 1938* (Czernin Verlag, 2011)

Grunwald, Max, *Samuel Oppenheimer und Sein Kreis* (Wilhelm Braumuller, 1913)

Grunsfeld, Max, My Life (Unpublished)

Grunsfeld, Max, *Eine Judische Familie im Burgenland* (Studien Verlag, 2013)

Gulick, Charles, *Austria From Hapsburg to Hitler*, Volume 1 (University of California 1980)

Halkin, Hillel, *Jabotinsky* (Yale University Press, 2014)

Bibliography

Hamann, Briggitte, *Hitler's Vienna* (Oxford University Press, 1999)

Hamerow, Theodore S., *Why We Watched: Europe America and the Holocaust* (W.W. Norton & Co, 2008)

Hammurabi, *The Code of Hammurabi*, trans. Claude Johns (Amazon Digital Services, 2019)

Hausner, Gideon, *Justice in Jerusalem* (Harper & Row, 1966)

Helperin, David, *Shabbatai Tsvi: Testimonies to a Fallen Messiah* (Littman, 2007)

Hemingway, Ernest, *Homage to Catalonia* (Secker & Warburg, 1938)

------ 'On the American Dead in Spain', *New Masses*, 30 (1939), 3

Herzl, Theodor, *Der Judenstaat* (Judischer Verlag, 1896)

----- *Altneuland* Seemann Nachfolger, 1902)

Hobsbawn, E.J., *The Age of Extremes* (Michael Joseph, 1994)

Hofrichter, Robert, Janovicek, Peter Von *Pressburg nach Salzburg* (Styria Premium, 2014)

Hughes, Ben, *They Shall Not Pass: The British Battalion at Jarama* (Osprey, 2011)

Jacobs, Joseph (ed.), *The Jewish Encyclopedia* (Funk & Wagnalls, 1906)

Jahner, Harald, *Aftermath: Life in the Fallout of the Third Reich* (Penguin Random House, 2021)

Kaminski, Lukas and Jan Zaryn (eds), *Reflections on the Kielce Pogrom* (Institute of National Remembrance, 2006)

Karniel, J., *Die Toleranzpolitik Kaiser Josephs II* (Bleicher, 1985)

Kastztner, Resso, *The Kasztner Report* (Yad Vashem Press, 2013)

Kister, Joseph, *The Irgun* (Jabotinsky Institute, 2000)

Klee, Ernst, *Das Personelexikon zum Dritten Reich* (Nikol, 2021)

Kochan, Lionel, *The Making of Western Jewry, 1600–1819* (Palgrave Macmillan, 2004)

Koeslter, Arthur, *Thieves in the Night* (Macmillan, 1946)

----- *Darkness at Noon* (Macmillan, 1940)

Krammer, Arnold, 'Germans against Hitler: The Thaelmann Brigade', *Journal of Contemporary History*, 4 (1969), 65–83

Kranzler, David, *Holocaust Hero: The Untold Story of Solomon Schonfeld* (Ktav, 2003)

Kravitt, Edward F., '"Ein hypermoderner Dirigent": Mahler and Anti-Semitism in *fin de siècle* Vienna', *19th Century Music*, 18 (1994–5), 257–76

----- 'Mahler, Victim of the "New" Anti- Semitism', *Journal of the Royal Musical Association*, 127 (2002), 72–94

Robbins Landon, H.C, Wyn Jones, David, *Haydn His Life and Music* (Thames & Hudson, 1988)

----- *Haydn at Esterhazy 1760 – 1790* (Thames & Hudson, 1978)

Landau, Ronnie, *The Nazi Holocaust* (Ivan R Dee, 1994)

Landis, Arthur, *Lincoln Brigade* (Citadel Press, 1968)

Leff, Laurel, *Buried by The Times: The Holocaust and America's Most Important Newspaper* (Cambridge University Press, 2005)

Leser, Norbert and Paul Sailer-Wlasits, *Als die Republik brannte, von Schattendorf bis Wien,* (Va Bene, 2002)

Less, Avner (ed.), *Eichmann Interrogated* (Lester & Orpen Dennys, 1983)

Lever, Walter, *Jerusalem Is Called Liberty* (Massadah Publishing, 1953)

Levinson, Joshua, *The Life of Koppel Theben (Leader of Israel)* (Warsaw, 1898)

Lewy, Guenter, *The Nazi Persecution of the Gypsies* (Oxford University Press, 2000)

Lipstadt, Deborah, *Beyond Belief: The American Press and the Coming of the Holocaust 1933–1945* (Simon & Schuster, 1993)

London, Louise, *Whitehall and the Jews 1933–1948* (Cambridge University Press, 2000)

Lowry, Fern et al., 'The Evian Conference on Political Refugees', *Social Service Review*, 12 (September 1938), 514–18

Lutgenau, Stefan, *Paul Esterhazy, 1901–1989: Ein Leben im Zeitalter der Extreme* (Studien Verlag, 2005)

Macartney, C.A. (ed.), *The Hapsburg and Hohenzollern Dynasties in the Seventeenth and Eighteenth Centuries* (Macmillan, 1970)

MacGregor, Neil, *Germany, Memories of a Nation* (Allen Lane, 2014)

Macleod, Iain, *Neville Chamberlain* (Frederick Muller Limited, 1961)

Malkin, Peter Z. and Harry Stein, *Eichmann in my Hands* (Grand Central Publishers, 1990)

Mallmann, Klaus-Michael and Martin Cuppers, *Nazi Palestine: The Plans for the Extermination of the Jews in Palestine* (Engima Books, 1990)

Markova, Ina, 'Austrian Victims and Austria as Victim in the Short 1940s', in *Austrian Federalism in Comparative Perspective*, ed. Gunther Bischof and Ferdinand Karlhofer (University of New Orleans Press, 2015), pp. 172–98

Martens, Bob and Peter Herbert, *The Destroyed Synagogues of Vienna* (Lit Verlag, 1998)

Marx, Karl, 'Zur Judenfrage', in *Deutsch-Französische Jahrbücher*, ed. Arnold Ruge and Karl Marx (Bureau der Jahrbücher, 1844), pp. 182–214

McCullough, David, *Truman* (Simon & Schuster, 1992)

Menascé, Esther Fintz, *A History of Jewish Rhodes* (Rhodes Jewish Historical Foundation, 2014)

Metzker, Isaac and Harry Golden, *A Bintel Brief: Sixty Years of Letters From The Lower East Side to the Jewish Daily 'Forward'* (Schocken, 1971)

Morris, Marla, *Jewish Intellectuals and the University* (Palgrave Macmillan, 2007)

Mugnai, Bruno, *Foreign Volunteers in the Spanish Civil War 1936–1939* (Soldiershop Publishing, 2019)

Neville, Peter, *Appeasement: The Diplomacy of Sir Nevile Henderson* (Open University, 1988)

Nicolas Esterhazy II, Un Prince Hongrois Collectionneur, catalogue of exhibition at Chateau de Compiegne (Réunion des musées nationaux, 2007)

Nirenberg, David, 'The Rhineland Massacres of the Jews in the First Crusade', in *Memories Medieval & Modern*, ed. Gerd Althoff (Cambridge University Press, 2002), pp. 279–309

Ofer, Dalia, *Escaping the Holocaust: Illegal Immigration to the Land of Israel, 1939–1994* (Oxford University Press, 1990)

Offenberger, Ilana Fritz, *The Jews of Nazi Vienna 1938–1945* (Palgrave Macmillan, 2017)

Olusoga, David, *Black and British* (Pan Macmillan, 2017)

Patai, Raphael, *The Jews of Hungary* (Wayne State University Press, 1996)

Patek, Artur, *Jews On Route To Palestine 1934–1944* (Jagiellonian Press, 2013)

Pedersen, Susan, *The Guardians: The League of Nations and the Crisis of Empire* (Oxford University Press, 2015)

Bibliography

Pelinka, Anton, 'SPO, OVP – Isolation or Integration', in *Conquering the Past, Austria, Nazism Yesterday and Today*, ed. F. Parkinson (Wayne State University Press 1989), pp. 245–56

Perl, Willy, *The Four Fronted War* (Crown Publishers, 1988)

Pitot, Genevieve, *The Mauritian Shekel: The Story of Jewish Detainees in Mauritius* (Rowman & Littlefield, 2000)

Poliakov, Leon, *The History of Anti-Semitism, Volume 1 : From the Time of Christ to the Court Jews* (University of Pennsylvania Press, 2003)

----- *The History of Anti-Semitism, Volume 2: From Mohammed to the Marranos* (University of Pennsylvania Press, 2003)

----- *The History of Anti-Semitism, Volume 4: Suicidal Europe 1870–1933* (University of Pennsylvania Press, 2003)

Popplewell, Oliver, *Munich Why?* (Austin Macauley, 2022)

Portschy, Tobias, *Die Ziegeunefrage* (Kurt Bauer-Gesichte, 1938)

Pulzer, Peter, *The Rise of Political Anti-Semitism in Germany and Austria* (Harvard University Press, 1988)

Rabinovici, Doron, *Eichmann's Jews* (Politi, 2011)

Rady, Martyn, *Customary Law in Hungary* (Oxford, 2015)

Radványi, Orsolya, 'Les collections d'art de la famille Esterhazy aux XVIIIe et XIXe siècles et la naissance de la Pinacothèque nationale', in *Nicolas II Esterhazy 1765–1833, un prince hongrois collectionneur*, ed. Laurence Posselle (Réunion des musées nationaux, 2007), pp. 86–91

Reich, Herta and Heimo Halbraine, *Zwei Tage Zeit, Die Flucht einer Murzzuschlager Judin 1938-1944* (ABC-CLIO, 2014)

Reinharz, Yehuda and Yaacov Shavit, *The Road to September 1939* (University of Chicago Press, 2018)

Roberts, Andrew, *The Holy Fox: A Biography of Lord Halifax* (Weidenfeld & Nicolson, 1997)

Rosenblum, Yonason, *They Called Him Mike* (Mesorah Publications, 1995)

Rosenkranz, Herbert, 'The Anschluss and the Tragedy of Austrian Jewry, 1938 to 1945', in *The Jews of Austria: Essays on their Life, History and Destruction*, ed. Josef Fraenkel (Valentine Mitchell, 1967)

Roth, Joseph, *Job, The Story of a Simple Man* (Kiepenheuer Verlag, 1930)

Rubin, Barry and Wolfgang G. Schwanitz, *Nazis, Islamists and the Making of the Modern Middle East* (Yale University Press, 2014)

Russell of Liverpool, Lord, *The Record: The Trial of Adolf Eichmann for his Crimes against the Jewish People and against Humanity* (Knopf, 1963)

Salner, Peter and Martin Kvasnica, *The Chatam Sofer Memorial* (Institute of Ethnology of Slovak Academy of Sciences, 2013)

Samuel, Viscount, *Memoirs* (Cresset Press, 1945)

Schama, Simon, *Belonging, The Story of the Jews 1492-1900* (Bodley Head, 2017)

Schuschnnigg, Kurt, *Austrian Requiem* (Victor Gollancz, 1947)

Bamuel-Schwartz, Judith, *Never Look Back, Jewish Refugee Children in Great Britain 1938–1945* (Purdue University Press, 2012)

Segev, Tom, *One Palestine Complete: Jews and Arabs Under the British Mandate* (Macmillan, 2001)

----- *A State at Any Cost: The Life of David Ben Gurion* (Macmillan, 2018)

Vinitzky-Seroussi, Vered and Teeger Chana, *Silence and Memory* (OUP, 2019)

Sherman, A.J., *Island Refuge* (University of California Press, 1973)

----- *Mandate Days, British Lives in Mandate Palestine 1918–1948* (Thames & Hudson, 1997)

Shirer, William, *Berlin Diary* (Alfred A. Knopf, 1941)

----- *The Rise and Fall of the Third Reich* (Simon & Schuster, 1960)

Silber, Michael K., 'From Tolerated Aliens to Citizen Soldiers, Jewish Military Service in the Era of Joseph II', in *Constructing in Eastern Central Europe*, ed. Pieter M. Judson and Marcia L. Rozenblit (Berghahn, 2004), pp. 19–36

----- 'Hungary Before 1918', in *The YIVO Encyclopaedia of Jews in Eastern Europe*, ed. Gershon Hundert (Yale University Press, 2008)

----- 'Habsburg Jewry in the Long Eighteenth Century', in *The Cambridge History of Judaism, Volume 7: The Early Modern World, 1500–1815*, ed. Jonathan Karp and Adam Sutcliffe (Cambridge University Press, 2019), 763–97

Silverman, Lisa, 'Absent Jews and Invisible Antisemitism in Postwar Vienna: *Der Prozess* (1948) and *The Third Man* (1949)', *Journal of Contemporary History*, 52 (2017), 211–28

Simon, Walter B., 'The Jewish Vote in Vienna', *Jewish Social Studies*, 23 (1961), 38–48

Sofer, Chatam, *Pressburg Under Siege* (CIS Publishers, 1991)

Sonabend, Daniel, *We Fight Fascists: The 43 Group and their Forgotten Battle for Post-war Britain* (Verso Books, 2019)

Stangneth, Bettina, *Eichmann Before Jerusalem: The Unexamined Life of a Mass Murderer* (Vintage, 2014)

Steinmetz, Selma *Osterreichs Zigeuner im NS Staat* (Europa Verlag, 1966)

Stern, Selma, *The Court Jew: A Contribution to the History of the Period of Absolutism in Central Europe* (Taylor & Francis, 2020)

Strang, Bruce, 'Two Unequal Tempers; Sir George Ogilvie Forbes and Sir Nevile Henderson and British Foreign Policy 1938–1939', *Diplomacy and Statecraft*, 5 (2007), 107–37

Taylor, Derek, *Solomon Schonfeld: A Purpose in Life* (Valentine Mitchell, 2009)

Teveth, Shabtai, *Ben Gurion: The Burning Ground 1886–1948* (Houghton Mifflin School, 1987)

----- *Ben Gurion and the Holocaust* (Thomson Learning, 1997)

Thomas, Hugh, *The Spanish Civil War*, 4th ed. (Penguin, 2012)

Thurner, Erika, *National Socialism and the Gypsies in Austria* (University of Alabama, 1998)

Tremlett, Giles, *The International Brigades: Fascism, Freedom and the Spanish Civil War* (Bloomsbury, 2020)

Utgaard, Peter, *Remembering and Forgetting the Holocaust in Austrian Schools 1955–1996* (Routledge, 1999)

Vuillard, Eric, *The Order of the Day* (Pan Macmillan Picador, 2019)

de Waal, Edmund, *The Hare with Amber Eyes* (Vintage, 2011)

----- *Letters to Camondo* (Macmillan, 2021)

Wainewright, Will, *Reporting on Hitler* (Biteback, 2017)

Wagner, Markus, 'Sozialisation und Integration eines ewig Gestrigen', *Tobias Portschy, Ein Leben fur die volkischdeutschnationale Idee*, (University of Vienna, 2013)

Wallace, Max, *In The Name of Humanity: The Secret Deal to End The Holocaust* (Allen Lane, 2017)

Walters, Guy, *Hunting Evil: How the Nazi War Criminals Escaped and the Hunt to Bring Them To Justice* (Bantam Press, 2009)

Warnock, Barbara, *Forgotten Victims: The Nazi Genocide of the Roma and Sinti* (Wiener Holocaust Library, 2019)

Wasserstein, Bernard, *Britain and The Jews of Europe 1939–1945* (Oxford University Press, 1979)

----- *The Assassination of Lord Moyne*, (Jewish Historical Society of England, Vol 27 pp72-83, 1979)

----- *On The Eve: The Jews of Europe Before the Second World War* (Profile Books, 2012)

Weidermann, Volker, *Ostend, The Summer Before the Dark* (Pantheon, 2016)

von Weisl, Wolfgang, *The Jews of Austria, Collected Essays, Illegale Transporte* (Valentine Mitchell, 1967)

Weissberg, Alex, *Advocate for the Dead: The Story of Joel Brand* (André Deutsch, 1958)

Weizmann, Chaim, *The Letters and Papers of Chaim Weizmann*, 13 vols (Oxford University Press and Rutgers, 1968–79)

Wilkie, Wendell, *One World* (Simon & Schuster, 1943)

Zalmon, Milka, *Forced Emigration of the Burgenland Jews*, PhD thesis, Bar Ilan University, 1999

Zweig, Stefan, *Beware of Pity* (NYRB Classics, 2006; originally published in German in 1939)

----- *The World of Yesterday* (University of Nebraska Press, 2013; originally published in German in 1942)

Newspapers and News Websites

BBC Online

Belfast Newsletter

British Movietone News

Bulletin of International News

Daily Express

Daily Herald

Daily Mirror

Daily Telegraph

Der Spiegel

Die Arbeiter-Zeitung

Die Judenpresse

Die Neue Welt

Die Stimme

Ha'aretz

Haboker

Jewish Chronicle

Jewish Telegraph Agency

Jüdische Familienforschung

Le Soldat de la Republique

Manchester Evening News

Manchester Guardian

New Republic

New York Times

Palestine Post

Tablet Magazine

The Spectator

The Sunday Times

The Times

Times Literary Supplement

Wiener Morgenzeitung

Index